Kant and the Early Moderns

Kant and the Early Moderns

EDITED BY

Daniel Garber
and Béatrice Longuenesse

PRINCETON UNIVERSITY PRESS
PRINCETON AND OXFORD

Published by Princeton University Press, 41 William Street,
Princeton, New Jersey 08540
In the United Kingdom: Princeton University Press, 6 Oxford Street,
Woodstock, Oxfordshire OX20 1TW

Library of Congress Cataloging-in-Publication Data

Kant and the early moderns / edited by Daniel Garber and Béatrice Longuenesse.
p. cm.
Includes bibliographical references and index.
ISBN 978-0-691-13700-1 (cloth : alk. paper)—
ISBN 978-0-691-13701-8 (pbk. : alk. paper)
1. Kant, Immanuel, 1724–1804. 2. Philosophy, Modern.
I. Garber, Daniel, 1949– II. Longuenesse, Béatrice, 1950–
B2798.K22273 2008
193—dc22   2008016892

British Library Cataloging-in-Publication Data is available

This book has been composed in Sabon

Printed on acid-free paper. ∞

press.princeton.edu

Printed in the United States of America

10 9 8 7 6 5 4 3 2 1

TO THE MEMORY OF

MARGARET DAULER WILSON

scholar, teacher, friend

Contents

Preface

THE ESSAYS INCLUDED in this volume were originally prepared for a conference held at Princeton in May 2004 around the theme "Kant and the Early Moderns." The content of the volume is actually more modest than this ambitious title might lead the reader to believe. Only a few of the early-modern figures discussed by Kant are under consideration here, and to ensure the unity of the volume, the ten essays selected for it are all focused on issues in metaphysics and what we today call epistemology and philosophy of mind. Nevertheless, the chosen figures are sufficiently prominent, both in their own right and in relation to Kant's explicit discussion of them, for this selection to offer a significant glimpse into the myths and realities of Kant's philosophical heritage.

The conference was organized as a series of dialogues between Kant specialists and early-modern specialists. To the former we asked to present, in its historical context as well as its internal argumentative coherence, Kant's view of his own relation to a chosen early-modern figure. To the latter we asked to outline in its own terms and context the view Kant is purportedly addressing, laying out differences in philosophical methods and backgrounds, perhaps tracing the sources of Kant's reading or misreading of them. Thus, the present volume consists of five pairs of essays involving Kant's relations to Descartes, Locke, Leibniz, Berkeley, and Hume. The first essay in each pair is primarily "Kant on . . . " or "Kant and . . . ," and the second essay is on the corresponding early-modern figure. Beyond this common pattern there turned out to be, as the reader will discover, about as many different ways to conceive the confrontation as there were presenters. What emerges from these dialogues is a richer and more complex picture than usually acknowledged, of the concepts and arguments that bind or pull apart Kant and his early-modern forebears. Our hope is that this volume will be an invitation to continue filling in the multifarious nuances of that picture. This is one of the ways in which we might also clarify the nature of our own debts, to Kant and to his early-modern predecessors.

We wish to express our gratitude to the philosophy department at Princeton University for its financial and organizational support, which was an immeasurable help in putting together this conference. Special thanks to Agnieszka Gerwel, whose energy and dedication greatly contributed to the conference running as smoothly as it did. Ian Malcolm supported from the earliest stage the project of publishing the papers that resulted from the conference, and exercised exemplary patience in waiting for the final draft of the volume. A special note of thanks to the Wissenschaftskolleg in Berlin, which offered one of us ideal conditions to work on the final preparation of the volume, and to the Faculty of Arts and Sciences at New York University, for supporting the leave that allowed her to spend the year at the Wissenschaftskolleg.

The conference was organized in memory of Margaret Wilson, who taught at Princeton for almost thirty years before her untimely death in 1998. To many of us she was an incomparable friend and teacher. The breadth and rigor of her expertise in early-modern philosophy all the way down to Kant was unparalleled. Her influence is present explicitly or implicitly throughout this volume.

DANIEL GARBER BÉATRICE LONGUENESSE
Princeton, NJ *New York, NY*
and
Berlin, Germany

Abbreviations and References for Primary Sources

GEORGE BERKELEY

Bk Works: Berkeley, George, 1948–1957: *The Works of George Berkeley, Bishop of Cloyne*, Luce, A. and Jessop, T. (eds.), 9 vols. (London: Thomas Nelson). Cited by volume and page numbers.

PHK: *A Treatise Concerning the Principles of Human Knowledge*. In *Bk Works* 2. Cited by section number.

[Berkeley, George,] 1737: *Alciphron ou le petit Philosophe: Das ist: Schutz-Schrifft Für die Wahrheit Der Christlichen Religion, wider die so genannten starcken Geister . . .* , Kahler, W. (ed. and trans.) (Lemgo: Meyer).

Berkeley, George, 1781: *Philosophische Werke, Erster Theil* (Leipzig: Schwickert).

RENÉ DESCARTES

AT: Descartes, René, 1981: *Oeuvres*, Adam, C., and Tannery, P. (eds.) (re-edition, Centre National de la Recherche Scientifique), 11 vols. (Paris: Librairie Philosophique J.Vrin). Cited by volume and page numbers.

CSMK: Descartes, René, 1984–1991: *The Philosophical Writings of Descartes*, Cottingham, J., Stoothoff, R., Murdoch, D., and Kenny, A. (eds. and trans.), 3 vols. (Cambridge: Cambridge University Press). Cited by volume and page numbers.

All works of Descartes are cited by volume and page numbers in *AT* and *CSMK*, except for the *Passions* and the *Principles*. Abbreviations for individual works are as follows:

Burman: *Conversation with Burman.*

DM: *Discourse on the Method.*

Meds: *Meditations.*

(Med II: Second Meditation.)

Second Replies: *Second Replies to Objections.*

Passions: *The Passions of the Soul* (cited by part and section).

Principles: *Principles of Philosophy* (cited by part and section).

Search: *The Search for Truth by Means of the Natural Light.*

DAVID HUME

EHU: Hume, David, 2000a: *An Enquiry Concerning Human Under-standing*, Beauchamp, T. L. (ed.) (Oxford: Oxford University Press). Cited by section and paragraph numbers.

EPM: Hume, David, 1998: *An Enquiry Concerning the Principles of Morals*, Beauchamp, T. L. (ed.) (Oxford: Oxford University Press). Cited by section and paragraph numbers.

THN: Hume, David, 2000b: *A Treatise of Human Nature*, Norton, D. F., and Norton, M. J. (eds.) (Oxford: Oxford University Press). Cited by book, part, section, and (where given) paragraph numbers.

IMMANUEL KANT

AA: Kant, Immanuel, 1900–: *Kants Gesammelte Schriften*, Deutsche Akademie der Wissenschaften (eds.), 29 vols. (Berlin: George Reimer/ Walter de Gruyter). Cited by volume and page numbers.

A—/B—: *Critique of Pure Reason*, cited by page numbers in Kant's first (A) and second (B) editions. The following translations are used:

Kant, Immanuel, 1933: *Critique of Pure Reason*, 2nd ed., Kemp Smith, N. (trans.) (London: Macmillan; repr. St. Martin's Press, 1961).
OR
Kant, Immanuel, 1998: *Critique of Pure Reason*, Guyer, P., and Wood, A. (trans.) (Cambridge: Cambridge University Press).

Except when noted, all of the following works of Kant's are cited by volume and page in *AA*:

CJ: Kant, Immanuel, 2000: *Critique of the Power of Judgment*, Guyer, P., and Matthews, E. (trans.) (Cambridge: Cambridge University Press). Cited by section number, as well as volume and page numbers in *AA*.

Corr.: Kant, Immanuel, 1967: *Philosophical Correspondence, 1759–99*, Zweig, A. (ed. and trans.) (Chicago: University of Chicago Press). Cited by page number.

CPrR: Kant, Immanuel, 1997: *Critique of Practical Reason*, Gregor, M. (trans.) (Cambridge: Cambridge University Press).

Dilucidatio: *A New Elucidation of the First Principles of Metaphysical Cognition*, in Kant, Immanuel, 1992: *Theoretical Philosophy before 1781*, Walford, D., and Meerbote, R. (eds. and trans.) (Cambridge: Cambridge University Press).

Discovery: *On a Discovery Whereby Any New Critique of Pure Reason Is to Be Made Superfluous by an Older One*, in Kant, Immanuel, 2002: *Theoretical Philosophy after 1781*, Allison, H., Heath, P., and Hat-field, G. (eds. and trans.) (Cambridge: Cambridge University Press).

Inaugural Dissertation: *On the Forms and Principles of the Sensible and the Intelligible World*, Meerbote, R. (trans.) in *Theoretical Philosophy before 1781*.

Logic: the *Jäsche Logic*, in Kant, Immanuel, 1995: *Lectures on Logic*, Young, J. M. (ed. and trans.) (Cambridge: Cambridge University Press).

Met.L₁: *Metaphysik L₁* in Kant, Immanuel, 1997: *Lectures on Metaphysics*, Ameriks, K., and Naragon, S. (eds. and trans.) (Cambridge: Cambridge University Press).

Met.Herder: *Metaphysik Herder*, in *Lectures on Metaphysics*.

Met.Mongrovius: *Metaphysik Mongrovius*, in *Lectures on Metaphysics*.

Met.Vigilantius: *Metaphysik Vigilantius*, in *Lectures on Metaphysics*.

MFNS: Kant, Immanuel, 2004: *Metaphysical Foundations of Natural Science*, Friedman, M. (ed. and trans.) (Cambridge: Cambridge University Press).

Negative Magnitudes: *Essay to Introduce the Concept of Negative Magnitude in Philosophy*, Walford, D. (trans.), in *Theoretical Philosophy before 1781*.

Notes: Kant, Immanuel, 2005: *Notes and Fragments*, Guyer, P. (ed.), Bowman, C., Guyer, P., and Rauscher, F. (trans.) (Cambridge: Cambridge University Press).

Progress: *What Real Progress Has Metaphysics Made in Germany since the Time of Leibniz and Wolff?* in *Theoretical Philosophy after 1781*.

Prolegomena: Kant, Immanuel, 1977: *Prolegomena to Any Future Metaphysics That Will Be Able to Come Forward as Science*, Carus, P., Beck, L. W., and Ellington, J. (eds. and trans.) (Indianapolis: Bobbs-Merrill). OR

Kant, Emmanuel, 2004: *Prolegomena to Any Future Metaphysics*, Hatfield, G. (trans.) (Cambridge: Cambridge University Press).

R: Kant, Immanuel, *Reflexionen*.

Tone: *On a Recently Prominent Tone of Superiority in Philosophy*, in *Theoretical Philosophy after 1781*.

GOTTFRIED WILHELM LEIBNIZ

AL: Leibniz, G. W., 1923–: *Sämtliche Schriften und Briefe*, Berlin-Brandenburgische Akademie der Wissenschaften (eds.) (Berlin: Akademie Verlag). Cited by series, volume, and page numbers.

AG: Leibniz, G. W., 1989: *G. W. Leibniz: Philosophical Essays*, Ariew, R., and Garber, D. (eds. and trans.) (Indianapolis: Hackett).

B: Bodemann, Eduard, 1896: *Die Leibniz-Handschriften der Königlichen Öffentlichen Bibliothek zu Hannover* (Hannover/Leipzig: Hahnsche Buchhandlung).

C: Leibniz, G. W., 1903: *Opuscules et fragment inédits de Leibniz*, Couturat, L. (ed.) (Paris: Alcan).

F: Leibniz, G. W., 1857: *Nouvelles lettres et opuscules inédits de Leibniz*, Foucher de Careil, A. (ed.) (Paris: Durand).

FW: Leibniz, G. W., 1998: *G. W. Leibniz: Philosophical Texts*, Francks, R., and Woolhouse, R. S. (Oxford: Oxford University Press).

G: Leibniz, G. W., 1875–1890: *Die Philosophischen Schriften von Leibniz*, Gerhardt, C. I. (ed.), 7 vols. (Berlin: Wiedmann). Cited by volume and page numbers.

GM: Leibniz, G. W., 1849–1863: *Mathematische Schriften*, Gerhardt, C. I. (ed.), 7 vols. (Berlin: A. Asher/ Halle: H. W. Schmidt). Cited by volume and page numbers.

Gr: Leibniz, G. W., 1948: *Textes inédits d'après les manuscrits de la Bibiothèque provinciale de Hanovre*, Grua, G. (ed.), 2 vols. (Paris: Presses Universitaires de France).

L: Leibniz, G. W., 1969: *G. W. Leibniz: Philosophical Papers and Letters*, 2nd ed., Loemker, L. E. (ed. and trans.) (Dordrecht: Reidel).

LC: Leibniz, G. W., and Clarke, S., 1956: *Leibniz-Clarke Correspondence, Together with Abstracts from Newton's Principia and Opticks*, Alexander, H. G. (ed. and trans.) (Manchester: Manchester University Press).

Mon.: "*Monadology*," cited by section number.

NE: Leibniz, G. W., 1981: *New Essays on Human Understanding*, Remnant, P., and Bennett, J. (trans.) (Cambridge: Cambridge University Press).

JOHN LOCKE

LW: Locke, John, 1823: *The Works of John Locke*, 10 vols. (London: Thomas Davison, Whitefriars).

Drafts: Locke, John, 1990: *Drafts for the Essay Concerning Human Understanding, and Other Philosophical Writings*, Nidditch, P. H., and Rogers, G.A.J. (eds.) (Oxford: Oxford University Press).

Draft C: Ms. Draft C of Locke, *Essay Concerning Human Understanding*. In the Pierpont Morgan Library, New York. (Note that excerpts from the manuscript have been transcribed and published in Mattern 1981.) Cited by book, chapter, and section numbers.

E: Locke, John, 1975: *An Essay Concerning Human Understanding*, Nidditch, P. H. (ed.) (Oxford: Oxford University Press). Cited by book, chapter, and section numbers.

TCE: Locke, John, 1963: *Some Thoughts Concerning Education*, Yolton, J. W., and Yolton, J. S. (eds.) (Oxford: Oxford University Press).

Locke, John, 1688a: "Extrait d'un livre anglois qui n'est pas encore publié, intitulé *Essai philosophique concernant l'entendement, où l'on montre quelle est l'étenduë de nos connoissances certaines, & la maniere dont nous y parvenons,*" Le Clerc, J. (trans.) in *Bibliothèque universelle et historique* 8:49–142.

Locke, John, 1688b: "[Review of Isaac Newton,] *Philosophiæ naturalis principia mathematica,*" in *Bibliothèque universelle et historique* 8:436–50.

Kant and the Early Moderns

Daniel Garber and Béatrice Longuenesse

KANT'S WORK is replete with references to his predecessors, in ancient as well as in modern philosophy. Whether positive or negative, these references are always part of Kant's effort to set up a picture of the history of metaphysics understood as a "history of pure reason" in which each philosophical figure of the past is called upon to play its role and occupy its proper place in the gradual—albeit conflict-ridden—discovery by reason of its own power and limits, as brought to light by Kant's critical philosophy.

Indeed, the final chapter of the *Critique of Pure Reason*, chapter 4 of the Transcendental Doctrine of Method, is called "The History of Pure Reason." This title, says Kant, "stands here only to designate a place that is left open in the system and must be filled in the future" (A852/B880).[1] Kant never filled that place by actually writing a "history of pure reason." Nevertheless, the nature and goals of such a history are clearly sketched out in the few programmatic paragraphs to which the chapter in question is reduced. This sketch helps us understand what Kant means by a "history of pure reason" and thus what he is looking for in the authors he cites in the course of his own work.

A "history of pure reason," says Kant, is a history that would be written "from a transcendental point of view" (A853/B880). As we know from the introduction to the *Critique of Pure Reason*, a transcendental investigation, for Kant, is an investigation into the possibility of synthetic a priori cognition—namely, into the possibility of a cognition that does not derive its justification from experience (and thus is a priori) but nevertheless does not rely on the mere analysis of concepts (and thus is *synthetic*). According to Kant, metaphysics is a prime example of such synthetic a priori cognition if it is possible at all as knowledge of actually existing objects rather than as a system of empty thoughts to which human reason is inevitably drawn. Correspondingly, in the preamble to the *Prolegomena to Any Future Metaphysics*, Kant declares that all metaphysics should come to a stop until a clear answer has been given to this question: How are synthetic a priori judgments possible? Philosophies of the past have all collapsed in a heap because of their incapacity to provide an answer to that question, indeed even to formulate it (*AA* 4 275-78). A similarly damning appreciation of the metaphysical endeavors of the past opens the outline of a "history of pure reason" in the *Critique of Pure Reason*:

"I will content myself with casting a cursory glance, from a merely transcendental point of view, namely, that of the nature of pure reason, on the whole of its labors hitherto, which presents to my view edifices, to be sure, but only in ruins" (A852/B880).

But what exactly does it mean to consider the edifices of the past from the point of view of "the nature of pure reason"? It means, says Kant, examining the answers that past metaphysical systems respectively gave to three fundamental questions. First, what is the *object* of metaphysical cognition, namely, what is truly *real*? Is it an object given to sensibility, or an object accessible to the intellect alone? A prime example of the former position is Epicurus; a prime example of the latter is Plato. Second, what is the *origin* of metaphysical cognition: does it depend on experience or is it independent of it? A prime example of the former answer would be Aristotle and for the modern times, Locke. A prime example of the latter would be Plato and for the modern times, Leibniz. Third, what is the method to be adopted in answering the previously mentioned questions? Here Kant first distinguishes between *natural* and *scientific* method. He cannot heap enough scorn on the first (it is "mere misology brought to principles," a dismissive statement probably directed at the commonsense philosophers he also denounced in the *Prolegomena*: see AA 4 258). Kant then distinguishes two kinds of scientific method, the dogmatic (whose prime example is Christian Wolff) and the skeptical (whose prime example is Hume). None of these methods, he claims, have been able to offer a satisfactory answer to the first two questions, those concerning the *object* and the *origin* of pure cognitions of reason. There remains only one: the critical method, which has just proved its superiority by the clear answers the *Critique of Pure Reason* offers to the questions of the object and the origin of metaphysical cognition.

Let us briefly recall what these answers were. The only reality metaphysical cognition can tell us anything about is that of sensible objects or appearances. These are real in the sense that their existence is independent of our representations, although their formal features depend on the a priori forms of our cognition. Things in themselves, namely, things as they are independently of our cognition, are real in the same sense: they too exist independently of our representations (cf. Bxxvi–vii). But these things are not, at least for us humans, objects of a purely intellectual cognition, indeed they are not for us objects of theoretical cognition at all. There is thus no synthetic a priori cognition except of appearances, *sensible* objects. The origin of such cognition is in the combined forms of pure understanding and pure sensibility. No metaphysical cognition can be obtained at all, at least from the theoretical standpoint, except by applying the principles grounded on these forms to some minimal empirical content: the empirical concept of matter expounded in the *Metaphysical Principles of the Science of Nature* (see *AA* 4 470). The objects of traditional metaphysics: the soul, the world, God, are not objects of theoretical cognition at all, but mere objects of thought, the contents of Ideas that have their origin in reason alone and have no more than a regulative role in cognition. In addition, the ideas of the soul and of God will turn out to have an important role as the objects of postulates of pure practical reason.

The standpoint of pure reason, then, or transcendental standpoint on the metaphysical ruins of the past, is a standpoint that is meant to confirm *a contrario* the correctness of Kant's answers to the three fundamental questions on which hangs the future of metaphysics. Kant's "history of pure reason" is a history of reason's painful introduction to the knowledge of its own limitations. In other words, Kant's approach to the metaphysical systems of the past is driven by concepts and concerns deliberately internal to his own system.

Of course, Kant is not the first philosopher for whom the demonstration of the collapse of previous systems supports the demonstration of the virtues of his own. Other notable examples include, for instance, Book 1 of Aristotle's *Metaphysics* or Book 1, part 4 of Hume's *Treatise of Human Nature*, "Of the Skeptical and Other Systems of Philosophy." More directly close to Kant, Leibniz's *New Essays on Human Understanding* had a direct influence on Kant's presentation of the general structure of the history of metaphysics as defined by the opposition between those who think that "everything which is inscribed [on our souls] comes solely from the senses and experience"—Leibniz's examples are Aristotle and Locke—and those who think that "the soul inherently contains the sources of various notions and doctrines"— Leibniz's examples are Plato and himself (see *NE*, 48–49). And tracing back the concepts of metaphysics to the very nature of human cognitive powers is an idea that Hume, before Kant, had brought to a systematic development. But what is specific to Kant is the combined statement of the *illusory nature* of metaphysical endeavors, at least in the domain of "special metaphysics" (where the objects of investigation are the soul, the world, and God), the *inevitability* of the illusion, and its *fruitfulness* provided its theoretical and practical roles are carefully regimented. The history of metaphysics, conceived as a history of pure reason, thus becomes one more confirmation of the truth of the critical system. Kant gives unprecedented importance to the history of metaphysics by initiating a project in which investigating the history of metaphysics is part of investigating the nature of reason, and thus part of transcendental philosophy as the necessary preliminary to the "true" metaphysics. But precisely for that reason, the history thus expounded is, in a way, ahistorical since it is part of the timeless endeavor "to bring human reason to full satisfaction in that which has always, but until now vainly, occupied its lust for knowledge" (A855/B883).

Unsurprisingly, then, even though Kant never filled out the specific chapter on the "history of pure reason," we can find elements of it dispersed throughout the system. The preface of the *Critique of Pure Reason* opens with a reference to the sorry state of metaphysics and to the opposite methods of dogmatism and skepticism that have been unsuccessfully used in trying either to answer metaphysical questions or to put them to rest. And each part of the *Critique*, as Kant gradually unfolds his own answer to the question of the origin and object of metaphysical knowledge, contains extensive references to the authors whose answer to those two questions Kant takes himself to be directly opposing: Newton, Leibniz, Wolff, Berkeley in the Transcendental Aesthetic; Aristotle in the Metaphysical Deduction of the Categories; Plato in the Introduction to the Transcendental Dialectic; Hume in the Methodology, with a retrospective view on Kant's account of causality in the Second Analogy of Experience. Locke and Leibniz in the Amphiboly of the Concepts of Reflection. Descartes and Mendelssohn in the Paralogisms of Pure Reason. Newton and Leibniz, related back to the ancient opposition between Epicurians ("sensualists") and Platonists ("intellectualists) in the Antinomy of Pure Reason. Descartes again in the Ideal of Pure Reason. This list is not complete, and more examples can be found in all of Kant's published works.

This raises the question of what Kant had actually read of the authors he cites and discusses. In many cases, this question has no clear-cut answer. Kant's library is not a reliable indicator, for we know that Kant sold or gave away many of his books. Kant lived above Kanter's well-furnished bookstore, from which he could get a steady supply of new publications. Among the secondary sources that could have strongly influenced his view of the history of philosophy was Johann Jakob Brucker's 1766–1767 *Historia critica philosophiae a mundi incunabilis ad nostram usque aetetum deducta*, a mammoth work that influenced generations of German scholars and which Kant explicitly cites in the *Critique* (see A316/B372). In addition, Kant's account of historical figures was influenced by the works of post-Leibnizian German rationalists, which served as textbooks for his courses. For instance, even if it is possible that Kant read not only Descartes' *Discourse on the Method* but also the *Meditations* and *Objections and Replies*, nevertheless his presentation of the Cartesian views, for instance his very imperfect characterization of the Cogito argument, is probably influenced by the cursory account available in Wolff's *Psychologia Rationalis*, Wolff's *Psychologia Empirica*, and Baumgarten's *Metaphysica*. The only reasonably secure method to determine how much Kant actually knew and how he knew it, is thus to look at what Kant says, compare it to the primary sources that could actually have been available to him, and in case of discrepancies, look for other possible sources.

In any event, the systematic power of Kant's thought is such that to this day, what counts as, e.g., "Descartes" or "Hume" or "Leibniz" in our history textbooks and our historical conscience might well be Descartes or Hume or Leibniz read in light of Kant's reconstruction of their thought rather than those philosophers as they would have been read and understood before Kant. As a result, what exactly is novel about Kant's own philosophy is itself somewhat obscured. Each essay in this volume is an attempt to set the record straight on both counts.

Kant deals with a number of aspects of Descartes' philosophy. His most notorious discussion is contained in the Paralogisms of Pure Reason in the *Critique of Pure Reason*, in which he criticizes Descartes' move from the proposition "I think" to the assertion that I exist as a thinking substance, distinct from the body. Other important discussions, by Kant, of Descartes' philosophy, concern Descartes' assertion that the existence of the mind is more immediately known than the existence of bodies outside us, and Descartes' so-called ontological proof of the existence of God. Béatrice Longuenesse focuses her essay (chapter 1) on the first and second discussions just mentioned: Kant's criticism of Descartes' move from "I think" to "I am a substance whose sole attribute is to think," and Kant's refutation of Descartes' "problematic idealism." She analyzes the role Kant and Descartes respectively assign to the proposition "I think," in the argument of the Transcendental Deduction of the Categories (Kant) and in the Second Meditation (Descartes). She then evaluates Kant's criticism of Descartes' move from "I think, I exist" to "I exist as a thinking substance, distinct from the body" and Kant's refutation of Descartes' "problematic idealism." While endorsing, on the whole, Kant's argument against Descartes' move from "I think" to "I am a thinking substance," she suggests, in contrast, that Kant's refutation of Descartes' problematic idealism is less successful. In his own essay (chapter 2), Jean-Marie Beyssade undertakes to set the record straight on Descartes' behalf. He emphasizes the differences between Descartes' views and those that Kant attributes to him. Descartes' account of mind and its relation to body, he notes, is much more complex than Kant would have us believe. Descartes' doctrines that the mind is something whose essence is thought, is distinct from the body, and is better known than the body, are not a simple consequence of the premise "I think." Rather, they are established by a long and complex argument and the result of a process that takes place over the course of six "days" of meditation.

While Descartes' presence in Kant's work is narrowly focused on a few issues, the influence of Leibniz is much more pervasive, though ironically, more difficult to track and deal with. Leibniz was an *éminence grise* who stands behind much of German philosophy in the eighteenth century. His thought, as absorbed and transformed by figures such as Christian Wolff, made its way into every corner of the intellectual world. Because of that, separating out his influence from that of Wolff is very difficult. According to the standard story, while Kant began as a follower of the Leibniz-Wolffian philosophy, as he developed, he drifted further and further away. By the time of the *Critique of Pure Reason*, the story goes, he had fully repudiated the Leibniz-Wolffian philosophy. In her essay (chapter 3), Anja Jauernig offers an alternative account of Kant's relation to Leibniz. While she does not deny that Kant departs from Leibniz's philosophy in important ways, there is also an important sense in which Kant regarded himself as providing "the true apology for Leibniz," as he puts it in one of his last works (*Discovery*, AA 8 250). While Kant may have seen himself as rejecting the *Leibniz-Wolffian* philosophy, Jauernig argues that there is a way in which Kant saw himself as a defender of the *Leibnizian* philosophy. Daniel Garber (chapter 4), though, emphasizes the extent to which the true Leibniz was hidden from Kant. While Kant may have thought that he was defending Leibniz, the view of Leibniz that he held was deeply influenced by the historical tradition in which Leibniz was read in the eighteenth century—a tradition that was shaped by the relatively few texts that were available to the eighteenth-century reader. Most of the Leibnizian texts that are currently taken as central were only made available long after Kant's death. While the short and concise list of theses that, for Kant, define Leibniz's philosophy are not entirely misleading, they fall far short of characterizing Leibniz's complex thought, which evolved and changed throughout his career.

Both Locke and Kant were interested in the limits on our knowledge. In his *Essay Concerning Human Understanding*, Locke traces the path between experience and our ideas in order to determine the limits of what we can know about the world. His conclusion is that the sense organs we have determine the boundaries of knowledge. While we can have probable opinion about what lies behind those limits, the senses set strict boundaries. For Kant, too, the senses put boundaries on our knowledge, which is strictly limited to the phenomenal world of appearances. In his essay (chapter 5), Paul Guyer explores the relations between Locke and Kant on these questions. He emphasizes that while Locke's program is largely empirical, Kant's is transcendental. That is, while Locke argues from the empirical nature of our senses and the way in which we form ideas on the basis of the senses, Kant argues from the possibility of synthetic a priori knowledge: if synthetic a priori knowledge is to be possible, then knowledge must be limited to the phenomenal world. While Guyer acknowledges the limitations in Kant's transcendental argument, he argues that it allows a greater scope for empirical knowledge than Locke does. On Guyer's account, Kant believes that we can extend our knowledge beyond the deliverances of the senses through the discovery of causal laws. In that way he sees Kant's philosophy as superior to Locke's. Lisa Downing (chapter 6) considers these questions from the point of view of Locke. In the course of tracing the history of Locke's views on the limitations that the senses place on the scope of human knowledge, from the early drafts of the *Essay* to the *Essay* itself and beyond to the *Thoughts Concerning Education* and the polemical exchanges with Edward Stillingfleet, she sees an evolution in Locke's views that enables him to capture not only Boyle's empirical science, but also Newton's. In that context, she sees an openness toward new empirical knowledge in Locke's thought that goes beyond what Guyer argues for Kant.

There are some obvious connections between Berkeley's views and those of Kant. Both focus on the objects of our experience, and both claim that they constitute all that we can properly be said to know. There are also obvious differences, though. For Berkeley, there is nothing but minds and their ideas; Berkeley explicitly denies the mind-independent material things that others have supposed to exist. For Kant, on the other hand, while our knowledge is limited to the objects of possible experience, he does believe that behind them there are things in themselves that do have real existence, though they are beyond the possibility of our knowing. But still, one might wonder, how different are Berkeley and Kant on this question? Despite his insistent claims to the contrary, might Kant in fact be very close to Berkeley's position? In her essay (chapter 7), Dina Emundts explores this question. On Kant's view, Berkeley is to be understood as holding that the world of bodies is purely illusory, a position that he definitely did not want to hold. Though Emundts does consider it significant that Kant believes in the existence of things in themselves, she places more emphasis on Kant's conception of truth and objectivity. She argues that Kant has resources that Berkeley did not for constituting real objects in an objective world. It is on these grounds that she wants to claim that Kant's transcendental idealism does not reduce to Berkeley's world of illusion. Kenneth Winkler (chapter 8) expresses some reservations with respect to Emundts's readings of Berkeley and Kant. But the bulk of his essay is an explication and defense of Kant's understanding of Berkeley. Modern scholars of Berkeley's philosophy in general resist Kant's view of Berkeley's world as illusory. But, Winkler argues, there is real truth in Kant's characterization. Winkler contextualizes Kant's view of Berkeley in eighteenth-century conceptions of the history of philosophy. He sees Kant's reading of Berkeley's position—and Berkeley's conception of his own position—as linked to Plato's Battle of Gods and Giants, that is, the conflict between idealism and materialism, taken broadly, which eighteenth-century historians of philosophy took as a framework for understanding their contemporaries. Winkler argues that Kant, along with Berkeley himself, saw Berkeley's position in terms of that dispute, and saw Berkeley as being on the side of the gods. In the context of that philosophical vision, it is not improper to see the physical world as illusory in a sense and of less ultimate significance than the world of spirit—again, a perspective that can be attributed to Berkeley himself.

Hume's influence on Kant is well-known. As Kant famously put it, Hume is the philosopher who awoke him from his dogmatic slumbers (*Prolegomena*, preface, AA 4 260). In particular, Kant was drawn into philosophical speculation by Hume's thought about cause and effect. Hume was interested in the way in which a cause is necessarily connected with its effect. Hume's insight was to see the role that mind plays in determining the connection between the two. The connection between cause and effect is not something that we can learn directly from experience, Hume argues. Rather, like events associated with one another in experience produce an association between two kinds of events (fire and smoke, for example), so that when we see the one (fire), we expect the other (smoke). The necessary connection is, in that way, not in things themselves but in the mind that passes from the cause to the effect. This led Kant to appreciate the contribution that the mind could make to our perception of the world. In his essay (chapter 9), Wayne Waxman examines Kant's response to Hume. He argues that, in a way, the whole project of the *Critique of Pure Reason* is itself a response to Hume. Waxman argues that Kant uses Hume's basic strategy of looking to the senses to understand how the mind is furnished with its contents and what those contents are. But he shows how Kant had a source of sensible representation that Hume does not: for Kant, unlike Hume, the senses themselves are capable of a priori intuition. In that way, Waxman sees Kant's thought as a broader and corrected version of Hume's. Don Garrett (chapter 10), on the other hand, takes Hume's point of view on the matter. From Kant's point of view, there is something missing in Hume's thought: had Hume only realized that mathematics and metaphysics are synthetic a priori, Kant holds, then he would have been led to transcendental idealism, just as Kant himself was. Garrett tries to show that Hume did not really need Kant's help, and that his philosophy was quite adequate largely as it stood.

There is much left to do to understand the ways in which Kant contributed to our understanding (and perhaps misunderstanding) of the great philosophers who stood before him. The essays in this book represent first attempts at raising the right questions and sorting out the ways in which Kant related to early-modern philosophy.

CHAPTER 1

Kant's "I Think" versus Descartes' "I Am a Thing That Thinks"

Béatrice Longuenesse

WITH ONE EXCEPTION, all references to Descartes in Kant's *Critique of Pure Reason* occur in the Transcendental Dialectic. After having laid out in the Transcendental Aesthetic and Analytic what he takes to be the legitimate use of our understanding and reason—namely, that use that remains within the boundaries of possible sensory experience—in the Transcendental Dialectic Kant goes on to denounce the illusions of a metaphysical thinking that ignores those limits. His (mostly unnamed) targets are the metaphysicians of Leibnizian inspiration (primarily Wolff and Baumgarten), whose metaphysics textbooks Kant used as material for his own lectures. But Kant specifically addresses Descartes' own views and arguments on two occasions. First, in his criticism of rationalist theories of the mind as a thinking substance distinct from the body, in the first chapter of the Transcendental Dialectic, the Paralogisms of Pure Reason (A341/B399-A405/B432). Second, in his criticism of the so-called ontological proof of the existence of God, which Kant also calls the Cartesian proof, in the third chapter of the Transcendental Dialectic, the Transcendental Ideal (A592/B620-A603/B631). Moreover, Kant's "Refutation of Idealism," an addition to the Transcendental Analytic in the second edition of the *Critique*, is explicitly addressed at what Kant calls Descartes' "problematic idealism," namely, Descartes' statement that the existence of the mind is more immediately known and thus more certain than that of bodies, including our own (B274–79). And finally, we can read an implicit reference to Descartes in the famous statement that opens §16 of the Transcendental Deduction of the Categories, in the second edition of the *Critique*:

> The **I think** must be **able** to accompany all my representations: for otherwise something would be represented in me that could not be thought at all, which is as much as to say that the representation would either be impossible or else at least would be nothing to me. (B131–32)

In this chapter, I shall not consider Kant's criticism of the "Cartesian proof" of the existence of God. Not that it is any less important to Kant's criticism of Cartesian metaphysics than is his appropriation of Descartes'

"I think" and "I am, I exist." Quite the contrary: not only is it equally important, but there are interesting comparisons to be made between the two issues. Kant shares Descartes' conviction of the foundational role of the proposition "I think" on the one hand, of the concept of God on the other hand, in framing all cognitive use of reason. And in both cases, Kant's discussion of the Cartesian view is focused primarily on the *statements of existence* Descartes thinks he can derive from the proposition "I think" and from the concept of God, respectively. But Kant's attitude toward those derivations is very different. Kant notoriously criticizes the Cartesian proof of the existence of God, on the ground that existence is not a predicate of a thing or "real predicate," so that "God exists" cannot be analytically derived from "God is the most perfect being" (see A592/B620-A603/B631). In contrast, not only does Kant endorse Descartes' claim that the assertion "I think" entails the assertion "I exist," he even goes as far as to maintain that the latter is *contained* in the former (a point that I will examine later). But he criticizes Descartes for ignoring the fact that my consciousness of the existence of bodies outside me is just as immediate as my consciousness of the existence of my own mental states, at least insofar as I am conscious of this existence as *determined in time*.

I shall be considering the latter set of issues: the meaning of the proposition "I think" and the statements of existence Descartes and Kant respectively take to be necessarily connected with it. I shall do this in three steps:

1) I shall compare the contexts in which Descartes and Kant respectively discuss the proposition "I think": the first step out of radical doubt in the Second Meditation (Descartes, see Med II, *AT* VII 25; *AT* IX-1 19 (*CSMK* II 27)), the Transcendental Deduction of the Categories (Kant, see B131–32).[1] One striking fact here is that if Kant's concern is with "the 'I think' " (namely: the *proposition* "I think"), Descartes never mentions "I think" alone, but always "I think, therefore I am" or "I am, I exist as long as I think."[2] I shall try to elucidate the import of that initial difference for Descartes' and Kant's respective understanding of "I think," *cogito*.

2) Based on this first comparison, I shall endeavor to clarify the nature of Kant's criticism of Descartes in the Paralogisms of Pure Reason. To understand Kant's opposition to Descartes, it is first important to understand the points of proximity between them. As we shall see, Kant endorses the Cartesian claim that "I think" entails "I exist." He even maintains that one cannot think the one without thinking the other ("I think," insofar as it is actually thought, implicitly contains "I exist"). He also accepts the obvious point that "I" in "I think" refers to *something that thinks*. What he refuses is Descartes' assertion that we know this thing to be a thing whose *only* essential attribute is to think, namely, a thinking substance, or a mind distinct from the body.

3) Kant most definitely *disagrees* with Descartes' statement that my existence as a mind is more immediately known than the existence of bodies outside me, including my own. This point is addressed in the fourth Paralogism in the A edition of the *Critique of Pure Reason* (A366-A379). Significantly, this is the only instance in all four Paralogisms where Kant directs his criticism specifically at Descartes (rather than at some generic version of rationalist metaphysics). Descartes is again explicitly mentioned when Kant reformulates his Refutation of Idealism in the B edition of the Transcendental Analytic in the *Critique of Pure Reason* (B274–79). Those two versions of Kant's criticism of Descartes' "problematic idealism" will be the object of my investigation in the third part of this chapter.

There are systematic correlations between the three points I just mentioned, namely, (1) Kant's and Descartes' different concerns in considering the proposition "I think," (2) the interpretation of the proposition "I am a thinking thing" they respectively endorse, and finally (3) the certainty they respectively attach to the existence of bodies "outside me." I shall try to draw out these systematic correlations. On the whole, my conclusions are mixed. I think Kant gives a better account than does Descartes (indeed, he gives an account that is altogether absent from Descartes) of *why* thinking has to be attributed to the subject "I" (rather than, say, "it") in the proposition "I think" (rather than "it thinks" or "it is thought"). I also think that Kant's account of the difference between what he calls the "mere logical subject 'I' " in "I think," and any kind of thinking *thing*, or metaphysical substrate of thought, is the most interesting aspect of his anti-Cartesian interpretation of *cogito*. However, the sticking point, in Kant's confrontation with the Cartesian view, is Kant's purported refutation of idealism. I would like it to be a successful argument. But I am afraid I have to recognize, like many before me, that all I can do is throw up my arms in despair.

Having thus laid out my cards, let me now begin.

DESCARTES' *EGO COGITO, ERGO SUM*, KANT'S *I THINK*

The context of Descartes' so-called *cogito* argument is well-known: in the *Meditations on First Philosophy*, the meditator undertakes to accept as true only those beliefs that have survived the test of radical doubt, namely, that have survived all attempts at identifying a possible ground for disbelief. In the First Meditation, the meditator thus successively discards beliefs in the existence of ordinary objects of sensory perception, from the remotest to the closest and most familiar—including his own body—; he finds reasons to discard belief in the existence of even the simple phenomenal components of those objects of sensory perception, which one might initially have thought could not possibly be mere fictions, however deluded the representations of their composition might be. Finally he finds reasons to discard belief in even the seemingly most unassailable truths of mathematics. Reinforcing this last, most radical stage of the doubt is the supposition of a malicious demon that deceives me even in the most careful exercise of my perception and reason. This last, desperate stage of the doubt, however, is also what leads to light, at the beginning of the Second Meditation:

> I have convinced myself that there is absolutely nothing in the world, no sky, no earth, no mind, no bodies. Does it now follow that I too do not exist? No: if I convinced myself of something, then I certainly existed. But there is a deceiver of supreme power and cunning who is deliberately and constantly deceiving me. In that case I too undoubtedly exist, if he is deceiving me; and let him deceive me as much as he can, he will never bring it about that I am nothing as long as I think that I am something. So after considering everything very thoroughly I must finally conclude that this proposition *I am, I exist*, is necessarily true whenever it is put forward by me or conceived in my mind. (*AT* VII 25; *AT* IX-1 19 (*CSMK* II 17))

As is well-known, Descartes' famous formulation "I think, therefore I am" does not appear in the *Meditations*. It is present in this form in the *Discourse on Method* ("Je pense, donc je suis") and in the *Principles of Philosophy* ("Ego cogito, ergo sum") (*AT* VI 32 (*CSMK* I 127); *Principles* I.7). In the *Meditations*, the emphasis is directly on the statement of existence: "I am, I exist," although of course what grounds this statement of existence is the indubitable fact that "I convinced myself of something," namely, the indubitable fact that I think, however deluded my thoughts may be.

Innumerable attempts have been made at determining the exact nature of Descartes' move from the proposition "I think" to the proposition "I am, I exist," or indeed whether there is any inference at all from one to the other. Doing justice to that discussion is beyond the scope of this chapter. Let me just make two remarks that I hope will be helpful in comparing Descartes' "I think, therefore I am" to Kant's "I think."

The first concerns the nature of Descartes' move from "I think" to "I am, I exist." Contrary to Kant's charge (which we shall consider in a moment), Descartes does *not* derive the truth of the proposition "I exist" by a syllogistic inference from the major premise "Everything that thinks, exists" and the minor premise "I think." On the contrary, Descartes repeatedly insists that the proposition "I exist" is known with certainty to be true by virtue of our knowing that *the particular proposition* "I think" is indubitably true, and *not* from a prior knowledge of the universal proposition "Everything that thinks, exists." The classic reference here is from the Second Replies:

> When we perceive that we are things that think, this is a first notion that is derived from no syllogism; and when someone says, "I think, therefore I am, or I exist," he does not conclude his existence from his thought as if by the force of some syllogism, but as something known by itself; he sees it by a simple inspection of the mind. As it appears from the fact that, if he deduced it from the syllogism, he would first have had to know this major premise: Everything that thinks, is or exists. But on the contrary, it is taught to him from the fact that he feels in himself that it cannot be the case that he thinks, unless he exists. For it is in the nature of our mind to form general propositions from the knowledge of particular propositions. (*AT* VII 140–41, *AT* IX–1 110–11 (*CSMK* II 100). For a similar point, see also Letter to Clerselier on the Instances of Gassendi, *AT* IX 206 (*CSMK* II 271).)

However, the fact that the proposition "I exist" is not derived from "I think" by way of a *syllogistic* inference does not mean that its knowledge depends on no inference at all. It is true that in the Second Meditation (contrary to the formulations of the *Discourse on Method* or the *Principles*), there does not seem to be any mention of *inference* from "I think" to "I exist." Rather, the meditator directly asserts the certainty of the proposition "I exist": "The proposition I am, I exist, is necessarily true *whenever it is put forward by me or conceived in my mind*" (*AT* VII 25; *AT* IX–1 19 (*CSMK* II 17); emphasis mine). However, later in the *Meditations* Descartes does speak of an inference when he recapitulates the argument of the Second Meditation: "Natural light has formerly shown me that, *from the fact* that I doubted, *I could conclude* that I was." Or again: "Examining these past days whether anything at all existed in the world and knowing that, *from the sole fact* that I examined this question, *it followed very evidently* that I myself existed."[3] However, the striking fact here is that the inference is not from the statement of something's having a property (thinking) to the statement of its having another property (existing). Rather, the inference is from the statement of *a fact* (*that I think*) to the statement of an aspect of *this very same fact*, which is its necessary condition (*that I exist*). This being so, the assertion of my existence will be no more and no less indubitable than the assertion *that I think*. So what makes *this* assertion indubitable?

This question leads to my second remark, which concerns the role of 'I' in Descartes' argument. Two characteristics of the proposition "I think" make it indubitably true every time I actually think it. One is the peculiar relation that obtains between the *content* of the proposition and the *thinking* of the proposition (be it even in the attitude of doubt: "I doubt that I think"). The very fact of thinking the proposition "I think" makes the proposition true. Note, however, that we might make the same point about the proposition formulated impersonally: in being thought (by anybody at all, including me, or anyone else), the proposition "there is thought" is made true. Its truth-condition, that there *be* thought, is satisfied every time anyone or anything thinks: "there is thought." However—and this is the second aspect of the proposition to be taken into account—even under this impersonal form ("there is thought"), the proposition is not only true but also *known* to be true only by virtue of the fact that *the thinker of the proposition* "there is thought" is the truth maker of that proposition, precisely by virtue of the fact that he thinks it. In other words, the reason the thinker of the proposition "it is thought" or "there is thought" *knows* the proposition to be true is that it is he, himself, who is the bearer of the thought (the thinking) mentioned in the proposition "there is thought" (meaning: "there is thinking"). But this identity between the thinker of the proposition "there is thought" and the bearer of the thought (the thinking) mentioned in the proposition is precisely what is expressed by formulating the proposition in the first person: "I think." In thinking "I think," I refer the predicate of "thinking" to the one logical subject of whom I know indubitably, just by virtue of *thinking* the proposition "I think," that the predicate is true.[4]

To the question, why should thought be attributed in the first person rather than be expressed impersonally, I suggest that as far as Descartes' *cogito* argument is concerned, there is no other response to be sought than this: what 'I' in "I think" expresses is just this fact that in thinking "I think," the predicate "think" is attributed to the one subject of which it is indubitably *known to be true* just by virtue of thinking the proposition "I think." Descartes' Archimedean point, lifting him out of radical doubt, thus rests on two pillars: that "I exist" is a necessary condition of "I think"; and that "I think" is both *true* and *known to be true* just by virtue of being thought.

As we shall now see, the role of 'I' in Kant's "I think" is quite different from the role of 'I' in Descartes' *Cogito, ergo sum*. Not that they are incompatible. In fact, I shall suggest that Kant basically accepts Descartes' *Cogito, ergo sum* (or rather: *cogito = sum cogitans*) as I just analyzed it, although he rejects the syllogistic interpretation of it he wrongly attributes to Descartes. But Kant, I shall suggest, goes further in understanding the role of 'I' in "I think" by considering "I think" quite independently of any concern with the resolution of Cartesian doubts about existence.

The most famous statement in the *Critique of Pure Reason* is perhaps the following, which opens §16 of the Transcendental Deduction of the Categories in the B edition:

The **I think** must **be able** to accompany all my representations; for otherwise something would be represented in me that could not be thought at all, which is as much as to say that the representation would either be impossible or else at least would be nothing to me. (B131–32)

The "I think" means: the proposition, or the thought, "I think." When Kant says that "the thought 'I think' must be able to accompany all my representations," he is not claiming that it must *actually* accompany all of them, or even less that any time I think 'p' I necessarily also think "I think 'p' " or "I think that p." Rather, I suggest, he means that a representation is not *mine* ("*my* representation" in the text cited) unless I *can* ascribe it to myself, and moreover unless I can ascribe it to myself *under a description*, or as conceptualized in some determinate way. Consider, for instance, a case in which I say: "Look, that's a tower!" And someone will answer: "Are you sure?" To which I will reply: "Yeah, I *think* it's a tower." "I think," here, does not express a turning of my attention to myself as the thinker of the thought: "that's a tower." Rather, "I *think* it's a tower" summarizes some implicit process of combining and comparing the present object of my perceptual state with a whole array of previous objects of previous states, as well as taking stock of the location of the present object in space, the angle under which I perceive it, the quality of light, and so on, all factors that contribute to the identification of this particular object as a tower. When Kant says: "The 'I think' must be able to accompany all *my* representations," what he means is that in order to be mine (that is, to be such that it at least can be recognized, thought as *mine*, what *I* see, hear, imagine, and so on), a representation must be taken up in such a process of combination and comparison, which—the argument will continue—is also the process in virtue of which the *object* of the representation is *recognizable under a concept*, or thought.

This is a pretty minimal way of characterizing what Kant has in mind with the statement just quoted. Much more would need to be said, and is said by Kant, about what is presupposed by the ascription of my representations to myself in the proposition "I think." What I mainly want to stress here is that clearly, the emphasis on the relation of all my representations to the proposition "I think," in Kant's Transcendental Deduction, has quite a different role from the one it had in Descartes' Second Meditation. Kant's concern in the Transcendental Deduction is not any kind of skeptical doubt about *existence*, much less a doubt about the existence of the objects of our sensory experience. "I think" is not introduced as a solution to *that* kind of skepticism. Rather, it is part of Kant's response to a Humean brand of skepticism, a skepticism that is primarily directed at the objective validity of ideas of necessary connection. In other words, when Kant states that a representation is *mine* only if it can be accompanied by the thought "I think," he does *not* mean to move from there to the statement that a representation that is mine (or that I recognize as mine) is accompanied by the certainty of my own existence. Rather, he means to move from there to the statement that all *my* representations are taken up in one and the same act of combining and comparing them, an act that is determined according to some universal concepts of the understanding, among which is the concept of causal connection.

Note that the thought "I think" we are talking about in this context is a thought that "must be able to accompany" all my *perceptual* representations. According to Kant, all other modes of thinking, including the most abstract (mathematical thinking, and even logic), are premised on the most original function of thinking, whose role is to combine and compare objects of perceptual experience, and to recognize them under concepts. In this context, to say that representations are mine (i.e., possibly accompanied by the thought "I think") is to say three main things. *First*, I commit myself, as a thinker, to making consistent statements about those representations. Any inconsistency in the ways in which I describe the objects of my representations calls for evaluation, interpretation, and perhaps correction *by me*. For instance, if I think "the rose is in bloom," and I also think "the rose is faded," either I recognize that I am not thinking in both cases about one and the same rose, or I recognize that time has elapsed and that the very same rose that two hours ago appeared to me as in bloom now appears to me as faded. These evaluations have to be made from one and the same standpoint, mine. We make these kinds of judgments all the time, and in exercising judgment in this way, each of us implicitly commits himself to consistency in his judgments and is thus capable of making relatively reasonable sense of the world around him. The role of 'I' here is to express the fact that one and the same thinker, from one and the same standpoint, thinks the thoughts by which sense is made of a complex array of perceptual experiences. If the latter were attributed to *different* thinkers, no similar demand of consistency between the perceptual thoughts could be demanded—although of course *different* standpoints can themselves be evaluated within *one* standpoint that locates them with respect to one another: again, the standpoint of 'I' in "I think."

Second, it is not just conceptual coherence we endeavor to bring into our representations. Committing ourselves to thinking and recognizing the objects of our perceptual experiences under mutually consistent concepts is inseparable from supposing those objects to *belong in one space and one time*, in which all of them ought to be correlated. This is why for Kant, *conceptual* unity is inseparable from *unity of intuition*, whose forms are space and time: all objects have to be given or imagined in one space and one time.[5]

Third, both these unifying functions (thinking in one coherent and consistent conceptual space, intuiting in one space and one time) are at work in empirical circumstances specific to *a particular perceiver and thinker.* But those very same functions make it possible for any particular perceiver and thinker to recognize his standpoint as one particular standpoint, to be compared and combined with that of all other perceiving and thinking beings like him. This makes the use of 'I' in "I think" quite peculiar. For on the one hand, "I think" is a *universal* form of thought, which can be attributed to *any* thinker; on the other hand, this universal form is necessary for *particular, empirically determined perceivers and thinkers* to come up with thoughts about the world that *are independent of their own particular standpoint on the world.*[6]

There is nothing more to be known of 'I' in the context of this argument. It matters not at all what kind of entity is the bearer of the act whose peculiar kind of unity is expressed by the thought "I think." In referring his thoughts to 'I,' the thinker (perceiver, imaginer) is doing nothing more than committing himself to the unity and consistency of his thoughts, and committing himself to obtaining a unified standpoint that could be shared by all: an objective standpoint, also called by Kant "objective unity of apperception."

It is thus apparent that the function of 'I' in this context is quite different from what it was in Descartes' *cogito* argument. As we saw, there the use of 'I' served to express the identity between the subject *of which* "think" is asserted in the proposition "I think" and the subject *currently thinking* the proposition in which the predicate 'think' is attributed to a subject. In Kant's Transcendental Deduction, 'I' serves to express the identity of the subject that thinks a variety of thoughts about objects of perceptual experience and commits himself to the consistency of his thoughts about those objects. It is important to note, however, that the two approaches are not incompatible: the referent of Kant's 'I,' whoever s/he is, is obviously also the referent of Descartes' 'I,' the subject of the proposition "I think" identical to the thinker of the proposition. But again, the role of 'I' in Kant's "I think" is different from the role of 'I' in Descartes' "I think, therefore I am"; i.e., the function fulfilled by attributing 'think' to 'I' is in each case different.

An indication that the two approaches are not incompatible is that Kant *agrees* with Descartes that the proposition "I think" entails the proposition "I exist." Indeed, he thinks that the proposition "I think" just means "I exist thinking." He also notes that the notion of existence at work in this thought is prior to the *category* of existence or actuality, which applies to objects of experience. If anything, Kant claims to *improve* on Descartes' affirmation of the immediate certainty of "Ego sum, ego existo." For as I recalled earlier, if he has a reproach to make to

Descartes on this particular point, it is to have thought that the truth of *sum* is *inferred* from the truth of *cogito* rather than immediately contained in it. Kant's statement on this point is well-known, but still worth citing at some length:

> The 'I think' is, as has already been said, an empirical proposition, and contains within itself the proposition 'I exist'. But I cannot say "Everything that thinks, exists"; for then the property of thinking would make all beings possessing it into necessary beings. Hence my existence also cannot be regarded as inferred from the proposition 'I think,' as Descartes held (for otherwise the major premise, 'Everything that thinks, exists' would have to precede it) but rather it is identical with it. It expresses an indeterminate empirical intuition, i.e., a perception (hence it proves that sensation, which consequently belongs to sensibility, grounds this existential proposition) but it precedes the experience that is to determine the object of perception through the category in regard to time; and here existence is not yet a category, which is not related to an indeterminately given object, but rather to an object of which one has a concept, and of which one wants to know whether or not it is posited outside this concept. An indeterminate perception here signifies only something real which was given, [. . .] as something that in fact exists and is indicated as an existing thing in the proposition "I think." (B422n. See also B418, B428, B157n.)

As I noted already, Kant is mistaken when he attributes to Descartes the view that my existence is inferred from "I think" via a syllogistic inference. Descartes explicitly says the reverse more than once, and the existence that is, according to Kant, "prior to the category of existence" seems in fact strikingly similar to the existence that is asserted, according to Descartes, as a necessary condition of the very assertion "I think." Surprisingly enough, although Kant has clearly perceived the difference between Descartes' justification for asserting the existence of "myself as a thinking thing," and his justification for asserting the necessary existence of God as following from the ontological proof, he nevertheless treats Descartes' inference in the case of the *cogito* as if it followed the (illusion-driven) model of the ontological proof of the existence of God, where existence is derived from the *concept* of God and is thus asserted as absolutely necessary. Not only is Descartes not guilty as charged here, but I suggest that if Kant had correctly perceived the nature of Descartes' inference, he might have been able to clarify some of the more puzzling aspects of his own formulations, such as: the existence asserted in "I think" is that of the very act of thinking, or: the concept of existence at work here is prior to the *category* of existence (actuality, *Wirklichkeit*), which applies to objects given in sensation and connected to one another in time.

Whatever the case may be on this last point, let us accept, with Descartes *and* Kant, the statement "I think, I exist." *What* am I? This is the second point of contention between Kant and Descartes, to which I now turn.

DESCARTES' "SUM RES COGITANS" AND KANT'S "I, OR HE, OR IT (THE THING) THAT THINKS"

Having reached the Archimedean point of recognizing that "*I am, I exist*, is necessarily true whenever it is put forward by me or conceived in my mind," the meditator continues:

> But I do not yet have a sufficient understanding of what this 'I' is, that now necessarily exists. (*AT* VII 25; *AT* IX-1 20 (*CSMK* II 17). Descartes presumably means: this 'I' *whose existence follows necessarily from the fact that I assert it*.)

After careful investigation of the options left open in light of the radical doubt that precedes, he concludes that the only characterization he can confidently give of this 'I' that "exists" is: "Sum res cogitans." ("I am a thinking thing.") The earlier *Discourse on Method* was more emphatic:

> Next I examined attentively what I was. I saw that while I could pretend that I had no body and that there was no world and no place for me to be in it, I could not for all that pretend that I did not exist; and I saw that on the contrary from the mere fact that I thought of doubting the truth of other things, it followed quite evidently and certainly that I existed; whereas if I had merely ceased thinking, even if everything else I had ever imagined had been true, I should have had no reason to believe that I existed. From this I knew that I was *a substance whose whole essence or nature is simply to think* [emphasis mine], and which does not require any place, or depend on any material thing, in order to exist. (*AT* VI 33 (*CSMK* I, 127))

In the *Meditations*, the meditator gives himself more time before reaching such a strong conclusion. He recognizes that all he can say on the basis of the argument of the Second Meditation is that he is a thing that thinks. Whether thinking is an *essential attribute* of this thing (himself) that is now said with certainty to exist, and if so, whether it is the *only* essential attribute of this thing that is said to exist, such questions will find answers only after reasons have been provided to give credence to one's clear and distinct ideas, and to the judgments founded on them. Thus, only in the Sixth Meditation does the meditator allow himself to assert that the referent of 'I' in "I think" is *only* a thing that thinks, *really distinct* from a body or extended thing, albeit substantially united with a body.

In her characteristically lucid analysis of the different stages of Descartes' arguments in the *Meditations*, Margaret Wilson made the following comment concerning the statement "I am a thinking thing" as it first appears in the Second Meditation:

> *Sum res cogitans* ultimately includes at least five distinguishable claims (each one stronger than the one before):
>
> (1) I think
> (2) I am a thinking thing.
> (3) Thought is a property essential to me.
> (4) Thought is the only property essential to me.
> (5) I am essentially a thinking thing, and not essentially material.[7]

In the Second Meditation, she argues, Descartes has established (and indeed takes himself to have established) (1) and (2) and to have gestured toward (3). Only in the Sixth Meditation (having proved that God exists, that he is not deceiving, and that *we* do not deceive *ourselves* as long as we assent only to propositions formed on the basis of clear and distinct ideas) does Descartes have the resources to claim that he is justified in asserting (3), as well as (4) and (5).

Now strikingly, (1) and (2), and perhaps also, cautiously, (3), are the extent to which Kant can be taken to endorse Descartes' statement: *Sum res cogitans*.[8] He definitely parts company with Descartes on the last two. What, then, *is* Kant's quarrel with Descartes? How does this quarrel relate to the different contexts in which the proposition "I think" is introduced respectively by Descartes, and by Kant? This is what I now want to explore.

Kant's criticism of rationalist doctrines of the soul as a thinking substance is expounded in the Paralogisms of Pure Reason. The criticism is not directed only or even primarily at Descartes. Kant's most direct interlocutors are the post-Leibnizian Schulphilosophen, mainly Wolff, Baumgarten, and (on the particular issue of the immortality of the soul) Mendelssohn. The name "Descartes" appears only in the course of Kant's criticism of the fourth Paralogism, where what is under discussion is the respective certainty of our own existence as thinking beings, and of the existence of things outside us: extended things. Nevertheless, with the exception of Mendelssohn's, Descartes' is the *only* name explicitly mentioned in any of the Paralogisms. This is understandable: Kant's general thesis in the Paralogisms is that rationalist metaphysicians illicitly translated into real features of a *thing* the mere "logical features" of the thought 'I' in the proposition "I think." Kant would certainly be justified in claiming that Descartes was the originator of such a move. After all, reference to Descartes' *cogito* is invariably present in all early-modern rationalist theories of the mind. And as we shall see, each and every one of the features Kant claims rationalist metaphysicians attribute to the mind, as a thinking substance distinct from the body, do hold of Descartes' notion of the mind.

Nevertheless, as Jean-Marie Beyssade convincingly shows,[9] in the *Meditations* Descartes arrives at his statement that "I am a thing whose sole attribute is thinking" by a long and careful process of analysis, which starts in the final paragraphs of the Second Meditation and is painstakingly developed all the way to its conclusion in the Sixth Meditation. Kant ignores these developments when he traces the Cartesian/rationalist notion of mind to a fundamental illusion of reason that can be sketched out in the form of four "Paralogisms of Pure Reason." In fact, Kant makes no claim that what he lays out in these Paralogisms is an argument actually defended by Descartes or by any of the rational psychologists whose system he is criticizing. Rather, what he is claiming is that behind the explicit arguments or views defended by Descartes, Wolff, Baumgarten, or Mendelssohn lies an implicit logical structure of their thoughts that is more primitive than the step-by-step procedures by which they establish their conclusions, and that determines the contents of those conclusions more surely than any of the arguments they explicitly appeal to. Although the limits of this chapter make it impossible to consider in any detail Kant's argument in each of the Paralogisms of Pure Reason, let me nevertheless try to sketch out their common pattern.

Kant's general point in the Paralogisms is the following: given the role of the proposition "I think" in reflecting the act by which we bring about overall unity and consistency of our representations (as outlined in the first part of the present essay), there are ways in which we necessarily think of ourselves when we refer to ourselves by the subject-pronoun 'I' in "I think." We can lay out those ways just by considering the proposition and analyzing it in light of the four titles of the table of logical forms of judgment. The features attributed to *myself* as the referent of 'I' in "I think" are described by Kant as "logical" or "merely logical" precisely because they are merely ways in which we *think* of ourselves, or form a *concept* of ourselves by virtue of the sole proposition "I think," "which must be able to accompany all our representations." We form these thoughts or concepts just by virtue of the function fulfilled by relating our representations to one and the same 'I,' and thus independently of any corresponding *intuition* or "immediate and singular representation" of ourselves as objects given in space and time, referred to by 'I.' Let me now sketch out what this means when we consider 'I' under each of the four titles of the table of logical functions of judgment.

1) In the proposition "I think," 'I' is necessarily subject; it cannot be predicate. Although Kant gives no reason for this affirmation, we may suppose at least two explanations: 'I' is a singular term, which as such cannot be predicated of something else, but of which other things (properties or kinds) can be predicated. This general logical point is reinforced by the role of "I think" in the context of the Transcendental Deduction of the Categories. For as we saw, it is by being *attributed* to one and the same 'I' that the activity of thinking is unified and subject to norms of consistency. So 'I' in "I think" so understood is necessarily subject, not predicate. But, Kant claims, because of the position 'I' thus necessarily occupies in the thought "I think," one tends to think of the logical subject ('I' in thought) as a real subject, a metaphysical substrate or bearer of properties: a substance.

Now Kant has no objection to describing the referent of 'I' as *a thing that thinks*. Witness Kant's striking phrase expanding on the thought 'I', in the opening paragraphs of the Paralogisms, in both editions: "the 'I' or he or it (the thing) that thinks."[10] Surely, if there is thinking there is a thing that thinks. However, from Kant's standpoint, the problem with calling that thing a "substance" is that one then forgets that *of that thing we know nothing at all*, except that it has some activity present to us as our own thinking. But according to the account that was given of the category of substance in the Transcendental Analytic, this category is applicable only insofar as it serves to distinguish between permanent (substance) and changing (accidents) and thus to identify and reidentify objects of experience, and develop knowledge of them. None of this occurs with 'I.' 'I' in "I think" does not refer to a permanent *object* whose properties *change*. 'I' is just the term to which we refer our thoughts in order to think of them as unified by one standpoint and bound by rules that commit us ("me") to bring about unity and consistency under a unifying standpoint. Even if we grant that there can be no activity of thinking without a thing (or things) whose activity it is, the formal features of 'I' in "I think" give us no indication at all about *what kind of a thing* (or things) might be active in this way. Characterizing it as a substance, however, puts us on the slippery slope of trying further to determine, in light of the logical features of 'I' in "I think," what the real features of that substance might be.

2) The first of these features is simplicity, characterized under the title of "quality," the second title in the table of categories. In attributing thought to 'I,' we take the act of thinking to be one and indivisible. Not that it does not have any components, but each of its components is inseparable from all the others and derives its meaning from its relation to all

others, a relation expressed, again, by the fact that all thoughts are attributed to one 'I': 'I' is not plural; it is a first person *singular*. Correspondingly, the referent of 'I' is thought to have the property of indivisibility or simplicity. But this is a mere thought. It could well be that a thing given in intuition is indivisible in its action while being divisible by virtue of its extension in space. A fortiori, we can conclude nothing at all about the unknown subject of the activity of thinking from the simplicity of 'I in the thought "I think."

3) Under the title of "quantity," the referent of 'I' is thought to be numerically identical through time. In other words, in attributing 'think' to 'I' in "I think," not only do we think of 'I' as simple at any instant (as we saw in 2), we also think of 'I' as one and the same through time (numerically identical at any point in time). These two features, simplicity and numerical identity, are really two faces of one coin, consisting in the way we think of whatever is designated by 'I' in the context of the unifying and logically binding thought "I think." As we saw under the previous two titles of categories, we slip from the fact that 'I' in "I think" is (logically) necessarily subject, not predicate, to the thought of the "thing that thinks" as being a substance, indeed asserting that it is a substance. And we slip from the fact that 'I' in "I think" is (logically) one, not many (first person singular), to the thought that the "thing that thinks" is a *simple* substance. Similarly in the present case, we slip from the fact that 'I' in 'I think' is (logically) one and the same at any time at which we think, to the assertion that the simple (immaterial) thinking substance that is the bearer of these thoughts remains numerically identical, and indeed is conscious of its own numerical identity through time. Here Kant's denunciation of the illusion that plagues the rational psychologist is even more forceful than in the previous cases. He reminds us that according to the Transcendental Aesthetic and Analytic, time is *transcendentally ideal*: as a mode of ordering our intuitions, it is a feature of our own sensibility. And insofar as it is itself an intuition, it derives its unity from precisely the unifying standpoint, or transcendental unity of apperception, whose analytic (conceptual) expression is the proposition "I think," which "must be able to accompany all *my* representations." This being so, of course what we refer to by 'I' has to be one and the same through the whole time of our experience. And of course this identity is prior to and different from the identity of any object identifiable and reidentifiable *in* time, although it may readily be mistaken for such an identity:

In the whole time in which I am conscious of myself, I am conscious of this time as belonging to the unity of my self, and it is all the same whether I say that this whole time is in me, as an individual unity, or that I am to be found with numerical identity in all of this time. (A362)

And again:

> The identity of the consciousness of myself in different times is therefore only a formal condition of my thoughts and their connection, but it does not prove at all the numerical identity of my subject [here Kant means, of course, *metaphysical* or *real* subject: substrate or substance (B. L.)], in which—despite the logical identity of the I—a change can go on that does not allow it to keep its identity. (A363)[11]

4) This takes us back to the issue of existence (which corresponds to the fourth title of the table of logical forms and categories, modality). As we saw in part 1 of this essay, Kant acknowledges that an existence *is* asserted, and justifiably so, in the proposition "I think." "I think" is an assertoric proposition; it asserts a predicate ('think') of a subject ('I'). At least, this is what happens in any particular case in which any of us actually binds representations in such a way that "I think" actually accompanies them, whether explicitly or implicitly. However, a puzzling aspect of Kant's argument in the Paralogisms may be worth noting here. "I think," Kant says, is "the sole text of rational psychology." In other words, from the sole proposition "I think" and more particularly, from the role of 'I' in "I think," rational psychologists derive their whole doctrine of the soul as a thinking substance. But this means that "I think" is not treated as a singular proposition where a predicate, 'think' is asserted of a singular term, 'I.' Rather, the proposition "I think" is held to be true *of all thinkers*, and from the logical features of 'I' in "I think," real properties are derived that are themselves *true of all thinkers*. Moreover, even while denouncing the rationalist psychologist's move from the logical features of 'I' to real features of a thinking substance, Kant himself does accept that "I think" is a form universally shared by all thinkers. *For all thinkers*, 'I' in "I think" is subject, not predicate. *For all thinkers*, 'I' in "I think" is one, not many. *For all thinkers*, 'I' is, at every instant in time, one and the same. No *particular* act of thinking needs to *actually occur* for these features to be universally thought to belong to any subject that thinks. Here, says Kant, "I think" is "taken problematically" (see A346–47, A353–54). Not so with the fourth title: on pains of falling into the error Kant (wrongly) accuses Descartes of having fallen into, that of deriving existence from thought taken *as a concept*, one must go back to the proposition "I think" *as an assertion*, where the content of the proposition is made true by the *individual act of asserting it*, and known to be true *by the agent of the act referred to by 'I.'*

This, I suggest, explains why, on the one hand, Kant describes 'I think' as "a mere form of thought" or "a mere form of consciousness" (here we have 'I think' "taken problematically," i.e., *the* 'I think' that "must *be able to* accompany all my representations"). But on the other hand, when (and only when) Kant considers "I think" under the fourth title of the logical forms and categories (modality), he describes it as "an empirical proposition, which means as much as: "*I exist* thinking" (B428). However, he adds, the existence thus asserted of 'I' is not the *category* of existence, or actuality. One way to explain this point might be the following: just as the numerical identity of the subject thought by 'I' is *not* the identity of an identifiable and reidentifiable object, recognized under a concept and connected to other objects in space and time, similarly what is asserted to exist in the proposition "I exist" *insofar as this proposition is contained in "I think,"* is *not* an identifiable object connected to other objects in space and time. In other words, our access to its existence cannot be of the same kind as the access we have to the existence of identifiable and reidentifiable objects. This is why, as Kant insists, the concept of existence at work in thinking "I think," i.e., "I exist thinking," is not the category of actuality at work when we say that an object of experience exists, i.e., is actual (actually exists) (see B423n. cited earlier).

To return to Descartes' "Sum res cogitans" and Kant's "I or he or it (the thing) that thinks": Kant agrees with Descartes that "I" refers to something that thinks, and that "I think" entails (indeed, for Kant, contains) "I exist." He probably agrees that it is part of the essence of that thing, that it thinks.[12] But he disagrees that we have any warrant to assert that its only essential attribute is to think, or that it is a mind, distinct from the body, and whose existence is more certain than that of bodies. Indeed, when we make this kind of statement we make a category mistake. For we compare the certainty of the pre-categorial existence contained in "I think" and the certainty of the *actuality* of objects given, identified, and reidentified in space and time.

What does make sense is to consider the respective certainty of the existence (actuality) of the thoughts ordered in time by 'I' in "I think" and the existence (actuality) of bodies outside these thoughts, including the body empirically connected to *my* representations. Here Kant adamantly opposes what he calls Descartes' "problematic idealism." This point is the last I want to address.

DESCARTES AND KANT ON THE CERTAINTY OF MY OWN EXISTENCE AND THE CERTAINTY OF THE EXISTENCE OF THINGS OUTSIDE ME

The fourth Paralogism (the "Paralogism of Ideality") does not have the same structure as the previous three, at least in the first edition of the *Critique*. It is beyond the scope of the present chapter to try to explain this striking difference. Instead I shall briefly summarize Kant's argument in the fourth Paralogism in the A edition and then analyze its relation to the Refutation of Idealism whose place, in the B edition of the *Critique*, has been shifted to the Transcendental Analytic (B274–79).

I shall then relate these two versions of Kant's refutation of Descartes' "problematic idealism" to the aspects of Kant's relation to Descartes' *Ego cogito, ergo sum* I analyzed in the earlier parts of this chapter.

In the fourth Paralogism, in the first edition of the *Critique of Pure Reason*, the inference Kant refutes is roughly the following.

(1) Only those things of which we are immediately conscious have indubitable existence.

(2) Objects outside us are *not* objects of which we are immediately conscious. Rather, their existence is inferred, as a cause, from the immediate consciousness we have of our own representations.

(3) So the existence of objects outside us is dubitable. It is possible, but not certain, that objects outside us exist. Only our own existence as thinking beings, and that of our own representations, is indubitable. (A366–67) [13]

In his comments on the fourth Paralogism, Kant attributes the conclusion (and the inference it implicitly rests on) to Descartes, and in the Refutation of Idealism added to the Transcendental Analytic in the second edition of the *Critique*, he describes as Descartes' "problematic idealism" the view that the existence of objects outside us is merely probable, not certain.

Now it is true that a causal reasoning of the kind described in the fourth Paralogism can be found in Descartes' *Meditations*. The first instance of it is in the Third Meditation, where Descartes claims that there must be at least as much formal reality in the objects that *cause* ideas in us, as there is objective reality in our ideas themselves. According to this principle, only God is an object whose idea cannot have been caused by our own formal reality, i.e., by the degree of reality contained in our own existence. So only of God can we say with certainty that he exists as the cause of the idea of God in us. In contrast, the existence of all other objects is doubtful, for none of the ideas of those objects has more objective reality than there is formal reality in us, so that the degree of reality they contain "objectively" can have its source in the degree of reality there is "formally" in us just as well as by the degree of reality contained formally in objects outside us.[14]

A related (although different) causal reasoning is present again in the Sixth Meditation. At that point it has been established to Descartes' satisfaction that God exists and is not deceiving. There is therefore every reason to believe that I am not deceived when I think, after careful examination, that the passive capacity to receive ideas of sensible things that I experience in myself is related to a corresponding active capacity in things outside me, rather than in myself or in God. Nevertheless, of course in any particular case, if I do not exercise sufficient attention in determining the causes of my ideas, I can be deceived about them and in particular about their relation to outer objects.[15]

What Kant means to oppose, in criticizing what he calls Descartes' "problematic idealism," is *not* the claim that our belief in the existence of objects of outer sense (objects we perceive as existing in space) is sometimes deceptive, or the claim that in any particular case we may be deluded in believing a particular external object to exist. What he means to oppose is the idea that we have a stronger warrant (i.e., their being immediately presented, rather than inferred) for our belief in the existence of objects of inner sense (our own mental states, and thus ourselves as the subjects of those states) than we have for our belief in the existence of objects of outer sense *in general* (whatever the fate of any particular belief in the existence of any particular object of outer sense). Problematic idealism, he claims, rests on an equivocation on the concept of "object outside us." If by "object outside us" we mean an object considered independently of the way we perceive or cognize it, then indeed it is true to say that *of such an object* we are not immediately conscious, and that its existence can only be inferred. But this is not what is meant by "object outside us" when we talk of "objects of outer sense." Objects of outer sense are not objects considered independently of the way we perceive them. On the contrary, they are objects *of our outer intuition*, whose form is space. To *these* objects we do not have an inferential, but an immediate access: they are directly present to us by way of outer intuition, whose form is space, just as objects of inner sense (our own inner states) are directly present to us by way of inner intuition, whose form is time. (A367–79)

Of course, the sticking point here is Kant's restrictive clause, according to which objects of outer intuition are immediately present *only as appearances*, i.e., *only as representations in us*. How is this different from saying that only our representational states, and thus only our own existence as the bearers of those states, is an existence we are immediately conscious of? How is saying that objects of outer sense are present to us "only as representations in us" different from saying that they are present to us as determinations of our own existence, i.e., determinations of our existence as thinking (representing) beings?

In the refutation of idealism he offers in the fourth Paralogism (in the A edition of the *Critique*), I think Kant has two answers to offer to this question. First, "is in us" here does not mean "is within our minds" or "exists only as a determination of our own existence as minds," since what has been at issue all along was whether 'I' refers to a mind, i.e., to a thing whose sole essential determination is to think. So, "within us" just means: "within the scope of the thought 'I think,' " without any presumption as to the ontological status of what is thus described as "in us." Whether it is a merely mental or a material object is not thereby decided.

Second, the qualification "in us" so little prejudges the issue of the material or immaterial (mental) nature of the object of representation, that it applies *both* to objects of inner sense and to objects of outer sense, and that it applies to them *in the same way*, namely, as a restriction concerning the epistemic access we have to them. Both objects of inner sense (our own inner, mental states) and objects of outer sense (objects in space, represented as distinct from our own inner states) are *in us* in the sense of being *within the scope of "I think,"* i.e., *not* things as they are in themselves, independently of our cognitive access to them. For both kinds of objects, Kant claims, "the transcendental object" that corresponds to them is unknown to us. But *both* inner objects and outer objects, being "in us," within the scope of our own cognitive access, are objects of immediate consciousness, or immediately present to us. There is, in this respect, no privilege whatsoever of the objects of inner sense over the objects of outer sense.

Still, neither of these answers seems to block the possibility of idealism or to constitute a compelling answer to *problematic* idealism. Whatever the nature of mental states, and whatever the nature of the referent of the 'I' that is the logical subject of "I think," it still seems that the *only* existence for which we have sufficient warrant, so far, is on the one hand the pre-categorial existence of the act of thinking (and therefore of some unknown subject for that act) and, on the other hand, the actual, empirically given existence of the mental (representational) states whose intentional correlates are combined according to the forms of the transcendental unity of apperception. What reason are we given to think that the outer objects thus represented are outer, not just in the sense of being (represented) in space, but also in the stronger sense of being ontologically distinct from the mental states by way of which we have access to them?

That is the worry the Refutation of Idealism in the second edition of the *Critique* is supposed to address. Kant's argument is roughly the following:

(1) I am conscious of my own existence as determined in time. That is to say, I am conscious of my own inner states as occupying determinate positions in time.

(2) Now, the positions of anything at all in time are determined only with respect to something permanent, in relation to which everything else changes. (This is a point Kant made in the argument of the First Analogy of Experience, which I will not consider here.)

(3) But in inner sense, there is nothing permanent: inner states are constantly changing.

(4) So the permanent with respect to which the temporal order of my own inner states is determined, has to be outside me (i.e., it has to be in space, in objects of outer sense).

(5) So, the *empirically determined* consciousness of my own existence (i.e., the empirical consciousness I have of the temporal order of my own inner states) proves the existence of objects in space outside me.[16]

It is quite clear that in this argument, Kant means to be talking about the *existence* of a thing outside me, and not just of my *representation* of the existence of a thing outside me. *My* representations, he insists, are always successive. So the permanent with respect to which they are determined as successive has to be outside them in the stronger sense outlined in the fourth Paralogism in A: in the sense of being *distinct from* them, *ontologically independent* of them. But it also has to be outside them in the second sense outlined in the fourth Paralogism: outside them as (represented) in space. For this is the only way in which something permanent can actually be present to me. Only *in space* are things represented as permanent, because only in space can a distinction be made between simultaneous and successive existence, and thus only in space can things be presented as persisting while their states change (this argument was made in the Third Analogy of Experience, which we cannot analyze more fully here and will just accept for the sake of the present argument). So only by relating the succession of my mental states to the states of things existing in space can I assign them determinate positions in time, or can "the mere consciousness of my own existence" be "empirically determined." (B275)

Now it seems clear that with such an argument, all we are talking about are objects *of consciousness*. Whatever Kant's efforts to come up with an argument in which we move from an assertion of existence (the existence of my own mental states) to the assertion of another existence taken to be the necessary condition of the former (the existence of objects outside my mental states), what he is in fact doing is moving from the *consciousness* of a specific determination of my existence (its empirical determination in time) to a necessary condition of that consciousness, which is itself another consciousness (the consciousness of a permanent, which, he argues, has to be a consciousness of something in space). In other words, the most his new Refutation of Idealism seems to be establishing is that *in my consciousness* there is a necessary distinction between objects of inner sense and objects of outer sense, and the latter are just as immediately present as the former, indeed are a condition for the determinate consciousness of the former.

Of course, it remains true that "in my consciousness" does not mean, for Kant, "within a mind, as a thinking substance." The argument just summarized needs to be read in the context of Kant's anti-Cartesian view, according to which we have no warrant to characterize the referent of 'I' in "I think" as a mind or a thinking substance whose sole essential attribute is to think. Still, even keeping this point in mind, the question remains open whether the objects I am necessarily conscious of, *as* objects ontologically distinct from myself and my mental states, *are* actually distinct from me and my mental states. Despite his own indignant statement ("It is a scandal of philosophy and universal human reason that the existence of things outside us . . . should have to be assumed merely on faith, and that if it occurs to anyone to doubt it, we should be unable to answer him with a satisfactory proof") (BXXXIXn.)—despite this indignant statement, it does not seem that Kant, on this particular point, made any decisive progress over Descartes.[17]

Let us now take stock. In this essay, I have considered three aspects of Kant's relation to Descartes' "Cogito ergo sum" or "Ego sum, ego existo." The first was Kant's understanding of the proposition "I think," and of the role of 'I' in this proposition. The second was Kant's criticism of Descartes' move from "I think" to "I am a substance whose sole essential attribute is thought." And the third was Kant's criticism of Descartes' statement that the existence of the mind is more immediately certain than the existence of bodies outside the mind.

I have argued that Kant's analysis of the role of 'I' in "I think" is the truly original and groundbreaking aspect of his challenge to the Cartesian *cogito*. The bulk of that analysis is given not in the Paralogisms of Pure Reason, but in the Transcendental Deduction of the Categories. On the basis of that analysis, in the Paralogisms of Pure Reason, Kant provides a diagnosis of the illusions of rational psychology, which, although it does not do justice to the subtlety and care of Descartes' arguments in the *Meditations*, does capture an implicit logic by which features of 'I' as the logical subject of the proposition "I think" are thought to be features of a thing, a metaphysical subject, or substance. I submit that as far as these first two points are concerned, Kant's challenge to the Cartesian view is successful. It is all the more striking that as far as Descartes' *Cogito, ergo sum*, or *sum cogitans* is concerned, Kant's view is at least in one respect closer to Descartes' than Kant himself was ready to acknowledge. For like Descartes, Kant thinks that an assertion of existence is present in the very assertion "I think," although that assertion does *not* warrant asserting the existence of a substance "whose sole essential attribute is to think."

When it comes to the third point, Kant does not seem to have made any real progress over Descartes, even if he gives us good reason to reject the Cartesian solution to that problem. I suggest that this failure arose because Kant remained too Cartesian for his own good, that is to say, too bound to the early-modern theory of ideas. The idea of "turning the game that idealism plays . . . against it," as Kant proudly proclaimed in the Refutation of Idealism (B276), is perhaps what stopped him in his tracks. For it meant accepting Descartes' starting point (the immediate certainty of the existence of our ideas, or in Kant's vocabulary, of our representational states) and *from that point* trying to show that we are just as immediately certain of the existence of outer objects, indeed that our certainty of the latter is the condition of our empirical knowledge of the succession of the former. But this meant that the whole argument remained within the scope of objects *of consciousness*, and it remained unclear why we should necessarily take the latter to be ontologically independent of the consciousness we have of them, i.e., to be ontologically independent of our own states of consciousness. Perhaps the best we can do here is agree with Heidegger: Kant thought that "it was a scandal of philosophy and of human reason in general that there is still no cogent proof for the existence of things outside us." The real scandal, Heidegger rebutted, "is not that this proof has yet to be given, but that such proofs are expected and attempted again and again."[18] Perhaps, on this point at least, he was right.

CHAPTER 2

Descartes' "I Am a Thing That Thinks" versus Kant's "I Think"

Jean-Marie Beyssade

I SHALL RESTRICT MY COMMENTS, as Béatrice Longuenesse largely did with hers, to what is usually called Descartes' *cogito*, which Kant discussed and criticized on several occasions, both explicitly and implicitly, especially in the *Critique of Pure Reason*. I shall leave out of consideration, as she did, other points of Descartes' philosophy, such as the proof of the existence of God, which Kant and his contemporaries called "the Cartesian proof," the proof which we call, after Kant, "the ontological proof," and which Descartes himself called the "a priori" proof.[1] These other questions are certainly of great interest, but they appear secondary in comparison with what Descartes called "the first principle of the philosophy I was seeking" (*DM* IV, *AT* VI 32 l.23 (*CSMK* I, 127)).

This first principle for the complete philosophy which Descartes had been seeking from his youth (finally delivered only in the *Principia philosophiae* of 1644) is never expressed as *Cogito* or *Ego cogito* (I think; *Ich denke; Je pense*). Most often it is expressed as *Ego cogito, ergo sum sive existo* (in French, *Je pense, donc je suis*; in English, "I think, therefore I am or exist") or, in his definitive exposition, Meditation II of the *Meditationes de prima philosophia*, as *Ego sum, ego existo* (*Je suis, j'existe*; I am, I exist). This first principle is thus never expressed merely as a detached "I think"; rather, "I am, I exist" is always connected to, even deduced from, the experienced fact that I think: "I think, therefore I am," in *Discourse* (part 4), or "this proposition *I am, I exist*, is necessarily true whenever it is put forward by me or conceived in my mind"[2] in Meditation II (Med II, *AT* VII 25 l.11–13; *AT* IX–1 19 (*CSMK*, II, 17)). It is this that is the first principle. A bit later on in Meditation III it is further developed by way of the claim "I am a thing that thinks [*Sum res cogitans*],"[3] leading eventually to the full conclusion that I am a substance whose whole essence or nature consists only in thinking. In Discourse IV, this conclusion is drawn shortly after I have asserted my existence (*DM* IV, *AT* VI 33 l.4–5 (*CSMK* I 127)). In the *Meditations*, though, it is postponed until the Sixth and final Meditation.[4]

What can we expect from the confrontation between Kant's "I think" (*Ich denke*) and Descartes' *Cogito ergo sum*? To tell the truth, from a strictly historical point of view, not very much. Kant probably did not directly read Descartes' writings themselves; in general, he only knew Descartes secondhand, mainly from handbooks in the Leibnizian and Wolffian tradition. Kant was not interested in giving an accurate account of authors and their writings, of other philosophers and their philosophy. But this very lack of historical interest on Kant's part is a good reason for us to adopt a perspective more philosophical than strictly historical. Kant's criticism can display more clearly the specific character of each doctrine, both Kant's and Descartes'. Turning away from the view that Kant criticizes and too quickly ascribes to Descartes, we may be able to find in Descartes' own meditations a lengthier and more careful train of thought and a *Sum res cogitans* ("I am a thinking thing") immune from the criticisms we find in the Paralogisms Kant discusses in the Transcendental Dialectic of the *Critique of Pure Reason*. In the end, Descartes' thought may not altogether escape Kant's critique. But at least we are now put on our guard by Kant's criticism, which is less a comment on Descartes' philosophy than a moment of pure reason in its speculative use, or what is, according to Kant, a natural and necessary illusion of theoretical reason. With Kant in mind, we can now read Descartes again in order to better grasp how he proceeds, and to discover whether he can resist Kant's criticism of rational psychology.

The main point I intend to emphasize here is the delay or postponement between the proposition (*pronuntiatum*) "I am, I exist," at the beginning of Meditation II, and the statement "I am a substance of which the whole essence consists only in thinking" in the middle of Meditation VI. For the central point and the whole force of Kant's criticism in the Paralogisms, especially in the first one on substantiality, consists in ignoring the role that time plays in Descartes' reasoning, which, as a result, becomes sophistical. Kant's criticism proceeds as if in the quasi-instantaneousness of a mere syllogism, and in the logical timelessness of its three constitutive propositions, one proceeds directly from "I think" (as a logical function, an extra-temporal act) to "I am a thinking substance" (a simple, personal, permanently lasting mind, separate from the body). Kant points out a Paralogism that results from giving two different meanings to the term "thought," which functions as the middle term in the syllogistic inference he attributes to Descartes. According to Kant, the same procedure is at work in all four proofs of rational psychology, whose "sole text," he says, is one and the same proposition "I think."[5]

But this is not how Descartes proceeds. The delay in the *Meditations* reveals the difference between Descartes' rules and method, and the inferences that Kant attributes to him.

First, Descartes' starting point is not a logical subject, but the indubitable experience of an existence, my own existence: *Ego sum, ego existo* (I am, I exist). As I noted earlier, the proposition "I think" is never, even in the *Discourse*, asserted separately, nor is it asserted as the first truth. So what we need to observe is how patiently, step-by-step in the course of the metaphysical meditation, the idea of a thinking substance and the idea of its real distinction from the body (mind and body becoming two different and even opposite substances)[6] are attained.

Certainly, in Discourse IV, Descartes does draw the inference very quickly. He reasons *from* something *to* something else. What he infers *from* is "I think, therefore I am." This formula *as a whole*, consisting in the two connected propositions, is the first truth, "the principle of the philosophy I sought." *From* this he draws an inference *to* a (quite different) metaphysical thesis: "I am a substance whose whole essence or nature consists in thinking." This conclusion is drawn very quickly—too quickly. Descartes himself admits that this fourth part of the *Discourse* is a summary, an "epitome" of the *Meditations*, which needs to be explained by reference to the *Meditations* (*Burman, AT* V 153 (*CSMK* III 338 with notes 2 and 3)). Only the *Meditations* (which Kant probably never read) "give the true (and whole) way by means of which the thing in question is discovered methodically."[7] In fact, the idea of substance is progressively elicited through an analytic mode of exposition, which patiently prepares and justifies the final thesis, that I am a substance of which the whole essence is only to think.

Even though Descartes repeatedly writes "I am a thing that thinks" in Meditation II, nowhere in that text does the term "substance" even appear. Even if Descartes commonly uses "*res*" as an equivalent (*res sive substantia*), the technical term "substance" appears only in Meditation III, when Descartes explains the notions of "objective reality" of an idea, and of "degrees of reality" (Med III, *AT* VII 40 l.12 and 20; *AT* IX–1 31–32 (*CSMK* II 28)).[8] In that text, substances are now distinguished from modes or accidents, and the latter are said to have less reality than the former. Moreover, like a stone or a piece of wax, the *ego* is now explicitly called a substance: "*Item me esse substantiam*," "*Ego autem substantia*," "I too am a substance" (Med III, *AT* VII 44 l.23 and 45 l.7; *AT* IX–1 35 (*CSMK* II 30–31)). In the course of that same analysis, the notion of substance is generally described and defined as a *kind* of thing: a thing capable of existing independently: "*Res quae per se apta est existere.*" However, even if Meditation II contains neither the term "substance" nor the thesis that I am a substance, several philosophical moves in that meditation, in accordance with his analytic mode of exposition, prepare the ground for both of these theses, whose articulation is postponed until Meditation III. This, then, is the first delay.

Now, the formula that appears in the *Discourse* in the paragraph that immediately follows the assertion of my existence ("I am a substance whose whole essence consists in thinking") appears in the very same terms in the *Meditations*, but much farther along, in the French version of the last Meditation an addition to the original Latin text, an addition (quite legitimately) introduced either by the translator or perhaps by Descartes himself.[9] The addition occurs when Descartes is at last in a position to gather up all the elements he needs for demonstrating the real distinction between mind and body, that is, a distinction between two substances, a thinking substance and an extended substance.[10] It is important to note just how long Descartes delayed this demonstration: from Tuesday, as it were, the second day of the meditator's retreat, to Saturday, the day of the Sixth and final Meditation.[11] As Descartes announces in the synopsis, we are first obligated to clarify both the essence of mind and the essence of body, a task started with the analysis of the piece of wax in the second half of Meditation II and continued in the Fifth and Sixth Meditations, where the authority of those two clear and distinct conceptions is further secured by the certainty that a nondeceiving God exists, a certainty acquired only after Meditation III (*Synopsis, AT* VII 13–14; IX–1 9–10 (*CSMK* II 9)). At the same, time in accordance with the analytic mode of exposition, these reasonings contribute toward clarifying the idea of substance (the thinking substance, the extended substance) as they relate to the two principal attributes of thought and extension, and as they relate to the ideas of modes (understanding, will, imagination, and so on; figure, motion, situation, and so on).[12] These long delays, the second such delays, which are deliberate, intentional, skillfully contrived and controlled, and conceptually justified, make it easier to conceive a substance that is a thinking, and *only* a thinking, substance.

In contrast, Kant turns Descartes' long meditative path, with its breaks and returns, with its slow explication of the concept of a thinking substance, into a procedure that is strictly logical and quasi-instantaneous, one that he took to be illegitimate. To reply to Kant's criticism, one must recall Descartes' analytic path in its different moments, spread over six days, whose specific requirements allow him to call his method of setting out his philosophy "the true way by means of which the thing in question was discovered methodically," as he defines the analytic way of demonstration.

In the rest of this chapter, I will limit myself to commenting on the first of the delays just outlined, those in Meditation II, and to showing how this Meditation paves the way for the idea of the *ego* as something that is *only* a thinking substance, but without actually advancing the thesis. *I am, I exist. But what am I?* This question is the question "*quid?*" ("*what*" am I?) a question asked in Meditation II just after my own existence has been posited or asserted, an assertion often called by Cartesian scholars the assertion "*quod*" ("that" I am). I myself, the *ego* of *Ego sum, ego existo,* will later be called a substance, but nowhere in Meditation II does this term occur. Nonetheless, in each of my thoughts *ego* is that something which maintains them in existence; or rather, since each of them may at any time cease to be, *ego* is that which gives them being or existence. *Ego* is a *res cogitans,* and *res* will later turn into *substantia,* of which all my thoughts are so many different modes, or qualities, or ways of being, or attributes (*Principles* I.56). But substance-and-mode terminology would be scholarly gibberish, so to speak, if cut off from the analytic steps that approach and prepare it, and are carefully introduced in nontechnical language. *I am a thinking thing, I am a thing that thinks, sum res cogitans*: so many sentences in ordinary language, which will have to be turned into *I am a substance whose whole essence or nature consists in thinking.* Long before Kant, Father Bourdin, the author of the Seventh Objections against the *Meditations,* joked about it: "You exist, I allow it; you are thinking, I grant you this. You may even add that you are a thinking thing, or a thinking substance, since you are so fond of high-sounding phrases" (Seventh Objections, *AT* VII 503 l.15–18 (*CSMK* II 342)).

Between the more modest-sounding "thinking thing" and the high-sounding "thinking substance," there is a great distance. In Meditation II, where we are now, we can follow the beginning of the path. It contains at least three different steps along the path of our analytic mode of exposition.

The first step gives me the certainty that I do not need a body to be certain of my existence, this very existence I assume when I say or con-ceive: *I think, therefore I am.* A first answer to the question *quid* is thus found by *excluding* whatever is corporeal in the ideas I previously had of myself. I am neither a body, nor a biological *anima,*[13] nor even any kind of subject of sense and imagination, something that would imply a real body. All these can be doubted and separated from me, from the *ego* whose existence I am sure of whenever I think. So I am only a thinking thing, "that is a mind, or intelligence, or understanding, or reason" (*mens sive animus sive intellectus, sive ratio: anima* is necessarily excluded here), "words whose meaning I have been ignorant of until now" (Med II, *AT* VII 27 l.13–15; *AT* IX–1 21 (*CSMK* II 18)). Let us linger for a moment on this last phrase. There is no predetermined meaning for these words—a mind, or intelligence, or understanding, or reason—under which I should subsume my experience as a thinking thing. On the contrary, I have to determine their correct meaning, and now I can do it, according to my experience of doubting, by excluding everything that in any way implies having a body. This process of exclusion takes some time. The first answer to the question *quid* (*what* am I?), the first *quid*, is: "I am, then, in the strict sense only a thing that thinks," constricted, restrained within the boundaries of its thoughts. But for sure, a true and real thing, a thing that is something real and that truly exists, even if I cannot say, for now, that it is anything more than "a thinking thing." For Descartes starts from an existence, as we have already noted.[14] Only this existential experience of a thinking thing, which gives meaning to the words *mens sive animus*, makes it possible to reply to Kant that the word "thought" does not change its meaning from the beginning to the end of the process.

I next try to find something else: *Quid praeterea*? What else am I? But Descartes (or the meditator) can only repeat that he is nothing more: "I am not that structure of limbs which is called a human body . . . not even some thin vapour which permeates the limbs, a wind, fire, air, breath or whatever I depict in my imagination, for these are things which I have supposed to be nothing. Let this supposition stand. For all that, I am still something."[15]

"Let this supposition stand" (*Maneat positio*). In the first Latin edition of the *Meditations* (1641), it is a subjunctive, rendered in Cottingham's English translation by "Let it stand," *it* meaning that the *positio*, the position, which we are invited to maintain, is the same as the previous suppositions, *supposui*, the fictitious or factitious reasons for doubting (the dreams, the evil genius, and so on). The second Latin edition of 1642, however, gives the verb in the indicative: *Manet positio*. ("The position does remain"). But the position at issue may perhaps be very different from the presuppositions or reasons for doubt. In fact, it may be their exact opposite, namely, the so-called *cogito* itself, my own existence as a thinking thing. If so, it is possible (though perhaps not necessary) to read: "I have supposed all these material things to be nothing. (But) the proposition (*positio*, position) still stands, viz., that I am nonetheless something." The position, or even the self-positing (to speak like Kant, let us use the German words *setzen*, *Setzung* or even *Selbstsetzen*, *Selbstsetzung*, all of those terms referring to the spontaneous act of positing oneself as an "*Ich denke*," "I think") remains (*manet*), inasmuch as it is necessarily connected with the doubt and its assumptions. It is worth noting, by the way, that two of the first and best readers of the *Meditations*, Arnauld and Gassendi, read the *Maneat positio* in the two conflicting ways just outlined. Arnauld adopted the second reading of *position*, taking it to refer to the Cartesian *cogito*, and he agreed with Descartes, concluding with him that "the (pro)position still stands, and hence I am not a body" (Fourth Objections, *AT* VII 198 l.17–19; *AT* IX–1, 154 (*CSMK* II 139)). Gassendi adopted the first reading, taking *positio* to refer to the Cartesian reasons for doubt, and he disagreed, rejecting all those metaphysical fictions: "Let this (sup)position stand? No, but stop here, O Mind, and let those (sup)positions, or rather fictions, finally depart" (Fifth Objections (on Med II), *AT* VII 264–65 (*CSMK* II 184–85)). Descartes did not explicitly choose between their two readings. For him, what is important is for us to linger for a long time with the two ideas (or thoughts, or opinions, call them positions or propositions or suppositions or whatever you want), with the two ideas working together, against one another, inside the meditator's mind. The two ideas? Namely, (1) first idea, no body exists; (2) second idea, I do exist, I am something that exists and thinks my thoughts. A long time? Long enough to become accustomed to, to become acquainted with a bodiless thing. This acquaintance is the first step toward acknowledging an immaterial substance.

In any event, at this stage of the reasoning, my perception of myself as a thinking thing and *only* a thinking thing must, of course, be understood in the context of an epistemological order: not in an order pertaining to the actual truth of the thing itself (*in ordine ad ipsam rei veritatem*), but merely in an order pertaining to my own perception (*in ordine ad meam perceptionem*) (*Meds*, preface, *AT* VII 7–8 (*CSMK* II 7 and note 2)). To validate the reasoning as displaying the true essence of the thing, we must dispel all suspicion of our clear and distinct ideas, i.e., a nondeceiving God must license us to derive knowledge of the real essence of things from the evidence of our cognition. This is the reason for another delay we have noticed, the delay that postpones the high-sounding statement ("I am a substance whose essence consists in thinking") until Meditation VI. However, within its own order, the order of my perceptions, the clear and distinct perception I acquire of myself in Meditation II is careful, rigorous, and scrupulous, not hasty and temporary. I completely perceive myself as a thinking thing, apart from any corporeal things or qualities.[16]

Let us now consider again the order of my perception. In order to assert the independence of thought from the material world, that is, in order to maintain that every thought requires a thinker, a thing that thinks, while at the same time I deny that this thing is a material or corporeal or extended thing, an independence that is the main feature of a substance, it is not required that I should have several thoughts. Nor is it required that I should endure, that I should continue to exist from one thought to another. Even if I had only one thought, and the latter were instantaneous, even if I should disappear with it, it seems that the general principle ("he who thinks cannot but exist while he is thinking") would remain valid. Even having just one thought would compel us to posit a thing that thinks this thought and that with it makes up a true and genuine *ens per se* (as Descartes and his contemporaries would say), a being through itself, or a *res quae per se apta est existere*, a thing capable of existing by itself, that is, independently.[17] Let us call this feature, this kind of independence, "perseity." If we deny a thinking substance any duration, any plurality of thoughts, and any subsistence from one thought to the next, this perseity would hardly allow the notion of a substance to be in any way significant, and for there to be any difference between a mode (such as a thought) and the "metaphysical matter" that is supposed to support it (*Third Replies*, II, *AT* VII 175 l.13; *AT* IX–1 136 (*CSMK* II 124)).

But the analysis of *ego* does not stop here in Meditation II. A second move in the analytic exposition takes us in an opposite direction. A second step reveals a second *quid* (*Sed quid igitur sum?* What then am I?) and opens up a wider horizon. I am a thing that thinks, yes; I am a thought, or one thought, no. Rather a swarm or a throng, a multitude of modes of thinking, whether countless or numerable, finite, infinite, or indefinite. I quote: "A thing that thinks. What is that? A thing that doubts, understands, affirms, denies, is willing, is unwilling, and also imagines and feels" (Med II, *AT* VII 28 l.20–23; *AT* IX–1 22 (*CSMK* II 19)). This phrasing is repeated at the very beginning of Meditation III, with an interesting addition that appears only in the French translation of 1647: "*qui aime, qui hait*" ("that loves, that hates"), before and not after the break introduced by the word "also" ("and also imagines and feels," *imaginans quoque et sentiens*), which separates the modes pertaining to the pure mind and those pertaining to a mind intimately united with a human body.[18] But this is another story.

Here Descartes emphasizes the multiplicity of my thoughts, and the gathering of this diversity in the undivided unity of one and the same self, or *ego*. "Indeed, this is a considerable list [*non pauca sane hæc sunt*], if all these belong to me" (Med II, *AT* VII 28 l.23–29 l.18; *AT* IX–1 22–23 (*CSMK* II 19)). But why not? Why should they not belong to me? Here, according to the Cartesian analysis, from within the doubting that was initiated in Meditation I,[19] I observe all the activities just listed in an orderly way. "Is it not I who now doubt almost everything, I who nevertheless understand something, I who affirm that this one thing is true, I who deny other things, I who desire to know more things." In each of these "activities,"[20] I, the *ego*, the self, reasserts itself. Each of these "modes" (to anticipate by a "day" the introduction of the technical terminology of substance–mode–attribute) is undistinguished from my thought (". . . which of these activities is distinct from my thinking?"). Each mode is unseparated from myself (". . . which can be said to be separate from myself?"). Beyond my thought, I myself make up an *ens per se*: this is the perseity mentioned earlier. And a bit further, when speaking of imagination and sensation, identity: "But it is also the case that the 'I' who imagines is the same 'I'. . . . Lastly, it is also the same 'I' who has sensory perceptions." I am the same *ego* behind each particular way of thinking: we are stepping toward the permanence of a substance that remains the same through time.

But it is only a step. We have not yet mentioned duration explicitly. Identity of the same thinker with a diversity of many thoughts, which may be simultaneous, is one point. Identity of the same body through the innumerable states of a melting piece of wax is another. This third move in the analytic exposition is achieved only in the second half of Meditation II.

It is time to conclude. Let me return to Kant. In this essay, I have tried to understand what Descartes claimed, both in light of and in opposition to the well-known Kantian objections that have become part of our philosophical tradition, and are generally taken to be well-founded. I have tried to resurrect Descartes' point of view and to support Descartes' theses as well as I could against the attacks of a new objector. It is as if Béatrice Longuenesse had written an Eighth Set of Objections with a Kantian pen, and I had to gather from Descartes' writings the elements of an answer on Descartes' behalf, his Replies to these Eighth Objections.

It is for the reader to judge whether this kind of "disputation" can highlight any real issues in philosophy and in the history of philosophy. In any event, we know that Kant was not very concerned with what his actual predecessors had really said or thought. He was chiefly interested in what he called, in the last chapter of his first *Critique*, "the history of pure reason." From this point of view, the names of philosophers, such as Descartes or Leibniz, are chiefly conventional marks to denote the main intellectual positions inside the field ("the battlefield") of philosophy. As for Descartes, I have only tried to show a different Descartes (to my mind, the real Descartes) behind the simplified and somewhat distorted Descartes that Kant so harshly criticized. Like many of his contemporaries, Kant quite honestly believed this false Descartes was the true one. And so he directed his strongest blows in his direction, and often with good philosophical effect. But since this pseudo-Cartesius was at least in part a fiction, it is not surprising that those blows sometimes failed to reach their mark.

Kant's Critique of the Leibnizian Philosophy: *Contra* the Leibnizians, but *Pro* Leibniz

Anja Jauernig

A COMPUTER COUNT of the number of explicit references in Kant's writings to the early-modern philosophers who are discussed in this volume returns the most hits for Leibniz, by a wide margin, both in the precritical and the critical period, in the *Critique of Pure Reason* itself, and even in the correspondence and the *Nachlaß*. In fact, with the exception of God, Leibniz is the most mentioned individual in the Kantian corpus overall.[1] Of course, this hit count in itself does not justify the conclusion that Leibniz is the most important and influential thinker for Kant's philosophy and philosophical development, but it at least indicates that Leibniz plays a prominent role in Kant's thinking during the latter's whole philosophical career. In order to establish that Leibniz indeed occupies a special place among the philosophers who were important for Kant, and in order to identify what exactly this importance consists in, one has to look for more evidence and for more of an argument than a mere hit count. To provide more evidence, a rough sketch of such an argument, and the beginning of a more detailed account of the relation between Kant and Leibniz is the project of this essay.

An influential and popular story about Kant's philosophical development and about his relation to Leibniz portrays him as, roughly speaking and briefly put, a Leibniz-Wolffian by education, who, after an eye-opening encounter with Newton's *Principia*, embarks on the project of reconciling Leibniz-Wolffian metaphysics with Newtonian science in order to provide a unified picture of reality and metaphysical foundations for the Newtonian theory. This project gradually leads Kant further and further away from his Leibniz-Wolffian starting point, and ultimately culminates in the total rejection of the Leibniz-Wolffian philosophy in the *Critique of Pure Reason* as a paradigm example of the kind of dogmatic metaphysics that Kant's critical philosophy is designed to put out of business. This story has a lot going for it and is convincing with respect to several aspects of Kant's philosophical development and his relation to Leibniz-Wolff. But, I want to suggest, without several qualifications, and without the addition of further chapters on the rather complex relation between Kant and the Leibnizian philosophy, the story is one-sided and potentially misleading.[2]

One misleading feature of the indicated story is that it tends to overemphasize Newton's role in Kant's gradual emancipation from Leibniz-Wolff and in the development of transcendental idealism. Substantiating this charge would require an in-depth analysis and discussion of Kant's precritical writings, which cannot be provided in the space available here and which will be left for another occasion. For the present, I can only express my allegiance to an alternative reading, according to which Kant's philosophical development is primarily driven by Kant's desire to solve general, mostly metaphysical problems that arose within or were left unanswered by the Leibniz-Wolffian philosophy that Kant was familiar with, as opposed to the alleged desire to develop a philosophical system that is compatible with and can serve as a foundation for the new science of the famous Englishman. These internal problems of the Leibniz-Wolffian philosophy include, for instance, the problem of the possibility of a community or connection of substances in one world, of the nature of space and the composition of matter, or the problem of individuation, all of which, *qua* problems, are home-bred and independent of the new scientific developments in England, and all of which continued to represent key problems in Kant's philosophical inquiries well into the critical period. In particular, this also holds for the problem of how to reconcile the new mechanistic science with a metaphysical view of the world that asserts the existence of final causes or purposes, of human freedom, immortal souls, and of God, and for the problem of how to provide metaphysical foundations for the new science, which are ur-Leibnizian problems that Leibniz himself wrote about *in extenso*. This is not to say that there were no further influences from other, non-Leibnizian quarters that helped to shape Kant's philosophical path, but, to my mind, the relevance of most other early-modern thinkers, Newton included, remains restricted to a suggestive, as opposed to a formative, role in Kant's philosophical life, as one might put it. The writings of these other early moderns either indicated ways to Kant in which the problems that he had previously identified within the Leibniz-Wolffian framework might be overcome—often by combining their proposals with elements of the Leibnizian canon—or they helped him to narrow the range of possible answers to these problems, namely, by proposing solutions that Kant judged to be unacceptable. For example, with regard to the problem of the possibility of a community or connection of substances in one world, we might mention in the latter category Malebranche's occasionalism, which Kant rejected, and in the former category the physical influx theory of Kant's teacher Martin Knutzen, which Kant tried to combine with the Leibnizian doctrine of the preestablished harmony, modifying both in the process. It is also in this category that Newtonian science should be listed, which, in several ways, helped Kant to formulate new or better solutions to old

Leibniz-Wolffian problems, as, for instance, an improved explanation of the possibility of a community or connection of substances in one world by appeal to certain aspects of Newton's theory of gravitation (cf. *Nova Dilucidatio*, AA 1 413ff.; *Inaugural Dissertation*, AA 2 406ff.). In addition to the Leibnizians, there were very few other early-modern thinkers whose writings posed problems to Kant that he adopted as his own, and which catalyzed important steps in his philosophical maturation. Hume deserves to be mentioned in this context, because his critique of the concept of cause, or of necessary connection, figured prominently in Kant's philosophical awakening, according to Kant's own famous testimony (cf. *Prolegomena*, AA 4 260). Kant's relation to Hume is the topic of another essay in this volume, and considering it here would amount to trespassing, but it should be noted that, even for the discovery of the problem of how to understand the necessary connection between causes and effects, Hume's wake-up call was not essential for an inquisitive Leibnizian like Kant. The function of Hume's analysis is best understood as emphasizing the importance of the problem of causality to Kant rather than, literally, first opening his eyes to it.[3] For this problem already naturally arises in the Leibnizian philosophy itself, namely, with respect to the Leibnizian conception of truth and its relation to the principle of sufficient reason, of which Kant was fully aware.[4] So, one qualification that should be added to the sketched popular story about Kant's philosophical development is that the problems of reconciling the new science with Leibniz-Wolffian philosophy and of providing metaphysical foundations for the new science are only two among many, equally important problems that shaped the direction of Kant's philosophical journey to his critical philosophy. Most importantly, in essence these two problems are of thoroughly Leibniz-Wolffian provenance, as are the overwhelming majority (and maybe all) of the problems that defined Kant's philosophical path. That the specific version of mechanistic philosophy that Kant wanted to reconcile with Leibnizian philosophy incorporated more and more elements of Newtonian physics as the years went by is an undeniable fact and a topic worth discussing, but its role in Kant's development of his transcendental idealism is, to my mind, not essential.[5]

The main topic of the present essay concerns a more serious problem with the popular story about Kant's philosophical development and his relation to the Leibniz-Wolffian philosophy, namely, that in the absence of further chapters that would complete and balance it, the story obscures the true relation between Kant and Leibniz by creating the false impression that Kant's rejection of Leibniz-Wolffian metaphysics in his critical philosophy was decisive and total, and by leaving the reader to surmise wrongly that Kant's criticisms were as much directed at Leibniz's original philosophy as at Wolff's elaboration of it. A closer examination of the relation between the Kantian and the Leibnizian philosophy reveals that none of these contentions is true. Not only are Kant's focal problems Leibnizian problems, it is also the case that no other early-modern philosopher was as close to Kant with regard to their respective positive (metaphysical) views as Leibniz—and this holds not only for the young Kant but for the critical Kant as well. Far from rejecting Leibniz's philosophy in the *Critique of Pure Reason*, Kant even conceives of his main work as "the true apology for Leibniz," as he himself puts it (cf. *Discovery*, AA 8 250).[6] It is true that as far as Kant's physical theory of the sensible world in the critical period is concerned, Kant is quite close to Newton, which is one of the reasons why the popular story seems so attractive, and which is one of the aspects of Kant's philosophy with respect to which the popular story is right on the mark. But Kant's metaphysics—which is what he himself most cared about—is and remains very much Leibnizian, and, to the extent that Wolff is faithful to Leibniz, even Leibniz-Wolffian throughout the critical writings. Perhaps more surprisingly, it can be argued that even the transcendental philosophy of the first *Critique* itself, i.e., the non- or antimetaphysical part of Kant's mature theory, shares many aspects with Leibniz's philosophy, so that it would be deeply mistaken to view the *Critique of Pure Reason* as an intended final death knell for Leibniz's system. The limited and modest project for the rest of this essay will be to give a general, programmatic advertisement for these claims, and to try to convince the reader that at least this part of the sketched reading of Kant's development and his relation to Leibniz represents a genuine interpretative option that merits our attention.[7]

Relevant Textual Evidence

Let us start by looking at the textual evidence that defenders of a "rejection" view might adduce for their interpretation, according to which Kant's gradual emancipation from the Leibnizian philosophy culminated in a thorough rejection by the time of the publication of the *Critique of Pure Reason*. This view receives its strongest support from Kant's multiple and rather fierce objections against central Leibnizian tenets, which can be found in the precritical and critical period, most of which are poignantly summarized in the *Critique of Pure Reason* in the chapter "On the Amphiboly of Concepts of Reflection." Many of the problems with the Leibnizian philosophy, or at least precursors of the problems with the Leibnizian philosophy, that are discussed in the critical writings were recognized by Kant quite early in his career. Those are among the problems that motivated Kant's departure from school orthodoxy and that set him on his long journey to transcendental idealism. Length constraints will not permit a detailed discussion of Kant's objections, but in order to see how thoroughly he distances himself from the Leibnizians, and in order to have the criticisms on the table for future reference, it will be helpful to give a (shamefully) brief sketch of them.[8] Kant's critique centers on the following nine central Leibnizian doctrines:

1. The "merely logical" distinction between sensibility and understanding, and the doctrine that we confusedly perceive things in themselves (cf. B60/A43). According to Kant, the Leibnizians mischaracterize the difference between sensibility and understanding as consisting in the different degrees of distinctness of the representations provided by these faculties. This leads the Leibnizians to the identification of our sensible representations of the *phenomena* with confused representations of *noumena* (cf. B60/A43ff.; B320/A264; B326/A270ff.; *Progress, AA* 20 278). Kant argues against this identification that no analysis of our sensible representations of objects will ever put us in the possession of representations of things in themselves, since the former belong to a different species of representations altogether, or, more precisely, since the former essentially include representations that belong to a different species of representations, namely, intuitions as opposed to (mere) concepts. Through our sensible representations in perception we do not apprehend things in themselves confusedly, but only the way in which we are affected by them, while things in themselves are not perceivable, or sensibly representable at all (cf. B60/A43; *Prolegomena, AA* 4 290; *Discovery, AA* 8 219).[9]

2. The conception of substances as individuated by their intrinsic properties alone, and the corresponding principle of the identity of indiscernibles (PII), according to which intrinsically indiscernible objects, i.e., objects that are indistinguishable with regard to their intrinsic properties, are identical. To Kant's mind, this conception of substances and their identity conditions could, if at all, only be applied to intelligible objects, since a "*substantia phenomenon* . . . consists one and all of relations" (B321/A265; cf. B335/A279ff.).[10] Already in the *Nova Dilucidatio*, Kant refutes the "intrinsic" version of PII for phenomenal objects by imagining a counterexample in which intrinsically indiscernibles are located at different spatial positions, which suffices to mark their distinctness (cf. *Nova Dilucidatio, AA* 1 409ff.). From a fully critical point of view, even the restricted version of the Leibnizian conception of substance, understood as applying to intelligible objects only, cannot be defended, since it transcends the bounds of sense by purporting to represent knowledge of things as they are in themselves, namely, about how *noumenal* substances are individuated (cf. B319/A263ff.; B327/A271ff.; *Progress, AA* 20 282).[11]

3. The preestablished harmony as an account of the community of substances, which is explicated as a preordained coordination between the

perceptual states of all monads. In addition to complaining about its intuitive implausibility—Kant calls the preestablished harmony "the most miraculous figment that philosophy has ever come up with" (*Progress, AA* 20 284)—Kant's main objection is that the preestablished harmony falls short of the task of explaining the possibility of a real community of substances in one world, since a community of substances that consists in the mutual harmony of their perceptual states is only ideal or sympathetic (cf. *Inaugural Dissertation,* AA 2 409; B330/A274–B331/A275).[12]

4. The twofold use of the principle of sufficient reason as a logical principle, according to which there is a reason or "ground" for every truth, and as a causal principle, according to which every event has a cause. While agreeing with the legitimacy of the logical principle, at least in this general formulation, Kant complains that the Leibnizians owe a proof for the causal principle, which is synthetic and not obviously true (cf. *Discovery, AA* 8 193ff., 239ff.; *Logic, AA* 9 51; Letter to Reinhold, 1789, *AA* 11 36ff.; *Progress, AA* 20 277ff.; see also note 4 in this essay).

5. The non-opposition of positive determinations. According to Kant, this principle is not unrestrictedly valid. It holds for the logical opposition of predicates, i.e., it is indeed true that any two predicates that contain no negations on any level of analysis are not contradictory from a purely logical point of view. But the principle does not hold for the real opposition of sensible properties, as is illustrated by what one might call "directional" properties, for which the principle fails. For instance, although having a velocity of 10 mph to the east and having a velocity of 10 mph to the west are arguably both positive properties, they nevertheless stand in opposition to each other and cancel each other out. According to Kant, the difference in directionality can ultimately only be represented in intuition, i.e., by means of sensible representations, which is why the Leibnizians, who exclusively focused on intellectual representations, failed to realize that the principle of the non-opposition of realities can, at most, be valid for the predicates composing the concepts of objects, but not for the properties of objects (cf. B320/A264–B321/A265; B329/A272ff.).[13]

6. The "monadology," according to which monads, i.e., simple, mind-like substances, are the most fundamental building blocks of the universe (B330/A273). According to Kant, the monadology leads to a dilemma: it implies that matter is composed of ultimate simple elements and, thus, not infinitely divisible, which, on the assumption that matter and space are structurally identical, implies that space is not infinitely divisible either. This result conflicts with an accepted theorem of geometry, according to which space is infinitely divisible.[14] The inference to the merely finite divisibility of matter from its composition out of ultimate, simple elements can be explained by appeal to the additional assumption, which

the Leibnizians endorse, according to Kant, that infinite real wholes, i.e., wholes that are composed of an infinite number of actual (as opposed to merely potential) parts, are impossible (cf. *Inaugural Dissertation*, AA 2 387ff.; B458/A430; B532/A503ff.; B551/A523ff.; *Prolegomena*, AA 4 342; *Progress*, AA 20 289–90; *MFNS*, AA 4 506ff.). If matter were infinitely divisible and composed of ultimate simple elements, it would amount to an infinite real whole, which is impossible.

A comment in passing regarding Kant's philosophical development may be permitted: to my mind, the problems concerning the infinite divisibility of space, and the existence of infinite real wholes, are of utmost importance in Kant's philosophical maturation. They represent precursors to the first two antinomies, which are at least partly responsible for Kant's philosophical awakening. The eventual solution to the problem of infinite real wholes and its application to the problem of the extent of the world might even be what Kant is alluding to with the famous "great light" of the year 1769, which marks a decisive step forward, and toward the critical philosophy (cf. R 5037, AA 18 69).[15]

7. The relational theory of space and time. According to Kant, the Leibnizians conceive of space as an order in the community of simple substances, and of time as an order in the series of states of these substances. Thus, for the Leibnizians, space and time are ultimately reducible to properties of intelligible objects. Furthermore, they regard our representations of space and time as empirical concepts, which are acquired through abstraction from the confusedly perceived spatio-temporal relations between substances. Their classification of our representations of space and time as confused permits them to account for space and time's seeming independence and logical priority with respect to physical objects, which are commonly ascribed to them in the mathematical sciences (cf. B331/A267ff.; B323/A267; B326/A270). According to Kant, this view of our representations of space and time involves the fundamental Leibnizian misconception of the difference between sensibility and understanding described earlier under (1). Furthermore, it renders the apriority and necessity of the mathematical sciences unintelligible, since, on the sketched view, our concepts, on which these sciences rest, must be classified as empirical. On the other hand, if the Leibnizians resort to the move of distinguishing between the ideal space of the geometer and the real space of the physical world—in which case they can account for the a priori nature of geometry—they are left with the new problem of not being able to explain how mathematics is possible as an a priori synthetic science, i.e., a science that is independent of experience *and* applies to the world.[16]

The last two objections are not explicitly raised by Kant but are implied in his discussion(s). They concern:

8. The doctrine of the reducibility of relations or of extrinsic properties, according to which relations or extrinsic properties can be reduced to intrinsic properties without ontological remainder. Kant is committed to denying the doctrine of the reducibility of relations. For if all extrinsic properties of substances could be shown to be nothing but complex combinations of intrinsic properties, or at least to be (strongly) supervenient on intrinsic properties, Kant's alleged counterexample to PII, i.e., the thought experiment of the intrinsically indiscernible objects at different spatial positions, and his objections to the Leibnizian conception of substance, namely, that phenomenal substances are (at least partly) individuated by their extrinsic properties, would no longer be decisive.[17]

9. The classification of all judgments as analytic, which follows from the Leibnizian conception of truth, as understood by Kant, according to which a proposition is true if, and only if, the predicate concept is contained in the subject concept. Kant agrees that this containment condition is necessary and sufficient for the truth of analytic judgments, which, accordingly, can be verified through conceptual analysis by application of the principle of noncontradiction alone. But, Kant objects, not all judgments can be classified as analytic in this way. There are certain judgments, the synthetic ones, whose truth cannot be ascertained by the application of the principle of noncontradiction alone, and whose predicate concept is not included in the subject concept.[18]

Surveying this list of objections, it indeed seems to be the case that by the time of the *Critique of Pure Reason*, Kant has completely broken with the Leibnizian philosophy that had dominated the early stages of his career, as is claimed by the "rejection" view. But in addition to the more familiar texts in which Kant attacks the Leibnizians, there are several curious, less well-discussed passages, in which Kant speaks in highly approving terms of Leibniz. In these passages, Kant self-avowedly defends Leibniz against his self-appointed disciples who, according to Kant, have seriously misunderstood Leibniz's original position.[19] Kant maintains that a correct reading of Leibniz reveals that his own and Leibniz's views are in fact very close, and that with regard to many issues, Leibniz had already tried and intended to say what Kant then made explicit in his critical philosophy. More specifically, Kant proposes to understand Leibniz's emphasis on the importance of the principle of sufficient reason as an (implicit) recognition of the need for a special principle of justification for synthetic judgments, in addition to the principle of noncontradiction, which can only "ground" analytic judgments (cf. *Discovery*, AA 8 248; draft notes for *Discovery*, AA 20 363–64). Moreover, Kant argues that Leibniz should not be understood to hold that matter is composed of monads, but only that it has its ground in an intelligible substratum, which is unknowable for us, but which, due to the constitution of our minds, is conceived of as composed of simple parts (cf. *Discovery, AA* 8 203). Correspondingly, Leibniz's proposal to treat space as ideal must not be misunderstood as suggesting a distinction between the ideal space of the geometer and the physical space of the actual world, which supposedly corresponds to the order of relations between things in themselves; rather, Leibniz should be understood as saying that space is the order of relations between appearances in the phenomenal world (cf. *MFNS, AA* 4 507–8; *Discovery, AA* 13 248–49). Finally, what Leibniz dimly saw in his doctrine of the preestablished harmony between mind and body, Kant speculates, is the harmony between our two main faculties of knowledge, i.e., sensibility and understanding, whose mutual correspondence, indeed, cannot be explained otherwise than by ascribing it to the purposeful arrangement of a divine designer (cf. Letter to Marcus Herz, May 26, 1789, *AA* 11 52; *Discovery, AA* 8 249–50). In *On a Discovery*, Kant's reply to the (self-proclaimed) Leibnizian Eberhard, Kant goes so far as to assert that

> the *Critique of Pure Reason* might thus very well be the true apology for Leibniz, even against his own disciples who extol him with non-honoring praises, as it can be for various older philosophers, who many a historian of philosophy presents as talking mere non-sense, despite all of the praise administered to them, and whose intention is not guessed by neglecting the key to all exegesis of pure products of reason from mere concepts, i.e., the critique of pure reason itself (as the common source for all), and by not seeing what they wanted to say in the word-for-word examination of what they actually said. (*Discovery, AA* 8 250–51)

What shall we make of these pro-Leibnizian passages? There are several possibilities. It might be that these passages are meant ironically: even the *Critique of Pure Reason*, which is thoroughly anti-Leibnizian, does more justice to Leibniz's original position than Eberhard and his ilk. If Leibniz's friends are all like Eberhard, only God can save him.[20] Kant's capability of making ironical and witty remarks should certainly not be underestimated, but the occurrence of similar pro-Leibnizian passages in several different writings, especially also in writings whose nature is not polemical, casts severe doubts on this reading.

Another option would be to take Kant at his word: when rightly understood, Leibniz is indeed very close to the teachings of the *Critique of Pure Reason*, but not in the respects latched onto by Eberhard and his friends, who got it all wrong, but in the respects highlighted by Kant. This pro-

posal is more plausible than the suggestion that Kant is speaking ironically, and it is the proposal that I would like to defend.

Toward a Reading of the Critical Philosophy as the True Apology for Leibniz

The proposed reading, according to which Leibniz's philosophy and
Kant's transcendental idealism are much closer than commonly recognized, faces an immediate challenge: how are we, then, to understand
Kant's thorough critique of the Leibnizian philosophy in the *Critique of
Pure Reason* and other critical and precritical writings? Did Kant inter-
mittently forget about his earlier reading of Leibniz and his objections
that we listed in the previous section?

The following suggestion seems promising to me: Kant's critique of the
Leibnizian philosophy in the *Critique of Pure Reason* and other critical
works is motivated partly by rhetorical and pedagogical considerations
and partly by a polemical intention, which, however, is not primarily directed at Leibniz himself, but at the Leibniz-Wolffian *Schulphilosophie*.
As for the first point, it is a reasonable strategy for the initial presentation
and advertisement of a new philosophical system to emphasize differences
and novel doctrines and methods compared to the earlier views and methods of the towering figures of the history of philosophy, rather than dwell-
ing on commonalities that the new philosophy shares with the venerable
old ones. As for the second, more important point, it is a plausible reading
that many of the objections in the *Critique of Pure Reason* that are presented as objections to Leibniz or the Leibnizian philosophy in general
are really objections to a particular version of Leibnizianism, namely the
Wolffian, or Wolff-Baumgartenian one, which is the version that Kant
was introduced to in his early days. Furthermore, it is not out of the question—although, at this point, not much more than a plausible speculation—that Kant *closely* read several of the relevant original Leibnizian
texts only relatively late in his career, after having become interested in
the question of how much of a discrepancy or of common ground there
really was between him and the original Leibniz.[21]

More generally, in addition to Kant's pro-Leibnizian remarks, there are
other reasons that recommend caution about too hastily adopting the
prevalent "rejection" view of the relation between the critical Kant and
Leibniz's philosophy. In fact, even with regard to the Wolffian version of
Leibnizianism, the break might not go as deep as is commonly assumed.
It is certainly true that Kant moves beyond Leibniz and Wolff in important
respects, but these corrections and additions mainly concern issues in epistemology, philosophical methodology, the philosophy of mind, and ethics.

Kant's metaphysical or ontological views, however, I want to suggest, remain very much Leibnizian from the very start to the very end—views, we might add, central aspects of which are also shared by Wolff and the Leibniz-Wolffian Schulphilosophie.

How so? According to Kant, metaphysics is "the science which proceeds through reason from the cognition [*Erkenntnis*] of the sensible to the cognition [*Erkenntnis*] of the supersensible" (*Progress*, AA 20 260). As the *Critique* explains, we cannot arrive at knowledge of the supersensible by theoretical means, or, put differently, we cannot be assured of the "objective reality" or even of the "objective validity" of our cognitions of the supersensible from a theoretical point of view; that is, we cannot be certain that there are actual or even really possible objects corresponding to these cognitions. This demarcation of the limits of our theoretical knowledge represents the core of Kant's epistemological/methodological correction to Leibniz-Wolff. From a practical point of view, objectively valid or even objectively real cognition of the supersensible is possible, according to Kant, which, however, differs in kind from the theoretical knowledge that we can attain about appearances. As one might put it in modern terms, the propositional attitude expressed in a state of practical objectively valid/real cognition is different from the one expressed in a state of theoretical objectively valid/real cognition even if the two attitudes are taken toward the same proposition. If the proposition in question concerns the supersensible, an attitude of practical objectively valid/ real cognition is possible, according to Kant, whereas an attitude of theoretical objectively valid/real cognition is not. The first step in proceeding to this practical "knowledge" of the supersensible is made through the cognition of the supersensible "in us," namely, through the concept of freedom, whose objective reality, or at least objective validity, is vouched for by the moral law. Eventually, this path will lead us to the cognition of the supersensible "above us," i.e., of God, and "after us," i.e., of the immortality of the soul (*Progress*, AA 20 295; cf. also *CPrR*, AA 5 141ff.; *CJ*, AA 6 175ff., 195ff.). Through this methodological correction to Leibniz-Wolff, Kant opens up a different path to a similar destination, so to speak, namely, to the objectively real or at least objectively valid cognition of the supersensible that represents the "final end" of metaphysics (*Progress*, AA 20 260). As Kant puts it in a letter to Kästner:

At the same time I shall be permitted to state that my efforts, which so far have been directed at critique, are by no means intended to work against the Leibniz-Wolffian philosophy, as it might have appeared, (for I have been finding it [the Leibniz-Wolffian philosophy] neglected for quite some time now). Rather they are intended to lead this philosophy through a roundabout route onto the same track of a schooled procedure, which these great men, it seems to me, judged superfluous, and [to lead it] through it [the procedure] to the very same end, but only through the combination of the theoretical philosophy with the practical philosophy—an intention that will become clearer if I live long enough to present metaphysics in the form of a coherent system, as I am planning to do. (Letter to Kästner, August 5, 1790, *AA* 11 186)

One might think that in order to understand and appreciate Kant's critical work in theoretical philosophy, and maybe even in ethics or aesthetics, it is not necessary to pay attention to this metaphysical undercurrent of his thinking. After all, Kant did not live long enough to finish his coherent system of metaphysics, and although the doctrine of the Postulates in the *Second Critique* and some aspects of the theory of the beautiful and the sublime in the *Third Critique* might give us a sense of where Kant was planning to go, there is no way of knowing what the envisioned work would have looked like in detail. Moreover, many contemporary interpreters who follow a long-standing and still prevalent antimetaphysical trend in Kant scholarship would no doubt want to argue that it is good that Kant never got around to writing his metaphysics, since without it his philosophy still has a chance of being acceptable to the contemporary, sober philosopher as well.[22] But here it seems only fair to Kant to take him at his word that transcendental philosophy is a true system, in which each part is connected with any other "as in an organized body," and where "the exposition of the whole is required in order to set each part straight [*jeden Teil zu rectifizieren*]" (BXXIII, and Letter to Christian Garve, August 7, 1783, *AA* 10 339; cf. B27/A13, B860/A832ff.). And the whole includes, in addition to Kant's critical work, his envisioned alternative path to the supersensible through the combination of the theoretical with the practical philosophy, which, therefore, has to be taken into account if the project is to understand *Kant's* transcendental philosophy—even if this means leaving the contemporary, sober philosopher behind.[23]

For there are two hinges around which it [metaphysics] turns: first, the doctrine of the ideality of space and time, which, with respect to theoretical principles, merely hints at the for us unknowable supersensible, while, on its way to this end [i.e., the supersensible], metaphysics is theoretical-dogmatic where it deals with a priori knowledge [*Erkenntnis*] of the objects of sense; second, the doctrine of the reality of the concept of freedom, as the concept of a knowable [*erkennbaren*] supersensible, where metaphysics is merely practical-dogmatic. (*Progress*, *AA* 20 311)

In sum, I want to submit that the real importance of Leibniz's philosophy for the critical Kant does not consist in the fact that it provides a useful contrast to Kant's own critical philosophy, and a paradigm example of a metaphysical system that deserves to be committed to the flames, which is how Leibniz's role is usually understood. In my view, this is the polemical and pedagogical function in Kant's critical philosophy that pertains to (many parts of) the Leibniz-Wolff-Baumgartenian Schulphilosophie. Leibniz's own importance, by contrast, consists in the fact that Kant agrees with several of Leibniz's central doctrines (as understood by Kant), most prominently—but not exclusively, as we will see later—with central aspects of the underlying metaphysical picture of the supersensible world, fundamental disagreements concerning methodological and epistemological questions notwithstanding. Moreover, the case can be made that Kant is not only serious when he claims that Leibniz's philosophy and his own transcendental idealism are very close in important respects, but that he is actually *correct*. In other words, it can be argued that most of the objections against the Leibniz-Wolffian Schulphilosophie in the precritical writings and the *Critique* in fact do not, or at least not straightforwardly, apply to Leibniz's own philosophy, if correctly understood, and that the interpretation of Leibniz that is suggested by Kant in the mentioned curious, less-known passages is, on the whole, defensible.[24] This result, furthermore, makes it possible to take Kant at his word and use his claim that the *Critique of Pure Reason* might very well be the true apology for Leibniz as a key to a whole-scale interpretation of Kant's philosophy from an unorthodox point of view that promises to shed new light on both Kant and Leibniz.[25]

In order to prevent a likely misunderstanding, let me hasten to add that the overall point of the suggested interpretation is not to argue that Kant is basically Leibniz all over again. In addition to bringing the similarities between Kant's and Leibniz's thinking into sharper focus, the projected interpretation will also honor the dissimilarities between them and pay close attention to those aspects of Kant's philosophy that represent a departure from and an improvement upon Leibniz's, in particular Kant's theory of the mind, his result that our theoretical knowledge is limited to possible experience (and its conditions), and his roundabout route to the supersensible through the combination of the theoretical with the practical philosophy. The overall point of the suggested interpretation should rather be characterized as the attempt to counterbalance a widespread and very much slanted *"Alleszermalmer"* reading of Kant, by emphasizing that Kant's and Leibniz's mature philosophies bear a strong family resemblance and fall squarely into the same philosophical tradition.[26]

In this context, it should also be acknowledged that the success of such a project, both regarding the verification of Kant's reading of Leibniz and regarding the interpretation of Kant's critical philosophy as the true apology for Leibniz, depends on certain assumptions, which can be called into question. For instance, it depends on the assumption that there is such a thing as *the* philosophy of Leibniz, understood as a relatively well-circumscribed, coherent system of interrelated philosophical doctrines, or, at the very least, that those Leibnizian doctrines that Kant explicitly discusses admit of a coherent reading that stays sufficiently stable over the course of Leibniz's mature writings. Otherwise, all that could be claimed is that Kant's transcendental idealism shares certain aspects with philosophical doctrines that, at some point or other, were articulated by Leibniz in one of his many and varied "phases," which would be a far weaker and less interesting claim. The suggested reading also depends on the assumption that a sufficient number of the writings in which Leibniz's philosophical system is articulated were accessible to Kant.[27] This is not the place to enter into a detailed discussion of these issues, and nothing will be said about the first one here, except to register my view, which is not unique to me, that despite undeniable changes in emphasis and perspective in Leibniz's thinking, there is an intellectual edifice that can be called "the philosophy of Leibniz," which, in essence, is in place by the mid-1680s.[28] With regard to the second assumption, a couple of brief remarks might be permitted. Strictly speaking, all that needs to be shown in this context is that the views that Kant ascribes to Leibniz can already be gathered from, or at least are not incompatible with, the texts that were, possibly, available to Kant.[29] To my mind, this is plainly the case. Although many of Leibniz's works that play an important role in our contemporary understanding of Leibniz were not published during his lifetime, Kant knew, or could have known, a substantial number of Leibniz's writings, including—but not limited to—such important works as the *New Essays*, the *Conversation between Philarète and Ariste*, the *Principles of Nature and Grace*, the *Monadology*, and the Leibniz-Clarke correspondence. Moreover, Leibniz himself seems to think that his (then) published writings are sufficient for an adequate presentation of at least the fundamental core of his philosophy:

> It is true that my Theodicy does not suffice to present my system as a whole. But if it is joined with what I have published in various journals, those of Leipzig, Paris, and those of Mr. Bayle and Mr. Basnage, it will not fall far short of doing so, at least for the principles. (Letter to Remond, July 1714, G III 618 (*L* 657))

At any rate, as long as the then unpublished writings do not contradict Kant's conviction of the closeness between him and Leibniz, there is no reason to worry about our interpretation. And if it should turn out that the unpublished writings support Kant's conviction, and maybe even reveal further similarities in Kant's and Leibniz's thinking—as, I think, is indeed the case—this will be an added bonus, and additional support for the claim that Kant and Leibniz's philosophical systems are closely linked and belong in the same family. Not only will such a finding be an added bonus, it will also be very much in line with the fact that Kant is explicitly not engaged in a word-for-word examination of what Leibniz actually said, but in an attempted reconstruction of what Leibniz wanted to say. Kant does not judge Leibniz's philosophy according to its letter, but according to its spirit in accordance with his belief that it is "nothing extraordinary at all" to understand an author even better than he understood himself if one diligently compares the thoughts that the author has expressed about a certain topic at various places (cf. B370/A314).

After this general sketch and advertisement of my preferred reading of the relation between Kant and Leibniz, the last section of this essay will be devoted to a brief discussion about how the suggested reading plays out with regard to one central topic in Kant and Leibniz's philosophical theories, namely, the nature of space, which, so to speak, corresponds to one-half of one of the two mentioned "hinges" around which metaphysics turns, according to Kant.[30]

SPACE IN KANT AND LEIBNIZ

According to the reading I propose, a closer examination of the relation between Kant and Leibniz reveals that Kant's philosophical position is indeed quite close to Leibniz's, as Kant claims. This especially holds for Kant's metaphysical views, but also for doctrines that form a central part of what one might call Kant's a-metaphysical, critical theory of the *Critique of Pure Reason*. One case in point is, for instance, Kant's theory of space. What needs to be shown in order to substantiate the suggested interpretation with respect to the question of the nature of space is that Leibniz's own conception of space is not subject to the Kantian objections against the Leibniz-Wolffians listed earlier under (7), and that Kant's reading of Leibniz's theory of space, in which he likens Leibniz's views to his own, is defensible. That is, it needs to be shown that Leibniz himself does not conceive of space as an order in the community of monads, nor does he regard our representation of space as an empirical concept that is acquired through abstraction from the confusedly perceived spatial relations of substances, and that he agrees with Kant that space is an a priori scheme ordering appearances in the phenomenal world.

In order to make some headway in this regard, we need to take a brief look at Leibniz's general conception of reality. For Leibniz, reality comprises several ontological levels. This level-distinction is widely acknowledged in the literature, although there is disagreement about the number of distinct levels, their distinguishing characteristics, and the kinds of entities that are supposed to exist at each level. Most commentators favor some version of a three-level scheme distinguishing the ultimately real realm of simple substances, the phenomenal realm of physical bodies, and the ideal realm of abstract objects or *entia rationis*.[31] To my mind, this three-level interpretation is basically correct, but I would like to add a further distinction between different sublevels at the phenomenal level, and leave room for a second substantial level that one might want to include depending on the particular reading of Leibniz's theory of corporeal substance that one wants to adopt.[32] The first, more fundamental substantial level comprises individual substances or monads equipped with perceptions and appetitions, and (possibly) corporeal substances understood as aggregates of monads that are unified by the substantial forms of their respective master-monads. The second substantial level, which, to my mind, is ultimately dispensable and is dispensed with by Leibniz in his later writings, is inhabited by corporeal substances of a second kind, to be understood either as aggregates of monads unified by additional substantial principles of unity, i.e., so-called substantial chains, or as quasi-Aristotelian substances composed of substantial forms and primary matter, where the latter is "truly" material in the sense of being ontologically distinct from soul-like substances, or from constructions out of soul-like substances. The second main level is the level of phenomenal reality. Briefly put, phenomena are characterized by their dependence on the perceptions or cognitions of minds, where "real," "true," or (minimally) "well-founded" phenomena can be conceived of as the common intentional objects of the perceptions and cognitions of all monads existing in a given possible world.[33] As I understand Leibniz, the phenomenal level itself can be divided into three sublevels, namely, the intersubjective phenomenal world of common sense, the phenomenal world of physical science proper, and the phenomenal world of Leibniz's new (metaphysical) science of dynamics. It is at the latter level that a third kind of corporeal substances or, more precisely, the organic bodies of a third kind of corporeal substances, and their aggregates appear in Leibniz's scheme.[34] Corporeal substances on the phenomenal level, or rather their organic bodies, are to be understood as the intentional objects of Leibniz's new science of dynamics; at the same time, they can also be seen as the phenomenal expressions of the corporeal substances at the substantial level, i.e., of aggregates of monads that are unified by the substantial forms of their respective master-monads. The three listed phenomenal levels differ with respect to the criteria of "reality" or "well-foundedness" that their respective phenomena have to conform to, in the degree of "distinctness" of the respective representations describing their phenomena, and in how closely these representations approximate God's privileged view of the phenomenal world. The closer they are to God's view, the closer they are to the (phenomenal) truth, for God's representation of the phenomenal world, which is free of confusions and perspectival distortions, ultimately defines what counts as phenomenal reality.[35] Among the representations corresponding to the three phenomenal levels just indicated, Leibniz's science of dynamics is the most distinct, and the closest to God's privileged representation. For ease of reference—and other reasons, whose explanation would lead us too far afield—I shall call this phenomenal level "metaphysically grounded," while the other two phenomenal levels will be referred to as "merely phenomenal."[36]

Now, according to Leibniz, or at least the mature Leibniz, space proper is an abstract order of actual and possible spatial relations between actual material bodies.[37] Understood in this way, space must be classified as an ideal entity on Leibniz's view. For Leibniz, the ideal character of space is manifested in its topological and structural properties, as, for instance, its continuity, its logical priority compared to its parts, and its infinite wholeness,[38] and in that it is conceived of as comprising actual and *possible* spatial relations, which, in turn, is reflected in the common understanding that bodies are capable of exchanging their positions without exchanging any of their other attributes, and in the conceivability of a vacuum.[39]

According to my reading of Leibniz, even though space, understood in the indicated sense, is ideal, it does not only "live" at the ideal level of Leibniz's scheme. Versions of it also exist on the phenomenal levels of reality, namely, on the two less "real," merely phenomenal levels. These merely phenomenal levels are characterized by incorporating ideal features that are confused appearances of, or mental constructions from, features existing at the metaphysically grounded level of phenomenal reality, as, for instance, extension, which is the appearance of an abstract aspect of corporeal substances, or rather their organic bodies, namely, their *materia prima*.[40] Phenomenal space turns out to be such a mental construction as well, namely, a construction from the actually instantiated spatial relations between corporeal substances as they appear in perception.[41] The difference between the ideal mathematical space at the ideal level of abstract entities and the ideal phenomenal space at the merely phenomenal levels can be understood by thinking of phenomenal space as mathematical space "anchored" to the phenomenal physical world. This "anchoring" comprises two aspects: first, phenomenal space is the result of a mental construction based on the perceived spatial relations between physical bodies, as just mentioned; second, a certain system of physical bodies is used to pick out a privileged frame of reference in phenomenal space, which serves as a global rest frame, in relation to which the spatial positions and motions of all other bodies are determined.[42] Despite this difference, mathematical and phenomenal space are geometrically and topologically identical, and thus both ideal, according to Leibniz's criteria of ideality that were mentioned earlier.

In asserting that versions of ideal space exist on the ideal *and* the merely phenomenal levels of Leibniz's ontological scheme, I am in disagreement with Glenn Hartz and Jan Cover's influential interpretation of Leibniz's theory of space (and time). These authors argue that Leibniz changed his views about space and time between 1696 and 1709, classifying them as well-founded phenomena before the transition and as *entia rationis* afterward, so that for the mature Leibniz, there is no sense at all in which space and time are well-founded phenomena.[43] As already indicated in the previous section, to my mind Leibniz is a conservative thinker, in the literal sense of the word. With respect to the topic in question, this means that the changes one can detect in Leibniz's thinking do not have to be read as amounting to a dismissal of his earlier teachings of space and time as well-founded phenomena. They might also be taken as indications of an expansion of his view, presumably motivated by his struggles to come to grips with the labyrinth of the continuum, which resulted in the addition of a further ontological level to his scheme, namely, the ideal realm of abstract entities. There is ample textual evidence that the mature Leibniz still regards space and time, understood as abstract orders of possible situations, as part of phenomenal reality as well. (Cf. esp. LC and letter to de Volder, Oct. 11, 1705, G II 278.) Our proposed three-level distinction of the phenomenal realm helps to make sense of these passages *and* of the ones in which Leibniz classifies space and time as ideal. Apart from the level of metaphysically grounded phenomenal reality, which is inhabited by corporeal substances (or, rather, their organic bodies), i.e., "actual bodies," which, indeed, "have properties which are logically incompatible with those of ideal things,"[44] as Hartz and Cover insist, Leibniz recognizes further phenomenal levels, i.e., the merely phenomenal realms of our everyday experience and of physics proper, which *do* include ideal features, as just explained. The merely phenomenal realms are connected to both the underlying level of substantial reality, via the metaphysically grounded phenomenal level, and the ideal realm, via the confused and ideal features introduced into our representation of the world by the perceiving mind or soul.[45] For completeness' sake, it should also be mentioned that apart from ideal phenomenal space, we can also identify what Leibniz calls "concrete" or "real" space at the merely phenomenal levels, which consists in the totality of occupied places at a given time, i.e., the totality of all coexisting "filled" extensions instantiating spatial relations.[46]

On the metaphysically grounded level of phenomenal reality, no ideal or confused features are admitted. Given that phenomenal bodies at the merely phenomenal levels are supposed to be the appearances of corporeal substances in perception, it is plausible to identify the "real" in phenomenal space, i.e., space at the metaphysically grounded level of phenomenal reality, with the totality of all actual spatial relational properties of corporeal substances.

Finally, on the assumption that the only kind of genuine substances in Leibniz's ontology are immaterial monads, one has to conclude that there is no correlate of space or spatial relations at the substantial level of reality that could ground the spatial aspects of the phenomenal world. Of course, via their perceptual states monads do stand in quasi-spatial relations. In this way of looking at it, monads can be regarded as located in an abstract space where neighborhood or even distance relations are determined by the closeness of the corresponding points of view in the common phenomenal space. But far from being the metaphysical ground of the spatial relations between phenomenal bodies, this quasi-spatial arrangement of monads is itself the result of a construction based on the coherently perceived spatial relations between phenomenal bodies and the perspectival nature of monadic perceptions. It must be admitted that Leibniz's language sometimes suggests that monads are aggregated in space, but in his more careful moments he makes clear that the use of spatial vocabulary in the description of monads is only an analogical way of speaking, which, when taken literally, "contains a certain confusion of classes, so to speak" (Letter to des Bosses, April 30, 1709, G II 372 (L 599)). For, strictly speaking,

> [t]here is no spatial or absolute nearness of distance between the monads. And to say that they are crowded together in a point or disseminated in space is to use certain fictions of our mind when we seek to visualize freely what can only be understood. (Letter to des Bosses, June 16, 1712, G II 450–51 (L 604))[47]

The question of whether the mature Leibniz is committed to the existence of any kind of corporeal substances on the substantial level of his ontology is trickier and cannot be adequately discussed here. But if Leibniz's own explicit assertions on this topic count for something, the answer to this question must be a clear no. For "when considering the matter carefully," he invariably comes to the conclusion that "there is nothing in the world except simple substances and, in them, perception and appetite" (To de Volder, G II 270 (L 537)). This is also the answer I would want to defend in detail if there were enough room. For now, I will restrict myself to an argument by authority and let Leibniz settle the question:

> This . . . at last brought me to understand, after many corrections and forward steps in my thinking, that monads or simple substances are the only true substances and that material things are only phenomena, though well founded and well connected. (Letter to Remond, January 10, 1714, G III 606 (L 655))[48]

This general sketch of Leibniz's conception of space at the different levels of his ontological scheme already puts us in the position to ascertain that for Leibniz, space is not an order in the community of monads or of things in themselves, since it does not even exist on the relevant level of reality. Moreover, it is indeed the case that for Leibniz space is an ideal order of appearances in the phenomenal world.

But what about the a priori nature of our representation of space and the constitutive function that is attributed to it on the Kantian view? Against the background of Leibniz's famous discussion of our acquisition of the notion of space by observation, comparison, and abstraction in his fifth letter to Clarke, one might be inclined to judge that our concept of space is empirical for Leibniz, and, thus, a fortiori cannot be constitutive of the phenomenal world in the Kantian sense, nor can it ground mathematics as an a priori discipline (cf. *LC*, 69ff., *G* VII 400ff.). But, I want to suggest, this impression is mistaken. To see this, one has to remind oneself that for Leibniz, all our knowledge of necessary truths is based on innate ideas.[49] Leibniz's frequent classification of the propositions of the mathematical sciences as necessary implies, then, that the concepts of space and time, on which these sciences are based, according to Leibniz, are innate as well.[50] An important aspect of Leibniz's theory of innate ideas in this context is that, despite their innateness, these ideas have to be *learned*, namely, by reflection on our own acts of thinking. In much the same way as Kant conceives of the original acquisition of our representations of space and time and the categories, Leibniz also holds that the learning of innate ideas requires experience, on the occasion of which we consciously apprehend innate ideas for the first time.[51] So, instead of taking Leibniz's description of our acquisition of the concept of space in his letter to Clarke as a story about the empirical genesis of this concept, one might rather read it as part of an account of the original acquisition of the innate and, thus, a priori concept of space on the occasion of the perception of spatial relations between phenomenal bodies.[52]

But how about the constitutive function of our representation of space, which alone, according to Kant, explains how geometry can be an a priori synthetic science, i.e., can be a priori and true of the actual world? Kant's own famous explanation is, of course, that the a priori theorems of Euclidean geometry are true of the actual world because, due to our cognitive makeup, the Euclidean spatial form is one of the two forms under which a world can appear to us at all (time being the other one) (cf. B XVI–VII; B41/A24–25). Perhaps surprisingly at first glance, it turns out that Leibniz can give a structurally very similar explanation. Given that the ultimate ground for our innate ideas and the necessary truths based on them are ideas in God's mind, and given that it is God's privileged description of phenomenal reality that determines what the phenomenal world looks like, Leibniz can explain the possibility of geometry as an a priori science by appeal to the fact that in God's privileged description, phenomenal bodies are arranged in a universal spatial order in conformity with His idea of space, which, as harmony will have it, corresponds to our innate idea of space.[53] The a priori theorems of Euclidean geometry are true of the actual world because the Euclidean form is the spatial form that God uses in his privileged description of possible phenomenal worlds, or, at the very least, of the best of all possible worlds, and because the perceptions of monads are modeled on the divine privileged description.[54] This Leibnizian account of the applicability of Euclidean geometry to the world is less elegant and ontologically more expensive than Kant's, but structurally their respective accounts are not that far apart. At the very least, the suggested explanation on behalf of Leibniz shows that he is not "obliged to deny that a priori mathematical doctrines have any validity in respect of real things" (B56–57/A39–40).

The similarity between Leibniz's and Kant's accounts of the constitutive function of the a priori representations of space, and time, can be brought out more sharply by taking a closer look at Leibniz's view of the role of these representations in God's design of possible worlds. An analysis of Leibniz's conception of how God goes about "composing" possible worlds—or at least, of how He goes about designing the plan of the actual world—suggests that Leibniz thinks of God as using His ideas of space and time as a map of the terrain, so to speak, which indicates the possible spatio-temporal positions that can be assigned to the various representatives of the species chosen for creation:

> [T]ime and place, or, in a word, the receptivity or capacity of the world, can be taken for the outlay, or the terrain on which a building is to be erected as commodiously as possible, the variety of forms corresponding to the spaciousness of the building and the number and elegance of its chambers. . . . [T]here does exist the greatest amount possible in proportion to the given capacity of time and space (or the possible order of existence), in much the same way as tiles are laid so that as many as possible are contained in a given space. (*On the Radical Origination of Things*, G VII 303–4 (L 4870))[55]

Together with the fact that for Leibniz the participation of all phenomenal objects and events in a universal spatio-temporal order is what unifies them in one common world, this and other similar passages suggest that, on Leibniz's view, the ideas of space and time in God's mind function as conditions for the possibility of the unity of a given collection of phenomenal bodies in one world, which is precisely the role that our representations of space and time play in Kant's theory as well.[56] It will be left to Kant, however, to transfer the "construction" of the phenomenal world according to this spatio-temporal scheme of order from God's mind to the human mind, which is one of the aspects with respect to which Kant provides an apology for Leibniz that goes beyond the original Leibnizian theory.[57]

It should be clearly stated that this is not the only aspect with respect to which Kant departs from Leibniz in his views about space (and time). A further important dissimilarity concerns the particular representational format that these philosophers ascribe to our representation of space— Leibniz takes himself to be talking about a concept, Kant about an intuition.[58] This dissimilarity is related to further differences in emphasis regarding particular features of this representation that play an important role in Kant's theory, whereas Leibniz does not make much of them.[59] These features include that our representation of space is singular, i.e., that there is only one thing falling under it, and that we conceive of the parts of space as "cut out" from or delineated in the one underlying space. We also have not had time to say anything about Kant's and Leibniz's views on absolute motion, and the implications of these views for the question of what kind of geometrical structure they want to ascribe to space-time, with regard to which further differences in their approaches, but also further similarities in their final positive accounts, can be identified.[60] But at the end of the day, after all dissimilarities have been taken into account, it still seems fair to say that there is a substantial and, at first, surprising agreement between our two protagonists with regard to the question of the nature of space: space is an a priori ideal system of order of appearances that is (partly) constitutive of the phenomenal world. The agreement would not be so surprising if this is the right way to think about space—which it might very well be.

Two final, related worries deserve to be addressed before closing the case for the time being: (1) Do the indicated similarities between Kant and Leibniz mean that, on the proposed interpretation, Leibniz should be regarded as a transcendental idealist about space? (2) Doesn't the fact that, on the proposed interpretation of Leibniz, God's privileged description of reality determines the spatial structure of the phenomenal world imply that Leibniz should be regarded as a transcendental realist about space?[61] The answer to both of these questions, I want to suggest, is no. That is, in my view the distinction between transcendental idealism and transcendental realism, understood on the basis of Kant's explicit characterizations of this distinction at several places of his work, is not an exhaustive one, at least as far as the theory of space is concerned—despite the fact that Kant himself might have *believed* the distinction to be exhaustive.[62]

It is a matter of some controversy in the literature how exactly Kant's transcendental idealism should be characterized, and how it should be distinguished from other forms of idealism and from transcendental realism. There is not enough room to rehearse the debate here, so let me just briefly state how I think the transcendental realism-idealism distinction with respect to space should be best understood based on Kant's explicit assertions on the topic.[63] As I see it, according to Kant's explicit pronouncements on the matter, a necessary and sufficient condition for being a transcendental idealist about space is to hold that space is nothing but a form of human sensibility—which implies, among other things, that space is not a thing in itself or an affection of things in themselves.[64] Together with the assumption that only through sensibility can empirical objects be given to us, transcendental idealism about space implies that space is empirically real, which means, minimally, that empirical objects really possess spatial properties, as opposed to merely appearing to have them. A necessary and sufficient condition for being a transcendental realist about space, according to Kant's explicit pronouncements on the matter, is to take space to be a thing in itself or an affection of things in themselves—which implies, among other things, that space is not only a form of our sensibility.[65] That is, being a transcendental realist about space in the indicated sense implies not being a transcendental idealist about space in the indicated sense, and vice versa. But holding space to be nothing but a form of human sensibility is not the only way of disagreeing with the claim that space is a thing in itself or an affection of things in themselves, just as holding space to be a thing in itself or an affection of things in themselves is not the only way of disagreeing with the claim that space is nothing but a form of human sensibility. There is a third way of disagreeing with these claims, namely, by endorsing Leibniz's view, according to which space is an abstract system of actual and possible spatial relations among (phenomenal) coexistences in God's mind.[66] On this view, space is neither only a form of our human sensibility nor a thing in itself or an affection of things in themselves.

If one bears in mind the differences between Leibniz's and Kant's accounts of (the representation of) space, which were briefly sketched in our previous discussion, one might go so far as to say that for Leibniz, space plays the role of a "form of God's intuition," in the sense that the function of the idea of space in God's design of His privileged description of the world in Leibniz's theory is structurally similar to the function of the intuition of space in our constitution of (our representation of) the phenomenal world in the Kantian theory. Given this agreement, and given that Leibniz would also agree with Kant's classification of space as not being a thing in itself, or not pertaining to things in themselves, while still being empirically real, it seems fair to say that Leibniz's position on space is much closer to transcendental idealism than to transcendental realism, even though it also differs from the former in certain respects, which is why, ideally, it should be listed as a separate, third category in the set of possible positions on the ontological status of space.[67]

CHAPTER 4

What Leibniz Really Said?

Daniel Garber

ANJA JAUERNIG HAS OFFERED an able defense of Kant's reading of Leibniz. On the story that she has told us, quite convincingly, Kant should be understood not as an opponent of Leibniz, but as one of his great defenders, a philosopher who understood Leibniz and offered a philosophical elaboration and defense of his views, in distinction with the somewhat different views of the Leibnizian school of eighteenth-century German philosophy, as exemplified most notably by Christian Wolff. In this essay I would like to offer a complementary view to the one that Jauernig presented in the previous chapter.

I will say, at the very beginning, that I am no Kant scholar. What I want to do is look at some of the issues that Jauernig has raised from the point of view of someone whose primary competence is in Leibniz's thought. I certainly appreciate her attempt to present a more sympathetic view of Kant's reaction to Leibniz. In a philosophical world in which Kant has many more contemporary followers than Leibniz does, it is no small thing to be told that Kant did not, after all, reject Leibniz's metaphysical views. But without wanting to sound too ungrateful for what Jauernig has attempted to do for Leibniz, I want to sound a note of mild dissent.

The main theme of this volume is Kant's treatment of his early-modern predecessors. Now, this can be understood in a number of different ways. As someone whose scholarly life has been centered on early-modern philosophy, I interpreted this theme in a rather special way. Kant, of course, was a major turning point in the history of philosophy. How he represented earlier thinkers in his influential works had a major role to play in how later readers understood them: Kant was, in a way, and for many people remains a filter through which we read the philosophical past. But Kant, of course, was not a scholar in the history of philosophy; he read earlier thinkers as he was taught them, and interpreted them through the lens of his own particular philosophical commitments. Nor could it have been any other way. So for me, as a scholar of early-modern thought, the question is really the way in which Kant *distorted* the history of early-modern thought. In saying this, I do not mean to blame Kant for having committed any intellectual misdeed. My interest as an historian of early-modern philosophy is just to set the record straight.

When we are discussing this question, we must remember how little of Leibniz's own work Kant and his eighteenth-century contemporaries had to go on. For Leibniz's metaphysics, the main source was the "*Monadology*," published in German and Latin shortly after Leibniz's death.[1] Other important works included *Theodicy*, published in 1710, and the Leibniz-Clarke letters, also published shortly after Leibniz's death.[2] Those were supplemented by some of the articles he had published in learned journals, including the "*Meditationes de cognitione, veritate, et ideis*" (published in the *Acta eruditorum* in 1684), the "*Système nouveau . . .* " (*Journal des sçavans*, 1695), the "*Specimen dynamicum*" (*Acta eruditorum*, 1695), and "*De ipsa natura*" (*Acta eruditorum*, 1698), which were republished in some later collections of Leibniz's writings. After 1765, readers also had the *Nouveaux essais*, though by the time that appeared, the general picture of Leibniz's thought had already pretty well solidified.[3] Much of the material that we now depend on for understanding Leibniz's thought, including the "*Discourse on Metaphysics*," the "*First Truths*" paper, the correspondence with Arnauld, the correspondences with de Volder and (for the most part) Des Bosses, and many, many more texts now regarded as central were not published until the nineteenth or twentieth century.[4]

I should note that from the point of view of contemporary Leibniz scholarship, the philosophical texts Kant had available give us a very slanted view of Leibniz's philosophical thought. As Russell and Couturat pointed out at the beginning of the twentieth century, these texts contain only a hint of Leibniz's logic and the contribution it makes to his philosophy. But more than that, these texts give us no real understanding of Leibniz's earlier thought and where his mature thought comes from. Also missing are the central texts and series of letters that illuminate and nuance his thought. The "*Monadology*" is a particularly unfortunate text on which to ground an understanding of Leibniz's philosophy. The "*Monadology*" is, indeed, a kind of canonical statement of his view. But it is not clear why it was written or the status it had in Leibniz's own mind.[5] The text was never published, and was probably not intended for publication, nor was it widely circulated. It sets Leibniz's views out in neat little packages and misses the richness of dialogue and discussion characteristic of Leibniz's letters and other writings. It also misses the way in which Leibniz's thought fits into the dialectic of different views at the end of the seventeenth century, and gives almost nothing of the motivation that drove Leibniz to introduce monads into the world.

An illustration of how this limitation of sources affected the understanding of Leibniz can be seen in the essay on Leibniz in Johann Jacob Brucker's monumental and highly influential *Historia Critica Philosophiae* (Leipzig, 1742–1744).[6] Leibniz was clearly a figure of great importance to Brucker. The essay on Leibniz is the penultimate modern philosopher discussed in the last volume (*"pars altera"* of volume 4) of the first edition. The essay is over one hundred pages and discusses at length Leibniz's intellectual development and the larger social and political context of his thought. Brucker surveys not only his philosophical thought but also a wide variety of his other pursuits, including his work as a diplomat and historian. However, the essay ends with roughly forty pages summarizing his philosophy. Brucker begins with a few short pages on logic, taken from the *"Meditationes de cognitione, veritate, et ideis"* of 1684 (Brucker 1742–1744, vol. 4-2, pp. 398–401). This is followed by an extensive presentation of *"metaphysica Leibnizii,"* the longest section in the summary of Leibniz's philosophy, a Latin translation of the *"Monadology,"* expanded with extensive commentary (Ibid., pp. 401–32). The *"theologia naturalis Leibnizii"* is represented by an annotated and abridged version of Leibniz's *"Causa Dei"* (Ibid., pp. 432–40), a kind of methodical summary of the argument of the *Theodicy,* originally published as an independent work in 1710 but integrated with the *Theodicy* as an appendix starting in the second edition of 1712 and in all subsequent editions. Brucker ends with a short summary of theses taken from the Leibniz-Clarke letters (Ibid., pp. 441–44) and some moral precepts taken from the end of the *"Monadology"* and the preface to the *Codex Juris Gentium Diplomaticus* (1692) (Ibid., pp. 444–46). In this way, his reading of Leibniz's philosophy is shaped by a relatively small body of texts.

Because of his general importance for German philosophy, Leibniz's thought had been taken up by others, most notably Christian Wolff, and interpreted, altered, adopted, and transformed in various ways.[7] Wolff did his best in his writings to distinguish his views from those of Leibniz, both for philosophical reasons (he really did disagree with Leibniz on a number of crucial points) and for polemical reasons (the Pietist controversy made being associated with Leibniz highly undesirable). But as with Descartes and the Cartesians in the century before, people did not always distinguish carefully between Leibniz and his later followers. For that reason, some of the doctrines that Kant attributes to Leibniz are actually those of later Leibnizians. For example, Kant's most celebrated criticism of Leibniz in the *Critique of Pure Reason* is that he "intellectualized the appearances":

> He [Leibniz] compared all things with each other solely through concepts, and found, naturally, no other differences than those through which the understanding distinguishes its pure concepts from each other. The conditions of sensible intuition . . . he did not regard as original; for sensibility was only a confused kind of representation for him, and not a special source of representations; for him appearance was the representation **of the thing in itself**, although distinguished from

cognition through the understanding in its logical form, since with its customary lack of analysis the former draws a certain mixture of subsidiary representations into the concept of the thing, from which the understanding knows how to abstract. In a word, Leibniz **intellectualized** the appearances, just as Locke totally **sensitivized** the concepts of understanding. (A270/B326)

The view that sensation is continuous with the concepts of the understanding is not found anywhere in Leibniz himself, so far as I can see. It seems to derive from Wolff's reading of Leibniz's "*Meditationes de cognitione, veritate, et ideis*" in his German Logic of 1713.[8] It can also be found in Baumgarten's *Metaphysica*.[9] But even so, it is not surprising that later readers would attribute that doctrine not to Wolff or Baumgarten but, as Kant did, to Leibniz himself. (We shall return to this criticism of Kant's later in this essay and examine it more carefully.)

Kant's Leibniz is not a fabrication by any means, and I do not want to suggest that his readings of Leibniz are not in some way grounded in Leibnizian texts or, at least, in texts that he had good reason to believe were genuinely Leibnizian. But based as it was on a reasonably small number of Leibniz's texts, read through the filter of Leibniz's contemporary advocates, I want to argue that the Leibniz that Kant presents in his main later writings is a gross oversimplification of the real Leibniz. The real Leibniz, I would argue, is a subtle, complex thinker, constantly rethinking his views and willing to explore new paths. In Kant's hands, he is reduced to a few dogmatic precepts, a caricature of his real thought.

Kant offers a succinct summary of Leibniz's philosophy in a number of places in his critical writings. The most extended and detailed is probably in the Amphiboly section of the *Critique of Pure Reason*, where he outlines what he takes Leibniz's "intellectual system of the world" to be, and offers some of his most direct criticisms (A270ff./B326ff.). The discussion wanders a bit, but in his characterization of Leibniz's position he includes the doctrine of the monads as things in themselves, the principle of sufficient reason, the principle that basic concepts cannot contradict one another, the principle of preestablished harmony, and the doctrine of space and time. But there are even more succinct summaries of Leibniz's philosophy in two later texts. The first occurs in the treatise *On a Discovery Whereby Any New Critique of Pure Reason Is to Be Made Superfluous by an Older One*, published in 1790 in connection with Kant's controversy with Eberhard. There he writes:

Leibniz's metaphysics contained primarily three peculiarities: (1) the principle of sufficient reason, and that so far as it was merely meant to indicate the insufficiency of the principle of contradiction for the knowledge of necessary truths; (2) the doctrine of monads; (3) the doctrine of pre-established harmony. (*Discovery*, AA 8 247)

In *On a Discovery*, Kant goes on to elaborate on each of these points. His account of the Leibnizian philosophy is very similar in another late work, *What Real Progress Has Metaphysics Made in Germany Since the Time of Leibniz and Wolff?* written between 1788 and 1795, but first published only after Kant's death in 1804. There he dispenses with the neat summary. However, three of the four points Kant elaborates in his exposition of Leibniz's philosophy correspond exactly to the three points in *On a Discovery*. To them Kant adds a fourth, the principle of the identity of indiscernibles.

One quite striking thing about reading these characterizations of Leibniz, as well as those found, for example, in Wolff, is the emphasis on principles. Principles certainly are very important to Leibniz. In the "*Monadology*," he announces:

> Our reasonings are based on *two great principles, that of contradiction*, in virtue of which we judge that which involves a contradiction to be false, and that which is opposed or contradictory to the false to be true ... and *that of sufficient reason*, by virtue of which we consider that we can find no true or existent fact, no true assertion, without there being a sufficient reason why it is thus and not otherwise, although most of the time these reasons cannot be known to us. (*Mon.* 31–32)

And in the Leibniz-Clarke correspondence, Leibniz certainly makes considerable use of the Principle of Sufficient Reason, particularly in his discussions of space and time. However, one can exaggerate the centrality of these principles. On other occasions, Leibniz uses many other principles: the Principle of Continuity, the Principle of Perfection, the Principle of the Equality of Cause and Effect, and so on, without in any way attempting to reduce them to these two principles. And there is nothing in Leibniz's genuine texts that could prepare one for the role that they play in Wolff's *Vernünftige Gedanken von Gott, der Welt und der Seele des Menschen* (1720), the so-called *German Metaphysics*. There, after a very brief chapter on our own existence (chapter 1, which contains only five pages), Wolff launches into a long discussion of these same two principles as the foundation of all knowledge, principles that he will hark back to again and again in later discussions. It is not surprising that Kant will later see the centrality of certain metaphysical principles as constitutive of a Leibnizian approach to philosophy. Again, it is not that they are not important, it is just that they probably are not quite as important to Leibniz himself as they came to be for later Leibnizians, their followers, and their opponents.

But I do not want to dwell on these issues. Rather, I would like to look more closely at Kant's treatment of the relation between monads and bodies. There, I shall argue, one can see clearly some of the consequences of the rather narrow view Kant and his contemporaries had of Leibniz's philosophy.

On Kant's predominant reading, Leibniz held that bodies are actually made up of an infinity of monads. Because each monad represents the entire world in which it exists, bodies are represented in monads through the representation of the monads that compose them. However, because of the imperfection of monads and their inability to perceive each of the monads that compose a body distinctly, bodies are confused representations of the monads that compose them, and thus are phenomena. And so, he writes in the *Critique of Pure Reason*:

> Leibniz took the appearances for things in themselves, thus for *intelligibilia*, i.e., objects of the pure understanding (although on account of the confusion of their representations he labeled them with the name of phenomena). (A264/B320)

Kant is a bit clearer in *Progress*:

> But as to Leibniz's principle of the logical difference between the indistinctness and the distinctness of representations, when he claims that the former, that mode of presentation which we were calling mere intuition, is actually only the confused concept of its object, so that intuition differs from concepts of things, not in kind, but only according to the degree of consciousness, and thus the intuition, for example, of a body in thoroughgoing consciousness of all the presentations contained in it would yield the concept of it as an aggregate of monads—to this the critical philosopher will reply that in that way the proposition "bodies consist of monads" could arise from experience, merely by analysis of perception, if only we could see sharply enough (with appropriate awareness of part-representations). (*Progress*, AA 20: 278)

This reading of Leibniz is closely connected with Kant's claim that the supposed intellectualization of appearances was the fatal flaw in Leibniz's thought. For Kant, things in themselves are not accessible through sensible intuition, but only through the intellect. Thus, if our representations of bodies were to be a representation of the infinity of monads that make them up, a representation of things in themselves, it would have to be through the intellect. But insofar as Leibniz wants to say that our sensible representation of bodies is just a confused representation of the monads that make up bodies, our outer senses must thus be confused products of the intellect. That is, Leibniz must (wrongly) think of the senses and the intellect as being on a continuum, instead of being quite distinct faculties.

What Kant wants to do (if I understand him) is to make the knowledge we have of things in themselves (which comes from the intellect) radically distinct from the knowledge we have of appearances (which comes from sensibility).

In his discussion of Leibniz in *On a Discovery*, Kant is somewhat more generous toward Leibniz on this score, and gives him the benefit of the doubt:

> Is it really believable that Leibniz, such a great mathematician! wanted to compose bodies out of monads . . . ? He did not mean the physical world, but rather its substrate, unknowable by us, the intelligible world, which lies merely in the Idea of reason and in which we really do have to represent everything we think therein as composite substance to be composed of simple substances. He also seems, with Plato, to attribute to the human mind an original, though by now dim, intellectual intuition of these super-sensible beings, though from this he inferred nothing concerning sensible beings, which he would wish to be taken for things related to a special mode of intuition, of which we are capable solely with regard to cognitions that are possible for us, in the strictest sense as mere appearances, tied to (specific, particular) forms of intuition; we should not therefore let ourselves be disturbed by his account of sensibility as a confused mode of representation, but must rather replace it by another, more suited to his purpose; for otherwise his system will be inconsistent. (*Discovery*, AA 8 248–49)

Here Kant attributes to Leibniz something closer to his own position, the view that bodies are not really composed of monads and that our sensory perception of bodies is not just a confused perception of the monads that make them up. Kant charitably assumes here that Leibniz *must* have realized that monads, things in themselves, are only conceivable through the intellect, and that while *in a sense* they must ground the bodies we experience, they do not contribute in any way to our experience of them, even if other strands in Leibniz's thought suggest otherwise. This more generous attitude is consistent with the strategy of *On a Discovery*. In response to Eberhard's attack on Kant for not being sufficiently Leibnizian, Kant replies in that essay by showing that he is more Leibnizian than thou. It is in this context that he presents himself as offering "the true apology for Leibniz" in his *Critique of Pure Reason* (*Discovery*, AA 8 250).

The question, then is: Did Kant get Leibniz right in his account of the relation between monads and bodies? The answer is clear: solidly yes and solidly no. Let me explain.

First of all, there is a part of the story that Kant was almost completely unaware of. On my reading of Leibniz, at least, the monadology, the idea of a metaphysics grounded in simple and unextended substances comes rather late in his career, perhaps in the mid-1690s, perhaps in 1700 or so; at the moment we lack the documents to determine an exact date or even the exact path by which he came to his views of a monadological metaphysics. Before he discovered monads, I would argue, the fundamental notion in Leibniz's metaphysics was that of an individual substance, a corporeal substance understood on the model of an organism, a body connected with a soul. This is the position one finds, for example, prominently discussed in the Correspondence with Arnauld from 1686 and 1687.[10] But Kant and his contemporaries had no real inkling of this earlier view, and generally assumed that it was monads all the way back to the earliest writings that they read. The main texts in which Leibniz advanced such a metaphysics grounded in corporeal substance, the Correspondence with Arnauld, for example, were simply unknown before the nineteenth century. And when these earlier texts did become known, the idea of Leibniz as a monadologist was deeply entrenched by more than a century of philosophical tradition. As a consequence, the newly published texts were read through the lens of the view of Leibniz that Kant and others had assumed, a view that takes the monadology as central. Insofar as Kant was ignorant of that theme in Leibniz's thought, he certainly could not be said to understand Leibniz's views on body.

But let us leave aside this period in Leibniz's thought and focus on the later writings, which do deal with monads. What, then, was Leibniz's view of the relation of monads to bodies? And did Kant get *that* right? It is very interesting that the relation between monads and bodies is not really discussed in the "*Monadology*," the work on which Kant and his contemporaries largely depended for Leibniz's metaphysics: it is a gaping hole in that work. Leibniz begins that work with an extended discussion of monads, what they are, their perceptions and appetitions, a total of sixty paragraphs, including a digression on necessary truth, the principles of reasoning, and the creator of the world of monads. But then, quite abruptly, in §61 he turns to composites and to bodies. Nowhere in the "*Monadology*" does Leibniz address the question as to how monads are related to bodies. My conjecture is that Leibniz was not really sure what he wanted to say here, and so in the "*Monadology*" he said nothing. The serious discussions of the issue are found in two sets of correspondence that Kant and his contemporaries did not have access to, the correspondence with de Volder and the later correspondence with Des Bosses. What, then, was the view Leibniz advanced in those documents?

Burcher de Volder (1643–1709) was the professor of physics and philosophy at the University of Leiden. He was a committed Cartesian, though he rejected Malebranchian occasionalism. He was prominent enough that when Huygens died, he named de Volder as his literary executor.

The correspondence is a very interesting set of letters, very important for understanding Leibniz's thought. In those letters, Leibniz is attempting to explain himself to someone he generally regards as a smart and worthy correspondent, even though he is a Cartesian. There we find one of the most careful developments of Leibniz's views on the metaphysics of monads. In particular, Leibniz is trying to contrast his own views on body and extension with those of someone who believes that the essence of body is extension and that there is nothing more to body than its geometrical properties. Here are the kinds of things that Leibniz writes to de Volder. The first is from a letter written on June 20, 1703:

> I therefore distinguish: (1) the primitive entelechy or soul; (2) matter, namely primary matter or primitive passive power; (3) the monad completed by these two things; (4) the mass or secondary matter, or organic machine for which innumerable subordinate monads come together; and (5) the animal, or corporeal substance, which the monad dominating in the machine makes into one thing. (G II 252)[11]

In this passage, well-known to later commentators, Leibniz seems to conceive of the monad as consisting of a soul and primary matter. However, "mass or secondary matter" consists of an aggregate of monads. When such an aggregate itself is appropriately organized and has a dominant monad, it constitutes "one thing." Leibniz even suggests in this connection (as Kant assumes that he would have to, on this view) that monads have a kind of spatial dimension:

> For even if monads are not extended, they nonetheless have a certain kind of situation in extension, that is, they have a certain relation of coexistence to other things which is ordered, namely, through the machine over which they preside. I do not think that there exist any finite substances which are separated from every body and, therefore, lack situation or order in relation to the other coexisting things in the universe. Extended things involve in themselves many things endowed with situation. But things that are simple, even if they do not have extension, must have a situation in extension, although it may not be possible to designate it precisely, as with incomplete phenomena. (G II 253)

What are the phenomena in question here? Here is a passage written a few paragraphs earlier in the same letter, where Leibniz gives some indications of what he has in mind:

> But in the phenomena, or the resulting aggregate, everything is indeed explained mechanically, and masses are understood to impel one another. And in these phenomena nothing is needed except the consideration of derivative forces, once it is agreed where they result from, namely, the phenomena of aggregates from the reality of monads. (G II 250)

There are obscurities here, to be sure. But even so, it seems that bodies are understood as aggregates of monads. Such aggregates are phenomenal insofar as they are unified not in themselves, but by us: "But since simple things alone are true things, the rest are only beings through aggregation, and therefore phenomena, and, as Democritus used to say, exist by convention not by nature" (G II 252). And so Leibniz writes: "Bodies, which are commonly taken for substances, are nothing but real phenomena, and are no more substances than perihelia or rainbows, and this is not something that is overturned by touch any more than by sight. The monad alone is a substance, a body is substances not a substance" (G II 262).

This is close to the view that Kant attributes to Leibniz in the passages from the *Critique of Pure Reason* and *Progress* that I quoted earlier. But this is not to say that he got Leibniz's view correct. Elsewhere Leibniz says things that would seem to be a bit different. For example, in a letter to de Volder from mid-1704 he writes:

> But accurately speaking matter is not composed of constitutive unities, rather it results from them, since matter or extended mass is nothing but a phenomenon founded in things, like the rainbow or the parhelion. And there is no reality in anything except the reality of unities, and so phenomena can always be divided into lesser phenomena which could appear to other more subtle animals, and the smallest phenomena may never be reached. Substantial unities are not really parts, but the foundations of the phenomena. (G II 268)

Here he explicitly denies what he had suggested earlier, that bodies are made up of monads. Instead, monads are "the foundations of the phenomena." Whatever exactly that means. Similarly, in a letter written to de Volder shortly after, Leibniz writes:

> I do not really do away with body, but restore it to what it is; for I show that corporeal mass which is believed to have something besides simple substances, is not a substance, but a phenomenon resulting from simple substances, which alone have unity and absolute reality. (G II 275)[12]

Here Leibniz makes the claim that body is a "phenomenon *resulting from* simple substances." What exactly this means, though, is not at all clear.

Elsewhere still in this series of letters there is something that looks very much like the kind of view that Kant charitably attributed to Leibniz in *Progress*:

> I do not see what argument could prove that there is anything in extension, mass, or motion beyond the phenomena, that is, beyond the perceptions of simple substances. And so the active and passive force which is conceived of as a certain something in mass outside perceiving things, is nothing other than a phenomenon, like the rainbow,

or an image in a mirror, or a dream, but wholly consistent with itself. And the reality of sensible things consists in nothing other than the agreement of the phenomena.[13]

On this view, the physical world would seem to be the common dream of a multitude of monads. On this view, monads do not perceive or represent one another: the world exists insofar as they perceive it in common with one another.[14]

Can we then say that Kant got Leibniz right in *Progress*? In a way, yes. Something like the view that he attributed to Leibniz out of charity can really be found in Leibniz's texts, even though Kant could not have known that. But one should not be so hasty to conclude in Kant's favor.

In the letters to de Volder we can find a variety of positions on the relations between monads and bodies. Leibniz's uncertainty on the issue continues into his correspondence with Des Bosses, which begins shortly after the correspondence with de Volder begins to peter out. Bartholomaeus Des Bosses (1668–1728) was a Jesuit mathematician. Des Bosses also became the Latin translator of the *Theodicy*. In a way, these letters form a nice complement to the de Volder correspondence. De Volder was a Cartesian, whereas Des Bosses was a Scholastic. The correspondence extended from January 25, 1706, until May 29 1716, just a few months before Leibniz's death.

A number of passages in the early part of the correspondence would seem to identify bodies as aggregates of monads:

> Matter (i.e. secondary matter), or a part of matter, exists in the same manner as a herd or a house, that is, as a being by aggregation. (Leibniz to Des Bosses, March 11, 1706, G II 304)[15]

> [F]rom many monads there results secondary matter, together with derivative forces, actions and passions, which are only beings through aggregation, and thus semi-mental things, like the rainbow and other well-founded phenomena. (Leibniz to Des Bosses, March 11, 1706, G II 306)

There is even a passage that suggests that monads have position:

> [A] simple substance, even though it does not have extension in itself, nonetheless has position, which is the foundation of extension, since extension is the simultaneous continuous repetition of position. (Leibniz to Des Bosses, July 21, 1707, G II 339)

But in the letter of January 28, 1712, Des Bosses raises a new topic: corporeal substance. This changes the conversation and starts a new discussion. As in Leibniz's earlier writings, before monads were introduced into the picture, corporeal substances were understood to be complex substances, such as human beings and other living things. In these later letters with Des Bosses, Leibniz is working out the question as to how a group of monads could come together to form a genuine complex substance. The solution that he develops is that for a group of monads to come together and form a complex corporeal substance, God would have to add a substantial bond, a *vinculum substantiale*. From this moment on to the end of the exchange, the doctrine of corporeal substance and the substantial bond become central topics of discussion.

The doctrine is complicated and at various moments verges on the incoherent. But briefly, in these letters, which stretch from late January 1712 to the end of his life, Leibniz argues for the following main theses:

(1) For there to be corporeal substance, something is needed over and above the monads.
(2) That something is itself substantial, rather than modal.
(3) The substantial bond is distinct from the monads, and is something over and above them.
(4) Such a substantial bond will be the seat of form and matter, which arise from the form and matter of the individual monads.
(5) Such a substantial bond is not a soul (a monad), but exists over and above a soul in an organic body.
(6) A substantial bond can only attach to a collection of monads that constitutes an organic body.[16]

It is important to note here that this view is clearly inconsistent with the pure monadological view as expressed to de Volder or in the "*Monadology.*" In the classic monadological texts, all there are are monads and in them, perception and appetition. But the view of corporeal substance that Leibniz outlines to Des Bosses requires something over and above the monads, a substantial bond that links them together.

In the course of the discussion of the substantial bond, Leibniz considers some very significant revisions of his view of body. For example, he writes:

> Thus, one of two things must be said: either bodies are mere phenomena, and so extension also will be only a phenomenon, and monads alone will be real, but with a union supplied by the operation of the perceiving soul on the phenomenon; or, if faith drives us to corporeal substances, this substance consists in that unifying reality, which adds *something absolute* (and therefore substantial), albeit impermanent, to the things to be unified. (Leibniz to Des Bosses, February 15, 1712, G II 435)[17]

You say that bodies can be something other than phenomena, even if they are not substances. I think that unless there are corporeal sub-

stances, bodies collapse into phenomena. And aggregates themselves
are nothing but phenomena, since besides the ingredient monads, everything else is added through perception alone, by virtue of the fact that
they are perceived at the same time. (Leibniz to Des Bosses, May 29,
1716, G II 517)

Here the view seems to be that if there are no substantial bonds, then
bodies are aggregates of monads, which we unite through an operation
of the mind. Add a substantial bond, though, and the situation is different: the bodies of our experience are themselves real, genuine things in
themselves.

But elsewhere, the suggestion is that if there were no substantial bonds,
then the world of bodies would be just the coordinated dreams of an
infinity of monads:

If that substantial bond of monads were absent, then all bodies with
all their qualities would be only well-founded phenomena, like a rain-
bow or an image in a mirror, in a word, continuous dreams that agree
perfectly with each other; and in this alone would consist the reality of
those phenomena. For it should no more be said that monads are parts
of bodies, that they touch each other, that they compose bodies, than
it is right to say this of points and souls. And a monad, like a soul, is,
as it were, a certain world of its own, having no relationship of dependence except with God. Therefore, if a body is a substance, it is the
realization of phenomena going beyond their agreement. (Leibniz to
Des Bosses, February 15, 1712, G II 435–36)

If bodies are phenomena, and are judged by our appearances, they will
not be real, since they will appear differently to others. Thus, the reality
of bodies, of space, motion and time seems to consist in this: that they
are the phenomena of God, i.e., the object of his knowledge of vision.
And the difference between the appearance of bodies with respect to us
and their appearance with respect to God is in some way like the difference between a drawing in perspective and a ground plan. For whereas
drawings in perspective differ according to the position of the viewer,
a ground plan or geometrical representation is unique. God certainly
sees things exactly such as they are according to geometrical truth, although likewise he also knows how each thing appears to every other,
and thus he contains in himself eminently all the other appearances.
(Study for Leibniz to Des Bosses, February 15, 1712, G II 438)

On the substantial bond view, we seem to be faced with real things
in themselves in our experience: genuine corporeal substances. But what
becomes of the monads on this view? Here is what Leibniz says:

Hence corporeal substance, or the substantial bond of monads, although it requires monads naturally or physically, does not require them metaphysically, since it is nonetheless not in them as in a subject; and so it can be destroyed or changed, while the monads are preserved, and accommodated to monads that do not naturally belong to it. Nor is any monad besides the dominant monad even naturally attached to the substantial bond, since the other monads are in a perpetual flux. (Leibniz to Des Bosses, August 23, 1713, G II 482)

Monads are still there, at a deeper level, underlying the substantial bond and the corporeal substance that it creates. More than that it is hard to say.

It is not entirely clear just how seriously Leibniz took the substantial bond and his account of corporeal substance. Precisely because the substantial bond theory is inconsistent with the monadology, commentators have been reluctant to admit that Leibniz seriously advanced it. But, indeed, in the correspondence, it is not clear just how committed Leibniz is to the view. Particularly at the beginning of the discussion, Leibniz carefully distances himself from the view. But as the correspondence proceeds, it looks more and more as if he is seriously considering it. It seems clear that Leibniz is worried about the reality of body, and is experimenting around with a way of reviving his earlier and more robustly realistic view. He seems willing to entertain giving up the monadology—and to introduce something new in nature—in order to save the reality of bodies. (It makes it easier to take it seriously if you accept the view that monads only represent the last stage of Leibniz's metaphysics; viewed in that way, the substantial bond just represents a step toward the next stage in Leibniz's thought.) At very least, one can say that Leibniz is seriously examining whether to abandon the strict monadological idealism and add something that will ground the full-blown reality of composite bodies.

So, what does this show? It may be too strong to say that Kant gets Leibniz's story about the relation between monads and bodies wrong. The account he gives in the *Critique of Pure Reason* and *Progress*, and against which he argues, the account that a body is an aggregate of monads confusedly perceived together is certainly *Leibnizian*: it is a view held by Leibniz himself, if you know where to look for it. It is also true that Leibniz held the view that Kant allows Leibniz in *On a Discovery*, the view that Jauernig wants to attribute to him, the view of bodies as the common dream of a multitude of monads. That too can be found in genuine Leibnizian texts. As can other views, including the early view of bodies as grounded corporeal substance understood independently of monads, or bodies as grounded in collections of monads united by substantial chains, as he argues in his letters to Des Bosses. During the later part of his life, Leibniz was definitely committed to the view that monads, simple substances are at the metaphysical ground-level of the world. And he was committed to the existence of the bodies of sensory experience. But he did not seem to have a fixed view of what exactly the relation is between those two realms. In his writings we can find a number of different accounts of that relation, and no clear reasons for saying that one or another of these accounts is his clear favorite.

In his letters and private papers, Leibniz seems remarkably open to articulating and exploring the consequences of different positions without necessarily committing himself to any. In those papers, we see an active, curious, and very creative mind hard at work sorting things out. These are thought in process, a remarkable record of a remarkable mind trying to sort things out and figure out what he should believe. In these letters and notes we have an intimate view of Leibniz's philosophical practice. There is a kind of dialogue among these notes, as if Leibniz were conducting a kind of learned debate within the confines of his study. The idea that the world is made up of monads at its most basic level, for example, is certainly one of his important doctrines, and quite central to his thought in later years. But, as we have seen in the Des Bosses letters, Leibniz is willing to question even that late in life, and experiment with an alternative, even as he is penning the "*Monadology*," the essay that will be the primary source for his metaphysics for the generations that follow. In a sense, it was impossible for Kant to get Leibniz right simply because there was no single Leibniz to get right!

It is always tempting to ask what Leibniz really thinks, and to try to set out in clear and simple terms just what the Leibnizian philosophy comes to. And given the small number of texts that Kant and his contemporaries had available, this seems like a very reasonable project. But when we look at the larger context, the full complexity of his literary remains, Leibniz comes out as a very different kind of thinker. The project of reconstructing the doctrine that Leibniz held, explicitly or under wraps, is fundamentally misguided. What we should be doing, instead, is trying to capture the complexity of his thought, its twists and turns, its hesitations and its affirmations. What, then, *did* Leibniz *really* think? On some issues, such as the relation between monads and bodies, perhaps that question does not even make sense to ask.

And here, I think, is where we find the greatest distortion in Kant's representation of Leibniz's thought: the idea that his philosophy can be captured in a short list of cut-and-dried theses, and put into neat textbook form. In a way, it is no accident that Leibniz never wrote the single work that could serve as the authoritative account of his philosophy. Leibniz's philosophical spirit is too rambling and messy to fit so neatly between two covers.

Kant's Transcendental Idealism and the Limits of Knowledge: Kant's Alternative to Locke's Physiology

Paul Guyer

KANT'S AIM in the *Critique of Pure Reason* was "a critique of the faculty of reason in general, in respect of all the cognition after which reason might strive **independently of all experience,** and hence [a] decision about the possibility or impossibility of a metaphysics in general, and the determination of its sources, as well as its extent and boundaries, all, however, from principles" (A xii).[1] Kant's project sounds very similar to the project for his *Essay Concerning Human Understanding* that John Locke had announced almost a century earlier when he stated that it was his "*Purpose* to enquire into the Original, Certainty, and Extent of humane Knowledge; together with the Grounds and Degrees of Belief, Opinion, and Assent" (*E* 1.1.2). Like Kant, Locke supposed that the extent and thus the boundaries of human knowledge can be determined by scrutiny of our own cognitive capacities: "were the Capacities of our Understanding once discovered," then "the Horizon" would be "found, which sets the Bounds between the enlightned and dark Parts of Things; between what is, and what is not comprehensible by us" (*E* 1.1.7). Kant clearly saw a relation between his project and Locke's; indeed, "the famous Locke" is the first philosopher named in the *Critique* (A ix). Yet Kant rejected Locke's own examination of the "capacities of our understanding" as an inadequate "**physiology** of the human understanding" (A x). It cannot have been the general project of determining the limits of human knowledge by any examination of our own cognitive capacities that Kant meant to reject under the name of "physiology." Instead, Kant's problem with Locke's "physiology" was that it was *empirical*, that is, that it attempted to determine both the contents of human knowledge and its boundaries through a purely empirical investigation of the human capacity for cognition (see B127). Kant, by contrast, supposed that he could provide what he called a "transcendental" determination of the fundamental structures of our cognition, and therefore that he could also provide a transcendental rather than an empirical determination of its limits.

Kant's explicit criticism of Locke, repeated over many years, was that Locke's "physiological" attempt to give a purely empiricist account of human knowledge could yield neither the contents nor the necessity of the a priori concepts on which all our empirical knowledge rests. Thus, Kant did not explicitly assert that Locke's determination of the *limits* of human knowledge uses an empirical method. But he would have been right to do so, for Locke's determination of these limits is in fact largely based on his estimates of the scope and powers of the human senses, estimates that are themselves empirical in character. Kant, by contrast, derives both the foundations and the limits of human knowledge from his transcendental inquiry into the conditions of its possibility: for Kant, the necessity of space and time as the a priori forms of sensible intuition and of the categories of the understanding as the a priori forms of all thought can be explained only if these forms of intuition and thought apply only to our experience of objects rather than to objects themselves, that is, to appearances rather than to things as they are in themselves. However, although Locke's determination of the limits of human knowledge was not only empirical but also thoroughly premature, Kant's own transcendental determination of the limits of human knowledge is founded upon claims to necessity to which he had no right. Nevertheless, Kant's own conception of *empirical* knowledge and its principles suggests a far more plausible picture of the limits of such knowledge than Locke does, for Kant argues that the scope and power of our senses may be indefinitely extended by empirical science itself. For Kant, while there can never be anything that would count as complete empirical knowledge of the sensible world, there is also never any reason to believe that any particular stage in the progression of empirical knowledge represents an ultimate limit to it. This is the enduring lesson about the limits of human knowledge that we should draw from Kant.

LOCKE: THE EMPIRICAL LIMITS OF HUMAN KNOWLEDGE

In this section, I first recount Kant's explicit charge that Locke's account of knowledge is merely physiological, and will then address the less obvious point that Locke's account of the limits of human knowledge can also be considered entirely physiological.

Locke, of course, held that all of our knowledge arises from the "several distinct *Perceptions* of things" that "*Our Senses*, conversant about particular sensible Objects, do *convey into the Mind*" (*E* 2.1.3) as well as from "the *Perception of the Operations of our own Minds* within us, as it is employ'd about the Ideas it has got" from sensation (*E* 2.1.4). Thus, for Locke all the contents of our concepts must be traced to perceptions of external objects or perceptions of our perceptions, and there is no room for any additional origins for or constraints upon the contents of our concepts. Kant was obviously responding to this empiricist program when he started the *Critique of Pure Reason* by rejecting "a certain **physiology** of the human understanding (by the famous Locke)" (A ix), and when he famously claimed, later in the work, that while "Leibniz **intellectualized** the appearances . . . Locke totally **sensitivized** the concepts of understanding in accordance with his system of **noogony** . . . i.e., interpreted them as nothing but empirical or abstracted concepts of reflection" (A271/B327). The latter way of putting his objection seems unique, but the claim that Locke offered only a physiology of knowledge was one that Kant repeated frequently in his notes and lectures. One of Kant's pithiest statements of the charge comes in a note from 1776–1778, in which he states that

> Locke [is] a physiologist of reason, [concerning] the origin of concepts. He commits the error of taking the occasion for the acquisition of these concepts, namely experience, as its source. Nevertheless he makes use of these concepts beyond the boundaries of experience. (*R* 4866, *AA* 18 14)[2]

By the last remark, Kant presumably means that Locke inconsistently thinks he can conceive of the existence of a nonsensible object, namely God, by means of concepts drawn entirely from the senses, a point that Kant at least once made explicit in his lectures when he said that Locke (along with Aristotle) acts "inconsistently," "For if all concepts are borrowed from experience, then they can assume nothing other than what [rests] on experience," "But God is not in any experience."[3] But more typically, Kant just emphasized the shortcomings but not the inconsistency of Locke's attempt to ground all of our knowledge solely on ideas provided by the sensory experience or reflection upon it.

First, as in *R* 4866, Kant stressed that Locke confused the *occasion* on which we become conscious of a concept with the *origin* of the concept and the source of its validity. He then charged that this was to overlook the contribution of the laws of the mind itself, in the first instance the laws of the understanding, to the contents of our concepts. Both of these charges were made in a note from 1769:

> Some concepts are abstracted from sensations, others merely from the law of the understanding for comparing, combining, or separating abstracted concepts. The origin of the latter is in the understanding; of the former, in the senses. All concepts of the latter sort are called pure concepts of the understanding, *conceptus intellectus puri*. We can of course set these activities of the understanding in motion only when occasioned to do so by sensible impressions and can become aware of

certain concepts of the general relations of abstracted ideas in accordance with the laws of the understanding; and thus Locke's rule that no idea becomes clear in us without sensible impression is valid here as well; the *notiones rationales*, however, arise no doubt by means of sensations and can also only be thought in application to the ideas abstracted from them, but they do not lie in them and are not abstracted from them. Just as in geometry we do not derive the idea of space from the sensation of extended beings, although we can clarify this concept only on the occasion of the sensation of corporeal things. Hence the idea of space is a *notio intellectus puri* which can be applied to the abstracted idea of mountains and of kegs. (*R* 3930, *AA* 17 352)[4]

Locke was, of course, aware that we perform operations of comparing, combining, and separating ideas that are furnished to us by the senses: he devotes a chapter to these operations of the mind, arguing that they are the means by which simple ideas are transformed into abstract and/or complex ideas (*E* 2.11). So if Kant's objection is to have any bite, he must mean that although sensible impressions first occasion us to form abstract concepts by means of processes of comparison, combination, and separation and provide ineliminable elements of the contents of such ideas, the understanding also brings its own "laws" to that activity, so that the concepts thus formed must reflect not only the character of the input from experience but also the structures of the laws of thought. Further, however, the conclusion of Kant's remark implies that it is not just the laws of the understanding, but also the inherent forms of pure intuition that structure our sensory experiences of external objects, so that the concepts we form on the basis of our "sensations of corporeal things" are structured by the laws of both sensibility and understanding as well as by the contents of the sensations themselves—although Kant does not distinguish sensibility from understanding as clearly in this note from 1769 as he would a year later in his Inaugural Dissertation, and thus he calls our pure intuition of space, which cannot be derived merely from the contents of our sensations of external objects, a *notio intellectus puri*.

In a note from later in the 1770s, when Kant had more clearly drawn the key distinction between sensibility and understanding that would structure the first *Critique*, he defined the issue between him and Locke as whether "concepts are merely *educta* or *producta*," whether, in terms of a biological contrast that he often employed, they are the products of mere "preformation" through the senses alone or of a genuine "*epigenesis*" involving both the senses and the mind: that is, whether concepts arise "either through physical (empirical) influence or through consciousness of the formal constitution of our sensibility and understanding, on the occasion of experience, hence yet as *producta a priori*, not *a posteriori*"

(*R* 4851, *AA* 18 8).[5] He makes it clear that Locke's view is the former, whereas his is the latter (*AA* 18 9). And this leads to the heart of his objection to Locke, namely, that Locke's physiological approach, attempting to derive the whole content of all of our ideas from the senses or from reflection on ideas of the senses but without the recognition of any additional structure imported by the constitution of the mind in both sensibility and understanding, is not only incapable of fully explaining the content of our ideas, but a fortiori is also incapable of explaining the *necessity* of the most fundamental ideas of both sensibility and understanding. This is made clear in another note from the years of the genesis of the first *Critique* (1776–1778), where Kant writes, "According to Priestly and Locke, all cognition must be empirical, and nothing synthetic can possess true necessity" (*R* 5021, *AA* 18 63).[6] Kant recognizes that Locke can explain analytic necessities, but holds that he has no way of explaining synthetic a priori cognition, the acceptance of which, he rather confidently maintains in this same note, is "universal without exception."

Kant expands upon this conclusion in an important note from the period of the first publication of the *Critique of Pure Reason* (1780–1783); I quote only its last part:

> Among all of our thoughts there is not the least trace of the intuition of objects other than those of the senses and no thoughts that pertain to anything other than the exposition of appearances. An intellectual intuition of objects outside of us, that do not exist through us, also seems to be impossible.
>
> If one assumes intellectual intuitions, this yields no cognition of the understanding through concepts and thus no thought and also no communicable cognition.
>
> If it were supposed that we had everything a posteriori through experience and the immediate perception of objects, thus even space and time, then we would not know anything of them other than contingent truths. We cannot cognize anything of them synthetically a priori unless these intuitions are given to us a priori, consequently not through objects, but through the subject, although its relation to the objects, since these are given as appearances through those subjective conditions. . . .
>
> Now the logical system of the cognitions of the understanding is either empirical or transcendental. The former Aristotle and Locke, the latter either the system of epigenesis or that of involution, acquired or inborn. The so-called healthy understanding is an *asylum ignorantiae*. (*R* 5637, *AA* 18 274–75)[7]

On the one hand, Kant agrees with Locke, we cannot suppose that we have any determinate ideas of objects without input from the senses, and therefore, although Locke does not always realize this, we cannot have any determinate ideas about objects not accessible to our senses. On the other hand, Kant objects to Locke, if we assume that the content of our ideas is exhausted by the input of the senses in experience, we will not be able to explain any synthetic a priori cognition. In his own view, however, our concepts of objects apply both pure forms of sensibility and pure forms of understanding to the inputs of the senses, and these, singly and in combination, do yield synthetic a priori cognition in spite of the necessity of experience for occasioning the application of these forms and for partially determining the content of our abstract but still empirical concepts.

Usually Kant is content to suggest that Locke simply failed to recognize the possibility of synthetic a priori cognition, and thus never even considered whether his empiricism could be adequate to explain such cognition. In one striking passage from late lectures on metaphysics (1794–1795), however, Kant talks as if Locke did recognize the problem, but thought it could be solved, at least asymptotically, by empirical methods:

> Aristotle and later Locke set up a (so-called) physiology of reason, because they viewed a priori cognition as something which can be acquired empirically, and which we have elevated by generalization to an a priori cognition from the determination of things drawn from experience. They thus assumed, in view of the origin, all cognition as sensible . . . and believed that the more a proposition is raised up through abstraction, the more it approaches an a priori proposition.[8]

It would be hard to find a place where Locke does make such a claim; perhaps by the time Kant made this striking remark, it had been a long time since he had last read the *Essay*. Leaving this isolated remark aside, Kant's general criticism of Locke was simply that his "physiological" derivation of all concepts from inputs from the senses and unstructured reflection upon them cannot explain any of the synthetic a priori knowledge that we have in pure mathematics, applied mathematics, or pure physics of nature.

Kant's description of Locke's physiological method seems to be a fair account of the latter's procedure in such well-known passages of his work as his attempt to explain how we get all our ideas of space from our experience of particular spaces (*E* 2.13), all our ideas of time from our experience of particular durations (*E* 2.14), and all our ideas of substances from our experiences of their particular powers (*E* 2.23); and Kant's theory of knowledge, with its characteristic arguments that we cannot experience particular spaces and times without the a priori intuitions of space and time nor particular substances without a priori concepts of substance, causation, and interaction, is meant to undermine precisely such characteristic Lockean accounts. I will not attempt now to say whose account is more plausible (although I will criticize some aspects of

Kant's position in the section of this essay entitled "Kant: The Transcendental Limits of Human Knowledge"). What I now want to establish is that in Locke's *Essay*, the thesis that all of our knowledge arises from sensory perception can itself be seen as the premise of Locke's determination of the *limits* of human knowledge: Locke's larger argument is precisely that because all of our knowledge is founded upon sensory perception, the limits of our senses set limits for the knowledge that we can obtain by the empirical methods of science. Locke is often considered the publicist of the new science of the Royal Society and Isaac Newton; but his *Essay* is thus at least as much a warning against the pretensions of the new science, based on its own epistemological premises, as an advertisement for it.

Locke's assessment of the limits of human knowledge is founded, even before he has expanded on how our complex concepts are formed from our simple ideas, upon his distinction between primary and secondary qualities:[9] our knowledge of the properties of material substances is largely confined to their secondary qualities; but since the secondary qualities are only the effects of the causally significant primary qualities, and those are largely hidden from us because of the limits of our senses, our knowledge of the causal connections both among the properties of any single substance and between the properties of different substances is necessarily limited to the fragmentary and unreliable generalizations we can make from our observation of secondary qualities.

To understand Locke's empiricism, it is important to see that the distinction between primary and secondary qualities is both grounded in sensory perception and expresses the limits of such perception. First, the thesis that all the perceptible qualities of objects are grounded in the primary qualities—the "*Solidity, Extension, Figure, and Motion*"—of their smallest particles is presented by Locke as something that is grounded on observation of macroscopic bodies and their properties and behavior, and inference to the microphysical from such observation of the macrophysical. That is, Locke justifies his claim that the primary qualities "are utterly inseparable from Body, in what estate soever it be; such as in all the alterations and changes it suffers," by the statement that "Sense constantly finds" those qualities "in every particle of Matter, which has bulk enough to be perceived," and the further statement that "the Mind," which can apparently only extrapolate from what it observes, therefore finds "them inseparable from every particle of Matter, though less than to make it self singly be perceived by our Senses" (*E* 2.8.9). While the reference to the "Mind" might make it sound as if Locke thinks it some sort of conceptual truth that any particle of matter has primary qualities, in fact he seems to think that the "Mind" reaches this conclusion because it can extrapolate only from what the senses observe. Thus, he argues that if we divide something visible, such as a grain of wheat, which we can observe to have primary qualities, until it becomes invisible, we will still assume it to have primary qualities, although these are now insensible because "division (which is all that a Mill, or Pestel, or any other Body, does upon another, in reducing it to insensible parts) can never take away either Solidity, Extension, Figure, or Mobility from any Body, but only makes two, or more distinct separate masses of Matter, of that which was but one before"; and the premise that all that a "Mill, or Pestel" can do to a body is divide it must itself be grounded in observation. Further, it seems at least likely that Locke also bases the view that bodies act only by "impulse" and contact, thus that the only causally efficacious properties of bodies are those that determine the results of such impulse and contact, namely, the primary qualities, and therefore that all other properties of objects, including such secondary qualities as their color, taste, and the like, must be products of their primary qualities, on observation.[10] So it seems that Locke's thesis that all bodies, even imperceptible ones, have primary qualities, and that they produce all of their effects by the mechanical results of those primary qualities in impulse and contact, is intended to be founded on observation and reasonable inference from observation.[11]

Yet although we are supposed to know by sensory observation that bodies act by impulse and thus that our perception of secondary qualities is caused by the primary qualities of the smallest particles of bodies, the limits of the acuity and extent of our sensory perception also imply ineluctable limits on how much we can actually know about the secondary qualities of objects and their causal connections. Following the paragraphs just cited, Locke argues first that it is the primary qualities of their particles that cause our perceptions of the primary qualities of "Bodies of an observable bigness" (E 2.8.12) and that it is the same qualities that cause our "*Ideas of secondary Qualities*," but then that in both cases, the particles and their qualities which we have inferred to be the cause of all of our ideas fall below the threshold of our senses (E 2.8.13). The consequence of the imperceptibility of the particles of matter is that although we should be confident that such particular qualities as, for example, the "blue Colour" and "sweet Scent" of a violet are caused by the primary qualities of the particles of that flower, we can have no knowledge of just why or how the particles of that flower produce those particular ideas.

The imperceptibility of the fundamental particles of matter is the basis for the limits on our knowledge of physical bodies that Locke draws in his discussion of substance in E 2.23, in his discussion of adequate and inadequate ideas in E 2.31, and in his discussion of the extent of human knowledge in E 4.3. In the first of these chapters, Locke presents his thesis that "*Powers . . . make a great part of our complex* Ideas *of Substances*"

(*E* 2.23.10) as a consequence of the limits that our senses place upon the discovery of the primary qualities of their causally efficacious particles: "our Senses failing us, in the discovery of the Bulk, Texture, and Figure of the minute parts of Bodies, on which their real Constitutions and Differences depend, we are fain to make use of their secondary Qualities, as the characteristical Notes and Marks, whereby to frame *Ideas* of them in our Minds, and distinguish them one from another" (*E* 2.23.8). In the subsequent chapters, he further argues that our inability to discover by means of our senses the precise primary qualities of the particles of particular kinds of substances means that we cannot have deductive or "scientifical" knowledge of their causal powers, and thus cannot have genuine knowledge of the necessary coexistence of the macroscopic powers of any particular substance or of the necessary effects of one kind of substance upon another. Locke makes the first of these points in both *E* 2.31 and *E* 4.3. In the former, he argues that our complex ideas of substances are inadequate because we can have no "distinct perception at all . . . no *Idea* of its Essence, which is the cause that" any particular substance has the conjunction of secondary qualities or powers that it has been observed to have, for example, in the case of gold, "that particular shining yellowness; a greater weight than anything I know of the same bulk; and a fitness to have its Colour changed by the touch of Quicksilver" (*E* 2.31.6). In the latter chapter, he again argues that the ignorance imposed by the limits of our senses upon our knowledge of the particular primary qualities of any substance prevents us from having genuine knowledge of the necessary coexistence of its qualities: "For not knowing the Root they spring from, not knowing what size, figure, and texture of Parts they are, on which depend and from which result those Qualities which make our complex *Idea* of Gold, 'tis impossible we should know what other Qualities result from, or are incompatible with the same Constitution of the insensible parts of *Gold*" (*E* 4.3.11). Later in this chapter, Locke also argues that our ignorance of the particular primary qualities of the causally efficacious particles of substances prevents us from having deductive knowledge of their effects on each other. In one passage he writes:

> If a great, nay far the greatest part of the several ranks of *Bodies* in the Universe, scape our notice by their remoteness, there are others that are no less concealed from us by their *Minuteness*. These insensible Corpuscles, being the active parts of Matter, and the great Instruments of Nature, on which depend not only all their secondary Qualities, but also most of their natural Operations, our want of precise distinct *Ideas* of their primary Qualities, keeps us in an incurable Ignorance of what we desire to know about them. I doubt not but if we could discover the

Figure, Size, Texture, and Motion of the minute Constituent parts of any two Bodies, we should know without Trial several of their operations one upon another, as we do now the Properties of a Square, or a Triangle. (*E* 4.3.25)

But the limits of our senses prevent us from having such knowledge, and therefore we cannot know "their operations one upon another" with the necessity and universality that we should expect in genuine science. Locke is explicit that the limits of our senses prevent us from having knowledge of truly universal as well as necessary causal connections among substances: "whilst we are destitute of Senses acute enough, to discover the minute Particles of Bodies, and to give us *Ideas* of their mechanical Affections, we must be content to be ignorant of their properties and ways of Operation; nor can we be assured about them any farther, than some few Trials we make, are able to reach." But whether such trials "will succeed again another time," Locke continues, "we cannot be certain" (*E* 4.3.25)[12]

Locke's point here is different from the complaint about experience that Hume would later make. Hume makes the general point that no number of observations of objects in any class, no matter how large that number, logically implies anything about the unobserved members of the class. Locke thinks that if we did have experiential knowledge of the primary qualities of the constituent particles of a kind of substance, we could safely make truly universal inferences about the causal dispositions of all instances of that kind; but since we cannot observe those particles, and a fortiori cannot even confirm that all instances of a macroscopically similar kind are microscopically similar, we cannot infer that all instances of an apparently single kind of substance will have the same causal dispositions.

Locke holds not only that the acuity of our senses is inadequate to the minuteness of the causally efficacious parts of objects, but also that their range is inadequate to the vastness of the universe and therefore incapable of observing many substances which influence the behavior even of the substances that we can observe. "When we consider the vast distance of the known and visible parts of the World, and the Reasons we have to think, that what lies within our Ken, is but a small part of the immense Universe, we shall then discover an huge Abyss of Ignorance" (*E* 4.3.24) not just of what sorts of substances may lie in the distant reaches of the universe, but also of what influence those substances may have upon the behavior of the substances that we can observe in our own part of the universe (*E* 4.6.11). To be sure, it can only be on the basis of sensory observation that we have some idea of the vastness of the universe, but reflection upon the same senses that give us this sense of vastness also leads us to recognize the inadequacy of our senses for giving us any determinate knowledge of the substances in those remote regions of the universe and their effects on the behavior of those observable substances closer to home.

In all of these arguments, Locke's claim is that precisely because all our knowledge must be based on ideas furnished by our senses, the limits of our senses represent ineluctable limitations on the possibility of knowledge. Locke piously maintains that the acuity of our senses has been calibrated by God to make them most useful to us for successfully navigating our macroscopic environment (*E* 2.23.12). Since God has already treated us with infinite wisdom, we have no reason to believe that the limits of our senses either should be or can be recalibrated. For Locke, the limitations of our senses and thus the limits of our knowledge are God-given.

Kant: The Transcendental Limits of Human Knowledge

Kant's arguments for the limitation of human knowledge in ways determined by the constitution of human subjectivity are not based on any empirical claims about the limits of the human senses. They are transcendental, in the Kantian sense of following from the explanation of the possibility of substantive or synthetic a priori knowledge (see B40, A85/B117). Kant's argument is that we have knowledge of certain substantive or synthetic universal and necessary truths; that such universal and necessary truths must be known a priori; that we can have substantive a priori knowledge only of our own forms of representation and of the representations of things constituted in accord with those forms, not of things as they may be in themselves independent of those forms; and thus that the explanation of the possibility of our knowledge of substantive, as opposed to merely definitional, necessities at the same time limits our knowledge of such necessities to our own representations, barring us from knowledge of how things might be in themselves. The plausibility of any argument of this form rests, of course, on both the initial claim to knowledge of substantive necessary truth and the assumption that such knowledge can be explained only by interpreting it as a mere reflection of the essential forms of human subjectivity. In fact, in each of Kant's central arguments from necessity to the limits of subjectivity, his assumptions concerning each of these points are at least as dubious as Locke's assumption that the natural limits of our sensory acuity are God-given and essentially unalterable.

Kant often suggests that his argument for the limitation of human knowledge to mere appearance turns entirely on the transcendental ideality of the spatial and temporal form of the objects of experience, with the restriction of all further forms of thought to mere appearance due entirely to the fact that such further forms of thought can yield cognition only when applied to objects in space and time. Thus, in the preface to the second edition of the *Critique*, Kant writes:

> In the analytical part of the critique it is proved that space and time are only forms of sensible intuition, and therefore only conditions of the existence of things as appearances, further that we have no concepts of the understanding and hence no elements for the cognition of things except insofar as an intuition can be given corresponding to these concepts, consequently that we can have cognition of no object as a thing in itself, but only insofar as it is an object of sensible intuition, i.e., as an appearance; from which follows the limitation of all even possible speculative cognition of reason to mere objects of **experience**. (Bxxv–vi)

Of course, it was one of Kant's enduring accomplishments to show that concepts yield cognition only when applied to intuitions, so that any feature that is essential to intuition must indeed be true for all cognition. Thus, if Kant really had shown that space and time are only features of appearance, he would also have shown that all of our cognition is restricted to appearance. But he does not in fact confine himself to this argument. He offers another argument for the limitation of our knowledge to mere appearance from an independent necessity, namely, the necessity of the unity of apperception itself, which he also holds can be explained only on the assumption that through the concepts of our understanding we can always impose order on our own representations, but an order that is therefore valid only for those representations. The structure of this argument is parallel to that of his argument from the necessity to the transcendental ideality of space and time, but its premise is different.

Kant begins the argument from the necessity to the transcendental ideality of space and time in two different ways, distinguished as the "metaphysical" and "transcendental" expositions in the second edition of the *Critique*, and corresponding, although Kant does not say this, to the distinction between "synthetic" and "analytic" methods suggested by the *Prolegomena*.[13] In the metaphysical and synthetic approach, Kant does not begin with the assumption that we have any a priori knowledge of universal and necessary truths about space and time. Rather, he argues that the representation of any ordinary object in space and time depends upon a priori cognition of certain universal and necessary truths about space and time, which can then be explained only by the assumption that space and time themselves are mere forms of intuition, not things as they are in themselves or any properties of them. To take the case of space, what he argues is, first, that we cannot individuate external objects from each other or from ourselves at all except by situating them in space (thus at distinct spatial locations), so that the representation of space is necessary as "the ground of all outer intuitions" (A23–24/B38). Then he argues that any particular space, or the space occupied by any particular object, is necessarily represented as part of a larger space surrounding it, from which it follows (by iteration) that we necessarily represent space as a "unique" and "all-encompassing space" (*CPrR*, A25/B39). The necessity of certain features of space itself, hence our possession of a priori knowledge about space, will in turn have to be explained by the Copernican hypothesis that the form of space reflects our own form of intuition rather than anything inherent in things in themselves.

The "transcendental" and analytic argument about space, by contrast, starts off with an explicit assumption that we possess some synthetic a priori cognition, namely, synthetic a priori cognition of geometrical propositions describing the structure of space and of objects in them, rather than purporting to derive the existence of such a priori cognition from any apparently merely empirical cognition. But it then continues as before by arguing that such synthetic a priori cognition can be explained only by our possession of an a priori intuition of the form of space, and that "an outer intuition . . . that precedes the objects themselves, and in which the concept of the latter can be determined a priori," can only "inhabit the mind" insofar "as it has its seat merely in the subject, as its formal constitution for being affected by objects" (B41) and does not represent any "property at all of any things in themselves nor any relation of them to each other" (A26/B42).

To reach the conclusion of transcendental ideality, Kant claims that we cannot have a priori knowledge of the necessity of any "absolute" or "relative determinations" that inhere in things themselves rather than only in our representations of them, and therefore infers from our alleged a priori cognition of the necessity of space and its geometrical structure that "Space is nothing other than merely the form of all appearances of outer sense, i.e., the subjective condition of sensibility" (A26/B42). Why? Why does he not infer what might seem to be an obvious alternative, namely, that since their location in space and possession of spatial properties are necessary conditions for our intuition of any objects, any objects that we do succeed in intuiting must really be located and structured in space? Would not the fact that objects we intuit actually satisfy our conditions for intuiting them be the best explanation for the fact that we do intuit them? Kant's answer to this question comes out some pages later, and depends upon his interpretation of the necessity that we supposedly know in our a priori cognition of space and spatiality. The key to Kant's argument is that he does not restrict himself to the conditional or *de dicto* necessity that since any objects we can perceive must satisfy the constraints imposed by our forms of intuitions, then whatever objects we do perceive must in fact satisfy those conditions. Rather, he thinks that he is entitled to assert the *de re* necessity of the spatiality of any objects that are spatial at all; that he can justify this assumption in the case of our representations of objects, because they are made in accordance with our own forms of intuition and therefore in some sense *must* be spatial; but that he would not be justified in asserting such necessity of objects other than our representations, and therefore must deny that such objects are spatial at all in order to avoid the conclusion that they are merely contingently so, which would, as he thinks, undermine the supposed necessity of spatiality throughout their entire domain. That this is how Kant thinks is evident in his most illuminating comment about his argument for transcendental idealism in the Transcendental Aesthetic, where he asks

> If there did not lie in you a faculty for intuiting a priori; if this subjective condition regarding form were not at the same time the universal a priori condition under which alone the object of this (outer) intuition is itself possible; if the object ([e.g.,] the triangle) were something in itself without relation to your subject: then how could you say that what necessarily lies in your subjective conditions for constructing a triangle must also necessarily pertain to the triangle in itself? (A48/B65)

If we thought that both our representations of objects as well as the objects themselves were spatial, then while we could say that our representations of them are necessarily spatial, we could not say that the objects themselves are necessarily spatial. But since, Kant clearly assumes, our a priori knowledge implies that whatever is spatial is necessarily so, then objects other than our representations cannot be spatial at all, and our spatial representations of them cannot yield cognition of them as they are in themselves. The limitation of the validity of what we know a priori to our own representations rather than to things in themselves follows from Kant's assumption that whatever is known a priori must be necessarily true *de re* of all of its objects.[14]

Of course, Kant's premise for this argument is dubious. Radical empiricists such as Hume[15] and Mill have doubted that we are entitled to assert any necessary truths about the spatiality of external objects or the specific structure of their spatiality as described by mathematics. At least since Moses Mendelssohn's 1762 *Essay on Evidence*,[16] less radical thinkers have allowed that there is a sense in which we can think of necessity within a formal mathematical system, but that any assertion that such a system correctly describes any objects external to it, even if indubitable, must be regarded as contingent. But any merely conditional necessity that objects that we do perceive must satisfy the formal constraints inherent or necessary in our own system of representation is precisely what Kant rejects. His argument for transcendental idealism depends instead on the assumption that the necessity that we can know a priori must be *de re* rather than merely *de dicto*, absolute rather than relative. That is the only reason why he needs to think that the possibility of a priori knowledge depends on transcendental idealism's limitation of it to the structure of our own representations.

Although, as we saw, Kant prominently suggests that the limitation of the cognitive validity of any and all of our forms of thought depends entirely on the transcendental ideality of the forms of intuition, he in fact offers an independent argument for transcendental idealism with respect to the pure concepts of the understanding; yet this argument makes precisely the same sort of assumption about necessity that is at work in his argument for the transcendental ideality of space and time. The argument I have in mind is the central argument in the Transcendental Deduction of the Categories, in which Kant begins with the assumption that we have a cognition of the unity or numerical identity of our self throughout all of our representations, which is synthetic because it asserts a connection among all our representations, but which must be a priori precisely because it is necessary rather than conditional upon anything contingently true of the objects of our representations. He then argues that because this transcendental unity of apperception is a priori yet synthetic, it must presuppose an a priori synthesis of the contents of our apperception, and such a synthesis must take place in accordance with a priori rather than empirical concepts, namely, the pure concepts of the understanding. Kant's clearest statement of this argument is given in the third section of the first-edition deduction, which begins with the premise that "[w]e are conscious a priori of the thoroughgoing identity of ourselves with regard to all representations that can ever belong to our cognition, as a necessary condition of the possibility of all representations," and then goes on to state, first, that "[t]his synthetic unity . . . presupposes a synthesis, or includes it," and, second, that "if the former is to be necessary a priori then the latter must also be a synthesis a priori" (A116–18), which will in turn require the a priori categories of the understanding (A119). Kant concludes this argument by stating that "[t]he principle of the necessary unity of the pure (productive) synthesis of the imagination prior to apperception is thus the ground of the possibility of all cognition, especially that of experience" (A118).

Now one might be tempted to read Kant's conclusion as the assertion of a merely conditional necessity, that is, the necessity that *if* we are to enjoy apperception, *then* the objects of our representation must permit a synthesis of our representations of them. That would not by itself imply that we are always in a position to *impose* a synthesis in accordance with the categories upon our representations. But Kant assumes precisely that we are in such a position. If this is not sufficiently evident from his statement that the necessary unity of the pure synthesis of the imagination is prior to apperception, it certainly becomes evident in his doctrine of transcendental affinity, in which he asserts that it is "impossible for appearances to be apprehended by the imagination otherwise than under the condition of a possible synthetic unity of this apprehension." He explicitly rejects any supposition that it can be "contingent whether appearances fit into a connection of human cognitions" (A121). He says that "only because I ascribe all perceptions to one consciousness (of original apperception) can I say of all perceptions that I am conscious of them," but rejects any possibility that it might be contingent of any particular representations whether I *can* say that I am conscious of them; rather, "There must therefore be an objective ground, i.e., one that can be understood a priori prior to all empirical laws of the imagination," for the unity of our representations (A122). Kant calls this "objective ground" the transcendental "affinity" of appearances, and treats it precisely as something we impose on our representations of objects rather than anything inherent in the objects themselves: "as exaggerated and contradictory as it may sound to say that the understanding is itself the source of the laws of nature, and thus of the formal unity of nature, such an assertion is nevertheless correct" (A127).

Now it may not be clear from these quotations that Kant means to conclude, without presupposing the transcendental ideality of space and time, that the order that flows from the categories is true only of appearances and not of things in themselves, just like space and time. But that this is his intent becomes indubitable at the conclusion of the second-edition deduction. Here he rejects the possibility that the categories are "subjective predispositions for thinking, implanted in us along with our existence by our author in such a way that their use would agree exactly with the laws of nature along which experience runs (a kind of **preformation-system** of pure reason)," on the ground that in such a case, "I would not be able to say," for example, "that the effect is combined with the cause in the object (i.e., necessarily), but only that I am so constituted that I cannot think of this representation otherwise than as so connected; which is precisely what the skeptic wishes most" (B167–68). In other words, once again Kant explicitly rejects a merely conditional necessity that *if* we are to have an experience of the unity of apperception in our representations of objects, *then* those objects must be subject to causality; rather, he assumes that it is unconditionally necessary that the objects of our experience are subject to causality, something that can in turn be explained only if causality is inherent only in our own representations and not in the objects of our representations as they are in themselves at all. As in the first-edition deduction, this conclusion is ultimately derived from the premise that we have a priori knowledge of the fact of the necessary unity of apperception, not merely a priori knowledge of the conditional necessity that if we are to experience unity of apperception, then the objects of our experience must be subject to the categories.[17]

Of course, as in the case of Kant's assumption of the necessary spatiality and/or temporality of the objects of sensible intuition, it is by no means clear that he is entitled to his strong conception of the necessary unity of apperception. It may well be the case that I must be able to recognize a connection between any representation *I can call* "mine," that is, any representation of which I am actually self-conscious, but it is by no means clear that *I must be able to call* any representation I can have "my own"; there might be states of mind that satisfy various conditions for being representations without being accessible to self-consciousness or available for connection with other, self-conscious representations. If this is so, then Kant's argument that the order of nature is imposed upon our representations by ourselves and moreover limited to those representations, and does not represent any order inherent in the objects of our representations as they are in themselves, collapses.

Kant thus makes two separate arguments for the limitation of our knowledge to appearances rather than things in themselves, one concerning the spatiality and/or temporality of the objects of knowledge and the other their subjection to the categories. But in each case, the form of his argument is the same, namely, an inference from the unconditional necessity of the satisfaction of the conditions of the possibility of experience by the objects of that experience to the conclusion that it can only be appearances and not things in themselves that satisfy those conditions. Kant's arguments for the limitation of our knowledge to appearances rather than things in themselves are thus indeed transcendental rather than empirical, since they follow from an assumption of necessity known a priori. But in both cases, the assumption of necessity from which Kant begins is dubious, and it is far from clear that there is any more merit to Kant's transcendental limitation of knowledge than there is to Locke's empirical limitation.

Now it might seem that Kant succeeds in stating a transcendental limitation on the extent of our empirical knowledge that is independent of his distinction between appearances and things in themselves and can thus stand even if his arguments for that distinction fail. This would be the limitation that would result from reading the first two "mathematical" antinomies of pure reason (A426–43/B454–71) without invoking the distinction between appearances and things in themselves. We could read these arguments as implying that the indefinitely extendable character of our intuitions of space and time would prevent us from ever knowing that space and time are either finite and bounded or actually infinite and unbounded, even if one of these were actually true. The very form of our intuitions would prevent us from perceiving the boundary of space or time even if it had one, whereas the impossibility of ever actually completing an infinite synthesis would prevent us from knowing that space or time is actually infinite, even if it is. Surely such a result should count as a transcendental limitation on the extent of our empirical knowledge.

The problem with such an argument, however, is that it ultimately rests on the very same assumption as Kant's distinction between appearances and things in themselves, the assumption that we really have a priori knowledge of the structure of our intuition through acquaintance with its pure form. If we question the claim that we know that our spatial and temporal intuition is *necessarily* always infinitely extendable, however, the only alternative would be that we have some *empirical* basis for supposing that our intuitions are always indefinitely extendable and that we therefore cannot know space and time to be either genuinely finite or genuinely infinite. But if our basis for such a conclusion is in fact only empirical, then of course we do not have a transcendental limitation on the extent of our empirical knowledge, and could always discover that our current conception of its limitation is false.

Kant: Lifting the Empirical Limits of Knowledge

Of course, Kant himself did not recognize the failure of his own transcendental arguments for the limits of human knowledge. He did, however, recognize the weakness of Locke's empirical argument for the limitation of knowledge by the natural acuity of our senses. In his account of perception, he makes it clear that the informativeness of our natural senses can be extended by means of additional but still empirical science, and in his general account of empirical science in turn he makes it clear that while at any given time the results of empirical science will, of course, be limited to what has thus far been observed and extrapolated from observation, there is no particular point at which any such current limitation can be regarded as insuperable.

Kant takes the first step toward the revision of the Lockean conception of the empirical limits of human knowledge in his discussion of the "postulate" of actuality, that is, the rule for empirical use of the concept of actuality. The rule is "That which is connected with the material conditions of experience (of sensation) is **actual**" (A218/B265). As the ensuing discussion makes explicit, the requirement of connection with sensation as the material condition of experience means that our empirical knowledge of the real or actual is not confined to such qualities of it as are given immediately to our senses—thus, to the Lockean secondary qualities—but extends to all that can be connected to what is immediately given in sensation by empirically discovered causal laws—thus, the Lockean primary qualities. Thus, Kant writes that

> [t]he postulate for cognizing the **actuality** of things requires **perception**, thus sensation of which one is conscious—not immediate perception of the object itself the existence of which is to be cognized, but still its connection with some actual perception in accordance with the analogies of experience, which exhibit all real connection in an experience in general. (A225/B272)

This statement might be construed to mean that any and all knowledge of the existence of external objects is based on a causal inference from sensations regarded merely as events in inner sense. But such an interpretation is precluded by the Refutation of Idealism which Kant inserts into the discussion of the postulate of actuality in the second edition of the *Critique*, because it specifically abjures such a Cartesian model of knowledge of external objects. Instead, Kant's further comments make it clear that what he means is that we can use causal laws to take us from those macroscopic qualities of objects that we can, given our current sensory constitution, perceive without assistance, to other qualities that we cannot so directly perceive:

> Thus we cognize the existence of a magnetic matter penetrating all bodies from the perception of attracted iron filings, although an immediate perception of this matter is impossible for us given the constitution of our organs. For in accordance with the laws of sensibility and the context of our perceptions we could also happen upon the immediate empirical intuition of it in an experience if our senses, the crudeness of which does not affect the form of possible experience in general, were finer. (A226/B273)

For Kant, the limits of our empirical knowledge are not set by the constitution of our organs, but by what we can manage to connect to what the constitution of our organs allows us to perceive directly by the causal laws that we can discover, such as the laws of magnetism that we have discovered to explain the behavior of visible iron filings. Our inferences from the combination of our actual perceptions together with such causal laws can be represented in the form of what we would perceive if our senses were finer. While for Locke claims about what we or other creatures might perceive with finer senses are sheer speculation, meant only to emphasize the actual limits of our senses (see *E* 4.3.23), for Kant such claims are themselves products of empirical cognition.

The second key point in Kant's rejection of Locke's conception of the limits of empirical knowledge is that for Kant there is no fixed limit to the causal laws we can discover and thus to the empirical knowledge of reality that we can generate from what we most immediately perceive by the use of such causal laws. This thought is central to the model of the regulative principles of empirical knowledge of laws of nature that Kant presents in the appendix to the Transcendental Dialectic in the first *Critique* and in the introduction to the third *Critique*. Kant maintains that reason enjoins us to strive for maximal "manifoldness," "affinity," and "unity" in our knowledge of the laws of nature, and assumes that we can always come closer to satisfying these cognitive ideals without ever actually satisfying them. He illustrates his thought by arguing that we can apply these ideals to the concept of elliptical orbits for heavenly bodies, maintaining that "under the guidance of these principles we come to a unity of genera in the forms of these paths, but thereby also further to unity in the cause of all this motion (gravitation)" (A662/B690). Once we have introduced a general causal concept such as gravitation, Kant continues,

> we extend our conquests, seeking to explain all variations and apparent deviations from those rules on the basis of the same principle; finally we even add on more than experience can ever confirm, namely in accordance with the rules of affinity, even conceiving hyperbolical paths for comets in which these bodies leave our solar system entirely and, going from sun to sun, unite in their course the most remote parts of a world system, which for us is unbounded yet connected through one and the same moving force. (A663/B691)

The first thought to note here is that by means of a causal law formulated from and confirmed by our experience of observable bodies, we can form legitimate conjectures about the behavior of bodies beyond the limits of our senses, in this case because of their remoteness rather than because of their minuteness. Such conjectures may, as Kant suggests, lie beyond the boundaries of what current experience can confirm, but they are not, as Locke might have thought, pure speculations; they are connected "through one and the same moving force" to our well-founded explanations of readily observable phenomena.

Kant's reference to the remoteness of parts of the world system in this passage implies that there are at least two reasons, not just one, why any idea of completeness in empirical knowledge must always remain ideal: in Kant's view, the goal of completeness in the hierarchy of causal laws is always merely ideal (although he in fact never explains why we could not actually arrive at one absolutely "fundamental power"; see A649/B677), but in addition the domain of the *objects* of empirical science is necessarily unlimited because space and time themselves are "unbounded." We saw in the section entitled "Kant: The Transcendental Limits of Human Knowledge" that Kant may not be entitled to the claim that space and time are *necessarily* indefinitely extendable, and therefore, if not actually knowably infinite, certainly not finite. But even if our assumption that space and time are so extendable is itself merely empirical, we will still get as an *empirical* conclusion that although at any given time there will be a limit to the progress of our scientific knowledge, there can never be any particular ultimate limit to our scientific investigation. At any given time, there may be a limit in space to the domain of objects we have managed to explore and to connect to the most immediate objects of our perception by causal laws; but everything about our experience of space implies that there is nothing special about any region that is currently the boundary of our knowledge, and no reason why the domain of our knowledge should not subsequently be extended. Any given moment in time will likewise itself represent a current limit to the scientific investigations we have managed to complete, but since there is no essential difference between one moment in time and the next, we can never have any reason to conclude that the current limit of our scientific investigations is an ultimate limit. Once the naturally determined limits of our sensory acuity and scope have been allowed to be overcome by the addition of causal inferences to immediate observation, then there can be no further necessary limit to the progress of scientific inquiry, although of course at any particular moment our actual progress will be limited by our current but accidental position in space and time.

Kant thought he had replaced Locke's empirical theory of the limits of human knowledge with a transcendental argument for such limits. Kant's transcendental theory of the limits of our knowledge rests on claims about necessary truth that cannot survive scrutiny. But Kant's theory of empirical knowledge and empirical science suggests a fundamental revision of Locke's conception of the limits of our knowledge that is independent of Kant's transcendental idealism, and not subject to the objections to that controversial philosophy.[18]

CHAPTER 6

The "Sensible Object" and the "Uncertain Philosophical Cause"

Lisa Downing

BOTH IMMANUEL KANT AND PAUL GUYER have raised important concerns about the limitations of Lockean thought. Following Guyer, I will focus my attention on questions about the proper ambitions and likely achievements of inquiry into the natural/physical world. I will argue that there are at least two important respects, not discussed by Guyer, in which Locke's account of natural philosophy is much more flexible and accommodating than may be immediately apparent. (And, I am inclined to think, one of these respects represents a way in which Kant's system is objectionably constrained, where Locke's is in principle open.) On my interpretation, however, one crucial source of a too-limited vision of natural philosophy remains in Locke, where he is appropriately criticized by both Kant and Guyer.

My method will be to begin with a distinction that Locke draws in the very first draft of the *Essay*, between what he calls "the sensible object" and, on the other hand, "the uncertain philosophical cause." I believe that Locke's notion of "sensible object," *as opposed to* uncertain philosophical cause, retains a central place in his thought in the published *Essay*, even though this contrast is never made explicitly there. Tracing the evolution of these two concepts in his thought will allow us to track and better understand his developing views about the relation between the project of the *Essay* and natural philosophy and about the prospects for natural philosophy itself.

THE DISTINCTION

In the first extant draft of the *Essay* (Draft A), predating publication by eighteen years, Locke makes an intriguing distinction:

> for though white or sweet & many other sensations in us be perhaps causd in us constantly by particles of certein figures which figures are a relative consideration when the parts thereof are compard with one an other. yet the Idea of white or sweet &c being produced in me &

reteind in my memory without any relative consideration but as one simple positive Idea & when our senses are conversant about any object we take noe notice of any relation between the thing & our senses we ought to consider them as positive things, the uncertain philosophical cause of such a sensation in me being not here enquird into but the Idea & sensible object that produces it. & the greatest part of man kinde who never perplex their thoughts to examin wherein the nature of that thing which when they looke on they call white & feele the same sensation in them selves as a philosopher doth, have perfectly the same Idea of white that any philosopher hath who thinkes he hath found out the very essence nature or formality thereof or the way whereby it produces such a sensation in him. (*Drafts*, pp. 32–33)[1]

On the one hand, we have the idea of whiteness, which Locke here clearly treats as a sensation, a mental item. The interesting distinction comes on the side of the nonmental correlate of the idea. Locke singles out the "sensible object" that "produces" the idea as being a proper subject for his enquiry, along with the idea itself, while setting aside questions involving the "uncertain philosophical cause."

How should we understand Locke's sensible object, as he introduces it in Draft A? The sensible object apparently does not require special investigation or theoretical knowledge to identify. A Berkeleyan interpretation of the sensible object as a combination of ideas might seem to be suggested by Locke's insistence on the ready availability of the object to the ordinary person. This interpretation should be bracketed as unlikely, however, since (1) Locke describes the sensible object as *producing* the idea and (2) nowhere in his corpus does he betray any genuine attraction to idealism. (We will see later how to explain the occurrence of other passages that might seem amenable to an idealist reading.) If the sensible object is not something like a bundle of ideas, then, it is presumably not a different *thing* from the uncertain philosophical cause—both of the phrases in question refer to the physical thing that is the source of our ideas. Locke therefore must have in mind two different ways of understanding or conceptualizing this physical thing. The sensible object, I suggest, is the physical object as we are acquainted with it in sensory experience, the object *as known through* sense perception. The uncertain philosophical cause, on the other hand, is the object as it would be described in an ideal natural philosophy, i.e., scientia. Such a conception of the object is philosophical in the sense of belonging to natural philosophy. It is uncertain because we do not have access to such an ideal account.

On this interpretation, the basic thought expressed in the previous passage is a familiar one from the *Essay*: Locke does not want to enter into any controversial issues in natural philosophy; rather, he wants to work with and analyze what is available to everyman. In particular, he wants to discuss bodies, among other substances, as they are made epistemically available to us through sense perception. The suggestion, however, that sensible objects are objects as known to us through sense perception requires further elucidation. How should we understand sensible objects on this account?

Of course, for Locke all our sensory knowledge of objects comes down to sensory ideas. In an important sense, Locke holds that what we know of objects are our sensory ideas of them. This very modest point goes some way toward explaining a persistent puzzle about the *Essay*: Why does Locke slip as easily as he does between ideas and qualities, to the point that he is capable of writing passages that seem to imply that our very ideas inhere in bodies themselves?[2] Locke writes in this way so often because he holds that to talk of external objects as known to us through sense perception *is* to talk about our ideas.

As early as Draft A, however, he realizes that such talk needs reform. That draft ends with the following "memorandum":

> When I speak of simple Ideas as existing in things I would be understood to mean. such a constitution of that thing which produces that idea in our mindes. soe that Idea when it is spoken of as being in our understanding is the very perception or thought we have there, when it is spoken of as existing without is the cause of that perception. & is supposed to be resembled by it. & this also I call quality. whereby I meane anything existing without us which affecting any of our senses produces any simple Idea in us. (*Drafts*, pp. 82–83)

The same warning is repeated almost verbatim in Draft B (*Drafts*, p. 164), with "supposed" now strengthened to "vulgarly supposd." Note that Locke's understanding of quality here is still quite loose; it seems a new and only roughly defined concept in his thought.[3] What Locke clearly wants is a way of talking about that which, in the object, corresponds to the idea in us. He utilizes the term "quality" for this specific purpose. But in this paragraph, he characterizes this notion in too many ways. What seems constant is the thought that the quality is the cause of the perception/idea in us. In the last part of the paragraph, Locke characterizes this too broadly for his purposes, since a substance would count as a quality on that account. In the first part of the paragraph, he threatens to characterize it too deeply, since the "constitution of that thing" sounds like an aspect of the uncertain philosophical cause.

Locke's official characterization of quality in the published *Essay* is considerably more careful:

> Whatsoever the Mind perceives in itself, or is the immediate object of Perception, Thought, or Understanding, that I call *Idea*; and the Power

to produce any *Idea* in our mind I call a *Quality* of the Subject wherein that power is. Thus a Snow-ball having the power to produce in us the *Ideas* of *White, Cold,* and *Round,* the Powers to produce those *Ideas* in us, as they are in the Snow-ball, I call *Qualities*; and as they are Sensations or Perceptions in our Understandings, I call them *Ideas*; which *Ideas*, if I speak of sometimes, as in the things themselves, I would be understood to mean those Qualities in the Objects which produce them in us. (*E* 2.8.8)

Ideas "in the things themselves" are really qualities; qualities are powers to produce ideas. This definition seems carefully tuned to get the result that qualities are fully knowable through sensory experience, since Locke never questions that we can know, when we have an idea, that some thing without us has the power to cause that idea (*E* 4.11.2).[4] Qualities in objects are thus, as it were, interconvertible with ideas, even in epistemic contexts. The sensible object, rather than being a bundle of ideas, should be a bundle of powers, as is suggested by his remarks in A:

all the notion we have of substance amounting at last to noe more then the Ideas of certain powers i.e either of susteining in its self several simple Ideas or else altering or produceing other simple Ideas in other Beings. (*Drafts*, p. 20)

The bundled powers are of two sorts: (1) sensible qualities, that is, powers to produce ideas in us directly, and (2) powers to affect other objects such that they produce different ideas in us.

THE SENSIBLE OBJECT AND THE OBSCURE IDEA OF SUBSTANCE IN GENERAL

The notion of a bundle of powers, however, is conceptually problematic. This point is acknowledged in the early drafts, but becomes developed doctrine in the *Essay*. The idea of power that we glean from experience is a relative one, linking an item regarded as producing change to one regarded as receiving change. The idea of substance, by giving us a terminus for the power relation, unifies a bundle of powers and allows us to think in terms of *things with* powers.[5] It is this extra content that the general idea of substance supplies for us. Locke gives his best, most considered account of the content and origin of this idea in the correspondence with Stillingfleet:[6]

all the ideas of all the sensible qualities of a cherry come into my mind by sensation; the ideas of perceiving, thinking, reasoning, knowing, & c. come into my mind by reflection: the ideas of these qualities and actions, or powers, are perceived by the mind to be by themselves inconsistent with existence; . . . i.e. that they cannot exist or subsist of themselves. Hence the mind perceives their necessary connexion with inherence or being supported; which being a relative idea superadded to the red colour in a cherry, or to thinking in a man, the mind frames the correlative idea of a support. For I never denied, that the mind could frame to itself ideas of relation, but have showed the quite contrary in my chapters about relation. But because a relation cannot be founded in nothing, or be the relation of nothing, and the thing here related as a supporter or support is not represented to the mind by any clear and distinct idea; therefore *the obscure, indistinct, vague idea of thing or something, is all that is left to be the positive idea*, which has the relation of a support or substratum to modes or accidents; and that general indetermined idea of something, is, by the abstraction of the mind, derived also from the simple ideas of sensation and reflection: and thus the mind, from the positive, simple ideas got by sensation or reflection, comes to the general relative idea of substance; which, without the positive simple ideas, it would never have. (*LW* 4 21–22, emphasis mine)

Note that as Locke characterizes it, the idea *does* have positive content, exactly the modest content needed to fill out our idea of the sensible object, on the account just given. A sensible object is a thing with powers. Thus, Locke is completely sincere in his avowals to Stillingfleet that he denies neither the existence of substances nor the need for and existence of a general idea of substance.

Furthermore, if we keep in mind Locke's distinction between sensible object and uncertain philosophical cause, it is easy to see the truth of Michael Ayers's claim[7] that the obscure idea of substance in general is not, in Locke's view, *logically* required by the nature of predication, and it could (in principle) be supplanted by ideas of the real essences of things. We need the impoverished idea of substance because experience acquaints us with bodies only as bundles of powers, and we do not see what unites those powers.[8] If, on the other hand, we knew the real essence of an apple, we would understand the basis for all of its powers, we would grasp their necessary coexistence, and we would not need the idea of a bare thing to hang the bare powers on.[9]

CORPUSCULARIANISM AND THE UNCERTAIN PHILOSOPHICAL CAUSE:
LOCKE'S EVOLVING COMMITMENTS

That objects, as Locke is primarily concerned with them, are sensible objects is a point on which he remains firm throughout the development of the *Essay*. The object as it is known through sensory experience is a thing with powers. This view is manifest in his treatment of the reality, adequacy, and truth of our ideas, doctrines at the epistemological heart of the *Essay*. His views about what can and should be said about objects as uncertain philosophical causes, however, undergo considerable change over the course of the successive drafts and editions of the *Essay*, from 1671 through 1700.

If Locke wants to eschew all discussion of uncertain philosophical causes, as promised in the passage from Draft A with which we began, he ought not to commit himself to the truth of any particular scientific theory about the natures of bodies. In particular, of course, he ought not to commit himself to the truth of Boylean corpuscularianism as an account of the uncertain philosophical causes of our ideas. Drafts A and B from 1671 are consistent with Locke's declared intention to consider sensible objects rather than uncertain philosophical causes.[10] In these drafts, Locke employs the corpuscularian hypothesis in a circumscribed fashion, as a resource for the elucidation and defense of the following philosophical points: (1) We must distinguish between idea and corporeal cause. (2) We lack sensory access to the crucial micro-level of causal processes. (3) Extension and cohesion are central to our conception of body, and impulse to our understanding of body's activity. At the ontological level, Locke commits himself to no more than the uncontroversial view that macroscopic processes have causes that elude our senses. Moreover, the *effect* of Locke's limited deployment of corpuscularianism in the drafts is, as promised, to focus attention on the understanding, on our ideas (including our ideas of body) and the relations among them, and to emphasize exactly how uncertain is our access to the philosophical causes of those ideas.

In the much later Draft C (1685), however, Locke assigns a more prominent role to corpuscularianism.[11] Specifically, Locke's introductions, in this draft, of the primary/secondary quality distinction and the real/nominal essence distinction seem to commit him to the truth of corpuscularianism, for he characterizes both primary qualities and real essences exclusively or primarily in corpuscularian terms. These developments create severe tensions in Draft C which are not present in earlier drafts. The most basic tension is between assuming the truth of corpuscularianism and building further conclusions upon it, and, on the other hand, treating corpuscularianism as a probable hypothesis about matters beyond the scope of the *Essay*.[12] A still more serious tension arises between Locke's suggestion that corpuscularianism captures the nature of body qua body, evidenced in his treatment of primary qualities and real essence, and his periodic insistence that the ultimate nature of body is unknown to us.[13] Both tensions are produced by Locke's new inclination to suppose that corpuscularianism correctly characterizes the uncertain philosophical causes of our ideas.

Given the problems it created, why was Locke tempted to transgress the limits he had set to his own project? One set of motivations is not difficult to identify. In Drafts A and B, Locke employs a corpuscularian thought experiment in order to motivate the distinction between ideas and their causes. In Draft C, Locke stresses both this distinction and the pessimistic moral implicit in the example of positive ideas from privative causes, namely, that we cannot assume that our ideas "are Exactly the images and resemblances of something inherent in their subjects and Existing without us" (Draft C 2.7.8). Reifying the corpuscularian thought experiment allows Locke to make this point very forcefully indeed: assuming the truth of corpuscularianism, most of our sensory ideas fail to resemble their causes and are "no more the likenesse of something Existing without us then the names that stand for them are the likenesse of our Ideas" (Draft C 2.7.8). Likewise, the move permits a forceful presentation of the Lockean point that we do not sort bodies according to their real essences. For if the real essences of bodies are corpuscularian constitutions, we are quite ignorant of their real essences, and we obviously do not sort bodies according to them.

In the published *Essay*, Locke backs away from the Draft C commitment to corpuscularianism. This process occurs in two steps. The first is the articulation of an abstract notion of real essence, according to which each thing has a real constitution by which it is what it is. Aristotelianism and corpuscularianism, then, represent two different *hypotheses* as to what these real essences are like. This abstract understanding of real essence is suggested as early as Draft C 2.33.11 and is safely ensconced in the first edition of the *Essay* (E 3.3.15–17) in 1689.[14] It is a metaphysical notion in the sense of abstracting from particular physical theories to a notion that any natural philosophy would have to provide an account of. The abstract notion of real essence allows Locke to discuss uncertain philosophical causes without supposing that we are in a position to properly characterize them, that is, to render them certain.

It is not until the fourth (1700) edition of the *Essay* that Locke goes some ways toward alleviating the tensions involved in his discussion of primary and secondary qualities. The revisions are minimal, in keeping with Locke's general distaste for discarding his philosophical prose. First, as is relatively well-known, Locke modifies the claim of earlier editions that bodies can operate only by impulse by limiting its application to how bodies act upon us in sense perception. More importantly, he eliminates an argument that purported to establish the impossibility of action at a distance, making only the much more limited claim that impulse is the only sort of bodily action that we can conceive (E 2.8.11). It is less often noticed that Locke also modified *E* 2.8.9–10 in the fourth edition: rather than introducing the primary/secondary quality distinction, as in earlier versions, in terms of a *list* of properties that the strict corpuscularian theory takes to be basic, i.e., size, shape, solidity, number, mobility, Locke *first* introduces the notion of primary quality as an abstract, metaphysical notion:

> Qualities thus considered in Bodies are, First such as are utterly inseparable from the Body, in what estate soever it be; such as in all the alterations and changes it suffers, all the force can be used upon it, it constantly keeps. (*E* 2.8.9)

The primary/secondary quality distinction thus emerges as a distinction between the essential, intrinsic qualities of bodies, the qualities that "*are really in them,* whether any ones Senses perceive them or no" (*E* 2.8.17), and other apparent qualities reducible to the effects of those primary qualities on perceivers. This abstract notion of primary quality is logically linked to his abstract notion of real essence: the primary qualities of a body are the intrinsic and irreducible properties that ground all its other powers. The real essence of a substance is the source of its observable qualities, that which makes it the thing that it is. The real essence of a body of a certain kind, *X*, is thus constituted by that combination of the primary qualities of its constituents that are the causal source of those qualities according to which we classify it as an *X*. This notion of primary quality, then, like that of real essence, allows Locke to direct our attention toward uncertain philosophical causes, without attempting to definitively characterize them.[15]

How then should we understand Locke's famous thought experiment involving the grain of wheat? Here I think I am largely in agreement with Paul Guyer, at least to begin with. Locke is illustrating the use of sensory and conceptual criteria to isolate a list of qualities:

> Take a grain of Wheat, divide it into two parts, each part has still *Solidity, Extension, Figure,* and *Mobility*; divide it again, and it retains still the same qualities; and so divide it on, till the parts become insensible, they must retain still each of them all those qualities. For division (which is all that a Mill, or Pestel, or any other Body, does upon another, in reducing it to insensible parts) can never take away either Solidity, Extension, Figure, or Mobility from any Body, but only makes two, or more distinct separate masses of Matter, of that which was but one before, all which distinct masses, reckon'd as so many distinct Bodies, after division make a certain Number. These I call *original* or *primary Qualities* of Body, which I think we may observe to produce simple *Ideas* in us, *viz.* Solidity, Extension, Figure, Motion, or Rest, and Number. (*E* 2.8.9)

Locke's point is that observation and ordinary reflection upon it lead us to the view that the primary qualities of bodies are size, shape, solidity, motion/rest, and number. At least by the time of the fourth edition of the *Essay*, however, if not earlier, Locke is not officially committed to the correctness of this natural view. What we derive in this fashion is the *nominal essence* of body.[16] The nominal essence we assign to body represents one, uniquely natural, hypothesis about the real essence of body in general, and thus about what the primary qualities of bodies are,[17] that is, about the terms in which the real essences of individual bodies should be characterized.

Note that while Locke's notion of real essence applies to the uncertain philosophical cause—to specify a real essence is to characterize the uncertain philosophical cause—the paired notion of nominal essence, naturally enough, applies to sensible objects. We create a kind by selecting some set of observable properties (powers) that we will take to be necessary and sufficient to be of that kind. This allows us to divide the set of powers belonging to a sensible object into "essential" and "accidental" qualities, that is, to distinguish between those powers that make the object part of its kind, and those that are optional relative to that kind.[18]

Locke's discussion of our "primary ideas" of body and spirit must be understood as exemplifying this sort of partition among qualities. In that discussion, Locke seems to jump from the now-familiar view that we know the Substance of Body only as "the complex *Idea* of extended, figured, coloured, and all other sensible Qualities" (*E* 2.23.16) to the apparently unmotivated contention that "*the primary* Ideas *we have peculiar to Body . . . are the cohesion of solid*, and consequently separable *parts, and a power of communicating Motion by impulse*" (2.23.17). To locate our primary ideas of body, Locke considers the qualities belonging to the nominal essence of body, that is, those that we cannot conceive of bodies as lacking because they are definitive of our concept of body.[19] He then eliminates any common to both body and spirit, since the goal is to locate the ideas peculiar to body, in order to contrast them with those peculiar to spirit. The result (somewhat massaged, it seems, so as to secure parity between matter and spirit) is that there are two such primary ideas of body: the cohesion of solid parts and the power of communicating motion by impulse. The point is confined to the sensible object; Locke is tracking a conceptual priority among our ideas of bodies, derived from reflection on sensory experience. In this modest sense, then, some powers are more than mere powers, even at the level of the sensible object.

I maintain that, in the end, a similar account applies to Locke's treatment of primary qualities in *E* 2.8.9. Locke's point there is to remind us that the corpuscularian concept of body derives from the nominal essence we attach to body, and thus provides a peculiarly intelligible *example* of what the primary qualities of bodies could be. Through reflection on sensory experience, as exemplified in the thought experiment about the grain of wheat, we refine our conception of body. What Locke argues in *E* 2.8.9 is that the net result of this procedure, the conception of body that we distill from ordinary sensory experience, is the corpuscularian one.[20] To be a body is, we stipulate, to be something possessing size, shape, solidity, motion or rest, and number. This represents a stipulation in that all nominal essences, including the nominal essence of body, are made by us, not nature. They are not, of course, made arbitrarily, as Locke repeatedly emphasizes and as his *E* 2.8.9 account attempts to illustrate for the case of the nominal essence of body. That nominal essence, then, represents one uniquely natural hypothesis (the corpuscularian hypothesis) about what the real essences of bodies are like.

An obvious question to ask at this point is: Why *not* suppose that the uniquely natural hypothesis just *is* the correct one? I think Locke takes such an assumption to be entirely reasonable in the absence of any principled problem with corpuscularianism. Certainly, Locke does *not* simply assume that the uncertain philosophical causes of our ideas are unknowable in virtue of being the causes of our ideas. Were it the case that mechanism offered explanatory resources to account for our experience and manifested no obvious conflicts with our experience, Locke would take mechanism's truth to be a good bet. Indeed, this surely lies behind Locke's Draft C commitment to mechanism, as well as his persistent tendency to slide easily from an abstract understanding of real essence/primary quality to a mechanist one—that is, to the view of the uniquely natural scientific theory as to what fills the roles of real essence and primary quality.

However, as Margaret Wilson showed us in her influential and beautiful article, "Superadded Properties," Locke goes out of his way to *argue* in the *Essay* that mechanism cannot explain cohesion, impact, or body-mind causation (Wilson 1999a, pp. 196–208). This is the "more incurable . . . Ignorance" (*E* 4.3.12) that Locke discusses in conjunction with the less incurable ignorance emphasized by Guyer—that is, the limitations of our senses. In effect, *E* 4.3 provides a hierarchy of increasingly grave sources of limitations on our knowledge of physical substances:

(1) Supposing that mechanism is right, that is, that it correctly characterizes the uncertain philosophical causes of our ideas, the mechanist real essences of bodies elude us in virtue of their minuteness. [the less incurable ignorance]

(2) Even if we knew those mechanist real essences, we still would not understand how sensations are produced (nor would we understand cohesion or how motion is transferred at impact). [the more incurable ignorance]

(3) Mechanism might be the wrong theory, in which case the uncertain philosophical causes are "yet more remote from our Comprehension" (*E* 4.3.11).

Item (2) reinforces (3): mechanism's explanatory limitations give us reason to back away from our natural commitment to mechanism, for we see that it has no prospects for providing a complete scientia of body.

The last straw for Locke was provided by his growing appreciation of both the power of Newton's physics and the challenge it posed to strict mechanism.[21] What finally triggered the actual revisions to the fourth edition (1700) of the *Essay* was prodding from Edward Stillingfleet, to which Locke famously responded (in 1698):

> It is true, I say, "that bodies operate by impulse, and nothing else." And so I thought when I writ it, and can yet conceive no other way of their operation. But I am since convinced by the judicious Mr. Newton's incomparable book, that it is too bold a presumption to limit God's power, in this point, by my narrow conceptions. The gravitation of matter towards matter, by ways inconceivable to me, is not only a demonstration that God can, if he pleases, put into bodies powers and ways of operation above what can be derived from our idea of body, or can be explained by what we know of matter, but also an unquestionable and every where visible instance, that he has done so. And therefore in the next edition of my book I shall take care to have that passage rectified. (*LW* 4 467–68)

Newton's results undermine not only strict mechanism's contact action principle, but also its claim that the intrinsic qualities of bodies are exhausted by extension, solidity, and motion/rest. Responding to these developments, Locke finally and decisively retreats from speculation about the nature of uncertain philosophical causes, in keeping with his original proscription. What remains constitutes philosophical development of the very notion of uncertain philosophical cause, that is, explanation of what it would be to have a scientia of bodies, a scientific understanding of bodies as they are in themselves. To have a scientia of bodies would be to know what the primary qualities of bodies are—what sorts of qualities are intrinsic to them and irreducible to more basic qualities. Further, we would know what particular modifications of those qualities in particular bodies constitute the real essences from which all of their powers flow.

SUPERADDITION AND TWO MODELS OF NATURAL PHILOSOPHY

As we saw earlier, Locke's decisive retreat from commitment to mechanism is marked by the declaration (to Stillingfleet) that God has made matter gravitate toward matter by ways inconceivable to us. This led Leibniz to regard him as being among those who threatened the hard-won advances of the new science by advocating a return to occult and inexplicable qualities.[22] I will briefly argue in this section that, although there are real differences between the two philosophers here, Leibniz's central objection to Locke's position can be dissolved by a judicious application of Locke's distinction between sensible object and uncertain philosophical cause. In replying to Leibniz on Locke's behalf, I will also return to the set of questions raised by Paul Guyer—questions concerning whether, to what extent, and why Locke has foreclosed our prospects for scientific development.

What drew Leibniz's philosophical ire[23] was Locke's use of the notion of superaddition, according to which God may superadd qualities to substances even where we do not see how those substances are capable of such qualities. Locke applies this notion to both Newtonian attraction and to thought in matter (though Leibniz is surely malicious in suggesting that it is the latter that *motivates* the former). When forced to *defend* his view that, for all we know, God might allow matter to think, Locke appeals to the well-known example of Newtonian gravity:

> But it is farther urged, that we cannot conceive how matter can think. I grant it; but to argue from thence, that God therefore cannot give to matter a faculty of thinking, is to say God's omnipotency is limited to a narrow compass, because man's understanding is so; and brings down God's infinite power to the size of our capacities. If God can give no power to any parts of matter, but what men can account for from the essence of matter in general; if all such qualities and properties must destroy the essence, or change the essential properties of matter, which are to our conceptions above it, and we cannot conceive to be the natural consequence of that essence: it is plain, that the essence of matter is destroyed, and its essential properties changed in most of the sensible parts of this our system. For it is visible, that all the planets have revolutions about certain remote centres, which I would have any one explain, or make conceivable by the bare essence or natural powers depending on the essence of matter in general, without something added to that essence, which we cannot conceive: for the moving of matter in a crooked line, or the attraction of matter by matter, is all that can be said in the case; either of which it is above our reach to derive from the essence of matter, or body in general; though one of these two must unavoidably be allowed to be superadded in this instance to the essence of matter in general. The omnipotent Creator advised not with us in the making of the world, and his ways are not the less excellent, because they are past our finding out. (*LW* 4 461)

As Leibniz sees it, Locke here joins the Newtonians in proposing either occult qualities or a perpetual miracle; his response is to give

Locke a rather patronizing little lecture on the proper way to understand modifications:

> [I]t must be borne in mind above all that the modifications which can occur to a single subject naturally and without miracles must arise from limitations and variations of a real genus, i.e. of a constant and absolute inherent nature. For that is how philosophers distinguish the modes of an absolute being from that being itself; just as we know that size, shape and motion are obviously limitations and variations of corporeal nature (for it is plain how a limited extension yields shapes, and that changes occurring in it are nothing but motion). Whenever we find some quality in a subject, we ought to believe that if we understood the nature of both the subject and the quality we would conceive how the quality could arise from it. So within the order of nature (miracles apart) it is not at God's arbitrary discretion to attach this or that quality haphazardly to substances. He will never give them any which are not natural to them, that is, which cannot arise from their nature as explicable modifications. So we may take it that matter will not naturally possess the attractive power referred to above, and that it will not of itself move in a curved path, because it is impossible to conceive how this could happen—that is, to explain it mechanically—whereas what is natural must be such as could become distinctly conceivable by anyone admitted into the secrets of things. (*NE* 65–66; *AL* 6.6 65–66)

I submit that Locke has given us no reason to suppose that he actually disagrees with anything but the last sentence of Leibniz's lecture. Indeed, Locke's descriptions in the *Essay* of what it would be to know the real essences of things, that we would then understand how all of their properties followed from those essences, suggest a fundamental sympathy with Leibniz's picture, in particular, with the claim that "if we understood the nature of both the subject and the quality we would conceive how the quality could arise from it."[24] Superaddition is a notion we invoke from our position of ignorance; to say that God superadds a quality to body is to say that he bestows it upon bodies in some way which we do not comprehend. A quality that we must regard as superadded in this way is one that does not follow from our idea of matter as solid, extended stuff, but that is not to rule out that the quality might follow from the real essence of a body or of body in general.[25] The essences to which Locke refers in the previous famous passage are nominal essences.[26]

Locke says as much in another well-known passage that is easily misinterpreted:

> The idea of matter is an extended solid substance; wherever there is such a substance, there is matter, and the essence of matter, whatever other qualities, not contained in that essence, it shall please God to

superadd to it. For example, God creates an extended solid substance, without the superadding any thing else to it, and so we may consider it at rest: to some parts of it he superadds motion, but it has still the essence of matter: other parts of it he frames into plants, with all the excellencies of vegetation, life, and beauty, which are to be found in a rose or a peach-tree, &c. above the essence of matter in general, but it is still but matter: to other parts he adds sense and spontaneous motion, and those other properties that are to be found in an elephant. Hitherto it is not doubted but the power of God may go, and that the properties of a rose, a peach, or an elephant, superadded to matter, change not the properties of matter; but matter is in these things matter still. But if one venture to go on one step further, and say, God may give to matter thought, reason, and volition, as well as sense and spontaneous motion, there are men ready presently to limit the power of the omnipotent Creator, and tell us he cannot do it; because it destroys the essence, "changes the essential properties of matter." To make good which assertion, they have no more to say, but that thought and reason are not included in the essence of matter. I grant it; but whatever excellency, not contained in its essence, be superadded to matter, it does not destroy the essence of matter, if it leaves it an extended solid substance; wherever that is, there is the essence of matter: and if every thing of greater perfection, superadded to such a substance, destroys the essence of matter, what will become of the essence of matter in a plant, or an animal, whose properties far exceed those of a mere extended solid substance? (*LW* 4 460–61)

Locke clearly states at the beginning of the passage that we are talking about nominal essences—our idea of matter. Anything that causes in us ideas of extension and solidity satisfies the nominal essence of matter and thus is matter, whatever the uncertain philosophical cause. He ends with the very same point: wherever we have solid, extended stuff, we have the essence of matter; no essences have been violated. In fact, this is true in two senses: of course, the nominal essence remains the same, defined as it is by our abstract idea, and the stuff continues to satisfy it as long as it is solid and extended. We can also be sure that whatever is extended and solid has the real essence of body, since real essences of kinds are defined in relation to nominal ones.[27] Thus, Locke does not mean to be offering any models, by means of his examples, as to what superaddition amounts to and how it is accomplished.[28] Nothing Locke says, for example, rules out the thought that God bestows attraction on bodies by making the intrinsic and irreducible qualities of bodies such that attraction follows from them, that is, by building it into the nature of matter, as Leibniz might put it.[29]

If that is what God has done, of course, then the corpuscularian account of the real essence/nature of body is incorrect. Leibniz goes wrong in his Locke interpretation by supposing that Locke agrees with him in holding that intelligibility considerations allow us to definitively characterize the uncertain philosophical cause, and to do so along corpuscularian lines. Although, as we have seen, Locke is tempted in this direction around the time of Draft C and the first edition of the *Essay*, the correspondence with Stillingfleet marks an official repudiation of that temptation.

That superaddition is with respect to the sensible object is further supported by Locke's treatment of the thinking matter issue in his first letter, where he tells us that the question comes down to this: whether there exists any substance that has both the quality of solidity and the power of thought. Leibniz, like some later commentators, supposes that Locke has been misled by his obscure idea of substance in general (*NE* 63–64; *AL* VI.vi.63–64), but there is no such confusion. As Locke sees it, all we are in a position to rule out attributing to bodies are *contradictory* qualities/powers (*LW* 4 465), which again fits with his view that the sensible object, the object as known through sensory experience, is simply a thing with powers.

Locke defends the possibility of superaddition of thought to matter because we cannot rule it out; he maintains the fact of the superaddition of attraction because it has been empirically demonstrated. That is simply to say that empirical investigation can reveal to us that matter has more powers than are included in the nominal essence of matter that we derive from ordinary reflection on sensory experience. Locke has no difficulty in attributing those powers to sensible objects, without determining how they are grounded in the uncertain philosophical cause. This brings out very vividly the way in which Locke's thought contains two very different ideals of science or, better, ideals of two quite different practices, each of which might go under the modern label of "science." On the one hand, the *Essay* makes use of an old ideal of scientia, which seeks to deduce effects from causes, and thus to gain knowledge of necessary connections among qualities. Locke calls the uncertain philosophical cause "philosophical" because it is the proper concern of natural philosophers, who pursue such scientia, that is, "Knowledge of the Principles, Properties, and Operations of Things, as they are in themselves" (*TCE*, pp. 244–45). As we have seen, Locke holds that our prospects for scientia are grim, for the three reasons examined earlier, and we would do better to aim at nearer targets.[30] Locke's treatment of sensible objects suggests a model for the empirical study of the powers of bodies which fits both Boyle's experimental work and Newton's *Principia*, which, as Locke sees it, offers "Mathematicks, applied to some Parts of Nature" based on "Principles that Matter of Fact justifie," rather than a "*Natural Philosophy* from the first Principles of Bodies in general" (*TCE*, p. 248). This sort of empirical project results in judgment, not knowledge (*E* 4.12.10), but where knowledge is not to be had, we would be well-advised to seek judgment instead. The example of Newton's *Principia* clearly convinced Locke that the possible achievements of this sort of experimental natural philosophy could not be determined in advance. The example of Newton's optical researches certainly ought to have convinced him that we might in this way reach probable judgments about the submicroscopic.[31] Thus, Locke has available an account of disciplined inquiry into nature that is much more open than what is suggested by his pessimistic remarks about scientia.

Natural philosophy, so understood, would avoid speculation about uncertain philosophical causes, a general strategy endorsed by many prominent Newtonians. One might well wonder, however, whether working in this empirical way, generalizing from experience about the powers of bodies, might lead us in the end toward a new post-corpuscularian hypothesis about uncertain philosophical causes, a new attempt to characterize bodies as they are in themselves, that is, in terms of their ultimate intrinsic properties. It is clear that Locke holds out no real hope for such an eventuality. Here I do think that Locke went wrong. I conclude with some somewhat speculative suggestions about what led Locke to this overly pessimistic view.

(1) Locke's dogmatic empiricism severely restricts the basic *vocabulary* of natural philosophy. Because of this, any candidate for a primary quality must, it seems, be cashed out in one way or other in terms of sensory qualities. Presumably, Locke saw little room to maneuver here: although many theories could be invented which start from sensory qualities, why suppose that any of them could provide a better approximation of scientia than corpuscularianism? Here I think Kant's complaints about Locke's physiology of human understanding hit their mark—Kant is simply correct to see Locke's strict empiricism and doctrine of simple and complex ideas as providing an inadequate basis for the contents of human knowledge.

(2) Locke's standard for scientia is too high, requiring the deducibility of properties from essences in a way that parallels geometry. Here, I would argue that Locke's system is in principle more flexible than Locke himself saw, as well as being more flexible than Kant's. Locke's notions of real essence and primary quality must, like any other, be derived from reflection on experience. In *E* 2.8, one thing that Locke shows us is how reflection on sensory experience allows us to distinguish between appearance and reality and arrive at the very notion of a primary quality—a quality that bodies have intrinsically and that grounds other powers. In effect, Locke holds that we have a natural metaphysics, that it is the metaphysics

CHAPTER 7

Kant's Critique of Berkeley's Concept of Objectivity

Dina Emundts

IT IS WELL-KNOWN that Kant tries to distance himself from a position that he attributes to Berkeley, namely, the view that things are pure illusions. But is Kant right in claiming an essential difference between Berkeley's and his own philosophy? This is the main question of my essay. Interestingly, Kant does not simply treat Berkeley as someone who claims that things are mere illusions, but he also tries to explain why Berkeley holds this claim. According to Kant, Berkeley's position is unavoidable if one tries to think of the reality of space as something that is subject-independent. This is what Kant claims:

> Dogmatic idealism is unavoidable if one regards space as a property that is to pertain to things in themselves; for then it, along with everything for which it serves as condition, is a non-entity. (B274)

How are we to understand this diagnosis? In accordance with this passage, to regard space as a property that pertains to things in themselves leads to the thesis that space as a condition for spatial things must be an existing absolute space. According to Kant, Berkeley held that absolute space does not exist. The only alternative to absolute space that Berkeley could think of was to take space and all spatial things to be mere illusions. In denying that absolute space exists, Kant sides with Berkeley. Absolute space as an existing thing is a nonentity, namely, a thing whose concept is self-contradictory (A292/B349).[1] This is so because the concept of space as a real entity is supposed to describe a thing that contains all other things. Because things can be described as real only if they are in space, space itself cannot be regarded as a real thing.[2] In this context, we need not determine whether such a refutation of the assumption of the reality of absolute space is convincing. For Kant's criticism of Berkeley, this line of argument is only one of the background considerations. Kant's criticism can now be understood as follows: according to Kant, Berkeley drew the correct conclusion in refusing to think of space as belonging to things in themselves, but he failed to consider another possibility, i.e., that space is an a priori form of intuition. By providing this new conception of space, the Transcendental Aesthetic in the *Critique of Pure Reason* undermines the basis of Berkeley's position: things do not need to be reduced to mere illusions. Kant's philosophy can thus be seen not only as overcoming Berkeley's idealism, but also as preserving the lessons to be drawn from Berkeley's refutation of absolute space as an existing thing.

On this characterization of Kant's relation to Berkeley (a characterization that Kant himself offers more than once in the *Critique of Pure Reason*: see B71; B274; A491/B519), whether Berkeley's position can be defeated depends on whether we can prove that space and time are a priori representations. What is clear is that the claim Kant attributes to Berkeley—that space along with everything in it is an illusion—seems unreasonable. But this characterization of Berkeley's position is polemical and surely does not do justice to Berkeley's understanding of his own philosophy. Thus, one must examine in detail the nature of Kant's objections to Berkeley's position. However, even if Kant's description of Berkeley's position is correct, it is not at all clear what we achieve by substituting Kant's position for Berkeley's. This question is made especially pressing by the fact that although Kant and Berkeley are supposed to differ in their conception of space, Kant also maintains that space is neither a thing in itself nor a determination of a thing in itself, but rather a merely *subjective* form of intuition. So we need to ask how Kant's charge against Berkeley, that he makes everything an illusion, can be formulated more clearly and, above all, in a way that leaves room for Kant's own position.

One difficulty in answering this question comes from the fact that the concept of illusion is ambiguous. The opposite of illusion, for Kant, might be "truth" or "reality," but the intended opposite might also be "appearance," (cf. B69), "matter," or "things outside us." All of these concepts fall under what I shall call, in what follows, Kant's conception of objectivity. In exploring this conception of objectivity, I will focus on two main aspects, each of which plays an important role in Kant's strategy for opposing Berkeley's view. One is Kant's concept of truth in its relation to his notion of the objective validity of judgments. The other is Kant's notion of an empirical object. An empirical object for Kant is not a mere bundle of sensory data but a real entity in the world outside us. With respect to both of the aspects of Kant's notion of objectivity I just outlined, my central question will be: how does Kant's thesis that space and time are mere forms of intuition allow a concept of objectivity that not only differs from Berkeley's but also gives a foundation to Kant's critical reading of Berkeley's position?

KANT'S CONCEPTION OF OBJECTIVITY

First, I shall consider Kant's conception of truth. Second, I shall examine the benefits for his conception of objects Kant derives from his conception of space. Finally, I will confirm my thesis that Kant's notion of an empirical object is fundamentally different from Berkeley's by considering their respective account of primary and secondary qualities.

The Concept of Truth

For Kant, time and space are a priori intuitions and forms of intuition, namely, modes of ordering of anything given to us in sensible intuition. As such, they have their origin in us and not in things as they are in themselves. I will argue that for Kant, only if time and space are so understood are there anything like criteria of truth.[3] This is because (1) there is no empirical knowledge unless there is knowledge of universal and necessary laws, and (2) there is no knowledge of universal and necessary laws unless time and space are pure forms of intuition. Let me consider each of these points in turn.

(1) To argue for the claim that we need universal and necessary laws as a condition of truth, it is not sufficient simply to refer back to the fact that Kant takes the demonstration of the possibility of synthetic a priori judgments to be the main task of philosophy: one could, after all, argue for a conception of truth that includes only empirical knowledge claims and deny the importance of the demonstration of the possibility of synthetic a priori judgments. It is also not enough simply to show that the form of a law is the condition for the claim that a judgment is necessary, since someone interested in empirical knowledge could reply that this is convincing only in a Kantian framework. What one needs to show is that knowledge of universal, necessary laws is the precondition for *any* form of knowledge. Thus, the first point rests on the claim that only knowledge of necessary and universal laws provides us with a criterion of truth for empirical judgments.

The universal, necessary laws that come into play here must have a determinate content. They must contain more than rules for determining something as an object. For example, it is not sufficient for them to assert that all objects fall under necessary causal laws, but they must determine causes as forces. Thus, it is not the Principles (*Grundsätze*) laid out in the Transcendental Analytic of the *Critique of Pure Reason* that are relevant here, but rather the laws of nature laid out in the *Metaphysical Foundations of Natural Science*. Whereas the Principles (*Grundsätze*) only give the rules of what can be known in general about something possibly given to us—for example, that everything that is real has an intensive magnitude—the natural laws in the *Metaphysical Foundations of Natural Science* give us the specific principles and laws with which we have to explain what is really given—for example, that we have to explain something real in space with attractive and repulsive forces.[4]

The significance of these laws for empirical knowledge can be appreciated if we turn to a Kantian assumption about empirical knowledge.[5] This assumption is one that should be uncontroversial even in the eyes of someone who has no conception of a priori laws. On such a view, one can speak of "knowledge" only if a judgment can be justified by reference to other judgments. In the case of empirical judgments, other empirical judgments must always be taken into account: the truth of an empirical judgment is decidable only if the judgment can be integrated into a determinate context with a determinate content. For reasons that will not be discussed here, this leads Kant to the claim that judgments are determined as valid or invalid only in reference to a *system* of other judgments. This system is not fully given, but serves as a regulative idea for the ordering of empirical judgments.[6]

On the basis of this claim concerning empirical knowledge, we can now explain the importance of universal, necessary, i.e., a priori laws for empirical knowledge: only if we have knowledge of universal, necessary laws is it the case that some of the judgments in a system of knowledge can be singled out as certain, which means that the possibility of their revision can be excluded. These judgments provide the guiding principles for all the other judgments in the system. Without these a priori laws, not only could any judgment be fundamentally false, any system of judgments could as well. Without these laws, the only reasons for taking a judgment or system of judgments to be true would be purely pragmatic ones. If, however, some judgments are taken to be a priori true, then, first, no judgment that contradicts them can be (objectively) valid in the system; second, these judgments—and the concepts, such as forces and the like, which occur in them—must serve as the contentful basis of valid empirical judgments. In such empirical judgments, any entitlement to validity will depend on the kind of reference made to the judgments taken to be true a priori. In this way, the judgments taken to be true a priori are also a "criterion of truth" for any empirical knowledge.

This brings us to the second point: how knowledge of universal and necessary laws depends on our having a priori intuitions of time and space.

(2) Kant supports his claim with two considerations: (a) the fundamental laws of our experience—the Principles (*Grundsätze*)—are laws that describe what must be true in order for something to be an object of

experience for us.[7] They are not mere logical forms of thought, but are formulated, rather, in relation to what can be given to the senses. This is why they relate to our forms of intuition. That the form primarily under consideration is time has to do, among other things, with the fact that, for us, every sensible manifold is given in time. Thus, the relation of the a priori concepts (the categories) to time—that is, their schematization—is a condition for the formulation of the laws of experience. The Principles that are thus related to time also require some reference to space because they are to represent laws of objects of *outer* sense. This reference to space is indeed made explicitly by the Principles.[8] Note that it is possible to establish this relation because determinations of time can generally be related to determinations of space as a form of intuition (cf. B291).

So far I have only explained why the assumption that space and time are forms of intuition is a necessary condition for justifying a priori necessary laws, namely, the Principles of Pure Understanding in the *Critique of Pure Reason*. Remember, the Principles make no contentful claims about objects or events: they do not say anything about how an object realizes the conditions formulated by them. They are thus not suited to be contentful guidelines for knowledge. Such guidelines must, however, be given if necessary laws are to provide a criterion of truth as described earlier. (b) With this, we reach the second consideration necessary to justify the idea that space—as a form of intuition—is a condition for justifying necessary laws. We now have to show that space, as an a priori intuition, is to provide a condition justifying necessary and universal judgments with a determinate content. The argument is the following: in contrast to the Principles of Pure Understanding, natural laws must relate to the concept of matter as the concept of something given to the senses. These laws of the natural sciences are universal insofar as they must be valid for every object of the outer senses; in comparison with the Principles of Pure Understanding, however, they are also particular—namely, related to matter as a possible object of outer sense. The scope of these universal natural laws is determined by taking into account each of the Principles of Pure Understanding and determining what must be the case in order for something to become an object for us. Justifying natural laws formulated in relation to the concept of matter is, however, not achieved merely by calling upon the Principles of Pure Understanding. That the impenetrability of matter, for example, must be explained by an interaction of attractive and repulsive forces cannot be conceptually deduced from the Principles. The empirical concept of matter must also be taken into account in order to derive what can be known of impenetrability on the basis of the Principles of Pure Understanding.

Whatever can be said a priori about matter as an object of the outer senses must be necessary for matter to become an object for us. In order to have insight into these natural laws, which have—in contrast to the Principles—a specific content, we require some sort of procedure that would allow us to indicate a priori what must be the case in order for matter to be understood as the object of outer sense. Everything that is given to outer sense must be spatial. Since the faculty of spatial intuition has no empirical foundation, it can serve as a basis for the justification of a priori statements. Following the Transcendental Aesthetic, the faculty of spatial intuition is, with that of temporal intuition, the only faculty related to the sensible in an a priori way. Achieving an insight into the natural laws and into their validity should thus be possible by constructing in space—by means of mathematics—according to these laws the properties matter must have in order for it to be an object at all for us.

To sum up the preceding discussion: as a criterion of truth, we require something that can be recognized a priori as certain. Because the Principles of Pure Understanding (stated in the Analytic of Principles in the *Critique of Pure Reason*) have no specific contents, we must go beyond them in formulating contentful natural laws. As a procedure for ascertaining a priori the contents of those laws that relate to something given to the outer senses, only the verification of their spatial representability comes into question. The a priority of spatial representation is thus a necessary condition for a criterion of truth.

Let us now return to Berkeley. How do the points just laid out support Kant's claim that Berkeley lacks the criteria for truth and turns everything into mere illusions? We see how Kant can take himself to be justified in claiming that because for him space is a mere empirical representation, Berkeley lacks the resources for recognizing something as true (*Prolegomena*, appendix, AA 4, 374). One must remember that Kant agrees here with Berkeley that space and time are subjective, and that space is not a (subject-independent) real entity.[9] Kant's agreement with Berkeley on this point can be seen as the reason why Kant insists, in contrast to Berkeley, on the apriority of spatial representation. Only by asserting the apriority of space can Kant ground the possibility of cognition on our intuition of space, even though space remains something subjective.

If we now return to Kant's charge that Berkeley turns everything into mere illusion, we may attribute to Kant the following argument: if appearances correctly and consistently hang together according to empirical laws, then they are not mere "illusions." They can be distinguished from dreams or imaginings. "Real," for Kant, is what stands "in an empirical connection with my real consciousness" (A493/B521).[10] Of course, one can say that a similar feature distinguishes dreams and "reality" for Berkeley. He, too, can make the question of the reality of something dependent on the question as to whether something stands in connection with other things in accordance with empirical laws.[11] But what has been said previously should show where, in Kant's eyes, the problem lies. With a little bit of exaggeration, one could say: Berkeley cannot draw upon the criterion of correspondence with empirical laws of experience because he lacks the means to describe an objectively valid framework of empirical laws.

A passage relevant to this of consideration can be found in the *Prolegomena* (appendix, *AA* 4 374ff.). There, Kant claims to agree with Berkeley that space and time and everything in them are not things in themselves or properties of things in themselves, but merely belong to the appearances as such. "But these idealists," he continues,

> and among them especially Berkeley, viewed space as a merely empirical representation, . . . I show, on the contrary, first: that space . . . together with all its determinations, can be cognized by us a priori.

After thus distinguishing his position from Berkeley's through the thesis of the apriority of space and its determinations, Kant concludes:

> Since truth rests on universal and necessary laws as its criteria, for Berkeley experience could have no criteria of truth, because its appearances (according to him) had nothing underlying them a priori.

Note that so far I have not discussed Kant's conception of space in its own right. Of course, a specific conception of space lies at the basis of my reconstruction: space is taken to be a form according to which we order manifolds. Treating space as a form of ordering is a well-established reading of the Transcendental Aesthetic of the *Critique of Pure Reason*. We can hold that Kant assumes a faculty of sensible intuition whose form precedes experience and lies at the ground of every perception of an appearance in space, as well as every determinate representation of space. On this interpretation, the faculty of spatial intuition can be characterized—on the assumption that there is something given as real—as the faculty of relating sensations to things outside oneself. Note that this conception of space does not contradict the thesis that no perception of an object and no determinate representation of space are possible without the application of the Principles of the understanding.

The question arises here whether, following Kant, the faculty of spatial intuition implies a certain structural composition, or whether the structural composition of space (i.e., of every particular space) is more fully determined by the Principles of Pure Understanding. (One candidate for a property of space not to be traced back to the Principles is its three-dimensionality.) How one answers that question has consequences for the topic at hand. For Berkeley, spatial properties (such as "extended") are immediately given representations. Space is, for him, the result of an abstraction from these representations. It is not something that is itself structured in a determinate way. If Kant were to maintain that space has properties that are not given through the Principles of Pure Understanding, then he could claim that Berkeley is wrong in denying it a structure of its own. In this case, Berkeley's conception of mathematics or geometry—which is unacceptable to Kant—is not simply a consequence of the fact that he does not recognize synthetic a priori truths. Rather, it is grounded directly in his conception of space. The discussion of whether properties such as three-dimensionality are given through the structure of space as an a priori form of intuition is extremely complex.[12] As it is not especially germane to the subject at hand, I wish to suggest it only as a possible additional criticism, on Kant's part, of Berkeley's conception of space.

I now turn to the second aspect of what I have called Kant's notion of objectivity: his concept of an empirical object.

The Concept of an Empirical Object

Even if one grants Kant's point concerning the criteria of truth, one can still claim that more is required to distinguish Kant's conception of objectivity from Berkeley's. After all, one could say that Kant, just as much as Berkeley, lacks the resources to accommodate those aspects of objectivity we mean when, for instance, we speak of the existence of things outside ourselves. In what follows I will argue that Kant, in fact, has more resources than Berkeley for justifying statements concerning the existence of something real in space. These resources are (1) again, his conception of space as a pure form of intuition and (2) his conception of the role of conceptual elements in determining our representations of objects. I shall consider each of these two points in turn.

(1) Kant refers supporters of Berkeley's position to his Transcendental Aesthetic in the *Critique of Pure Reason*. More particularly, the first of the arguments concerning space is directed at such philosophers:

> Space is not an empirical concept that has been drawn from outer experience. For in order for certain sensations to be related to something outside me . . . thus in order for me to represent them as outside one another . . . the representation of space must already be their ground. (A23/B39)

We shall now investigate the importance of this consideration for Kant's response to Berkeley. If Kant wanted to link this consideration to the claim that Berkeley is not in a position to characterize things as real (cf. Berkeley, *PHK* §§29ff.) or spatial, Berkeley could easily counter this claim and point out that the predicate "is spatial" or "has a spatial property" can be used without problems on the basis of *his* philosophy (cf. *PHK* 43ff.). Kant's critique can, however, be reconstructed so that Berkeley has significantly fewer resources, compared to Kant, with which to justify talk of something real in space.

Berkeley's difficulties legitimating philosophical talk of something real in space is connected to the fact that Berkeley says that a thing can be described as "real" and spatial properties can be ascribed to it, even while claiming to have given up the concept of matter. Among the meanings of matter that Berkeley discusses in order to show they are contradictory or empty, two are particularly interesting in relation to Kant: first, the idea that matter is the cause of representations (of objects outside ourselves), and second, the idea that matter is the bearer of properties—a bearer that is not itself perceivable, or that is unknown to us. I will later discuss Kant's treatment of the position that there is something unknown to us which bears the properties we perceive when I discuss the concept of the *thing in itself*. The first meaning of matter, i.e., as the cause of ideas, is without doubt closer to Kant's conception, but the two certainly do not coincide entirely. Berkeley's proposal requires, namely, that that which we have immediately, as data, are ideas in the mind. As I will soon show, in Kant's conceptual framework, this assumption cannot be maintained in this crude form. Thus, one has to explain how Kant develops the concept of a representation in such a way that it allows for the justification of talk of the existence of matter. And as will be shown, this strategy for criticizing Berkeley is cogent especially if one assumes that Kant agrees with Berkeley that the second point made earlier—the idea that our representations are representations of an unknown object—has no theoretical utility.

According to Kant, one must distinguish "real" and "formal" components of representations. The "real" component is sensation. We cannot call it to mind at will, and we cannot think it a priori (A373). For this reason, it makes sense to call sensation the matter of perception (A50/B74; A268/B324). We must now examine the role played by the a priori forms of intuition: representations or perceptions are not the same as sensations, but rather require, in addition to matter, the form of intuition. In representation or perception, a sensation is to be related to the form of intuition. A result of this is that the real in a sensation need not be taken as something merely inner. Instead, there are two cases that must be distinguished from one another. When we relate that which is real as a sensation to the outer sense, we experience something as real in space; when we relate the sensation to the inner sense, we have an inner representation. To assume something real in space without having to think of it as something that is not immediately accessible to us is thus possible when we view space as a subjective form of intuition to which sensations must be related. In this context, we can call matter that which corresponds to sensation in space (A20/B34). As soon as the categories are applied, this matter can also be thought of as the cause of a modification of our senses, where the effect of matter is not an ideal representation, but rather a real sensation. Talk of the existence of matter and of things outside us is justified when one thereby refers to something real in space, that is, when a sensation is related to outer sense.

Because we claimed, in the previous consideration, that something is real when it "stands with my real consciousness in an empirical connection" (A493/B521; see also A377), we must explain how this is linked to the talk of something being real just discussed. The criterion of coherence discussed earlier is valid for every alleged experience (B279). That there must be something real in space, and that perceptions of something in space cannot all be imagined, cannot, however, be fully justified through this criterion. For that, we need an argument that shows that it is fundamentally—that is, not simply with respect to particular experiences—possible to prove the existence of objects outside of me. This argument is given in the Refutation of Idealism. The concept of existence that comes into play with this argument is addressed by the consideration at issue here. Talk of something being real can thus be justified not only on the basis of the coherence criterion: it can also be understood as meaning that this something is a real thing existing in space, even when one might be mistaken in individual cases.

As has already been emphasized, none of this is meant to be a direct refutation of Berkeley's position; it should only show why and in what sense Kant's philosophy can deal better with the concept of objectivity than Berkeley's. If, as is the case for Berkeley, things are in space only in the sense that they have spatial properties (such as extension, distance, etc.), and if matter cannot be seen as the source of a modification of our senses, talk of something real in space remains philosophically unacceptable (even if it is acceptable in everyday speech). This is where Kant's distinction between appearance and illusion comes into play. Saying that the real in space is dependent on our subjective forms of intuition makes it an appearance, not an illusion. What I predicate of appearance, according to Kant, is something I predicate of it as something outside me.[13]

In order to provide textual evidence for Kant's strategy against Berkeley as sketched here, it is not sufficient simply to refer to the first argument regarding space in the Transcendental Aesthetic. Rather, we must consult passages where Kant attempts to prove the existence of things outside us in space. This is done prominently in the fourth Paralogism in the first edition and in the Refutation of Idealism in the second edition of the *Critique of Pure Reason*. However, here we are confronted with the difficulty that Kant intends this proof not against Berkeley but against Descartes.[14] There are two reasons for this. First, Kant believes that with his demonstration of the apriority of space, he has already undermined Berkeley's idealism. Earlier I showed where in Berkeley's philosophy one can locate the defect Kant means to point out when he states that in it "everything is declared an illusion." Second, the Refutation of Idealism cannot be directed against Berkeley because it presupposes a philosophical notion of matter existing outside of us and which can affect us—and this is not an assumption that Berkeley shares, because for Berkeley the concept of matter is contradictory.[15] If this description of Kant's Refutation of Idealism is correct, these considerations cannot serve as a refutation of Berkeley, although one can turn to them if one wants to show that Kant's philosophy is able to make room for a concept of objectivity that can integrate the idea of real material things outside us.[16]

Strikingly, Kant's refutation of skepticism about the external world, especially the version in the first edition of the *Critique of Pure Reason*, contains formulations that bring, at first glance, Kant's position closer to Berkeley's than one could expect from my presentation of Kant's position.

Kant says, for instance, that matter "separated from our sensibility, is nothing": it is

> only a species of representations (intuition), which are called external, not as if they were related to objects that are external in themselves, but because they relate perceptions to space, where all things are external to one another, but that space itself is in us. (A370)

At the same time, though, he emphasizes a difference between his position and other idealist conceptions, a difference that can also be used against Berkeley:

> Thus the transcendental idealist is an empirical realist, and grants to matter, as appearance, a reality which need not be inferred, but is immediately perceived. (A371)

(2) If one keeps in mind the considerations thus far, it becomes plausible to think that the a priori elements of the understanding that Kant introduces also serve to make sense of his notion of objectivity. In order to speak of objects of experience, according to Kant, what has been said so far about the way something real is given to me in space is not at all sufficient. Talking of reality also requires conceptual elements.

Of course, the question of how to interpret the line of thought Kant uses to introduce the categories and determine their validity and scope is the object of a great deal of controversy. As far as Kant's criticism of Berkeley is concerned, and notwithstanding any problems one may have with Kant's Transcendental Deduction of the Categories, I want to call attention to a passage from the first edition:

> For only because I ascribe all perceptions to one consciousness (of original apperception) can I say of all perceptions that I am conscious of

them. There must therefore be an objective ground . . . on which rests the possibility, indeed even the necessity of a law extending through all appearances. (A122)

The manifold in space and time is, according to Kant, subject to a priori rules of ordering,[17] which account for the connectedness among appearances. For if we had merely empirical rules for the association of representations, any determinate collection of representations that we could describe as a thing could arise only randomly. According to Kant, the collection would be accidental even if the structure of things as bundles of representations were grounded in the things in themselves or in God, because this grounding would have nothing to do with whether we are in a position to associate these things according to rules. Thus, in order to justify the concept of an object, Kant's deduction must prove that universal rules are a necessary condition of experience. Universal rules are a necessary condition of experience because, according to Kant, the assumption of the contingency of associations—an assumption one is committed to if one relies solely on empirical rules—would imply the possibility of having to accept as *my* representations those which I am utterly unable to combine with others. To accept as my representations those which I am utterly unable to combine with others is taken to be impossible by Kant, because in order to understand the I as a unified consciousness (and not just as a consciousness that is only numerically the same), I must be in a position to think of myself as accompanying all my representations. This is possible only if all my representations can be connected according to rules. This, however, can be shown only by relying on a priori rules. If we wish to demonstrate that all (my) representations belong to a (unified) consciousness, then the rules according to which we synthesize the manifold cannot be merely empirical rules, but rather must be necessary a priori rules. These rules establish the concept of an object by indicating how something is to be determined in connection with other things.

If one attempts to use this point as a criticism of Berkeley's position, one is faced with the objection that it takes for granted Kant's concepts of the unity of consciousness and of objectivity. However, as I understand the matter, this point is not meant to count as a refutation of Berkeley's position. Rather, it is enough to say that Kant can show that we do not merely *say* that we make a judgment about an object or that an object has a property: instead, we can philosophically *justify* such talk. Let us again turn to the passage where it was said that assuming mere rules of association means being forced to take a determinate combination of representations as purely accidental. We can understand this to mean that, in such a case, we would not be able to claim that the connection of our representations has a *fundamentum in re*. Perhaps it will be said that God ensures an appropriate order of representations for us. Even then, though, one could not claim that we can *cognize* an order in the objects. The objection against Berkeley is, correspondingly, that he cannot give the concept of an object the meaning that we expect from a philosophical theory.

We can read in this light a passage from the A Deduction, where Kant raises the following objection against the idea that we have nothing we can take as the object corresponding to a cognition:

> We find, however, that our thought of the relation of all cognition to its object carries something of necessity with it, since namely the latter is regarded as that which is opposed to our cognitions being determined at pleasure or arbitrarily rather than being determined a priori, since insofar as they are to relate to an object, our cognitions must also necessarily agree with each other in relation to it, i.e. they must have that unity that constitutes the concept of an object. (A104ff.)

Kant believes his theory satisfies the explication of cognition of objects demanded here. The unity that the object makes necessary can be nothing other than

> the formal unity of consciousness in the synthesis of the manifold of the representations. (A105)

Against the interpretation given so far, one could argue that Kant overlooks the possibility that we can have a priori knowledge of God that provides us with information about the causes and the order of our representations. With respect to this objection, Kant's answer consists in proving that knowledge is possible only of objects of possible experience and that Berkeley's idealism is mystical and visionary (*Prolegomena*, §13, *AA* 4 293) because it transgresses these boundaries.[18] I will deal with an aspect of this critique, i.e., the problem of the thing in itself, in the second part of this essay.

I now want to turn to the third point I announced at the beginning: how the contrast between Kant's and Berkeley's notions of object is confirmed if one considers their respective views of primary and secondary qualities.

The Distinction between Primary and Secondary Qualities

The primary/secondary distinction is a natural topic to discuss when contrasting Berkeley and Kant: the two share the strategy of claiming that what is normally thought to be true of secondary qualities, namely, that they belong only to how things appear to us, is also true of primary qualities, i.e., real objects. At first glance, it seems that, in choosing such a strategy, Kant is siding with Berkeley. However, in light of the discussion so far, one can already guess that such a claim is shortsighted. For Kant wants to provide a theory that agrees with Berkeley that representations are not products of unknowable things in themselves, but which differs from him in that it can at the same time justify our concept of objectivity.

Once again, then, we can put forward a possible Kantian critique of Berkeley on the basis of common ground. Both Kant and Berkeley deny that the distinction between primary and secondary qualities is a metaphysical distinction, even while disagreeing about what can be said and philosophically justified about properties. Berkeley denies any ontological distinction between primary and secondary qualities because, according to him, both primary and secondary qualities are *in the mind*. He does not, however, refuse a distinction that would not have ontological implications.[19] As Berkeley suggests in *De Motu*, such a distinction could be based on the idea that primary and secondary qualities play different roles in scientific explanation. These different roles cannot, however, be justified by the notion that scientific explanations, in contrast to others, are objective. Rather, he suggests, by distinguishing between primary and secondary qualities, one refers to different roles in the process of scientific research (cf. *PHK* 101-11). For Kant, the distinction between primary and secondary qualities is an empirical one. Seen from the perspective of transcendental philosophy, every perception and every judgment is dependent upon our faculties of cognition. So far it seems that Kant is siding with Berkeley. However, the way Kant understands what other philosophers have said about secondary qualities suggests an argument against Berkeley. The traditional treatment of secondary qualities serves as an analogy for what Kant wants to say about appearances in the following way: as long as we bears in mind the real status of judgments of color properties, for example, there is no reason why we cannot apply a color predicate to an object itself. And the same is true of any predicate that pertains to appearances:

> It would be my own fault if I made that which I should count as appearance into a mere illusion. [In a footnote:] The predicates of appearance can be attributed to the object in itself, in relation to our sense, e.g., the red color to the rose. (B69ff.)[20]

Of course, one may ask whether in contrast to Berkeley, Kant does not in fact give a basis for a distinction between primary and secondary qualities through his transcendental philosophy. This suggestion is based, among other things, on the fact that Kant does believe he can justify parts of scientific knowledge as objective, in contrast to other cognitions. Might it be the case that the different ways we can relate to objects—considered transcendentally—could justify a distinction between primary and secondary qualities? Let us examine the distinction in Kant more closely.

Kant cannot distinguish between primary and secondary qualities through criteria that contradict his thesis that objects are given only as appearances. For instance, this would be the case if he were attempting to explain secondary qualities as those that must refer to mental events. Kant is also prohibited from making a distinction based on a representationalist view, according to which the primary qualities, unlike the secondary, apply to or are similar to the represented thing. On both these points, Kant roughly agrees with Berkeley in denying the distinction.

For Kant, concepts of secondary qualities are applicable in relation to the particular condition or organization of this or that sense (A45/B62). Concepts of primary qualities, in contrast, are applicable to their object under all states of the senses without restriction. Formulated in light of the transcendental philosophy, a primary quality is a quality that is ascribed to the object in relation to sensibility in general. Differentiating between primary and secondary qualities in this way is not open to Berkeley, for it requires that we be justified in ascribing properties to objects. In contrast, according to Berkeley, properties perceived by the senses are ideas that—without abstraction—are always related to one sense only. We have already discussed criticisms connected with this kind of consideration. However, it is not yet clear precisely what role the distinction between primary and secondary qualities plays for Kant.

Applying Kant's criterion for differentiating the two kinds of quality seems straightforward. For Kant, colors are not, strictly speaking, qualities of the body to whose intuition they are attached. Color sensations are sensations that arise from the effect of light reflected by a body, or of the ether, on the sense of sight (A29; CJ, §14, AA 5 224). The ether vibrations affecting the sense of sight and the surface structure of the body may jointly contribute to the explanation—to be specified more precisely—of color sensations,[21] but in any event the explanation of colors cannot proceed without reference to the particular organization of the sense of sight. Not so in the case of impenetrability, for example. The attribution of a property like impenetrability can also be based on a sensation, one that comes via the sense of touch. But in addition, impenetrability can be explained independently of the human sense of touch, by ascribing a force to the body which, whenever the body is penetrated, has an effect on the penetrating body, regardless of its structure. Thus, for Kant, impenetrability would be a primary quality. With respect to our question, though, we must note the following: the reason impenetrability is considered a primary quality is not that the *Metaphysical Foundations of Natural Science* demonstrated that it belongs to the essence of matter as object of outer sense (*MFNS, AA* 4 465-566).[22] On the contrary, it is characterized as a primary quality by virtue of the empirical criterion for differentiating primary and secondary qualities, namely, whether an empirical explanation of the property is possible without recourse to the constitution of a particular sense. The rigidity or physical state of a body is, for example, to be classified as a primary quality because it can be explained independently of the human sense of touch—namely, by forces within the body. They are, however, not material properties of which we have a priori knowledge, as in the case of impenetrability.[23]

If this is correct, it means that talk of a body having a property intrinsically can be understood in two ways. As transcendental philosophers, we know that matter and bodies must have certain properties, as these properties are the conditions for matter or bodies to be objects of experience. In the framework of Kant's philosophy, these properties are to be seen as a priori, and to be explained through a priori principles. For this we require that they be mathematically representable, and that is the case independently of whether the properties have to do with extensive or intensive magnitudes.[24] From the perspective of empirical research, however, a use of "intrinsic" can be established which signifies that a thing has a property regardless of the particular condition of whichever sense. This concept of "intrinsic" is not the same as the transcendental-philosophical one, and is not grounded through transcendental philosophical argument. Primary qualities may indeed admit of a mathematical representation better than secondary ones, but in Kant's eyes, mathematics plays a markedly subordinate role here in contradistinction to the role it plays with regard to those properties that can be recognized a priori. Moreover, Kant is a proponent of a dynamic theory of matter, and in many questions of empirical science, he takes a critical stance toward the criterion of mathematical representation or measurability. His suggestion for defining primary qualities—that the body has the property under all conditions of the senses—does not rest on the (quantitative) measurability or the mathematical representation of the property (Cf. *MFNS, AA* 4 532). Note, however, that it would be compatible with the perspective of the transcendental philosophy to take mathematical representation as the criterion of primary qualities. Kant's suggestion, according to which the distinction between primary and secondary qualities depends on the relation to our senses, is not determined by his transcendental philosophy. Further, for Kant it is not a foregone conclusion that secondary qualities play no role in natural science. That question depends, rather, on whether the corresponding judgments can be integrated in our system of empirical judgments. Thus, it could be that the explanation of a color perception falls within the scope of physical science, whereas a taste perception does not.[25]

The question as to what philosophical justification one has for ascribing a property to an object is thus to be strictly distinguished from the question as to whether a property is to be ascribed as primary or secondary. There is yet another philosophically grounded difference among properties that does not, for Kant, coincide with the primary/secondary distinction. According to Kant, there is a difference between properties based merely on sensations and those which are based on the forms of intuition. All primary and secondary properties named thus far are perceivable properties. For Kant they are, further, properties in which a sensation is related to something outside of me in space. The underlying sensation—for example, a sensation of red—cannot be imagined but rather must be experienced (cf. *Anthropology, AA* 7 167ff.). That something must be experienced and cannot be identified simply on the basis of a description is often seen as characteristic of the class of secondary qualities. According to Kant, however, the question whether something has to be experienced is to be distinguished from the question of whether it is a primary or secondary quality. Sensations can never be invented; nevertheless, differences in the explanations of properties of things must be discerned in accordance with differences in the corresponding sensations. In this context, we may ask how Kant deals with the spatial properties normally called primary, such as extension and shape. Regarded transcendentally, these are, for Kant, properties that must be distinguished from those which belong to mere sensation, as they are based on the condition of sensibility, that is, the forms of intuition (A20ff./B35). Unlike properties based only on sensations, extension and shape also apply to mathematically constructed objects. Regarded empirically, though, we can treat spatial properties as properties of things (*MFNS, AA* 4 484), and we can also perceive them in things (for example, through the sense of touch). Because they can be explained independently of the constitution of any particular sense, they are primary qualities—even though, from the transcendental-philosophical standpoint, they are a kind of property different from impenetrability, for instance.

Considering all of this, one could say that it is not the possibility of distinguishing between primary and secondary qualities that separates Kant and Berkeley. Rather, it is the fact that the two have, within the frameworks of their respective philosophies, very different resources for making the distinction. Above all, however, Kant's theory makes further distinctions independent of the primary/secondary quality distinction, which allow him to explain various possible forms of relating to an object given to us. We do not need the distinction between primary and secondary qualities in order to substantiate specific processes of natural science, to differentiate between intrinsic and extrinsic properties, or to distinguish various kinds of properties. We need this empirical distinction only in the context of explanations of properties that apply to empirically determinable objects. These differentiations can be used in criticizing Berkeley because they contribute to the concept of an object of experience more sophisticated and differentiated than the one that is possible for Berkeley.

The Bounds of Our Cognition

So far we have seen the following: Kant's theses regarding space make plausible a certain criticism of Berkeley, namely, that on Berkeley's view, the concept of objectivity cannot play the role that it can for Kant. It is worth noting that all the considerations so far are within the framework of a philosophy that, in agreement with Berkeley, does not try to use subject-independent things as a basis for its epistemology. In accordance with the discussions thus far, Berkeley's conception of objectivity is insufficient to warrant the possibility of objectively valid knowledge of nature and to give content to the concept of an object of experience. Nevertheless, one might suspect that the criticism of Berkeley presented here is not very far-reaching, since it is not directed against his idealism as expressed by the thesis *esse est percipi*. Thus, one might suppose, the criticism outlined earlier addresses only *certain* assumptions of Berkeley's, assumptions that could perhaps be rejected within a different but broadly Berkeleyan, idealistic framework. After all, it is not yet clear whether Kant's conception goes so far as to defend a notion of objectivity which includes, against Berkeley, "mind- or subject-independent" existence. With this question, we are directed back to Kant's concept of the thing in itself.

Kant uses the expression "thing in itself" in a number of different ways, some of which must remain out of consideration here.[26] In the context relevant to this essay, the important question is whether the assumption of mind-independent things in themselves, as the source of affections in us, is legitimate. If we were justified in using the concept of a thing in itself to refer to an existence independent of the cognizing subject, this would amount to a denial of Berkeley's principle *esse est percipi*.[27] As is well-known, the difficulty in assuming the thing in itself lies in finding an ontological reading for such an assumption. As will be shown in what follows, to give it ontological meaning does not mean merely committing oneself to an interpretation according to which things in themselves and appearances are two different kinds of entities, as one finds in the so-called Two-Worlds interpretation. The difficulty in finding an ontological reading is that it must somehow be managed without using the categories, since the application of the categories is restricted to objects of sensory intuition. One reading formulated in light of this difficulty says that Kant wanted to allow for the concept of a radically subject- or mind-independent world, but that he did not believe he could give ontological meaning to such a concept. For reference to the thing in itself to have any explanatory power, all we need is to be able to give it an epistemological meaning.

We can argue for such an epistemological meaning as follows: in the case of objects, the concept of the thing in itself allows us to get around their dependence on our merely subjective conditions of intuition. Because this representation of a thing in itself is the result of an abstraction, it need not have ontological implications. In this form, the thing in itself thesis cannot be used against Berkeley's principle *esse est percipi*. For that, it would need to be given an ontological meaning. However, against the thesis that the thing in itself need not be granted any ontological connotation it can be objected, quite independently of any criticism of Berkeley, that such a thesis does not square well with the role Kant assigns to the thing in itself—namely, that it can affect us.[28] In what follows I will present three interpretations of the thing in itself, which try to give this concept an ontological meaning. What I am interested in is to examine these interpretations with respect to their consequences for the *esse est percipi* principle. The first interpretation (1) takes the thing in itself as a limiting concept. The second interpretation (2) understands the thing in itself as a concept that indicates *that* something is given to us. The third interpretation (3) takes the thing in itself as something that gives us not only the material but also a quality of our intuitions. I will defend the first interpretation because it is in my view the only one that is possible without overstepping the boundaries of our possible cognition.

(1) According to the first reading presented here, the concept of a thing in itself is grounded in the notion that, in the framework of Kant's philosophy, we can give the concept of affection a twofold meaning. As mentioned earlier, Kant distinguishes between the form and the matter of a perception. The form is given through the pure forms of intuition, space and time. Not so for the matter, namely, sensation. A sensation can be understood as the result of an affection, for it is supposed to be something that is "in us" and not fabricated by us, but rather *given* to us. However, thinking of sensation as the result of affection raises a difficulty for Kant. Whatever is sensibly present to us depends on the subjective forms of intuition. If we relate the sensation to something outside ourselves, we conceive of it as something spatial. We can then take this spatial something to be that which affects us, and think of an object of experience as the source of the affection. In thinking this, however, we presuppose that the source of the affection is something that we can cognize. By this requirement, we also restrict the statement that it grounds: we can see something that affects us as something spatio-temporal only if that something also satisfies the conditions of the possibility of our experience. If we do not include this restriction, the prior statement is unacceptable. The difficulty in thinking of sensation as the result of an affection consists, then, in the fact that on the one hand, we must think of something or other as the source of the affection, and on the other hand, every object that we can think of carries with it the restrictions of the possibility of experience—restrictions that are in this case unac-

ceptable, because the source of affection does not in general have to meet the conditions of a possible object of experience. To avoid this difficulty, we must introduce the thought of the thing in itself. This thought makes room for the fact that—from the perspective of transcendental philosophy—the source of that which is given to us must be left *indeterminate*, even though everything that is something to us depends on the forms of intuition. This means that we think of things in themselves as existing mind-independent things that are the source of affection. The fact that with the concept "thing in itself" we indicate something that we must leave indeterminate is, in my view, the reason why Kant says that the thing in itself is a limiting concept (A255/B310).

If one asks whether this thought implies that something that is not spatio-temporal could still be given to us, we have to answer as follows: the thought that something subject-independent could exist does not mean that it would have to be given to us (in space and time). We do not need to equate "existing" with "being in space and time." It is enough to make clear in some respect or other what we mean by "existing," and this, in the case of the thing in itself as the source of affection, is the capacity to have an effect on us.[29]

Note that this thought of things in themselves does not justify the knowledge claim that things in themselves as mind-independent things exist. To sustain this knowledge claim, we would have to know that our affections are caused by something mind-independent, and this would certainly overstep the bounds of our cognition. Rather, we can only say that we can make sense of and cannot exclude the possibility of something mind- or subject-independent existing and having an effect on us. The thought of an existing something that is both subject-independent and the source of the affection is allowable,[30] but we cannot make it into a positive knowledge claim about the existence of something that is mind-independent.

This might be clarified by means of a comparison with Berkeley: if the concept of the thing in itself—as one might think in the context of a possible critique of Berkeley—is supposed to imply subject- or mind-independence, then the claim that things in themselves exist implies more than we can know, because the sensation could, after all, be the effect of a self-affection, or (as Berkeley positively asserts) of another mind. We just do not know. The concept of the thing in itself denotes only the indeterminateness of the source of affection. Thus, for Kant, there is no justification for the claim that things in themselves as mind- or subject-independent things exist.[31]

If one follows this interpretation of Kant's doctrine about things in themselves, it is easy to see that this doctrine is incompatible with the principle *esse est percipi*, since it allows for the possibility of mind- or subject-independent existence, whereas Berkeley's principle denies this possibility. According to this interpretation, one could also say: concerning the *esse est percipi* principle, Kant does not claim that Berkeley fails to establish a strong concept of objectivity. Rather, here Kant's objection against Berkeley consists in the claim that Berkeley's thesis about the source of our sensations goes beyond the boundaries of possible knowledge for us.[32]

One could object in Berkeley's defense that, even after all this, there is no motivation for the notion of mind-independent existence because everything that we have and that we refer to is subject- or mind-dependent. But this objection is based on a misunderstanding: in the previous discussion, we did not claim that we must make use of the concept of the thing in itself in our epistemology. Rather, the concept is supposed to show that we lack the means to make positive knowledge claims about the source of our affection from the perspective of transcendental philosophy. The principle *esse est percipi* is precisely such a positive claim in that it denies that mind-independent things in themselves can be the source of affection. The principle *esse est percipi* implies a priori cognition about the source of affection. Thus, Kant writes in the notes to the A edition (A29) of the *Critique of Pure Reason*:

> Pure idealism is concerned with the existence of things outside of ourselves. Critical idealism [i.e., Kant's] leaves this undecided, and claims only that the form of their intuition is merely in us. (*AA* 29 23)

(2) In contrast to the interpretation just suggested, one could argue that with respect to the source of affection, Kant must also consider yet another motivation for bringing into view the existence of things in themselves as mind-independent things. One may hold that the presence of a sensation must imply the existence of a thing in itself as a mind-independent thing, even if the latter cannot be experienced.[33] The problem mentioned earlier—that one may not call upon the categories in relation to the thing in itself—can be avoided by maintaining that talk of existence in the case of the thing in itself is different from such talk in the case of something based on the categories: in the former talk, "existence" does not represent the product of a synthesis, but rather expresses a sort of conceptual implication. The basis for this implication relation is that sensation is that matter in perception which is not caused by the self. "Thing in itself" is an expression for the fact *that* something is given to us, which we can then interpret in a certain way. Thus, the assumption of a real, not-self-caused sensation implies the concept of a thing in itself.

So far, the difference with the previous reading is that the concept of the thing in itself plays a role in our epistemology insofar as the concept of sensation does. This move seems to allow the suggestion of a kind of mind-independent existence with respect to our objects of experience.[34]

But if one argues that this concept of a thing in itself leads to the claim that the objects of our experience have a mind-independent existence, then one is faced with some problems. For instance, it is at least questionable whether such an existence assertion (of a mind-independent thing) can be grounded through a conceptual implication. If it cannot, and the assertion of the existence of a thing in itself as a mind-independent thing is based on a different thesis about affection, it is going to be hard to justify this thesis in a Kantian framework. Thus, the reading presented earlier seems to me to be more convincing.

Let us, though, concentrate on the potential of the alternative reading just outlined for a critique of Berkeley. To all appearances, this reading contains a stronger objection against Berkeley. For with this reading, not only is a mind- or subject-independent existence allowed for, it is (against Berkeley) positively asserted. However, one should keep in mind that the former reading has an advantage in terms of argumentative strategy: as we have seen, Berkeley cannot simply reply to it that the assumption of a thing in itself is irrelevant, even for Kant's epistemology or theory of perception (cf. Berkeley, *PHK* 67). Such a response would be based on a misunderstanding: even if the thing in itself had no relevance for Kant's epistemology, the equating of existence and mind-dependence put forward by Berkeley would be unacceptable for Kant. Against the reading currently under discussion, however, Berkeley could point out the fact that the assumption of a subject-independent existence remains dispensable for the theory. He could refer back to the givenness of every representation and sensation *in the subject*, and declare any deviation from this givenness an unacceptable and unnecessary abstraction. The earlier reading is thus not weaker than the latter, but it makes a *different* objection against Berkeley: the *esse est percipi* thesis (i.e., the thesis of the subject- or mind-dependence of any being) does not contradict anything that we have to introduce in our epistemology, but it claims more than we are justified to claim.

(3) Yet another reading that can be given goes beyond the one just discussed, in that it claims that not only *that* but also *how* a sensation is given to us must be explained through the assumption of a thing in itself. Again, I will discuss this reading with respect to the question as to whether it leads to the claim that things in themselves as mind-independent things exist. This reading is of particular interest, because it allows for an additional point against Berkeley's idealism. If one were, namely, to follow this reading, one could say that Berkeley's concept of an object is unacceptable because it takes the properties of an object to be those that must be attributed to the object only on the condition of the constitution of the subject, and is thus not suited to give properties a subject-independent basis.

The reason for making the thing in itself accountable for the quality of sensation can be stated succinctly:[35] without this function of the thing in itself, we would lack the means to explain why we have a variety of sensations that are not completely chaotic. Starting only from sensations, we cannot see reality, that is, our perceivable and conceivable world, as one whose structure can be traced back exclusively to the a priori conditions of our knowledge. We must assume that matter is structured in its content, or at least capable of affecting us in various ways, which appears to us through the conditions of intuition as a world whose matter is structured. There must then be an object (matter) which affects us, and which, though it has properties not recognizable by us, nevertheless has effects upon us that are not random and can indeed be structured in our representation of the world. Because we cannot obtain this concept of an object by abstracting from our subjective conditions of the experience of objects, this cannot be understood as simply an epistemic assumption; we must give the concept of the thing in itself ontological significance.[36]

One might argue against this reading as follows: if a particular sensation were to manifest a particular affection, then the degree of a sensation could not be dependent on accidental subjective conditions, such as attentiveness, sleepiness, and so on.[37] Kant asserts, however, that sensations do depend on such conditions (*Anthropology*, AA 7 162). This argument, however, is sufficient only to challenge a direct dependence relation between particular affections and sensations as effects. The reading in question can perhaps still be defended by insisting that there must be differences in the affection if there are differences in the sensation, even at the same degree of attentiveness. After all, one can also ascribe to Kant the idea that sensations somehow differ independently of individual ability and endowment. However, this last proposal is problematic for other reasons. If it were correct, then for Kant knowledge of the thing in itself would be required—namely, at least the knowledge that it has a structured effect on us—in order for us to have any sensible concept of reality. But such knowledge seems to be out of question in the framework of Kant's philosophy. Moreover, the assertion that such an assumption is required in order to explain the variety and order of sensations can be countered by virtue of the fact that the thing in itself is a limiting concept. Its theoretically relevant opposing concepts are those of sensation and appearance. Sensations are enough to account for the contingent matter of our experience. They can differ in quality regardless of whether we, for instance, view them more or less attentively. All we can know about the sensations, though, is that they are given to us. If we say that these differences are independent of us, or even that they exist independent of the subject, we go beyond the boundaries of the possibility of knowledge. In order to give meaning to these differing sensations, to tell others about them, or to explain them, we are simply referred back to possible objects of experience.

Of course, the question arises whether there are passages where Kant brings up the thing in itself in such a way that something positive can be said of it. And if so, we must also ask whether these passages can be brought into agreement with the reading given and defended earlier, according to which the concept of the thing in itself merely expresses the idea that the grounds of an affection must be left indeterminate. Let us examine a passage from the solution to the Antinomies of Pure Reason in the *Critique of Pure Reason* (A494/B522), according to which we must refer all our possible perceptions back to the transcendental object that is to be called the intelligible cause of appearances in general. First we must notice that it is at least an open question whether we should not make a distinction between the transcendental object and the thing in itself as the source of the affection, because the transcendental object is the object we constitute by our categories and not a thing that affects us. But even if one identifies the transcendental object with the thing in itself, this does not justify the previous reading of the thing in itself. True, this passage stands in tension with the reading discussed earlier, which says that the thing in itself is accountable exclusively for the *that* of our sensations. However, even if such an objection could legitimately be raised against the interpretation discussed earlier, that would not mean that the assumption of the existence of a thing in itself can be founded on the argument that the thing in itself is to be taken to be responsible for the quality of our sensations. Rather, it may be argued that if we do ascribe something to the thing in itself, then we do not ascribe it to the thing in itself as an existing object about which we know something, but rather to the thing in itself as something that we think of as the cause of appearances or as the source of the affection in us. Kant's conception of the thing in itself is thus well suited to a rejection of the *esse est percipi* principle. Within Kant's position, this rejection does not lead to a contradiction because Kant makes a distinction between the sensation and the form of intuition. The source of the affection that brings about our sensation can be thought of as something subject-independent.

In examining the various readings of Kant's doctrine about things in themselves, the following result arose: only on the variant (3) of the thing in itself thesis, which takes the thing in itself to be the ground for the *how* of sensation, can it be said that the properties of objects have a real, but to us unrecognizable, basis. Only in this case, moreover, are we justified in connecting the idea of "subject-independent existence" directly with the concept of the object. Not so on the reading of the thing in itself that I defended (1). According to this reading, we cannot (at least, strictly speaking) say of objects that they exist independently of a subject or even that "subject-independence" can be attributed to them in a definite sense. According to this interpretation, rather, this is precisely what is common to Kant and Berkeley: the denial of the (subject-independent) thing in itself as a component of a philosophical theory of knowledge. And this is what makes the defense of the representation of objectivity against Berkeley so important for Kant's philosophy. Note that this does not entail that Kant should be classified as a problematic idealist with respect to the thing in itself. A problematic idealist would take the existence of the thing in itself as a doubtful hypothesis. Kant, on the contrary, uses the concept of the thing in itself as a limiting concept; we cannot determine the source of the affection in us. To introduce the thing in itself as a limiting concept is possible for Kant because he also entertains a concept of an object of outer sense which does not need any reference to things in themselves. Kant classifies Berkeley as a *dogmatic* idealist because Berkeley does not merely *doubt* the existence of things (which would make him a *problematic* idealist like Descartes), but rather he denies their existence. *What* it is that Berkeley denies is an issue whose importance for Kant can hardly be overestimated: whether it is the existence of things outside us that he rejects, i.e., the existence of matter, or whether it is the existence of subject-independent entities. If it is the first, then his denial is nonsense. If it is the second, then caution is required in answering his claim. Certainly the denial is to be rejected. Dogmatic idealism claims something that it cannot claim. However, the claim cannot be answered by opposing a positive knowledge claim about the existence of subject-independent entities. Rather, the answer, for Kant, consists in the critique of the boundaries of our cognition.

Let me now come back to the question I started with. Is Kant justified in claiming that there is an essential difference between Berkeley's and his own philosophy? Because both Kant and Berkeley deny that the objects we perceive and cognize are things in themselves, it is all too common to reject Kant's claim that there is any essential difference between their positions. My claim in this essay has been that this is the wrong way to look at the contrast between Kant and Berkeley. The overwhelming difference between their views concerns their respective conceptions of truth and of objects. In other words, we should not seek the opposition between Kant and Berkeley in Kant's notion of the thing in itself, but in what I have called Kant's conception of objectivity.[38]

CHAPTER 8

Berkeley and Kant

Kenneth P. Winkler

I HAVE TO BEGIN by confessing that before being invited to the conference on which this volume is based, I had never thought seriously about Kant's response to Berkeley. And when, with the help of Dina Emundts and others, I looked closely at the passages in which Kant's response to Berkeley unfolds, I experienced a strange succession of feelings. The first was that Kant's comments on Berkeley are dismayingly off the mark. Kant himself condemned the "historian of philosophy" who "has [philosophers] talking utter nonsense,"[1] and at first it seemed to me that Kant was engaged in just that sort of hatchet job. But my second reaction—one that has lasted for quite a while now—was that Kant's response to Berkeley is very interesting, and although fair only up to a point, in many respects profoundly right. Kant directs our attention to aspects of Berkeley's thinking of which many of Berkeley's readers have lost sight.[2] This essay is, in large part, an attempt to motivate and defend that second (and so far final) reaction. I will be reviewing several passages, from both editions of the *Critique* and from the *Prolegomena*, in which Berkeley's idealism is analyzed and criticized, and in doing so I will be employing two main strategies. First, I will follow Kant in placing Berkeley, and his own response to Berkeley, against an ancient background. I will suggest that Kant saw his struggle with Berkeley as a reenactment of something very much like Plato's Battle of Gods and Giants. Second, I will explore Dina Emundts's observation that the Refutation of Idealism does not apply to Berkeley. Insofar as she is making a claim about Kant's professed intentions, Emundts is unquestionably correct. But I do think the Refutation brings interesting features of Berkeley's view to light, and that there are indications Kant was aware of this. In closing I comment briefly on what Emundts calls the "subject-independent existence" of the thing in itself,[3] and on the bearing of the distinction between primary and secondary qualities on the objectivity or externality of body.

BERKELEY'S AVAILABILITY TO KANT

Colin M. Turbayne and G. J. Mattey have shown that at least three of Berkeley's books were available to Kant (that is, published before the first edition of the *Critique*, in languages Kant was able to read): the *Three Dialogues between Hylas and Philonous*, in a 1756 German translation of the 1750 French translation of the first (1713) or second (1725) English edition; *De Motu*, published (but not, it seems, very widely distributed) in Latin in 1721; and *Siris*, translated into French in 1745 (and, in what Geoffrey Keynes describes as its medical parts, into German that same year).[4] A new German translation of the *Dialogues* appeared in 1781, in a volume included in Kant's library.[5] Neither the *Critique* nor the *Prolegomena* mentions any of these books by name, but *Siris* comes up briefly in Herder's notes on Kant's lectures, dated 1762–1764.[6] A passage in the *Prolegomena* (§13, *AA* 4 293), which I will discuss at length, may echo the *Three Dialogues* (*Bk Works* 2 244), but it may also reverberate Christian Garve's echoing of the *Dialogues* in his 1782 review of the *Critique*.[7]

For the most part, I will confine my quotations from Berkeley to the three books we know Kant could have read that defend immaterialism (the *Dialogues, Siris*) or some of its distinctive consequences (*De Motu*). But I should say at the outset that I differ from every writer on Kant's relationship to Berkeley known to me in believing, on grounds having nothing to do with that relationship, that the doctrines of *Siris* (1744) are by and large consistent with those of Berkeley's *Principles* (1710) and *Dialogues*. The early works differ markedly from the later one in their manner of presentation—the *Principles* and *Dialogues* confident, argumentative, and deliberately modern; *Siris* tentative, allusive, and almost nostalgically backward-looking—but in substance I believe they are the same. Some of my reasons for thinking this will emerge as we proceed.

KANT ON BERKELEY: AN OVERVIEW

Before looking closely at the passages that interest me most, I want to provide them with a context: four moments in Kant's relationship to Berkeley, between 1781 and 1787.

The first moment is the publication of the first edition of the *Critique*. Here, in a version of the fourth Paralogism omitted from the second edition, idealism is at first defined so as to exclude Berkeley. Idealism is the doctrine that "the existence of all objects of the outer senses is doubtful" (A367). Kant cautions that "by an **idealist**, . . . one must understand not someone who denies the existence of external objects of sense, but rather someone who only does not admit that it is cognized through immediate perception and infers from this that we can never be fully certain of their reality from any possible experience" (A368–69). He calls this *empirical* idealism, and traces it to the (transcendental realist) assumption that space is given in itself, independently of our sensibility.

> After [the transcendental realist] has falsely presupposed about objects of the senses that if they are to exist they must have their existence in themselves even apart from sense, he finds that from his point of view all our representations of sense are insufficient to make their reality certain. (A369)

After making his case against empirical idealism—a case that has struck many readers as markedly phenomenalist or Berkeleyan—Kant goes on to distinguish the *dogmatic* idealist, who denies the existence of matter, from the *skeptical* idealist, who merely deems it incapable of proof (A377). "The former," he writes,

> can be so only because he believes he can find contradictions in the possibility of a matter in general, and just now we are not dealing with that. The following section on dialectical inferences, which represents reason in its internal conflict regarding the concepts belonging to the possibility of the connection of experience, will also help us out of this difficulty. (A377)

The skeptical idealist is praised as "a benefactor to human reason, since he requires us to open our eyes well even in the smallest steps of common experience, and not immediately to take for a well-earned possession what we perhaps obtain only surreptitiously" (A377–78). The objections of the skeptical idealist force us, moreover, to acknowledge "the ideality of all appearances, which we have already established in the Transcendental Aesthetic independently of these consequences, which we could not then have foreseen" (A378–79).

Colin M. Turbayne speaks of "Kant's promise, in the first edition of the *Critique*, to deal with Berkeley's doctrine, and his failure to do so" (Turbayne 1955, p. 243). Indeed, Turbayne adds, "he did not even try." I am not persuaded of this.[8] Kant does not promise to deal with *Berkeley*, after all, but with supposed "contradictions in the possibility of a matter in general." And Kant does deal with this, in the Second Antinomy. The proof of the thesis shows that matter is made up of indivisible simple parts. The proof of the antithesis shows that matter is, instead, infinitely divisible. Kant observes that "on the presupposition that appearances, or a world of sense comprehending all of them within itself, are things in themselves," both proofs are "well grounded" (A507/B535). This suggests that we can use the Second Antinomy to construct a dilemmatic argument for transcendental idealism, modeled on one Kant himself constructs on the basis of the First Antinomy. Here is Kant:

> If the world is a whole existing in itself, then it is either finite or infinite. Now the first as well as the second alternative is false (according to the

proof offered above for the antithesis on the one side and the thesis on the other).

Thus it is also false that the world (the sum total of all appearances) is a whole existing in itself. (A506–7/B534–35)

Here is the construction modeled on the Second Antinomy:

If matter exists in itself, then it is either (in itself) finitely divisible or (in itself) infinitely divisible.

Now the first as well as the second alternative is false (according to the proof offered above for the antithesis on the one side and the thesis on the other).

Thus it is also false that matter exists in itself.

The argument Kant attributes to the dogmatic idealist is subtly but crucially different, because it denies that matter exists at all:

If matter exists, then it is either in itself finitely divisible or in itself infinitely divisible.

Now the first as well as the second alternative is false.

Thus it is also false that matter exists.

This is not an argument Berkeley actually makes. But the form of the argument had already been made familiar by Pierre Bayle, and Berkeley accepts the conclusion even if Bayle does not. Berkeley presents elements of the argument in the *Principles* (*PHK* 123–31) and alludes to these elements in both *De Motu* 57 (*Bk Works* 4 46–47, where they are, interestingly in view of some of Kant's other remarks on Berkeley, actually directed against space) and the *Dialogues* (*Bk Works* 2 258).

Kant's response to the dogmatic idealist's argument is to deny the first premise, if matter is interpreted as appearance:

Hence I will have to say: the multiplicity of parts in a given appearance is in itself neither finite nor infinite, because appearance is nothing existing in itself. (A505/B533)

By distinguishing between appearances and things in themselves, the transcendental idealist takes the wind out of the dogmatic idealist's sails.

The second moment is the Göttingen (or "Garve-Feder") review of the first edition (Garve 2004, the published version of a review originally drafted by Garve and edited by Johann Feder; for Garve's unedited review see Garve 2000), which spurred Kant, in the *Prolegomena* and the second edition of the *Critique*, to distinguish his views more aggressively from those of Berkeley. The review complains that according to the *Critique*,

[s]pace and time themselves are nothing real outside us, are not relations either, nor concepts we've abstracted, but are subjective laws of

our faculty of representation, forms of sensations, subjective conditions of sensory intuition. Upon these concepts of sensations as mere modifications of our self (upon which Berkeley also mainly built his idealism), of space, and of time, rests the one foundation pillar of the Kantian system. (Garve 2004, p. 202)

It concludes as follows:

If, accepting the most extreme thing the idealist wishes to assert, everything about which we can know and say anything, everything, is only representation and law of thought; if the representations in us, modified and ordered according to certain laws, are just what we call objects and world—to what end, then, the conflict with this commonly accepted language? *To what end* and *whence* the idealistic distinction? (Ibid., pp. 206–7)

The closing question (like a great deal else in this review) is not entirely clear; "the idealistic distinction" could be the distinction between two idealisms, transcendental and empirical, or the distinction between representations and objects that transcendental idealism insists upon. But the general point is clear enough. Why all the fuss? Why not, the review asks, be a plain-talking Berkeleyan?

The third moment is the appearance of the *Prolegomena*. Kant explains that

[i]dealism consists in the claim that there are none other than thinking beings; the other things that we believe we perceive in intuition are only representations in thinking beings, to which in fact no object existing outside these beings corresponds. I say in opposition: There are things given to us as objects of our senses existing outside us, yet we know nothing of them as they may be in themselves, but are acquainted only with their appearances, that is, with the representations that they produce in us because they affect our senses. Accordingly, I by all means avow that there are bodies outside us, that is, things which, though completely unknown to us as to what they may be in themselves, we know through the representations which their influence on our sensibility provides for us, and to which we give the name of a body—which word therefore merely signifies the appearance of this object that is unknown to us but is nonetheless real. Can this be called idealism? It is the very opposite of it. (*Prolegomena*, §13 Rem.1, *AA* 4 288–89)

Kant points out it has long been recognized that "without detracting from the actual existence of outer things," we can say that many of their predicates "belong not to these things in themselves, but only to their appearances and have no existence of their own outside our representation" (*AA* 4 289). Familiar examples are warmth, color, and taste. Kant says he includes "among mere appearances" not only these but also the primary qualities, yet he cannot be called an idealist "simply because [he finds] that . . . *all of the properties that make up the intuition of a body* belong merely to its appearances." After all, "the existence of the thing that appears is not thereby nullified, as with real idealism, but it is only shown that through the senses we cannot cognize it at all as it is in itself" (*AA* 4 289).

From this it follows, Kant claims, that he does not demote the sensible world into illusion. In fact, his doctrine alone secures "the application to actual objects" of the truths that "mathematics expounds a priori" (*Prolegomena*, §13, Rem.3, *AA* 4 292). He warns against confusing his transcendental idealism with

> the empirical idealism of *Descartes* . . . or with the mystical and vision-ary idealism of *Berkeley* (against which, along with other similar fanta-sies, our *Critique*, on the contrary, contains the proper antidote). For what I called idealism did not concern the existence of things (the doubting of which, however, properly constitutes idealism according to the received meaning), for it never came into my mind to doubt that, but only the sensory representation of things, to which space and time above all belong; and about these last, hence in general about all *ap-pearances*, I have only shown: that they are not things (but mere ways of representing), nor are they determinations that belong to things in themselves. (*AA* 4 293)

Finally, in an appendix responding specifically to the published review, Kant writes that

> the thesis of all genuine idealists, from the Eleatic School up to Bishop Berkeley, is contained in this formula: "All cognition through the senses and experience is nothing but sheer illusion, and there is truth only in the ideas of pure understanding and reason." (*Prolegomena*, appendix, *AA* 4 374)

His own idealism is governed, he explains, by a different principle: "All cognition of things out of mere pure understanding or pure reason is noth-ing but sheer illusion, and there is truth only in experience."

How did the reviewer end up seeing "genuine idealism" in Kant's *Cri-tique*? It was, Kant suggests, because space, time, and the things contained in them are conceived in the *Critique* not as "things (or properties of things) in themselves," but as belonging instead "to the appearances of such things." "Thus far," Kant writes, "I am of one creed with the previ-ous idealists." But, he continues, "these idealists, and among them espe-cially Berkeley, viewed space as a merely empirical representation," rather than as something that can be cognized a priori because it "inheres" in us as a form of sensibility (*AA* 4 374–75). Since "truth rests upon universal and necessary laws as its criteria, for *Berkeley* experience could have no criteria of truth, because its appearances (according to him) had nothing underlying them a priori; from which it then followed that experience is nothing but sheer illusion" (*AA* 4 375). Kant's own idealism is "therefore of a wholly peculiar kind, namely such that it overturns ordinary idealism." He suggests that it be called *critical* idealism, "to distinguish it from the dogmatic idealism of *Berkeley* and the skeptical idealism of *Descartes*" (*AA* 4 375).

The fourth and final moment is the publication of the second edition of the *Critique*, where Berkeley is now mentioned by name. In an addition to the Transcendental Aesthetic—intended to forestall the kind of objection made by Garve-Feder—Kant denies that his objects are illusions. That objects are illusions, he explains, follows only from the viewpoint he opposes:

> For if one regards space and time as properties that, as far as their possibility is concerned, must be encountered in things in themselves, and reflects on the absurdities in which one then becomes entangled, because two infinite things that are neither substances nor anything really inhering in substances must nevertheless be something existing, indeed the necessary condition for the existence of all things, which also remain even if all existing things are removed; then one cannot well blame the good Berkeley if he demotes bodies to mere illusion. (B70–71)

Kant does not actually say that *Berkeley* argues in this fashion: he claims only that we cannot fault Berkeley if we take space to be a property of things in themselves, because we will then be on our way to downgrading bodies just as Berkeley does.

The second mention of Berkeley in the second edition of the *Critique* comes in the Refutation of Idealism. Kant writes that

> [i]dealism (I mean **material** idealism) is the theory that declares the existence of objects in space outside us either to be merely doubtful and **indemonstrable** or to be false and **impossible**. The **former** is the **problematic** idealism of Descartes, which declares only one empirical assertion (*assertio*), namely **I am**, to be indubitable; the **latter** is the **dogmatic** idealism of Berkeley, who declares space, together with all the things to which it is attached as an inseparable condition, to be something that is impossible in itself, and who therefore also declares things in space to be merely imaginary. Dogmatic idealism is unavoidable if one regards space as a property that is to pertain to the things in themselves;

for then it, along with everything for which it serves as a condition, is a non-entity. The ground for this idealism, however, has been undercut by us in the Transcendental Aesthetic. (B274)

Problematic idealism is then praised, as it had been in the first-edition Paralogisms. Insofar as it allows "no decisive judgment until a sufficient proof has been found," it is "rational and appropriate for a thorough philosophical manner of thought" (B275). Kant then launches the Refutation, which is intended to show that "our *inner experience*, undoubted by Descartes, is possible only under the presupposition of outer experience."

The fourth moment I have identified may include not only the second edition of the *Critique* but also the *Metaphysical Foundations of Natural Science*, published one year before the second edition in 1786. For as Michael Friedman observes, certain passages in the *Metaphysical Foundations* closely resemble some of the second-edition changes meant to differentiate Kant from Berkeley.[9] I will discuss one such passage later on, but close study of the *Metaphysical Foundations* is beyond the scope of this essay.

Two Perplexing Passages in the *Prolegomena*

Of the passages I have reviewed, the one claiming that Berkeley finds nothing but illusion in the senses, and expects truth only from pure understanding, is the most startling. As Henry E. Allison writes, "it is perhaps this passage more than any other that has given rise to the charge that Kant's criticism of Berkeley was the product of ignorance" (Allison 1973a, p. 59).[10] I think that if we place the passage against an ancient background, we can see it, instead, as the work of someone who understands Berkeley quite well.

That placement against an ancient background is appropriate is suggested by Kant himself, who speaks of the "ancient name" of idealism (*Prolegomena*, §13, Rem.3, *AA* 4 293) and indicts Berkeley as a distant accomplice of Parmenides. These are, I think, powerful indications that Kant is viewing idealism in terms first set out by Plato in the *Sophist*:[11]

> STRANGER: What we shall see is something like a battle of gods and giants going on between them over their quarrel about reality.
> THEAETETUS: How so?
> STRANGER: One party is trying to drag everything down to earth out of heaven and the unseen, literally grasping rocks and trees in their hands, for they lay hold upon every stock and stone and strenuously affirm that real existence belongs only to that which can be handled and offers resistance to the touch. They define reality as

> the same thing as body, and as soon as one of the opposite party
> asserts that anything without a body is real, they are utterly con-
> temptuous and will not listen to another word.
>
> THEAETETUS: The people you describe are certainly a formidable
> crew. I have met quite a number of them before now.
>
> STRANGER: Yes, and accordingly their adversaries are very wary in
> defending their position somewhere in the heights of the unseen,
> maintaining with all their force that true reality consists in certain
> intelligible and bodiless forms. In the clash of argument they shat-
> ter and pulverize those bodies which their opponents wield, and
> what those others alleged to be true reality they call, not real being,
> but a sort of moving process of becoming. On this issue an intermi-
> nable battle is always going on between the two camps. (246 a–c,
> as translated in Cornford 1957, p. 230)

The division Plato lays down in this passage is related in various
ways to the more familiar division our teaching and scholarship sometimes enforces, and sometimes questions, between rationalists and empiricists, but it is importantly different from it. The distinction between rationalists and empiricists is post-Kantian; the distinction between Gods and
Giants (or idealists and materialists, as Cornford 1957 [p. 228], for example, speaks of it) is pre-Kantian. From the middle of the seventeenth century to the end of the eighteenth, English-speaking academic philosophers, among them Ralph Cudworth and Francis Hutcheson, standardly
viewed the history of philosophy largely as the history of *ancient* philosophy, or as the reenactment of ancient quarrels and the pursuit (or corrup-
tion) of ancient possibilities. One sees this even in Hume, who despite his
outbursts against the excesses of ancient philosophy (throughout *THN*
1.4.3, for example), uses ancient labels to mark out the various forms of
skepticism, and claims ancient origins for both sides of a central modern
debate about the source of our moral distinctions.[12] As I explain in the
following section, German scholarship in the history of philosophy was,
at least by the middle of the eighteenth century, significantly more ambitious than British scholarship, but there are reasons for thinking that
Kant, at least, viewed the history of philosophy much as his English-
speaking counterparts did.

Consider, to begin with, the evidence of his *Jäsche Logic*. This handbook is described by Gottlob Benjamin Jäsche, the editor commissioned
by Kant to prepare it, as "a *compendious manual*" of Kant's public lectures (*Logic, AA* 9 3). Like Hutcheson's *Logicae Compendium*, which in
this respect resembled many handbooks of instruction in logic published
in Britain in the seventeenth and early eighteenth centuries, Kant's manual
offers a "*Short sketch of a history of philosophy*" that begins—and very

nearly ends—with the ancient Greeks (*AA* 9 33–37). At least three pages (in the Akademie edition) are dedicated to their achievements. "When philosophy . . . passed from the Greeks to the Romans," the reader is then told, "it was not extended; for the Romans always remained just disciples" (*AA* 9 31). A single paragraph covers the Arabs (who followed Aristotle "in a slavish way"), the scholastics (who merely "*elucidated*" Aristotle), and the "*eclectics*" of the Reformation, who at last "acknowledged no school, but . . . instead sought the truth and accepted it where they found it" (*AA* 9 31). (Hutcheson [1756, p. 10] speaks similarly of "eclectics" who are not "pledged to any master," but embrace truth wherever they find it.[13]) Four paragraphs celebrate the advances of modern times, praising in particular Bacon, Descartes, Leibniz, Locke, and Newton (*AA* 9 31–32). (Wolff is mentioned, but not praised.) "Philosophy owes its improvements in modern times *partly* to the greater study of nature," Kant explains, and "*partly* to the combination of mathematics with natural science" (*AA* 9 31). Hutcheson (1756, p. 11) speaks more vaguely of modern thinkers who have, "not without great glory," "pointed out" or even "entered upon" new paths, but his very similar list of heroic reformers includes Descartes, Kepler, Galileo, and Newton (all in "physics") and Locke (in "logic and metaphysics").

Modern figures are obviously not ignored in these brief histories, but the space devoted to the Greek tradition, and to minor figures such as Plato's successors as head of the Academy, seems, to our eyes, disproportionately large. To the extent that the *Critique of Pure Reason* conveys a conception of its subject's history, it too is dominated by ancient patterns and concerns. In the closing chapter of the *Critique*, Kant presents, "in cursory outline," the three most significant points of disagreement in the history of philosophy (A853/B881). All but the third are characterized by means of ancient models. This first is actually Kant's account of Plato's Battle of Gods and Giants:

> **With regard to the object** of all our rational cognitions, some were merely **sensual philosophers**, others merely **intellectual philosophers**. Epicurus can be called the foremost philosopher of sensibility, and Plato that of the intellectual. This difference of schools, however, as subtle as it is, had already begun in the earliest times, and has long preserved itself without interruption. Those of the first school asserted that reality is in the objects of the senses alone, and that everything else is imagination; those of the second school, on the contrary, said that in the senses there is nothing but semblance [*Schein*], and that only the understanding cognizes that which is true. The former, however, did not on this account dispute the reality of the concepts of the understanding, but they were only **logical** for them, though they were **mystical** for the oth-

ers. The former admitted **intellectual concepts,** but accepted only **sensible objects.** The latter demanded that the true objects be merely **intelligible,** and asserted an **intuition** through pure understanding not accompanied by any senses, which in their opinion only confused it. (A853–54/B881–82)

As Kant's account shows, Plato's division was very durable. Its influence reached far beyond the eighteenth century. Here, for example, is Ralph Waldo Emerson, in his essay "The Transcendentalist," the text of a lecture first delivered late in 1841 or very early in the following year:

> As thinkers, mankind have ever been divided into two sects, Materialists and Idealists; the first class founding on experience, the second on consciousness; the first class beginning to think from the data of the senses, the second class perceive that the senses are not final, and say, The senses give us representations of things, but what are the things themselves, they cannot tell. The materialist insists on facts, on history, on the force of circumstances and the animal wants of man; the idealist on the power of Thought and of Will, on inspiration, on miracle, on individual culture. These two modes of thinking are both natural, but the idealist contends that his way of thinking is in higher nature. He concedes all that the other affirms, admits the impressions of sense, admits their coherency, their use and beauty, and then asks the materialist for his grounds of assurance that things are as his senses represent them. But I, he says, affirm facts not affected by the illusions of sense, facts which are of the same nature as the faculty which reports them, and not liable to doubt. (Emerson 1982, pp. 239–40)

Emerson's idealists, kin to Plato's gods, are of a "higher nature." And here, perhaps, we can begin to see why Kant was so rankled by the Garve-Feder description of his transcendental idealism as "higher" (Garve 2004, p. 201). Here is Kant's reaction:

> On no account *higher.* High towers and the metaphysically-great men that resemble them, around both of which there is usually much wind, are not for me. My place is the fertile *bathos* of experience. (*Prolegomena*, appendix, *AA* 4 374)

Kant's place is not on windblown Olympus with the gods, where Berkeley aspires to be, but nearer to the giants, on the firm and fertile earth.

It was entirely plausible for Kant to put Berkeley on the side of the gods, especially in view of *Siris* and *De Motu.* There is a clear sense in which bodies, as represented there, have diminished reality, and the features that diminish their reality are precisely those emphasized throughout Berkeley's writings, early and late. Berkeley's bodies (that is, ideas of sense) are caught in what the Stranger calls "a sort of moving process of becoming." They are fleeting, dependent beings. They have no permanence and no substance. Kant speaks of the "visionary purpose" of genuine idealism—a purpose he detects in its commitment to intuition by the intellect (*Prolegomena*, appendix, *AA* 4 375). Berkeley lays great emphasis on such intuition, not only in *Siris* and *De Motu*, but even in the *Three Dialogues*, as rendered, for example, by Eschenbach. Long passages distinguishing ideas and notions were added to the third edition of the *Dialogues* in 1734, as they were to the second edition of the *Principles* in 1732, but even in the first two editions of the *Dialogues*, one or another of which was the basis of the French translation Eschenbach relied on, Philonous says that he has, properly speaking, no idea of God or any other spirit ("these being active"), claiming instead to have a "*notion* . . . of God, . . . obtained by reflecting on my own soul[,] heightening its powers and removing its imperfections" (*Bk Works* 2 229–30; emphasis mine). Eschenbach follows Berkeley's terminology very faithfully: "idea" is rendered as *Gedanke* or *Vorstellung*; "notion" as *Begriff*.[14]

Turning now to the evidence for these interpretive claims in Berkeley's texts, we can begin with his own invocation of an ancient background, this time provided by Plato's *Theaetetus*:

> Socrates, in the *Theaetetus* of Plato, speaketh of two parties of philosophers[:] . . . the flowing philosophers who held all things to be in a perpetual flux, always generating and never existing, and those others who maintained the universe to be fixed and immovable. The difference seems to have been this, that Heraclitus, Protagoras, Empedocles, and in general those of the former sect, considered things sensible and natural; whereas Parmenides and his party considered [the universe] not as the sensible but as the intelligible world, abstracted from all sensible things. (*Siris* 348, *Bk Works* 5 157)

As the surrounding passages make clear, Berkeley thinks that the party of Parmenides has taken hold of the more important truth. "The Pythagoreans and Platonists," allies of Parmenides, had, he says, "a notion of the true system of the world." They realized that "mind, soul, or spirit *truly and really exists*: that bodies exist *only in a secondary and dependent sense*: that the soul is the place of forms [sensible forms, not Platonic Forms]: that the sensible qualities are to be regarded as acts only in the cause, and as passions in us" (*Siris* 266, *Bk Works* 5 125; emphasis mine). Our curiosity might at first be provoked by the sensible world, "but if, proceeding still in . . . analysis and inquiry, [we ascend] from the sensible into the intellectual world," we will change our system, and "perceive that what [we] took for substances and causes are but fleeting shadows" (*Siris* 295, *Bk Works* 5 137).

What is at bottom the same view is conveyed in the closing sections of
De Motu. There are, Berkeley explains as the work begins, "two supreme
classes of things, body and soul." They are "plainly different from one
another, and quite heterogeneous." We know the first by sense, and the
second by "a certain internal consciousness" (*De Motu* 21, *Bk Works* 4
36). The closing sections tell us which class is superior. In physics, the
study of body, things are not explained by assigning their "truly active
and incorporeal cause[s]" (*De Motu* 69, *Bk Works* 4 50–51). It is only in
first philosophy or metaphysics that "we are concerned with incorporeal
things, with causes, truth, and the existence of things" (*De Motu* 71, *Bk
Works* 4 51). He concludes:

> Only by meditation and reasoning can truly active causes be rescued
> from the surrounding darkness and be to some extent known. To deal
> with them is the business of first philosophy or metaphysics. Allot to
> each science its own province; assign its bounds; accurately distinguish
> the principles and objects belonging to each. Thus it will be possible to
> treat them with greater ease and clarity. (*De Motu* 72, *Bk Works* 4 52)

My suggestion is that the diminished reality of bodies—in particular,
their impermanence and insubstantiality—justifies Kant in placing Berkeley with the gods. To that extent, Kant's illusionist portrayal of Berkeley
is a fair one. I have also suggested that in placing Berkeley with the gods,
Kant is placing himself closer to the giants. Thus, Kant finds permanence
and substantiality just where Berkeley fails to find it, in our experience of
body, as he indicates in the following second-edition passage from
the Postulates:

> In order to give something that **persists** in intuition, corresponding to
> the concept of **substance** (and thereby to establish the objective reality
> of this concept) we need an intuition **in space** (of matter), since space
> alone persistently determines [*weil der Raum allein beharrlich be-
> stimmt ist*], while time, however, and thus everything that is in inner
> sense, constantly flows. (B291)

This is a passage anticipated, as Michael Friedman observes, in the *Metaphysical Foundations of Natural Science*, where Kant writes that[15]

> general metaphysics in all instances where it requires examples (intu-
> itions) in order to prove meaning for its pure concepts of the under-
> standing, must always take them from the general doctrine of body,
> and thus from the form and principles of outer intuition; and, if these
> are not exhibited completely, it gropes uncertainly and unsteadily
> among mere meaningless concepts. (*MFNS, AA* 4 478)

As I have so far described it, the diminished reality of bodies is a meta-physical matter. But Berkeley recognizes that it had, at least for Plato, epistemological bearing. He writes in *Siris* that

> there is, according to Plato, properly no knowledge, but only opinion, concerning things sensible and perishing; not because they are naturally abstruse and involved in darkness, but because their nature and existence is uncertain, ever fleeting and changing, or rather, because they do not in strict truth exist at all, being always generating or *in fieri*, that is, in a perpetual flux, without anything stable or permanent in them to constitute an object of real science. The Pythagoreans and Platonics distinguish between τὸ γενόμενου and τὸ ὄυ, that which is ever generated and that which exists. Sensible things and corporeal forms are perpetually producing and perishing, appearing and disappearing, never resting in one state, but always in motion and change; and therefore, in effect, not one being but a succession of beings: while τὸ ὄυ is understood to be somewhat of an abstract or spiritual nature, and the proper object of intellectual knowledge. Therefore, as there can be no knowledge of things flowing and unstable, the opinion of Protagoras and Theaetetus that sense was science is absurd. (*Siris* 304, *Bk Works* 5 140–41)

In another passage, though, Berkeley finds Plato more optimistic. He takes him to be suggesting that even though it is absurd to say that sense *is* science, it is not absurd—indeed, it is importantly correct—to say that sense provides reason with something it can work up into science:

> As understanding perceiveth not, that is, doth not hear, or see, or feel, so sense knoweth not: and although the mind may use both sense and fancy, as means whereby to arrive at knowledge, yet sense, or soul as far forth as sensitive, knoweth nothing. For, as it is rightly observed in the *Theaetetus* of Plato, science consists not in the passive perceptions, but in the reasoning upon them. (*Siris* 305, *Bk Works* 5 141)

Berkeley develops Plato's suggestion in section 253:

> We know a thing when we understand it; and we understand it when we can interpret or tell what it signifies. Strictly, the sense knows nothing. We perceive indeed sounds by hearing, and characters by sight; but we are not therefore said to understand them. After the same manner, the phenomena of nature are alike visible to all; but all have not alike learned the connexion of natural things; or understand what they signify, or know how to vaticinate by them. There is no question, saith Socrates *in Theaeteto*, concerning that which is agreeable to each person, but concerning what will in time to come be agreeable, of which

all men are not equally judges. He who foreknoweth what will be in every kind is the wisest. According to Socrates, you and the cook may judge of a dish on the table equally well, but while the dish is making, the cook can better foretell what will ensue from this or that manner of composing it. Nor is this manner of reasoning confined only to morals or politics, but extends also to natural science. (*Bk Works* 5 120)

This is the very model of science or natural knowledge advocated in both *De Motu* and the *Dialogues*. "The physicist," Berkeley writes in *De Motu*, "studies the series or successions of sensible things, noting by what laws they are connected, and in what order, what precedes as cause, and what follows as effect"—his point being that systematic precedence and following is all there is to what he calls "second corporeal causes" (71, *Bk Works* 4 51). As Philonous tells Hylas, "the more a man knows of the connexion of ideas, the more he is said to know of the nature of things" (*Bk Works* 2 245):

What therefore if our ideas are variable; what if our senses are not in all circumstances affected with the same appearances? It will not thence follow, they are not to be trusted, or that they are inconsistent either with themselves or anything else, except it be with your preconceived notion of (I know not what) one single, unchanged, unperceivable, real nature, marked by each name. (*Bk Works* 2 245)

Is not that opposition to all science whatsoever, that phrensy of the ancient and modern *sceptics*, built on the same foundation? Or can you produce so much as one argument against the reality of corporeal things, or in behalf of that avowed utter ignorance of their natures, which doth not suppose their reality to consist in an external absolute existence? Upon this supposition indeed, the objections from the change of colours in a pigeon's neck, or the appearances of a broken oar in water, must be allowed to have weight. But those and the like objections vanish, if we do not maintain the being of absolute external originals, but place the reality of things in ideas, fleeting indeed, and changeable; however not changed at random, but according to the fixed order of Nature. For herein consists that constancy and truth of things, which secures all the concerns of life, and distinguishes that which is *real* from the irregular visions of the fancy. (*Bk Works* 2 258)

Ideas may have diminished reality when compared to spirits, but this is no threat to their "reality" in the sense at work here (and in our ordinary, day-to-day lives).

Even in the *Principles*, immaterialism is presented as the only way of reconciling knowledge of nature with the perceptual relativity emphasized by the skeptics and by Plato before them. "It must be confessed that this method of arguing [from relativity] doth not so much prove that there is no extension or colour in an outward object, as that we do not know *by sense* which is the true extension or colour of the object," Berkeley writes at *Principles* 15 (emphasis mine). How then do we know it? By *reason*.[16] The opening sections of the introduction to the *Principles*, which introduce not just Berkeley's attack on abstraction but the entire book as well, are a sustained defense of reason or understanding against a skeptically inspired loss of confidence, and an affirmation of the authority of reason (a "superior principle," as it is called in *Principles* 1) over sense and instinct.[17]

The epistemology of body reaching from the *Principles* to *Siris* is a constructive one, and Kant doubtless makes less of it than he should have. But even if Berkeley thinks Plato was wrong to conclude that we can have no knowledge of the world of sense, he does not doubt for a moment that our knowledge of that world is of vastly diminished importance. "What deserves the *first* place in our studies," he writes in the culminating section of the *Principles* (where the emphasis so far is my own), "is the consideration of *God*, and our *duty*" (*PHK* 154). The being of a God is not just a truth but a "great truth" (*PHK* 149, 155). Although Berkeley does not speak here in terms of illusion, he does think that our passionate engagement in the whirl of sensory experience distracts us from things of more importance. "Intent on business or pleasure," we fall short of achieving "that conviction and evidence of the being of a God, which might be expected in reasonable creatures" (*PHK* 156). Vivid awareness of God's proximity is displaced by an opinion, "strangely [that is, very much] prevailing," that "all sensible objects have an existence natural or real, distinct from their being perceived by the understanding" (*PHK* 4). It is not altogether misleading to say that according to the author of the *Principles*, we are prone to a kind of illusion: an illusion of importance—of the suitability of sensible things as ultimate objects of concern.[18] The effect is a kind of practical atheism, against which our intuition of spirit, joined to reason, is the most effective antidote.

I want to turn now to another passage from the *Prolegomena*, a passage that may be even more perplexing than the last. The passage may include an echo of Berkeley's *Dialogues*:

> If it is an in fact reprehensible idealism to transform actual things (not appearances) into mere representations, with what name shall we christen that idealism which, conversely, makes mere representations into things? I think it could be called *dreaming* idealism, to distinguish it from the preceding, which may be called *visionary* idealism, both of which were to have been held off by my formerly so-called transcendental, or better, *critical* idealism. (*AA* 4 293)

Gary Hatfield also detects an echo of the *Dialogues* here (or the resounding of an echo first sounded in the Göttingen review), but not of the passage that comes to me.[19] The clearest echo, to my ear, is of Philonous's first speech in the following exchange from the Third Dialogue:

> PHILONOUS: You mistake me. I am not for changing things into ideas, but rather ideas into things; since those immediate objects of perception, which according to you, are only appearances of things, I take to be the real things themselves.
>
> HYLAS: Things! you may pretend what you please; but it is certain, you leave us nothing but the empty forms of things, the outside only which strikes the senses.
>
> PHILONOUS: What you call the empty forms and outside of things, seems to me the very things themselves. Nor are they empty or incomplete otherwise, than upon your supposition, that matter is an essential part of all corporeal things. We both therefore agree in this, that we perceive only sensible forms: but herein we differ, you will have them to be empty appearances, I real beings. In short you do not trust your senses, I do. (*Bk Works* 2 244–45)

Intriguingly, there seems to be an echo of the same passage in the unedited version of Garve's review:

> When the representations in us, modified, ordered, and connected according to this or that law, are completely identical with what we call objects, of which we speak and with all which our intelligence and science concerns ourselves, then it is completely irrelevant *whether we reduce things to ideas, or transform ideas into things*. The latter is more in accord with our nature—and is so much a part of our language that we cannot express ourselves in any other way. (Garve 2000, p. 77, emphasis mine)

Now there is no sign, in Kant's letter to Garve of August 7, 1783, that he had seen the original review before completing the *Prolegomena* (*Corr.*, pp. 98–105). The similarities could all be coincidental, but one possible explanation is that the very pregnant passage from Berkeley's *Dialogues* was widely known and available for recall. This is, at any rate, a conjecture I propose to investigate.

I have found very little on "*dreaming* idealism [*traümenden Idealismus*]" in the secondary literature. Kemp Smith (1950, p. 307) suggests that dreaming idealism is Cartesian idealism; Turbayne (perhaps following Kemp Smith) suggests the same (Turbayne 1955, p. 227), as does Hatfield in the introduction to his edition of the *Prolegomena* (p. xxix).[20] But it seems to me that this cannot be right:[21] in all other mentions of Descartes' idealism, Kant is careful to hold things and representations apart. In fact, he does exactly that earlier in the very paragraph in which the puzzling passage occurs. There he explains that Descartes' idealism "was only a problem, whose insolubility left everyone free, in *Descartes'* opinion, to deny the existence of the corporeal world, since the problem could never be answered satisfactorily" (*Prolegomena*, §13, Rem.3, *AA* 4 293). Mattey points out that dreaming idealism is "put forward as the converse of Berkeley's mystical attempt to change things into mere representations" (Mattey 1983, p. 171), but if it represents a distinct form of idealism, why does it seem to surface only here? And why does Kant claim that this newly visible idealistic target *was* to have been "held off" by transcendental idealism, suggesting that he had it in sight all along?

The most economical answer to these questions is that *"dreaming* idealism" is the one offered to Kant by the published Göttingen review, which concludes as follows:

> If, accepting the most extreme thing the idealist wishes to assert, everything about which we can know and say anything, everything, is only representation and law of thought; if the representations in us, modified and ordered according to certain laws, are just what we call objects and world—to what end, then, the conflict with commonly accepted language? *To what end* and *whence* the idealistic distinction? (Garve 2004, p. 207)

These lines offended Kant: "[A]fter having introduced me to the witty proposition that constant illusion is truth," he says, the review concludes with "the harsh, though paternal reprimand: To what end, then, the conflict with accepted language, to what end, and whence, the idealistic distinction?" (*Prolegomena*, appendix, *AA* 4 376). When he writes in the perplexing passage of the "reprehensible" idealism that turns things (considered not as appearances but as things in themselves) into representations, he is suggesting that *he* has shown it to be reprehensible. When he goes on to ask what we should make of an idealism that runs in the reverse direction, he is asking whether the reviewer's recommendation is any better off. (The answer is no.)

Now I think it is very likely that *Garve* is alluding to Berkeley at the end of his unedited review.[22] It is less clear that Kant is doing so: his reading of the published review, filtered through his interpretation of Berkeley as someone who transforms actual things (not appearances) into mere representations, may have left him, almost by accident, with a sentence sounding very much like the one that Garve had not yet published—the not-yet-published sentence sounding, in turn, very much like Philonous, and probably *not* by accident. Still, I would like to pursue the possibility that

Kant is responding (through the reviewer) to Berkeley. It is instructive to see how much interpretive weight the passage from the *Prolegomena* can bear; even if Kant is not responding to Berkeley firsthand, he is responding to someone who is representing Berkeley, as Kant has reason to believe. (Note that if dreaming idealism *was* to have been held off by transcendental idealism, then it must have been held off by Kant's points against Berkeley, rather than by his points against Descartes.)

Viewed as a response to Berkeley, the passage depicts him, correctly I think, as making a double movement. First comes the Parmenidean movement, a negative or destructive phase: we start with actual things (and note that they are, according to the passage, "not appearances," but things in themselves) and reduce them to representations. This is the movement to which Kant responds in the Antinomies, and in the material new to the B version of the Transcendental Aesthetic. It is a visionary idealism because it demotes or degrades bodies: compared to the persisting spiritual substances we know by intuition, they have diminished reality. The second movement is Heraclitean, or positive and constructive (and this, of course, is the phase being emphasized by Philonous in the final speech of the exchange I have quoted): we start with representations (the representations we are left with by the first movement) and find actual things among them, or construct actual things out of them. It is a dreaming idealism because, as Dina Emundts brings out so well, the bonds of Berkeleyan coherence are too weak to give rise to an objective world. (The second movement is not a visionary idealism, because the contrast with intellectual intuition, and with the undiminished reality it discloses, is no longer in play.) Transcendental idealism is opposed to both movements. It opposes the Parmenidean movement by distinguishing between appearances and things in themselves. As a result, Berkeley's negative arguments can no longer be made. And it opposes the Heraclitean movement by supplying the demanding "criteria of truth" that neither Berkeley nor the Göttingen reviewer can provide (*Prolegomena*, appendix, *AA* 4 375).

If my reading of this perplexing passage is along the right lines, Kant may understand Berkeley very well. He may see the constructive phase in Berkeley's thinking as well as the destructive one. If he does, his accusations of illusionism will be doubly justified: the destructive phase is illusionist because it leaves us with bodies of diminished reality; and the constructive phase is illusionist because it fails to establish that fugitive ideas can nonetheless be real.

Throughout this section of my essay, the intellectual intuition under discussion has not been what Kant, in an unpublished fragment on Berkeley, calls "the mystical [intuition] of God's ideas," but the intuition of spirit itself.[23] In my view, the human intuition of divine ideas plays no real role in Berkeley's thinking, not even in *Siris*. Kant at times may have thought it did, but I will now try to show that Kant had plenty to object to in Berkeley's appeals to intuition, even when they were confined to spirit itself.

THE GERMAN BACKGROUND

I suggested earlier that the German writing on the history of philosophy was, at least by the middle of the eighteenth century, more ambitious than British writing. I now want to explain what I meant by that, and to ask whether the German background of the *Critique* and the *Prolegomena* further assists us in making Kant's response to Berkeley comprehensible.

Alongside the textbook tradition typified by Hutcheson's *Logicae Compendium* stood the most ambitious early-modern English-language historical survey, Thomas Stanley's *History of Philosophy: Containing the Lives, Opinions, Actions, and Discourses of the Philosophers of Every Sect*, published over several years in three volumes, beginning with volume 1 in 1655. In the second edition of 1687, the thirteen parts in the three original volumes are brought together with a fourteenth, *The History of the Chaldaick Philosophy*, first published in 1662, forming an impressively large volume of about a thousand pages. Stanley's *History* is more closely detailed than anything one could expect to find in a conspectus designed for students, but it is even more decidedly ancient in its coverage: parts 1 through 13 are devoted entirely to ancient philosophy, and part 14 to its pre-Greek Eastern origins.

The book that so enriched German writing on the history of philosophy was Johann Jakob Brucker's *Historia critica philosophiae a mundi incunabulis ad nostram usque aetatem deducta*. It differs from Stanley's history in several striking ways. Large a book as Stanley's is, Brucker's colossal survey dwarfs it: the six volumes in its second edition, published in 1766–1767, average more than a thousand pages apiece. Brucker's book differs from Stanley's no less dramatically in coverage. In the first edition of 1742–1744, volume 1 covers Greek philosophy (concluding with the skeptics and the influence of Greek philosophy beyond Greek borders, supplemented by an appendix on philosophy in Asia and America), volume 3 covers medieval philosophy (concluding with scholasticism), and volume 2 the period in between. Volume 4, which is divided into two parts, bound separately, picks up the narrative with the "revival of letters" (see Brucker 1766–1767, vol. 1, p. 43, where a summary table is provided). Part 1 (which became volume 4 in the second edition) covers the philosophers Brucker classifies as "revivalists": skeptics, scripturalists, theosophists, and various enemies of philosophy. Part 2 (which became volume 5 in the second edition) covers the innovators of the sixteenth and seventeenth centuries, with separate chapters on Bruno, Bacon, Campanella, Hobbes, Descartes, Leibniz, and Thomasius, and succeeding chapters on developments in various subfields, among them natural philosophy (climaxing with Newton), metaphysics and pneumatology (where Spinoza is discussed), moral philosophy, and political philosophy. Volume 6, present only in the second edition, is an appendix of "additions, observations, changes, illustrations, and supplements" to all five of the volumes preceding it.

Despite its massive size and broad coverage of modern developments, Brucker's history resembles Kant's brief sketch in two respects: it sides wholeheartedly with the innovators, and it continues to rely on ancient terms of description. Kant speaks of "eclectics" in a way that may baffle present-day ears. Brucker speaks in the same way, anticipating Kant (and, very likely, influencing him) by fixing the label of "eclectic" even on the innovators. The label is derived from the Greek *eklektikos*, used by Diogenes Laertius for philosophers who refuse to align themselves with any one sect, preferring to "select" (*eklegein*), from among competing sects, the best material on offer.[24] In using the label for modern innovators who are nonsectarian partisans of truth, Brucker and Kant stretch its ancient meaning, but not beyond recognition.

For the impact of Brucker on a reader familiar with Stanley, we have the testimony of William Enfield (1741–1797), a Presbyterian preacher and tutor whose admiration for Brucker's history led him to produce not a full translation into English, but "a faithful *representation* of its general meaning and spirit"—a distillation of "the substance of this great, and . . . valuable work" (Enfield 1791, vol. 1 pp. v, vi). Enfield's book, published in two volumes, was entitled *The History of Philosophy, from the Earliest Times to the Beginning of the Present Century; Drawn up from Brucker's Historia critica philosophiae*. Enfield writes of Stanley that his plan "extended little further than to the history of the Grecian sects of philosophy; and . . . in executing it, he has rather performed the office of an industrious compiler, than that of a judicious critic" (Enfield 1791, vol. 1, p. iv). Enfield was preparing lectures when he first discovered Brucker, and the encounter left him a changed man. Regretting that "so valuable a fund of information should be accessible only to those, who had learning, leisure, and perseverance sufficient, to read in Latin six closely printed quarto volumes, containing on the average about a thousand pages each," he was inspired to assume the labor of his "representation." One great lesson of that labor is that the sectarian divisions marking earlier philosophy are inconsistent with a mature eclecticism (Enfield 1791, vol. 2, p. 512). Following Brucker, he explains that the "true eclectic method" calls for "rejecting prejudices of every kind, subjecting the opinions of former philosophers to the strict scrutiny of reason, and admitting no conclusions but such as may be clearly deduced from principles founded on the nature of things, and discovered by experience" (Enfield 1791, vol. 1, p. xxvii).

Kant was certainly familiar with Brucker (there is a specific reference to his history in the *Critique*, A316/B372), and in view of Brucker's breadth of coverage, it would be reasonable to seek, in his fifth or sixth volume, a treatment of Berkeley that could have shaped Kant's assessment of immaterialism. Here, though, our hopes are disappointed: Brucker's book pretty much ends with the seventeenth century, though volume 6 contains a "Mantissa" on Wolff, and volumes 5 and 6 now and then take note of developments since 1700. There is only one reference to Berkeley in Brucker, and it has nothing to do with immaterialism: it is a brief footnote in Brucker's account of Newton, acknowledging the attack on the calculus in Berkeley's *Analyst* (Brucker 1766–1767, vol. 5, pp. 644–45).

There is, however, something else in Brucker that may be almost as useful: a highly critical reading of Plato that is, in many respects, close to the reading of Plato that seems to have prepared the way for Kant's reception of Berkeley. Kant—whose reference to Brucker in the *Critique of Pure Reason* is precisely to Brucker's treatment of Plato[25]—says in the *Prolegomena* that "genuine idealism always has a visionary purpose and can have no other." It "was already to be seen with Plato," he explains, that genuine idealism "always inferred, from our cognitions a priori . . . to another sort of intuition (namely, intellectual) than that of the senses" (*Prolegomena*, appendix, AA 4 375). Reliance on intellectual intuition, he later wrote, made "*Plato the academic*" into "the father of all enthusiasm *by way of philosophy*" (*Tone*, AA 8 398). Brucker also takes Plato to task for his enthusiasm (Brucker 1766–1767, vol. 1, p. 664).[26] He quotes with approval an ancient complaint, which he attributes to Xenophon: instead of following the "sober [*sobrias*]" example of Socrates, Plato "reduced himself to an arrogant [*superciliosus*] teacher of wisdom" (Brucker 1766–1767, vol. 1, p. 664; or in Enfield's more colorful rendering, "a haughty professor of wisdom" [Enfield 1791, vol. 1, p. 218]).[27] Plato's turn away from Socrates was, in Brucker's view, in part a turn toward Pythagoras, who is himself condemned for enthusiasm later in the book (Brucker, 1766–1767, vol. 1, p. 1043).[28]

Brucker's interpretation of Plato was shaped by his reading of the *Didaskalikos*, or *Handbook of Platonism*, by Alcinous, a "Middle Platonist" of the second or third century c.e. That he wrote the *Handbook* and went by the name of "Alcinous" are perhaps the only things known about him, but his book deeply influenced the early-modern reception of Plato and Platonism. Stanley's *History* translates the book in full (it had already been translated into Latin three times in the fifteenth and sixteenth centuries),[29] and Brucker (followed by Enfield) borrows from it extensively.

Alcinous presents Platonism as a set of dogmas or defining commitments.[30] One of those commitments is to the diminished reality of body; another is to intellectual intuition as the only way of achieving knowledge of what is most real. Brucker, for example, follows Alcinous in defining philosophy (as seen by Plato) as the turning of the soul away from the body, toward the things that "truly are" and are perceptible only by the "intellect" (Brucker, 1766–1767, vol. 1, p. 670; see also Stanley 1687b, p. 180; Enfield 1791, vol. 1, p. 221; and the ultimate source in Alcinous 1995, p. 3). "In the strict sense," Brucker adds, wisdom for Plato is the knowledge of things "comprehended by the intellect"—things that "truly are" and concern, in particular, "God and the soul apart from the body" (Brucker, 1766–1767, vol. 1, p. 670, followed by Enfield 1791, vol. 1, p. 221–22).

Brucker, as I said, does not touch on Berkeley's immaterialism, but long before Kant, Berkeley had already been classified by several German readers—Christoph Pfaff, Wolff, and Eschenbach—as an idealist who denies the reality of body.[31] Kant's response to Berkeley *may* have been based on a reading of Berkeley in translation, or on conversations with his English-speaking friends.[32] But it may also have been based on an interpretation of Plato he found in Brucker, joined to a way of reading Berkeley already prevailing in Germany.

THE REFUTATION OF IDEALISM

My aim so far has been to contextualize, and to some extent support, Kant's reading of Berkeley as an ally of Plato and the gods. I turn now to the Refutation of Idealism in the second edition of the *Critique*. I believe there are signs that Kant understood the Refutation party as a blow against Berkeley and his party.

As Dina Emundts points out (see her essay in this volume, chapter 7), the Refutation of Idealism is not explicitly directed against Berkeley. But she also says that it "*cannot* be directed against Berkeley because it presupposes a philosophical notion of matter existing outside of us and which can affect us—and this is not an assumption that Berkeley shares" (emphasis mine).[33] Michael Ayers makes the same point. He writes that the Refutation "assumes the *concept* of a material permanent undergoing change, a concept which is not impugned by Descartes' scepticism but which Berkeley finds unintelligible and self-contradictory" (Ayers 1982, p. 68).[34] I am not entirely convinced that Emundts and Ayers are correct.

Note to begin with that if, as Henry Allison suggests (2004, p. 300), the Refutation of Idealism "presupposes" transcendental idealism, the concept of a material permanent presupposed by the Refutation (agreeing for the moment that some such concept *is* presupposed) will not be the transcendentally realist concept impugned by Berkeley. Note too that even if transcendental idealism is not presupposed in the proof itself, the Refutation follows the Transcendental Aesthetic, in which the grounds of Berkeley's idealism are, as Kant says, "undercut" (B274). Why, then, could the Refutation not be used to make a further point against Berkeley, who does after all say that even if the possibility of matter is granted, its existence cannot be proved (*PHK* 18–20)?

To some extent, the questions I am raising have to do with the burden of proof. In order for Kant's argument to be directed against Berkeley, is it enough for him to turn aside Berkeley's reasons for thinking that a "material permanent undergoing change" is impossible, or does he have to show, positively, that it is possible? It is, in fact, not at all easy to decide what role the possibility of matter is meant to play in the argument. The Refutation makes an existence claim: "the mere, but empirically determined, consciousness of my own existence proves the existence of objects in space outside me," and it sets out to force that claim on anyone who accepts the *cogito*. Now it may seem fair to demand of an existence proof that it furnish us, as it begins, with a definition of the thing whose existence it sets out to prove, and that it clear that definition of any imputation of contradictoriness or unintelligibility. Kant's proof certainly makes no such attempt. But does it have to? The proof contends that consciousness of my own existence in time is "possible only through the existence of actual things which I perceive outside me." Perhaps the proof can show us that persisting things do exist in space outside me, and therefore that the concept of such things *must* be both coherent and intelligible, even if it does not tell us why. A proof of this sort would be, in a certain sense, nonconstructive: it would establish the existence of a thing without "constructing" the concept under which it falls. It might be compared to a proof by reductio ad absurdum, which shows us *that* something is the case without explaining *why* or *how*. Arnauld and Nicole were among many who found indirect proofs less satisfying than their direct counterparts:

> This kind of demonstration, which shows that something is such-and-such not by its principles but by some absurdity that would follow if it were otherwise, is very common in Euclid. It is obvious, however, that it can convince the mind but it cannot enlighten it, which ought to be the main result of science. For the mind is not satisfied unless it knows not only that something is, but why it is, which is certainly not learned by a proof by reduction to absurdity. (Arnauld and Nicole 1996, p. 255)

But how, exactly, would conviction, even conviction short of enlighten-ment, be achieved? One way would be through the elimination of alterna-tives. Kant considers two: the consciousness of my own existence in time might presuppose a permanent in me, rather than a permanent in space; or it might presuppose no more than intellectual intuition can provide. Kant argues against both possibilities. Now *perhaps* it can be said that if someone has challenged the intelligibility of a concept, that challenge has to be met before the elimination of other alternatives can even be consid-ered. (The rough idea would be that conceptual objections take priority over objections of other kinds.) But I do not see why this has to be so, and if it does not have to be, the Refutation can challenge even Berkeley. If it is not the existence of matter that makes possible the consciousness of our own existence of time, what is it? Berkeley can, of course, shrug his shoulders, but it is not unfair to ask him to do more: to show that Kant's enumeration of alternatives is incomplete, that one of the two alter-natives Kant considers is dismissed too hastily, or that the consciousness of our own existence in time is simply unconditioned.

One objection to my suggestion is that Kant has his own suspicions about indirect proof, and he gives voice to those suspicions in terms strongly reminiscent of Arnauld and Nicole. According to one of several rules meant to "discipline" pure reason in its proof of transcendental truths,

[p]roofs must never be **apagogic** but always **ostensive**. The direct or ostensive proof is, in all kinds of cognition, that which is combined with the conviction of truth and simultaneously with insight into its sources; the apagogic proof, on the contrary, can produce certainty, to be sure, but never comprehensibility of the truth in regard to its connec-tion with the grounds of its possibility. Hence the latter are more of an emergency aid than a procedure which satisfies all the aims of reason. Yet they have an advantage in self-evidence over the direct proofs in this: that a contradiction always carries with it more clarity of represen-tation than the best connection, and thereby more closely approaches the intuitiveness of a demonstration. (A789–90/B817–18)

Kant goes on to examine the role of apagogic proofs in various domains, with the aim of showing that even when its goal is mere "certainty" (Ar-nauld and Nicole's "conviction"), its success depends on conditions that "the transcendental attempts of pure reason" cannot take for granted (A792/B820). "Here it simply cannot be allowed that assertions of syn-thetic propositions be justified by the refutation of their opposites" (A792/B820). But I do not think this caution necessarily applies to the Refutation of Idealism, whose conclusion—the existence of objects in space outside me—is not, like the proofs of pure reason under discussion in this part of the *Critique* (A782/B810), a synthetic a priori truth. It rests on what Kant repeatedly describes as an experience: the consciousness of my own existence in time.

I am therefore inclined to agree with Beiser (2002, p. 107) that the Refutation can at least be read as a refutation of Berkeley's idealism, and with Guyer and Wood (in their translation of the *Critique*, p. 72) that the Refutation can be viewed as "Kant's ultimate attempt" to distinguish his idealism from Berkeley's.[35] Perhaps Emundts at least would not in the end disagree. Even if the Refutation does not refute Berkeley, she writes, "one can turn to [it] if one wants to show that Kant's philosophy is able to make room for a concept of objectivity that can integrate the idea of real material things outside us" (see chapter 7 in this volume).[36]

I am interested in the possibility of bringing the Refutation to bear on Berkeley because it seems to me that his influence is present in it. He may not be Kant's target there, but there are indications that he has not been entirely forgotten. As we saw earlier, Berkeley claims to discover, by purely intellectual means, that he is a persisting substance. Kant repudiates this discovery, both in passages we have reviewed and in his lectures:

> If I maintain thinking beings of which I have intellectual intuition, then that is mystical. But intuition is only sensuous, for only the senses intuit. (Met.L₁, AA 28 207)

> Plato maintained mystical intellectual things. . . . Plato says we have concepts that are not borrowed from the senses, e.g., of a primordial being, etc. which we obtained through a higher intuition. (*Met.Mongrovius*, AA 29 760)

So when Kant includes the following caution in the Refutation, I think it is reasonable to suppose that Berkeley is among those he has in mind:

> The consciousness of myself in the representation *I* is no intuition at all, but a merely **intellectual** representation of the self-activity of a thinking subject. And hence this I does not have the least predicate of intuition that, as **persistent**, might serve as the correlate for time-determination in inner sense, as, say, **impenetrability** in matter, as **empirical** intuition, does. (B278; see also B157–58, A82, B407, and B416–18)

Earlier I quoted Kant's claim that only outer sense can provide an intuition corresponding to the concept of substance. He makes a similar claim about alteration in space with respect to causality, and about spatial co-presence with respect to community (B291–92).[37] These claims are then explicitly connected to the argument of the Refutation. As the section concludes, Kant writes that it can just as easily be established that the possibility of things as **magnitudes**, and thus the objective reality of the category of magnitude, can also be exhibited only in outer intuition, and that by means of that alone can it subsequently also be applied to inner sense. (B293)

He then observes that these remarks are of great importance, "not only in order to confirm our preceding refutation of idealism, but even more, when we come to talk of **self-cognition** from mere inner consciousness and the determinations of our nature without the assistance of outer empirical intuitions, to indicate to us the limits of the possibility of such a cognition" (B293–94). When he returns to the topic in the B version of the Paralogisms, Kant offers what seems to be a brief rehearsal of the Refutation of Idealism in which intellectual intuition is explicitly repudiated:[38]

> From all this one sees that rational psychology has its origin in a mere misunderstanding. The unity of consciousness, which grounds the categories, is here taken for an intuition of the subject as an object, and the category of substance is applied to it. But this unity is only the unity of **thinking**, through which no object is given; and thus the category of substance, which always presupposes a given **intuition**, cannot be applied to it, and hence this subject cannot be cognized at all. Thus the subject of the categories cannot, by thinking them, obtain a concept of itself as an object of the categories; for in order to think them, it must take its pure self-consciousness, which is just what is to be explained, as its ground. Likewise, the subject, in which the representation of time originally has its ground, cannot thereby determine its own existence in time, and if the latter cannot be, then the former as a determination of its self (as a thinking being in general) through categories can also not take place. (B421–22)

Ayers thinks that the Refutation actually makes two assumptions that Berkeley rejects. The second is the conception of the self "as a substance with objectively determined duration, its state being objectively determined in time." Given Berkeley's "official" view of time, he does not "allow" the self objective duration or "see its states as objectively determined in time—any more than he sees sensible bodies as objectively determined in space" (Ayers 1982, pp. 68–69).[39] Now Kant says in the *Prolegomena* that Berkeley gave no attention to time (*AA* 4 375; it is usually inferred from this, for example by Kemp Smith, that Kant was unfamiliar with Berkeley's *Principles*, the only one of his works in which time is discussed with any thoroughness). My point is not that Kant viewed Berkeley as unentitled to claims of empirical self-consciousness, but that he understood Berkeley to believe that the concepts of persistence and substance could be achieved (and given objective reality) by intellectual intuition alone. The Refutation, though it may be directed against Descartes, seems to me to strike one more blow against the claims made on behalf of intuition by Berkeley and the party of the gods.

The Thing in Itself

I have proposed that Kant saw in Berkeley what Brucker saw in Plato: a failure of humility. Kant's perception of Berkeley's failure is made vivid by the contrast between Emundt's cautious account of the thing in itself and Berkeley's confident affirmation of God as the cause of our sensations.

Emundts derives a notion of things in themselves, "ontologically" understood, from the givenness of sensation and from the fact that the source of sensation not only can but must be left indeterminate (see her essay in this volume, chapter 7). I am uncertain I fully understand why it must be, but perhaps she is reasoning as follows. If we are properly cautious, and build no more into givenness than it actually contains, we cannot, for example, say that the source that affects us lies in space. If it lies in space, then it must be an object of possible experience, but if we suppose that it is, we have ventured beyond what the sheer givenness of sensation can license. "To avoid this difficulty," Emundts writes, "we must introduce the thought of the thing in itself." Although we have no right to say that things in themselves exist, we have to allow for the possibility of a "subject-independent" source of affection.

I have two thoughts about this route to a notion of things in themselves, if I have understood Emundts correctly. First, the route will be a challenging one to follow. We are cautioned by Emundts not to go beyond sheer givenness. But it seems that in moving to the thought of a source, no matter how indeterminate, we are moving beyond it. The reply implicit in Emundt's account is that we are not: to think of sensations as given is to conceive of a source that gives it; to conceive of ourselves as affected is to conceive of a source that affects us. If we attribute no more to the source than this, we will have formed a properly austere notion of things in themselves. But then I am still left with a question, which Emundts herself raises. What keeps us from confidently asserting that the source of our affection exists, as Kant himself so often seems to do? Emundts writes that it is "at least questionable whether such an existence assertion (of a mind-independent thing) can be grounded through a conceptual implication," but here we seem to be dealing not merely with the *concept* of givenness, which contains, Emundts seems to agree, the concept of a source, but with the *fact* of givenness. Why is it that this fact, together with the conceptual implication, cannot support a confident existence claim?

My second thought concerns Berkeley. Emundts admits that the source of our affection could be either our own selves or another mind. This means that the source could also be Berkeley's God. Such sources do not seem incompatible with the principle that *esse* is *percipi*, suitably qualified, because as Berkeley himself indicates in his notebooks, his immaterialist formula should really be completed as follows:

> Existere is percipi or percipere. (*Philosophical Commentaries* 429, Bk Works 1 53)[40]

Berkeley can still be faulted for making "positive knowledge claims about the source of our affection" (Emundts, chapter 7, this volume), but if the thing in itself is, as Emundts says, "an expression for the fact *that* something is given to us," then Kant's own affirmation of the thing in itself is consistent with the particular interpretation Berkeley places on it, though not with Berkeley's dogmatic commitment to that interpretation. Berkeley should have said,

> *esse* is *percipi* or *affectere*,

but he is never so austere. He makes his closest approach to austerity in the following passage from the *Dialogues*:

> PHILONOUS: My meaning is only that the mind comprehends or perceives [bodies] and that it is affected from without, or by some being distinct from itself. (*Bk Works* 2 250)

Even this is not austere enough, because it rules out self-affection.

As Emundts says, the thing in itself is a limiting concept, and Berkeley, confidently intuiting spirits as uniquely active, transgresses the limits it imposes. But his failure is not, I think, one of insufficient objectivity, as Emundts seems to suggest, but of insufficient humility—the failure Brucker detected in Plato, and Kant subsequently found in Berkeley.

PRIMARY AND SECONDARY QUALITIES

When he condemned Berkeley's idealism as mystical or visionary, Kant's complaint was that it too readily detached certain conceptions from their conditions in sense. I want to conclude by suggesting that Berkeley's quarrel with Kantian conceptions of the primary qualities would, ironically, be roughly similar.

According to Emundts's very helpful account, primary qualities are (in Kant's view) ascribed to objects in relation to sensibility in general, whereas secondary qualities are ascribed to objects in relation to this or that sense. "The explanation of colors," for example, "cannot," as she writes, "proceed without reference to the particular organization of the sense of sight" (chapter 7, this volume). Impenetrability, by contrast, can be explained without reference to any particular sense, "by ascribing a force to the body which, whenever the body is penetrated, has an effect on the penetrating body." (This is not an explanation without reference to sensibility in general, because the explanation is cast in spatial and temporal terms.) The criterion, then, is whether we can devise an "empirical explanation" of the quality "without recourse to the constitution of a particular sense." If we can, the quality is primary; if we cannot, the quality is secondary.

The criterion Emundts attributes to Kant has a number of definite advantages. For one thing, to apply it we need not decide beforehand whether secondary qualities are ideas or sensations in the mind, or, instead, powers to cause ideas or sensations. (Perhaps this is why Kant does not labor over the distinction. I take it that in the passage Emundts quotes from *Critique* A70, Kant is thinking of secondary qualities in the second way. But Wilson [1999a, pp. 299–300] quotes many passages in which he adopts the first.) In either case, the quality is explained or characterized in relation to this or that sense.

Now Berkeley, as Emundts points out, though he can make a pragmatic distinction between primary qualities (considered as signs of great predictive power) and secondary qualities (considered as signs of more modest predictive power, or of predictive power more rigidly context-bound), cannot duplicate Kant's distinction, because Berkeley's explanations of qualities, primary as well as secondary, will always make reference to this or that sense. His qualities will be, as a result, more narrowly perspectival than Kant's primary qualities, and in that sense less objective.

I think all this is exactly right: Berkeley's primary qualities cannot be objective in the way Kant's are. Berkeley himself, though, would not regard this as a disadvantage, because Kant's less perspectival and allegedly more objective explanations could only be the result of illegitimate abstraction from our ideas of sense. Here, in Berkeley's view, it is Kant, not Berkeley himself, who would be left groping, "uncertainly and unsteadily," among mere concepts (*MFNS, AA* 4 478).[41]

CHAPTER 9

Kant's Humean Solution to Hume's Problem

Wayne Waxman

WHAT KANT TERMED "Hume's problem" (*Prolegomena*, AA 4 313) is a generalized version of Hume's skepticism, extending it from necessary relations between distinct existents to necessary relations between distinct determinations such as mathematical quantities, which, in its most fundamental formulation, is the question how are synthetic a priori judgments possible. Interpreters have always recognized that Kant's transcendental philosophy is directed to the solution of this problem. It is far less well appreciated, however, that the solution he offered is also based on a Humean model. In the preface to the *Prolegomena to Any Future Metaphysics*, Kant credited Hume with showing how questions about the meaning and application of concepts at the heart of age-old philosophical disputes can be resolved by tracing them to their sources as representations in the mind: "[I]f only the origin were ascertained, then everything concerning the conditions of its use and the sphere in which it can be valid would already of itself have been given" (*AA* 4 258–59). Kant recognized that Hume's concern with the mental origins of ideas was not limited to showing *how we form* such concepts as cause and effect, but, above all, how the psychological operations involved in their formation may contribute indispensable elements of their *content* as well. The importance of this "breakthrough" (*Eröffnung*) is evident. For if a concept can be shown to be bound up by content with the operations of conscious mind, then any attempt to employ it objectively in contexts in which abstraction is made from the mind and its representative constitution can have only one result: "[W]e either contradict ourselves, or talk without a meaning" (*THN* 175). If, for example, concepts of cause and effect owe even a single indispensable element of their content to the operations of conscious mind, it follows that any supposition that causes and effects exist mind-independently is not only false but also unintelligible, in the same sense that concepts of unfelt pain, joy, or hate would be. Thus did Hume open Kant's eyes to how psychological considerations could disclose inherent limitations on the scope of certain concepts that no amount of conceptual analysis is capable of revealing, particularly concepts whose unrestricted application seems a sine qua non of the very possibility of metaphysics: space and time, substance, quantity, existence, necessity, and, of course, cause and effect.

In what follows, I shall term Kant's Humean approach to metaphysical concepts *psychologism*. This psychologism, however, premises another doctrine, common to the apriorist Kant no less than to the empiricist Hume, which I shall call *sensibilism*: the thesis that no content of representation preexists its presence to consciousness in perception, whether in sensation or what Kant, Hume, and others termed, alternately, *inner sense, internal perception*, or *reflexion*: the mind's perception of its ongoing representational activity, particularly the operations whereby it synthesizes new representations from existing ones. Sensibilism contrasts not with innatism but what may be called *intellectualism*.[1] For, in relation to sensibilism, it is a subsidiary matter how intellectualists understand the contents of representation to preexist their presence to the senses in perception: innately, as Descartes and Leibniz supposed, or in the mind of God as Malebranche believed, or in some other way. What here is crucial is that, if ideas preexist the psychological operations whereby they are brought to consciousness in (clear or obscure, distinct or confused) perceptions, then *these operations are incapable of contributing anything essential to the content of these ideas and psychologism is not even so much as an option*. Thus, intellectualists relegated perceptual psychology to the margins and endeavored to explicate the content of ideas by purely analytic means to the end of formulating precise definitions.

For sensibilists like Hume, by contrast, psychology not only matters, it trumps definition. For if ideas never preexist their presence to consciousness in sensation or reflexion, nothing is capable of shedding more light on the content of our thoughts than the sense impressions from which they originate:

Complex ideas may, perhaps, be well known by definition, which is nothing but an enumeration of those parts or simple ideas, that compose them. But when we have pushed up definitions to the most simple ideas, and find still some ambiguity and obscurity; what resource are we then possessed of? By what invention can we throw light upon these ideas, and render them altogether precise and determinate to our intellectual view? Produce the impressions or original sentiments, from which the ideas are copied. These impressions are all strong and sensible. They admit not of ambiguity. They are not only placed in a full light themselves, but may throw light on their correspondent ideas, which lie in obscurity. And by this means, we may perhaps, attain a new microscope or species of optics, by which, in the moral sciences, the most minute, and most simple ideas may be so enlarged as to fall readily under our apprehension, and be equally known with the grossest and most sensible ideas, that can be the object of our enquiry. (*EHU* 7.4; also *THN* 105–6)

Hume's sensibilism is, in the first instance, a critique of traditional philo- sophical definitions whereby they are supplemented or, more usually, sup- planted, by psychological accounts tracing ideas to their originating im- pressions. But its most important consequence, so far as Kant was concerned, is to open up the possibility of psychologistically explicating concepts. For if, in providing a psychological account of the origin of a concept as a representation in our minds, we discover that the actions and/or affects whereby the representation is formed at the same time con- tribute ingredients indispensable to its *content,* then the psychologistic consequence is that the concept's *scope of application* is ipso facto limited to the experience of an appropriately constituted conscious mind in the same irreducibly subjective sense that pleasures or emotions are.

Since psychologism depends on sensibilism, the starting point for Kant's Humean response to Hume's problem must be Kant's own unique brand of sensibilism. Claims to complete originality are exceedingly rare in Kant, but he was saying nothing less than the truth when he declared that "it never occurred to anyone that the senses themselves might intuit a priori" (*Prolegomena, AA* 4 375n.). Like the proverbial flap of a butter- fly's wings in Brazil that can set off a tornado in Texas when the circum- stances requisite to exponentially amplify its force are in place, this seemingly minute divergence at the roots—Kant's addition of a single, thitherto unconsidered source of sensible representations—transforms ev- erything down the line, opening the way to an apriorist, yet still sensibilist understanding of fundamental metaphysical concepts, transcendental psychologistic limits to their application to objects, and—for Kant per- haps most important of all—the promise of a radically new conception of metaphysical freedom.

Of course, Kant faced innumerable obstacles to adapting Hume's sen- sibilist psychologism to his own anti-Humean purpose of showing that metaphysics is possible and, in the process, transforming it into a science capable of enduring without addition or revision. In what follows, we shall examine what these obstacles were and find that the endeavor to overcome them required nothing less than Kant's entire system of tran- scendental philosophy in all its complexity.

HUME'S TWOFOLD SKEPTICAL CHALLENGE

Hume's Conceptualist Doubt

Because of the prevailing epistemological focus in Hume interpretation, it is seldom appreciated that the problem he bequeathed Kant consists of two quite distinct skeptical challenges, with the conceptual taking prece- dence over the epistemic. The conceptual doubt concerns the very possi- bility of cause and effect and other concepts of fundamental importance to human understanding: failure to resolve it makes all questions as to their possible, actual, and necessary objective validity completely nugatory ("If we have really no idea of a power or efficacy in any object, or of any real connexion betwixt causes and effects, 'twill be to little purpose to prove than an efficacy is necessary in all operations," *THN* 113). Hume made the concept of cause and effect his principal focus because he deemed it so essential to the operation of human understanding that, without it, "[i]nference and reasoning concerning the operations of nature would, from that moment, be at an end; and the memory and senses remain the only canals, by which the knowledge of any real existence could possibly have access to the mind" (*EHU* 8.5; also *THN* 52–53 and 148). Attributing the cognitive and conative preeminence of the concept to its principal constituent, the idea of necessary connection, Hume consequently made this the principal focus of his inquiry.

To say that *X* is necessarily connected to *Y* as cause to effect is to say that *Y* cannot exist if *X* does not and must (cannot not) exist if *X* does. This means that, strictly speaking, enduring things are not causes because a cause cannot begin to exist without its effect ipso facto immediately coming into existence as well. In such cases, the causality of the cause is instead a state or action of a thing that, as soon as it comes into existence, immediately produces its effect. Since there may be different states or actions of the same or different things that have this effect, the cause, more precisely, is that which is common to all these states or actions. Similarly, where there are different states or actions of the same or different things that have the same cause, the effect is that which is common to them all. Thus, "[t]he same cause always produces the same effect, and the same effect never arises but from the same cause" (*THN* 117).

Now, the insight that led Kant to pronounce Hume's analysis of necessary connection the most decisive event in the history of metaphysics (*Prolegomena*, AA 4 257) is that the relation concerned in it is restricted to existents *distinct* in the sense specified by the separability principle (derived originally from Berkeley), according to which, "whatever objects are different are distinguishable, and whatever objects are distinguishable are separable by the thought and imagination . . . and whatever objects are separable are also distinguishable, and whatever objects are distinguishable are also different" (*THN* 17). This means that we cannot, for example, conceive mountains and valleys to be related as cause and effect because their necessary connection is purely conceptual, incorporated right into the ideas themselves: valleys cannot be conceived to exist in the absence of mountains and vice versa. By contrast, fire and smoke can be conceived to be so related precisely because each can be conceived to exist in the absence of the other. But there lies the rub: If to conceive cause and effect as distinct is to be able to conceive the existence of the one to be possible even in the absence of the other, but to conceive them as necessarily connected, is to be unable to conceive the existence of the effect to be possible if the cause does not exist (or the nonexistence of the effect if the cause exists), distinctness and necessary connection seem to be logically incompatible. Forced to choose, Hume opted to supplant the genuine, but seemingly impossible, concept of cause and effect—an *objectively* real necessary connection between distinct existents—with a *subjective* psychological surrogate, customary association.

In defense of this conclusion, Hume undertook to show that all the purposes of empirical reasoning are served quite satisfactorily by an idea of necessary connection that has its source in the customary association we experience in imagination: ordinary and scientific, cognitive and moral, probabilistic and certain, situational and universal. Only philosophical speculation suffers for want of the kind of objective necessary connection Hume showed human understanding to be incapable of conceiving. For only on the supposition that chains of such connections exist prior to and independently of associative imagination could we hope to extend our knowledge of matters of fact and real existence beyond anything experience is capable of disclosing. Lacking even the ability to conceive such connections, however, Hume concluded that such speculation is not merely deficient but vacuous, useful for nothing except kindling:

> When we run over libraries, persuaded of these principles, what havoc must we make? If we take in our hand any volume; of divinity or school metaphysics, for instance; let us ask, Does it contain any abstract reasoning concerning quantity or number? No. Does it contain any experimental reasoning concerning matter of fact and existence? No. Commit it then to the flames: for it can contain nothing but sophistry and illusion. (*EHU* 12.30)

Thus, to rescue metaphysics from such a fate, Kant's first Humean challenge was to demonstrate the possibility of a genuine concept of cause and effect, that is, the conceivability of a necessary connection between distinct existents.[2]

Hume's Epistemological Doubt

Interest in the epistemological side of Hume's consideration of cause and effect tends to focus on his analysis of causal inference, particularly the foundations of inductive reason. Far more pertinent to what Kant understood as "Hume's problem," however, is Hume's treatment of the putatively a priori (necessarily and universally valid) principle of cause and effect: the "general maxim in philosophy, that *whatever begins to exist, must have a cause of its existence*" (*THN* 56). So confident were Hume's predecessors, Empiricist no less than Rationalist, that this principle is known with such certainty that one cannot help but be sensible that its negation is a contradiction—something unintelligible rather than merely false—that they deemed it "one of those maxims, which tho' they may be deny'd with the lips, 'tis impossible for men in their hearts really to doubt of" (*THN* 56). But Hume did not share their confidence. (1) On the ground that the only candidates for terms of causal relations are distinct ideas, he argued that the possibility of conceiving "an object to be non-existent this moment, and existent the next, without conjoining to it the distinct idea of a cause or productive principle," is implicit in the very idea of such a relation. (2) Given that ideas, however complex, resolved into constituents that are nothing but direct copies of impressions of sensation or reflexion, Hume inferred from this conceptual possibility the possibility that something may really begin to exist without a cause. And (3) since all that is requisite to prove that the negation of the general causal maxim is intelligible is to show that their separation in reality implies no contradiction or absurdity, he concluded that "'tis impossible to demonstrate the necessity of a cause."

Of course, Hume was well aware that this conclusion does not imply that the general causal maxim is false, doubtful, or even dubitable. Quite the contrary, in endeavoring to show "Why a Cause Is Always Necessary" (title of *THN* I/iii/§3), Hume's purpose was not to challenge the certainty of the maxim, but only the consensus assumption regarding the *nature* of its certainty. Hume broke new ground by showing that the certainty of the maxim is not intuitive—not a purely intellectual affair of ideas alone—but rather something else entirely, involving the sensate, feeling part of our minds no less essentially than the conceiving part. Being a committed empiricist in his sensibilism, however, he saw no alternative but to trace its certainty to "observation and experience" (*THN* 58), and ultimately to the very same source to which he traced ideas of necessary connection: customary association.[3] Thus, Kant's second Humean challenge was to show that even if conceptual considerations alone are insufficient to establish the a priori objective validity of the general causal maxim, there is another source of a priori certainty, involving pure sensibility, sufficient to assure us that empirical objects are, in the strictest sense, *necessarily* and *universally* subject to causal laws.

KANT'S TWOFOLD EXTENSION OF THE SCOPE OF HUME'S SKEPTICAL CHALLENGE

Kant's first step in taking up Hume's twofold skeptical challenge was to determine whether its scope of the problem of necessary connections between distinct existents extends more widely, and reaches more deeply, than Hume himself appreciated. One area in which Kant thought it did is that of necessary relations between distinct *determinations*, considered independently of matters of fact and real existence. Quantitative relations of equality and inequality are a case in point: although abstract and indifferent to matters of fact and real existence, they are *distinct* in the same sense essential to Hume's skeptical reasoning regarding cause and effect. In equating 7 and 5 with 12, for example, I am conjoining quantitative determinations in a necessary relation that are as distinct as fire and smoke: I can think 12 without conceiving 5 and 7 just as easily as I can think 12 without conceiving the difference between 31 and 19, the square root of 144, or the cube root of 1,728. So, if the necessary relation between these determinations does not lie in the objects conceived in it, whence does it derive? In Kant's view, all the reasons that led Hume to look to experience and customary association to explicate causal understanding apply with equal force to mathematical understanding. In particular, a genuine concept of necessary relations of equality, or any other mathematical (and, one may add, mathematical logical) relation between determinations presupposed as distinct, seems as paradoxical, and impossible to form, as Hume showed the concept of a necessary connection between distinct existents to be.

Kant also extended the second, epistemological strand of Humean skepticism to mathematics, when he noted that even if necessary relations between distinct determinations were conceivable, the distinctness of the determinations already of itself implies that there can be no contradiction in the negation of even so elementary an equation as $2 + 2 = 4$. Yet, if the concepts alone do not suffice to establish the necessity of the relations, then, since necessity can only be cognized a priori, how is it possible to cognize the necessity of a relation of quantitative determinations at all? Either there must be some further, nonconceptual, yet still a priori basis that makes such cognition possible, or we must grant that mathematical truth can never have any but an empirical justification:

> In the end, however, we must admit that this science, so highly prized on account of its apodeictic certainty, must, despite all its pride, succumb to an *empiricism in principles* for the same reasons that *Hume* put custom in place of the objective necessity in the concept of cause, and must moderate its bold claims commanding assent (*Beistimmung*) a priori, expecting consent (*Beifall*) in the universal validity of its propositions from the favor of observers who, as witnesses, would not refuse to admit they had always perceived what the geometer proposes (*vorträgt*) as principles, and would allow that it may be expected to continue so in the future, though, to be sure, not necessarily. (*CPrR, AA 5* 52; also *Prolegomena, AA 4* 273)

Kant extended Hume's twofold skeptical challenge in a different direction as well, arguing that metaphysics depends, across the board, on concepts similar to cause and effect, in which necessary relations between distinct determinations or existents are to be conceived. Kant did not explain why Hume's doubt applies to other concepts in anything like the detail he did in the case of cause and effect, but presumably the reason is the same: where determinations or existents are presupposed as distinct, and so conceivable independently of one another, how can any relation between them be conceived as a necessary relation? To say they are distinct is to say that it is always possible to conceive one to exist or be posited in the absence of the other and never contradictory to suppose a relation between them not to hold, whereas to say they are necessarily related is to say that it is impossible for one to exist or to be posited except in relation to the other, and so, in effect, to deny their distinctness. Accordingly, just as with cause and effect and quantity, something has to give in the cases of subsistence/inherence, reciprocal interaction (community), quality (reality, negation, limitation), modality (possibility, existence, and necessity), and all other concepts of necessary relations. As before, it is the necessity of the relations stipulated in these concepts. For since the distinctness (manifoldness) of the terms capable of entering into each of the relations thought by means of these concepts is as much a precondition for them as for cause and effect and quantitative equality, the implications of this distinctness must take precedence over those of any necessity ostensibly conceived in their relation. In that case, however, only two choices remain, each fatal to the conceptual pretensions of metaphysics: either we must content ourselves with the pseudo-necessity of Humean-style subjective-psychological surrogates for metaphysical concepts, or we must accept that discourse employing terms for such concepts has nothing to underwrite it in the only objects ever present to the mind—Hume's perceptions, Kant's representations—with the implication that, objectively speaking, "these words are absolutely without any meaning, when employed either in philosophical reasonings, or common life" (*EHU* 7.26).

Nor is this extension of Hume's skepticism from cause and effect and quantity to metaphysical concepts generally the end of the story. For even if we did possess concepts of substance, reciprocal causation, and so on, is there any basis for supposing they *apply* to objects a priori (necessarily and universally)? Just as Hume argued that to conceive a thing to begin to exist we have only to think it absent one moment and present the next, so that there is no contradiction—nothing unthinkable—in supposing it not to have a cause of its existence, the same may be said with respect to every other metaphysical predicate: it is neither intuitively nor demonstrably knowable that every thing that begins to exist must exist either by subsisting or inhering, must be quantifiable (e.g., have a number), must have real qualities, and so on. To be sure, just as we draw a blank when we attempt to think the negations of arithmetical and geometrical propositions, so too we are helpless when it comes to imagining a world in which metaphysical predicates did not of necessity apply to all objects as such. Yet, this only shows that such concepts are indispensable to our *thought* of objects—something the Humean skeptic is the first to concede (*Prolegomena*, AA 4 258–59). But he will then ask to be told our reason for supposing that the *objects themselves* must be just as the natures of our understandings oblige us to represent them as being. After all, if no contradiction prevents us from conceiving objects that do not conform to these necessary conditions of our thought, then it will do no good to affirm their conformity to those conditions on the ground that such conformity is requisite to the truth—even the possibility of the truth—of the a priori principles in which fundamental metaphysical concepts, or "categories," are predicated of the objects that exist prior to and independently of our thought.[4] And Kant left it in no doubt that he accepted Hume's point that there indeed is no contradiction, nothing unthinkable, in the supposition that objects of the senses might continue to appear to us even if cause and effect and all our other concepts of objective necessary relations had no application to them.[5] To be sure, the failure of these objects to conform to metaphysical predicates might very well throw everything into confusion; but that is *our* problem, a crippling handicap for our understanding (thought and cognition) of objects, but by no means a problem for sensible objects themselves. And even if it so happened that objects did conform to the categories constitutive of our thought of objects, what basis would we have for affirming the necessity and universality of their conformity? If it were due to some accident, to divine beneficence, or some other cause distinct from our minds, then the kind of a priori knowledge that would permit us to affirm that metaphysical concepts apply necessarily and universally would be beyond our reach, and the Humean skeptic would still end up the victor (B167–68).

From Kant's perspective, the upshot of these considerations is this: so long as sensibilism is restricted to empiricism and psychologism lacks a transcendental (a priori) dimension, Humean skepticism (in Kant's generalized form) is irrefutable, so that "a *universal* skepticism would have to follow from these principles" (*CPrR*, AA 5 52). Accordingly, the twofold Humean challenge confronting metaphysicians is to show, first, how necessary relations between distinct determinations or existents are conceivable—how concepts of the necessary synthetic unity of the manifold can be formed—and, second, how, on the basis of these concepts, necessary and universal cognitions of objects—synthetic a priori judgments—are possible. And to meet and overcome it, Kant adopted the quintessentially

Humean strategy of exploiting the psychologistic potential of sensibilism—only this time sensibilism with an a priori dimension added.

KANT'S RESPONSE TO THE CONCEPTUAL
PHASE OF HUME'S SKEPTICISM

Whatever philosophers today may think of Hume's skepticism or Kant's
extension of it to include mathematics as well as the concepts and principles of metaphysics, there can be no question that, for Kant, the issue
hinges on whether objects are things in themselves or mere representations:

> *Hume* was quite right to explicate the concept of cause as a deceptive
> and false delusion (*Blendwerk*) when, as is almost always done, he took
> the objects of experience to be *things in themselves*. For of things in
> themselves and their determinations we can have no insight into how,
> because something A is posited, something else B must necessarily be
> posited as well. He thus could not at all admit any such a priori cogni-
> tion of things in themselves. (*CPrR, AA 5 53*)

Since the status of appearances as mere representations is a consequence
of Kant's transcendental idealism, his ascription of transcendental realism
to Hume brings us back to the pure sensible intuitions on which that
idealism depends. However, it is important not to limit its importance to
his response to Humean skepticism to resolving the secondary, epistemological doubt regarding the *application* of the categories to objects. For
Kant's a priori sensibilism proves no less crucial to his response to the
primary, conceptual phase of Hume's skepticism: the proof of the possibility of the *categories themselves* as pure concepts of the understanding.

In the metaphysical deduction of the categories (A76–81/B102–7),
Kant set out to prove the a priori origin of the categories by demonstrating
their correlation to the logical functions of judgment (B159). Yet, as he
made clear right from the outset, without the pure manifold of a priori
sensibility of the Transcendental Aesthetic as material (*Stoff*) for thought,
such concepts would be "altogether devoid of content and completely
empty" (A76–77/B103; also A15–16/B29–30 and A55–56/B79–80). A
short while later, after introducing the notion of the pure synthesis in the
imagination of this pure manifold, Kant tells us that a pure concept of the
understanding is first *given* when pure synthesis is represented universally
(A78/B104). Since this is just to say that pure concepts of the understanding have their source in the thought (discursive-universal representation)
of the pure synthesis in imagination of the pure manifold of sense as determined conformably to each logical function of judgment, he clearly regarded the psychological operations of sensible synthesis as indispensable

to their original formation by the mind ("through the relation of the manifold to the unity of apperception there arise concepts which belong to the understanding, but can only come into being by means of the imagination in relation to sensible intuition," A124). The question is whether the sensible conditions requisite in the initial formation of these concepts also enter into their *content,* thereby restricting their application in classic Humean-psychologistic fashion.

Most interpreters, I think it fair to say, would answer this in the negative, on the ground that a construal of the content of the categories that makes the manifold of sensibility an integral part of the content falsifies Kant's conception of them as pure concepts of the *understanding.* Kant left no doubt that the categories contain no sensible content, whether pure or empirical. Indeed, it was precisely for this reason that he deemed both a Transcendental Deduction of the Categories and a transcendental schematism absolutely indispensable (A87–91/B119–24, B144, B150–52, B158–59, and A137–39/B176–78). And, to be sure, the categories no more relate to pure intuition as concepts *of* space or time than they relate to empirical intuition as concepts *of* sensible qualities or sensible objects (colors, scents, etc., or trees, stones, psyches, etc.). Consequently, it may seem that the only reasonable construal of Kant's inclusion of sensibility and imagination in his account of the origin of the categories in the metaphysical deduction is one that does not restrict their content accordingly. That is, in much the same way we should not let the concept of the sun we obtain by sight determine the content of our astronomical concept of the sun, nor include in our arithmetical concepts any of the features of the apples, oranges, or whatever handy objects were used in our first addition lessons, so too it may seem imperative not to conclude that the a priori manifold of sense and its pure synthesis in imagination enter in any essential way into the content of the categories, however vital their role in the initial acquisition of these concepts.

Nevertheless, not only the metaphysical deduction but also the whole tenor of Kant's project seem to me to point directly to the conclusion that the senses do make an essential contribution to the content of the categories. It was certainly their content Kant had in mind when he asserted that pure concepts of the understanding "consist simply in the representation of this necessary synthetic unity" (A79/B104). As representations of the necessary synthetic unity of the manifold, the character of the categories depends essentially on the incorporation of manifoldness into their content. To abstract from all manifoldness would be to contradict this character and so nullify their anti-Humean status as concepts of the necessary relation of the distinct. And since Kant held that the senses are the only source of what is manifold in our representation, this is just to say that the manifold of sense and its synthesis in imagination are no less essential to the "transcendental content" (A79/B105) Kant imputed to the categories than the logical functions of judgment.[6] Indeed, so far as I can tell, the only real difference between Kant's psychologistic explication of the categories in the metaphysical deduction and its Humean model is that the psychological operations that here contribute elements indispensable to the content of concepts are strictly a priori: the *pure* manifold of sense and its *pure* synthesis in imagination. Otherwise, everything is the same, including the consequence—singled out by Kant himself in the *Prolegomena* preface—that apart from the conscious experience of an appropriately constituted mind, such concepts have, and can have, no application to objects whatsoever.

To be sure, the specific sensible content of the manifold itself—whether a mind is so constituted that it is spatial, temporal, or something else entirely—is irrelevant to the notion of a pure concept of a necessary relation between the distinct, and so can be excluded from the meaning of the categories. But that there must be *some* such manifold Kant left no doubt, just as he did that the senses alone, not the understanding, are capable of supplying it. For without this manifold and its synthesis in imagination, two indispensable elements of the content of any concept of a necessary relation of the distinct would be lacking: items that are genuinely distinct (determinations or existents) and the relation of those items. Insofar as Kant undeniably cast his doctrine of the categories as a response to Humean doubts regarding the possibility of concepts of necessary relations between distinct existents, he thus had no option but to proceed exactly as he did in the metaphysical deduction, and trace them to sources capable of providing all three elements indispensable to their content (A78–79/B104). Thus, even if in dealing with the question of their possibility (rather than their application to objects), abstraction has to be made from the *specifically* spatial and temporal character of the manifold in beings constituted like ourselves, we cannot abstract from the sensible manifold as such (irrespective of its particular character) and its synthesis in imagination without contradicting the transcendental content of the categories as representations of the necessary synthetic unity of that manifold.[7]

What might Hume have made of Kant's metaphysical deduction of the categories? Assuming that he could have been convinced that the senses intuit a priori, the remainder of Kant's psychological explication of the categories as concepts of objectively necessary relations seems comparatively unproblematic. If a manifold is given a priori, then the capacity to relate it a priori in imagination (pure synthesis) seems to follow as a matter of course. That the logical functions contribute necessity to the synthetic unity of the manifold Kant held to be thought in each category also seems unobjectionable: as purely formal (excluding all content), Hume would probably have conceded their apriority, and so too the necessity and universality of the synthesis of the manifold determined conformably to them. Thus, Kant's metaphysical deduction holds out at least the promise of a response to Hume's doubts regarding the intelligibility of concepts of necessary relations between the distinct.[8]

KANT'S RESPONSE TO THE EPISTEMOLOGICAL PHASE OF HUME'S SKEPTICISM

The metaphysical deduction of the categories also opens the way to a response to the second, epistemological strand of Humean skepticism concerning the application of pure concepts of the understanding to objects. We saw earlier that Kant considered this doubt ineliminable so long as objects, including those given immediately in perception to the inner and outer senses (sensations, reflexions, and thoughts), are taken to be things in themselves. Although he did not spell out why he considered Hume a transcendental realist regarding objects of the senses, Kant does seem to me to be on firm ground at least with respect to the first of the two theses he likened to Copernican revolutions: that the objects present to us immediately (pre-associatively) in perception must conform to our faculty of apprehending them in immediate intuition rather than vice versa (Bxvi–xvii). Hume gave no indication of holding this view, or even entertaining it as a possibility. For him, we apprehend all our perceptions as successive because they actually do, in transcendental reality, exist successively in our consciousness; and we apprehend visual and tactual sensations as extended and juxtaposed because that indeed is what these perceptions actually, in transcendental reality, are. Kant took the opposite view: without a pure intuition of time determining our apprehension of the data of inner sense (i.e., if our sensibility were constituted differently and some other pure intuition determined it otherwise), the manifold representations immediately present to that sense would appear not as a succession but as something else (A30/B46 and A36–38/B53–54 + n.); and without a pure intuition of space determining our apprehension of sensations (especially, but not exclusively, those of vision and touch: *Anthropology* §15), none of the manifold representations immediately present to us in outer sense would appear as extended or juxtaposed, but rather as something else (A41–44/B59–61). Thus, according to Kant's transcendental idealism, appearances are representations rather than things in themselves (even in Hume's attenuated sense) because they are constituted in conformity to a pure time and space that are nothing but modes of sensible representation rooted in the subjective constitution of our minds, and "it is a manifest contradiction to say that a mere mode of representation also exists outside our representation" (*Prolegomena*, AA 4 341–42).[9]

From this, it is easy to see just how transcendental idealism provided Kant with a means of responding to Humean doubts regarding the applicability of the categories to objects. On the reading of the metaphysical deduction sketched earlier, according to which the a priori manifold and its pure synthesis belong as essentially to the content thought in the categories as logical functions do, nothing more is needed to secure their application to the objects of the senses than to specify these representations of the necessary synthetic unity of the manifold of sense in general with respect to the specific character of the manifold—a process Kant termed transcendental schematism. For example, in minds with a sensibility constituted like ours, where appearances necessarily and universally conform to pure space and time, the specification of each category with respect to pure space and time—its transcendental schema—will yield the condition under which it becomes possible to subsume these appearances under categorial predicates a priori.

Of course, in realizing the categories with respect to the objects of our senses, their schemata do not confer on them any applicability to objects other than those that conform to these conditions. In particular, since schemata incorporate space and time—mere modes of representation— into their content, and since it is "manifest contradiction to say that a mere mode of representation also exists outside our representation," they do not enable us even so much as to *conceive* how the categories could apply to objects in general and in themselves. Still, by showing how these concepts can be supposed to apply a priori to the only objects that, according to Hume, are ever of concern to human understanding—sensible appearances—Kant's transcendental idealism does indeed hold out the prospect of laying to rest Humean doubts on this score.

That said, it is one thing to show that the categories *can* apply to sensible objects, quite another to overcome Humean doubts as to whether they actually *do*, and moreover do so universally and necessarily (i.e., a priori). This is where the second of Kant's Copernican theses comes in: if the objects present to us discursively in judgments of experience must conform to our faculty of cognizing them by means of concepts rather than vice versa, then we can cognize these objects a priori by means of pure concepts of the understanding. Establishing this thesis was the task Kant set himself in what he termed the *objective transcendental deduction of the categories* (Axvi–xvii). The proof rests on the principle of possible experience. In a nutshell, the claim is that Humean association by itself is insufficient to underpin experience of objects. For in order for an object to appear to us by means of our perceptions, there must, in addition to perceptions and their synthesis in imagination, be a concept in which the *necessary* unity of this synthesis is recognized. Hume—realizing, on the one hand, that any such necessary relation of the distinct can never be represented by means of any empirical concept, yet unable, on the other hand, to account for the possibility of a priori concepts to which appearances might conform—sought not so much to *explain* experience of objects as explain it *away* as the product of an illusion whereby we take the subjective necessity of customary association for an objective necessity governing the relations of appearances themselves (B127). But once the proof in the metaphysical deduction that pure concepts of objects are in our possession is accepted, the inadequacy of Hume's account becomes apparent. To begin with, utilizing these concepts, we can at the very least *think* objects as appearing through our perceptions, and so confer a genuinely objective form on our experiences a priori that can be neither explained nor explained away as mere subjective illusion. Only the a priori (necessary, universal) application of the categories to perceptions can explain this objective form (A93–94/B125–26). But in that case, it can no longer be denied *that* the objective experience, by virtue of its form, requires that the categories not only can but do, indeed must, determine appearances a priori. Thus, according to Kant, do the categories acquire *cognitive* validity as principles of possible experience (i.e., predicates of appearances in synthetic a priori judgments).

To be sure, the Humean may well wonder *how* the a priori determination of appearances by the categories can take place when the former can only be given a posteriori. But this is no mystery to the transcendental idealist. It was only because Hume was committed to transcendental realism regarding appearances that "it never entered his mind that perhaps the understanding, through these concepts themselves, is itself the creator (*Urheber*) of this experience in which its objects are found" (B127).[10] By determining space and time to yield transcendental schemata, the categories thereby also determine the appearances that necessarily and universally conform to these pure intuitions and do so completely a priori.

Humean Objections to Kant's Response to Hume's Problem

Yet, even if one grants that Kant's objective transcendental deduction rises to the challenge of Humean skepticism, that is not the same as saying there are no further hurdles the Humean skeptic might place in its way. Three obstacles in particular seem to me to have left Kant no choice but to supplement his objective transcendental deduction with the deeper, more complex *subjective transcendental deduction of the categories*:

1. *The heterogeneity problem.* The first concerns Kant's claim that the categories are concepts of necessary relations between distinct items (determinations or existents). How can the understanding confer necessity

on the synthesis in imagination of the a priori manifold of sense through things so entirely devoid of objective content as the merely logical forms of subject/predicate judgment, along with the rest of Kant's table of logical forms (A70/B95)? Certainly, they can confer a *logical* relation on given concepts, that is, enable us to combine them in a judgment. But the question is how they can be good for anything more. How, that is, can "the same understanding, through the very same actions whereby in concepts it brings about the logical form of a judgment by means of analytic unity also [bring] a transcendental content into its representations by means of the synthetic unity of the manifold in intuition in general" (A79/B105)? For Hume to concede defeat, Kant would have to explain how something so heterogeneous with respect to everything sensible as a logical function—something that seems usable for nothing else than forming judgments from given concepts—can confer necessary synthetic unity on the manifold right in sensible intuition itself.

2. *The objectivity problem.* Kant's claim that transcendental idealism can allay Hume's otherwise ineliminable doubts because it makes the understanding constitutive of the very objects we experience seems to depend on what seems like it might be an illicit *redefinition* of what an "object" is. In particular, Kantian "objectivity" precisely coincides with what the categories ostensibly represent: the necessary synthetic unity of the manifold. Thus, in the A edition of the Transcendental Deduction, Kant explicated the notion "an object of representations" as follows:

> [A]s we have to do only with the manifold of our representations, and that X which corresponds to them (the object), because it is supposed to be something distinct from all our representations, is for us nothing, the unity which the object makes necessary can be nothing else than the formal unity of consciousness in the synthesis of the manifold of representations. We then say: we cognize the object if we have effected (*bewirkt*) a synthetic unity in the manifold of the intuition. This however is impossible if the intuition cannot be generated (*hervorgebracht*) by means of a function of synthesis according to such a rule as to render the reproduction of the manifold necessary and make possible a concept in which this manifold is united. (A105; also B136–38, A197/B242–43, and A494/B522)

If the X corresponding to our representations is for us nothing, then the object of representations that *is* something for us can only be a feature of these representations themselves, namely, their necessary synthetic unity; and because the categories are the most fundamental concepts of that unity, so that without them it is unrepresentable, Kant felt warranted in portraying them as constitutive of objects as such. Against this the Humean skeptic might however object by asking what, beyond the name, warrants us in taking the representational results of our own acts of order-ing appearances to be "objects?" Certainly, the ingredients that enter into Kant's necessary synthetic unity are, on the face of it, merely subjective: the form, not the content, of judgments; the manifold of sense; and the relation of that manifold in imagination. If the objectivity of the "objects" constituted by the categories consists of no elements but these, how, other than being a priori, can they be distinguished from Humean fictions of associative imagination? One may be forgiven for thinking that a notion of "objectivity" so watered down that even a Humean skeptic might find it unexceptionable is unworthy of the name. What makes these "objects" any less subjective and fictitious than Humean fictions of space and time, necessary connection, identity over time, and individuality at a time, whereby "I paint the universe in my imagination" (*THN* 75)?

3. *The necessity problem.* Even if some fundamental difference could be specified to warrant according to the products of Kantian categories a kind of objectivity the products of Humean associationism lack, the fact remains that Kantian objects exist only in and for discursive thought, so that, apart from concepts whose only use consists in judging, they are nothing. Yet, by Kant's own admission, appearances are given to the senses in intuition, prior to and independently of thought and its logical functions (A89–90/B122–23). So, even if we grant his claim that these appearances are ideal, they still seem more deserving of the appellation of *object* than the products of the categories, by virtue of existing in us prior to and independently of discursive thought. After all, it is such ob-jects—corresponding to Humean perceptions as they exist pre-associa-tively—that are the true focus of Hume's skepticism regarding necessary connections between distinct existents. Moreover, like Humean percep-tions, Kantian appearances have no objectively ordered spatio-temporal existence by virtue of conforming to pure space and time,[11] but instead are nothing but a bare manifold of scattered, isolated perceptions (A120). So, what difference can it make if afterward, in *thought*, we represent these objects as conforming to pure concepts of necessary relations if they lack such determination in *intuition* itself? From the perspective of Hum-ean skepticism, the imposition of categorial conditions on our thought of objects, after the fact of their intuition, seems like a classic case of shutting the barn door after the horses have bolted.

INDICATIONS OF KANTIAN RESPONSES TO THESE OBJECTIONS

The foregoing objections should serve to make clearer the magnitude of the obstacles confronting Kant. Taken together, they suggest that the tran-scendental aesthetic, metaphysical deduction of the categories, and objective transcendental deduction of the categories are, in the end, insufficient to meet the Humean skeptical challenge. Our final question therefore is this: What did Kant require in order to overcome them, and what steps did he take in the subjective transcendental deduction of the categories to do so?

To solve Hume's problem, in the generalized form given to it by Kant, it has to be shown that Hume's skepticism presupposes something that only Kant's apriorism, grounded in pure sensibility, is capable of furnishing, at least in a manner consistent with the principles on which Hume's skepticism itself depends. This, in my view, is precisely what the subjective deduction does. Its brief is to investigate "pure understanding itself, according to its possibility and the cognitive faculties on which it rests," that is, to answer the question, "[H]ow is the *capacity to think* itself possible?" (Axvi–xvii) The principle of this inquiry, the basis of the possibility of pure understanding, is the original unity of apperception (B131, B134n., B137, and B153; also A97 and A128). Apperception is the ground to which Kant attributed the categories (A401–2 and B421–22) and even the logical functions of judgment (B131, B134n.). In so doing, he resolved the necessary synthetic unity of the metaphysical and objective deductions of the categories into a more fundamental demand for the necessary synthetic unity of the manifold in *one consciousness*. And with this we arrive at what, in my view, is a requirement that Humean skepticism can neither meet nor leave unmet.

In the A edition of the Transcendental Deduction, Kant advanced an argument intended to show that association is impossible unless there is necessary synthetic unity of the manifold in one consciousness a priori:

[T]hough we had a capacity to associate perceptions, it would nevertheless remain in itself entirely undetermined and contingent whether they were associable as well; and in the case where they were not, there would be a multitude (*Menge*) of perceptions and indeed an entire sensibility would be possible in which much empirical consciousness would be found but separately, without its belonging to a consciousness of myself, which however is impossible. For only by my ascribing all perceptions to one consciousness (original apperception) can I say of (*bei*) all perceptions that I am conscious of them. Hence, there must be an objective ground, i.e. one into which there is insight a priori, ahead of all empirical laws of the imagination, on which rests the possibility, nay even the necessity, of a law ranging through all appearances, namely, according to which appearances are one and all (*durchgängig*) regarded as data of the senses that are associable in themselves and subject to universal rules of a thoroughgoing connection in reproduction. This objective ground of all association I call their *affinity*. This, however, we can find nowhere else than in the principle of the unity of apperception in respect of all cognitions which are to belong to me. According to this, all appearances must generally (*durchaus*) so enter the mind, or be apprehended, that they accord with a unity of apperception which would be impossible without synthetic unity in their connection, which therefore is objectively necessary as well. (A121–22)

Kant's reasoning turns on the thesis that, in the absence of a necessary relation uniting distinct appearances (their affinity), these appearances might not belong to one and the same consciousness, and would then be, for all *conscious* intents and purposes—association not excepted— nothing to me (the *subject* of consciousness). For even if I still possess the capacity to associate perceptions, it would necessarily remain dormant so long as the appearances present before me were not in themselves associable, by virtue of being copresent, one and all, in the same unity of consciousness. And since the only thing that can guarantee such a unity is the subordination of appearances a priori (hence, necessarily and universally) to conditions of the necessary synthetic unity of the manifold in one consciousness, the objective deduction demonstration that the categories are precisely such conditions ("[they] make the formal unity of experience possible," A125) shows that association too must presuppose them.

A Humean skeptic might still object that an argument that turns on the contingency of the associability of appearances is insufficient to rebut his challenge. To be sure, if it happened that appearances were not associable in themselves, so that "a multitude of perceptions, indeed an entire sensibility would be possible, in which much empirical consciousness would be found, but separately and without its belonging to a consciousness of myself," then the cognitive implications might indeed be as devastating as Kant claimed. Yet, this is merely a possibility or, perhaps more accurately, something the impossibility of which we are not equipped to *know*. Might it not also be the case that there is some unknown factor, having nothing to do with the categories, that ensures that the appearances will one and all be associable?[12] However philosophically unsatisfying it may be to have to live with ignorance in this matter, that is no excuse for pretending to know that appearances conform a priori to the categories just because this is the only circumstance under which we can be *certain* of their associability a priori. A genuine refutation of the Humean skeptic must therefore be able to establish the stronger thesis that conscious representation, association included, is possible in no other way than by conformity to the categories as conditions for the original synthetic unity of apperception.

Hume himself may have inadvertently signaled where his skeptical principles are most vulnerable to such a challenge. In an appendix published with the second volume of the *Treatise*, he described a quandary implicit in the account of personal identity in the first volume from which he could discover no exit. There he psychologistically explicated "the true idea of the human mind" entirely in terms of associative relations specifically described as ideal (*THN* 169–71). The problem this creates is that "having thus loosen'd all our particular perceptions" from real bonds of every kind, "all my hopes vanish, when I come to explain the principles, that unite our successive perceptions in our thought or consciousness" (*THN* 400). As itself a condition of their associability, this unity of perceptions in one consciousness cannot be explicated associatively. Yet, Hume's refusal to renounce the fundamental principles of his skepticism—"*that all our distinct perceptions are distinct existences,* and *that the mind never perceives any real connexion among distinct existences*"—also prevented him from invoking a *real* substantial substrate in which successive perceptions inhere or real necessary connections link them to one another in a *real* system of causal relations (as opposed to the ideal-associative system described in *THN* 169–71). He thus had no option but to retract his claim in volume 1 that "[t]he intellectual world . . . is not perplex'd with any such contradictions, as those we have discover'd in the natural" (*THN* 152; cf. 399). In other words, Hume recognized that a quite new, fundamentally different theory of the unity of successive perceptions in consciousness is requisite to resolve the quandary, but he saw no way to provide it. At the same time, he did not pretend "to pronounce it absolutely insuperable. Others, perhaps, or myself, upon more mature reflection, may discover some hypothesis, that will reconcile those contradictions" (*THN* 400).

There is no evidence that Hume ever discovered a way out of his quandary. We hear no more on the subject of the unity of successive perceptions in consciousness in either the *Enquiry* or any of his other extant writings. Our question, then, is whether Kant's approach to the unity of consciousness in the subjective deduction can provide an exit. Already in the Transcendental Aesthetic there is the promise of one. For if time, and so too the succession of perceptions that presupposes it, is transcendentally *ideal*, what need is there for a principle of transcendentally *real* inherence, *real* causal connection, or *real* relation of any kind to explain how successive perceptions are united in our thought or consciousness? As a pure intuition that precedes and makes possible all appearances without exception, time is already as such the necessary unity of all the manifold in one consciousness, right in intuition itself. It thus explains the associability of appearances in strictly idealist terms that neither imply nor entail the kind of real necessary relation between distinct existents proscribed by the fundamental tenets of Humean skepticism.

What then does the subjective deduction add to a Kantian resolution of Hume's quandary? It shows that the unity of the manifold in pure time, "and in the consciousness of that representation, . . . is *synthetic* yet also

192 • Chapter 9

original" (B136n.). This means nothing less than that pure time, no less than the logical functions, categories, and categorially determinate objects of experience, is grounded on the principle of original apperception (A107 and B140), but with one crucial difference: pure time is unity of apperception right in intuition itself, prior to discursive representation under the categories (B160n.). Consequently, the Humean skeptic can no longer have recourse to an unknown factor, having nothing to do with the categories, capable of ensuring the associability of perceptions. For since, in conforming to pure time, perceptions ipso facto conform to the principle of original apperception, only something embodying the same principle can afterward account for the objective form prescribed in the objective transcendental deduction. This made it possible for Kant to argue that the categories not only embody this principle but also, as pure concepts of the understanding, are in the unique position of being able to confer objective form on appearances ahead of all experience. He was thus able to supplement the objective deduction with proof that conscious representation in general, and association in particular, is possible in no way other than the categories.

The full examination of Kant's Humean solution to Hume's problem, both in its generalized form (how are synthetic a priori judgments possible?) and his treatment of causation in particular, cannot be undertaken here.[13] For our purposes, it suffices merely to recognize two things. First, no one portion of Kant's philosophy can be singled out as containing the refutation of Hume. Instead, addressing and surmounting Hume's skeptical challenge requires the entirety of Kant's theoretical philosophy through the Transcendental Analytic (we should also perhaps include the Dialectic of the *Critique of Pure Reason* as well as the *Critique of Practical Reason*, esp. AA 5 54–57, since saving freedom from Humean necessitarianism was equally a part of Kant's anti-Humean program). Second, everything in this refutation is predicated on one simple psychological insight not vouchsafed Hume: the senses are a source of a priori, and not just empirical, intuition. From the seemingly small seed of Kant's a priori sensibilism grew all the vast differences between their philosophies.

CHAPTER 10

Should Hume Have Been a Transcendental Idealist?

Don Garrett

KANT ASSIGNS TO HUME—that "great thinker" and "acute man"—a crucial role in the history of metaphysics: it is "Hume's spark" that should have ignited, and in Kant's thinking did ignite, the flame that lights the way to transcendental idealism. This spark, on Kant's view, consisted chiefly in Hume's having posed a challenge:

> He [Hume] challenged reason, which pretends to have given birth to this concept [of cause and effect] of herself, to answer him by what right she thinks anything could be so constituted that if that thing be posited, something else also must necessarily be posited; for this is the meaning of the concept of cause. (*Prolegomena*, preface, *AA* 4 257)

On Kant's view, Hume concluded that his challenge could not be met, holding instead that

> reason was altogether deluded with reference to this concept, which she erroneously regarded as one of her children, whereas in reality it was nothing but a bastard of imagination, impregnated by experience, which subsumed certain representations under the law of association, and mistook a subjective necessity (custom) for an objective necessity arising from insight. (*Prolegomena*, preface, *AA* 4 257–58)

This outcome was not only unfortunate but also unnecessary, Kant held, for Hume would himself have been drawn to see the need for transcendental idealism and its distinctive account of causal necessity if only he had thought more carefully about the status of mathematics and its implications:

> For he imagined that its nature, or, so to speak, the constitution of this province, depended on totally different principles, namely, on the principle of contradiction alone, and although he did not divide judgments in this manner [i.e., into analytic and synthetic] formally and universally and did not use the same terminology as I have done here, what he said was equivalent to this: that pure mathematics contains only analytic, but metaphysics synthetic, a priori judgments. In this, however, he was greatly mistaken, and the mistake had a decidedly

injurious effect upon his whole conception. But for this, he would have extended his question concerning the origin of our synthetic judgments far beyond the metaphysical concept of causality and included in it the possibility of mathematics a priori also; for this latter he must have assumed to be equally synthetic. And then he could not have based his metaphysical judgments on mere experience without subjecting the axioms of mathematics equally to experience, a thing that he was far too acute to do. The good company into which metaphysics would thus have been brought would have saved it from the danger of a contemptuous ill-treatment; for the thrust intended for it must have reached mathematics, which was not and could not have been Hume's intention. Thus that acute man would have been led into considerations which must needs be similar to those that now occupy us, but which would have gained inestimably from his inimitable elegant style. (*Prolegomena*, §4, AA 4 272–73)

In consequence of this oversight, Kant alleges, Hume "did not suspect such a formal science [as metaphysics] but ran his ship ashore, for safety's sake, landing on skepticism, there to let it lie and rot" (*Prolegomena*, preface, AA 4 262). What Kant calls "Hume's problem"—namely, that of meeting the original challenge and thereby explaining the origin of the concept of causation in such a way as to "determine the conditions of its use and the sphere of its valid application" (*Prolegomena*, preface, AA 4 258–59)—was thus left to Kant for its solution.

What would Hume have made of this story of his role in the history of metaphysics as the forerunner of transcendental idealism? Did he actually pose the challenge that Kant describes concerning the concept of causation and find reason to be incapable of meeting it? Did he in effect suppose that mathematics consists only of necessary analytic judgments? Did he, as a result of his findings, abandon his ship of inquiry to "lie and rot" in skepticism? Would he have been obliged, in order to achieve a tenable position about causation, mathematics, and the scope of human knowledge, to become a transcendental idealist? Those are the questions that I shall try to answer.

HUME'S CHALLENGE CONCERNING CAUSATION:
THE ORIGIN OF THE CONCEPT

Kant represents Hume as challenging reason with respect to its right to regard a cause and its effect as such that, "if one is posited, the other must necessarily be posited." In characterizing Hume's challenge, Kant places it in the context of two claims that, he implies, Hume would endorse: (1)

that reason "pretends to give birth" to the concept of causation and (2) that a necessary connection is "the meaning" of the concept of cause. In order to determine whether Hume made such a challenge and denied that reason could meet it, it will be helpful first to determine his attitude toward these two claims. In the course of doing so, we will also have occasion to investigate Kant's further claim that Hume regarded reason as "mistaking a subjective necessity (custom) for an objective necessity arising from insight."

Reason, for Hume, is simply the faculty of making inferences, which may be either demonstrative or probable. Accordingly, reason, on his account, could "*pretend* to give birth" to the concept of causation only by yielding a (self-referential) *inference* to the conclusion that reason does give birth to that concept. On the face of it, such a conclusion about the concept's origin would seem to be unwarranted, however, since the characteristic outputs of reasoning are beliefs rather than new concepts. Indeed, Hume criticizes Locke for giving an essential but unexplained role to reasoning in his account of the origin of the idea or concept of causal power—an account that, as Hume remarks (*EHU* 7.8n.), violates Locke's own principle that reason can never give rise to any new idea. Yet there is nevertheless a way in which reason, for Hume, *does*—and does not merely pretend to—"give birth" to the concept of causation. In order to understand how this is so, it is necessary to understand his theory of causal inference and his theory of causal judgment—which, in turn, requires, respectively, an understanding of his theory of necessity and an understanding of his theory of concepts.[1]

Hume remarks that all reasoning, whether demonstrative or probable, is a "discovery of relations" (*THN* 1.3.2.2). Probable reasoning or inference, he holds, is always a "discovery" of specifically causal relations; and in this case, he declares, "the nature of the relation depends so much on that of the inference" that one cannot fully understand the former without first explaining the latter (*THN* 1.3.14.30). On his well-known account of it, probable reasoning or inference consists in a transition from an impression or memory to a lively idea, occurring after a previously experienced constant conjunction of objects that are like the former with objects like the latter, and accompanied by a distinctive internal impression that is the felt "determination of the thought to pass from causes to effects, and from effects to causes, according to their experienced union" (*THN* 1.3.14.1 and 1.3.14.22).[2] This impression of felt determination is the "impression of necessary connection" from which the idea of necessary connection is copied. It is properly termed an impression of *necessary* connection because, for Hume, the proper application of the term "necessity" always signifies a relation to some kind of mental determination to conceive things in a certain way—i.e., an inability of the mind to think or conceive otherwise. There are two kinds of such necessity. The first is that of self-evident or demonstrable "relations of ideas," for which the inability to conceive otherwise is grounded in the intrinsic nature of the ideas themselves. The second is that of causes, which involves instead a psychological difficulty in conceiving two things apart and an inability to avoid believing that they exist together—both of which arise after experience of constant conjunction. Thus, Hume writes:

> As the necessity, which makes two times two equal to four, or three angles of a triangle equal to two right ones, lies only in the act of the understanding, by which we consider and compare these ideas; in like manner the necessity or power, which unites causes and effects, lies in the determination of the mind to pass from the one to the other. (*THN* 1.3.14.23)

Probable or causal *inference*, as Hume describes it, presupposes no uniquely human capacities. Indeed, he argues (*THN* 1.3.16, "Of the reason of animals") that this fact constitutes an important point in favor of his account, since animals as well as humans show by their behavior that they perform causal inferences. But although animal reasoning implicitly discovers and depends on causal relations in order to infer one thing from another—and thereby implicitly represents things as standing in causal relations—animals do not make explicit judgments of the form: "Object *A* and Object *B* stand in the relation of cause and effect." This is because, while they perceive causes and make inferences from them, they lack a "general or abstract idea"—what we would call a "concept"—of causation.

Perceptions may have, and may represent their objects as having, many different qualities; for example, they may represent their objects as being round and a particular shade of red. Similarly, perceptions may stand in, and may represent their objects as standing in, many different relations;[3] for example, a pair of perceptions may represent one object as identical in shape but double in size to another while also representing the objects as existing simultaneously but at a distance equal to the height of the smaller. In order for perceptions to represent objects as having particular qualities and relations—and also in order for the perceptions themselves to *have* the qualities and relations that determine the nature of further cognitive operations—it is not necessary, or at least not always necessary, for the mind to have concepts *of* the qualities or relations in question. In order to think with generality *about* qualities and relations, however, or about the classes of things that have them, it *is* necessary to form concepts—that is, "general ideas"—of them.

Yet no idea, Hume argues, is general or indeterminate in its own nature. In order to have concepts or general ideas, therefore, the mind must employ what he calls the "imperfect" device of "abstract ideas" (*THN* 1.1.7.1). Such ideas arise in the mind, on Hume's view, in the following way. When perceptions resemble one another in some respect, it is psychologically natural to apply the same term to each, notwithstanding their difference. Later uses of the term come to elicit a particular and determinate idea (which we may call the "exemplar") together with a disposition to revive and "survey," as needed for reasoning or other purposes, the other ideas (which we may call, together with the exemplar, the "revival set") whose objects resemble one another in the operative respect (*THN* 1.1.7.7–8).[4] Similarly, the abstract idea of a *relation* consists, for Hume, of a determinate idea of a pair (triple, etc.) of particular things taken to stand in that relation and associated with a term in such a way that the mind is disposed to revive and survey for use as needed any of a set of ideas of other pairs (triples, etc.) whose objects strike the mind as similarly related.

To judge explicitly that a particular object has a specified *quality*, then, is to include a "lively" idea of that object—which, in virtue of its "liveliness," constitutes belief in the object's existence—within the revival set of the abstract idea of that quality; and to judge explicitly that two particular objects stand in a specified *relation* is to include a lively idea of that pair of objects in the revival set of the abstract idea of that relation. To judge that two objects *A* and *B* stand in the relation of cause and effect, therefore, is to include a lively idea of *A* and *B* in the revival set of the abstract idea of the causal relation. This is the revival set that has resulted from the effect on the mind of the resemblance holding among the various pairs of objects that, following experience of constant conjunction of like pairs, sustain causal inference with its characteristic impression of determination or necessary connection. Hume aims to capture this revival set with two definitions of 'cause', one in terms of constant conjunction and one in terms of association and inference:

> We may define a CAUSE to be "An object precedent and contiguous to another, and where all objects resembling the former are plac'd in like relations of precedency and contiguity to those objects, that resemble the latter."

> "A CAUSE is an object precedent and contiguous to another, and so united with it that the idea of the one determines the mind to form the idea of the other, and the impression of the one to form a more lively idea of the other." (*THN* 1.3.14.30–31)

These two definitions express what we might call the "external" and "internal" conditions, respectively, that lead to the impression of necessary connection and the inclusion of a pair of objects in the revival set of the abstract idea of cause and effect.

In Book 3 of the *Treatise*, Hume discusses distinctive sentiments of "moral approbation and disapprobation." Like the impression of necessary connection, these sentiments are what he calls "impressions of reflection"; and he characterizes our ability to feel them as a "moral sense" that enables us to discriminate vice and virtue (*THN* 3.1.2). He goes on to offer (in the *Treatise* and even more clearly in *An Enquiry Concerning the Principles of Morals*) two definitions of 'virtue', one of which involves a condition that is external to the moral judge ("the possession of mental qualities, *useful* or *agreeable* to the *person himself* or to *others*" [*EPM* 9.1]), and one of which involves a condition that is internal to the moral judge ("whatever mental action or quality gives to a spectator the pleasing sentiment of approbation" [*EPM* appendix 1.9]). At the same time, he also compares the perception of virtue and vice with the perception of secondary qualities. These analogies suggest that the mental operations by which constant conjunction leads to association, inference, and the impression of necessary connection may also be viewed as a kind of sense—a "causal sense"—that allows the mind to distinguish those pairs of objects that are *causally related* from those that are not.

Of course, senses need not be, and generally are not, infallible; not all things that appear to resemble one another in a given respect do resemble one another in that respect. Hence, not every object, or set of objects, that we might initially include in the revival set of an abstract idea is properly so classified, and principles to correct for idiosyncrasies of perspective are required. This is true, Hume notes, for primary and secondary qualities of bodies, for moral qualities of persons, and for aesthetic qualities of artifacts and other objects.[5] In parallel fashion, Hume offers, near the end of his discussion of causation in the *Treatise*, a set of eight "rules by which to judge of causes and effects" (*THN* 1.3.15), rules that serve precisely to guide the refinement of the revival set of one's abstract idea of the relation of cause and effect. These rules "are formed on the nature of our understanding, and on our experience of its operations in the judgments we form concerning objects"—that is, by reflection on the mechanism of causal reasoning in light of the past successes and failures of causal inferences of various kinds—and by means of them "we learn to distinguish the accidental circumstances from the efficacious causes" (*THN* 1.3.13.11).[6] Of course, the greatest problem of perspective or situation in discerning causal relations lies in the limitation of one's experience to only a small part of what actually occurs in the world, with the resulting danger of insufficient or unrepresentative samples. Enquiry into causes involves experimentation, conducted and evaluated in accordance with the rules by which to judge of causes and effects, that aims to mitigate this insufficiency. Just as the *correct* or *proper* revival set for the abstract idea of a sensible, moral, or aesthetic quality is the one that would arise in an *ideal-*

ized human observer possessing both the appropriate sense and a sufficient range of experience, judging in accordance with proper rules of correction, so the correct or proper revival set for the abstract idea of cause and effect is the one that would arise in an idealized observer having both the human causal sense and sufficient observations to constitute a representative sample for any causal judgment, and employing the proper rules by which to judge of causes and effects.

The *concept* of causation thus arises originally as the result of *probable inference*, in which the similarities (involving temporal priority, contiguity, and constant conjunction) among the various pairs between which inferences are made become salient and give rise to the abstract idea of the causal relation; and that idea is refined through the application of rules derived from further reasoning on the successes and failures of probable reasoning itself. Hence it is not unfair to say that reason, for Hume, does "give birth" to the concept of cause and effect. And since Hume thinks we can uncover this origin for ourselves through the elaborate causal reasoning presented in *Treatise*, Book 1, part 3, we may add that reason ultimately *claims* to do so as well.

Hume's Challenge concerning Causation:
Necessity, Subjectivity, and the Meaning of "Cause"

In addition to the errors of sensory perspective that require correction by rules, however, the mind is also subject, on Hume's view, to systematic errors of sensory mislocation or projection. Thus, he appears to suggest in *An Enquiry Concerning the Principles of Morals* that the mind has a tendency to *locate* both moral and aesthetic sentiments—which are in fact internal impressions that do not resemble any qualities in objects—in the objects of evaluation themselves, thereby "gilding or staining . . . natural objects with the colours, borrowed from internal sentiment" (*EPM* appendix 1.25). More explicitly in the *Treatise*, he compares similar errors concerning smells, sounds, and necessary connection:

> The mind has a great propensity to spread itself on external objects, and to conjoin with them any internal impressions which they occasion, and which always make their appearance at the same time that these objects discover themselves to the senses. Thus, as certain sounds and smells are always found to attend certain visible objects, we naturally imagine a conjunction, even in place, betwixt the objects and qualities, though the qualities be of such a nature as to admit of no such conjunction, and really exist no where. . . . [T]he same propensity is the reason why we suppose necessity and power to lie in the objects we consider,

not in our mind, that considers them; notwithstanding it is not possible for us to form the most distant idea of that quality, when it is not taken for the determination of the mind, to pass from the idea of an object to that of its usual attendant. (*THN* 1.3.14.25)

As a result of this projective mislocation, we often include an *idea* of necessary connection, as a part, in our ideas of cause and effect pairs themselves, and we erroneously suppose that we can *observe* causal power or necessity as a quality located in the causally related objects themselves.

This projective error of mislocation naturally leads, Hume thinks, to the further error of conflating the two distinct species of necessity with which we are acquainted. For it leads us to treat the necessity of causes, like the necessity that belongs to demonstrable or intuitable relations of ideas, as an inability-to-conceive-otherwise that is grounded in the intrinsic character of the ideas themselves—whereas in fact the necessity of causes lies in a psychological difficulty of separating two objects in thought and an inability to separate them in belief that results not from the intrinsic characters of the objects as we conceive them but rather from the habitual association that has been established between them by constant conjunction.[7] In this sense, Hume does maintain that we mistake a "subjective necessity for an objective necessity," just as Kant reports—for we often fail to realize that our *sense* of the necessity of causal relations derives from the effects of custom on subjects like ourselves rather than from observation of the intrinsic characteristics of the objects themselves.

It does not follow from this, however, that causal relations themselves are "subjective" in the further sense of depending on the mind for their existence. Hume considers explicitly the objection that his account of causation would "reverse the order of nature" by making "the efficacy of causes" depend on thought, imagining an objector who exclaims:

What! The efficacy of causes lie in the determination of the mind! As if causes did not operate entirely independent of the mind, and would not continue their operation, even tho' there was no mind existent to contemplate them, or reason concerning them. (*THN* 1.3.14.26)

To this he responds:

As to what may be said, *that the operations of nature are independent of our thought and reasoning, I allow it*; and accordingly have observ'd, that objects bear to each other the relations of contiguity and succession; that like objects may be observ'd in several instances to have like relations; and that all this is independent of, and antecedent to the operations of the understanding. But if we go any farther, and ascribe a power or necessary connexion to these objects; that is what we can never observe in them, but must draw the idea of it from what we feel internally in contemplating them. (*THN* 1.3.14.28; emphasis mine)

Resemblances among pairs of objects of the kind that the actual human causal sense happens to pick out would continue to hold, Hume thinks, whether there were human minds or not, and events in nature would continue to exemplify true generalizations. Furthermore, although the "necessity" of causal relations would no longer be felt, the *basis* of that necessity in constant conjunction would continue to exist, in much the same way that the *basis* of sensory "redness" would (at least according to what Hume calls "the modern philosophy") continue to exist in the corpuscular structure of bodies even if the impression of red (which, according to that same philosophy, does not resemble its basis in the bodies) were never to occur—and also in much the same way that the necessity of mathematical relations would never be felt in the absence of minds, even though the *basis* of that felt necessity would continue to exist in the intrinsic natures of related things. For this reason, Hume is willing to say that "the constant conjunction of objects constitutes the very essence of cause and effect" (*THN* 1.4.5.33) and that "'tis from the constant union that the necessity arises" (*THN* 2.3.1.4). The resemblances that are in fact detected among causal pairs by a feeling of necessity are not dependent for their existence on the existence of the human mind or of a causal sense that detects them.[8]

Does Hume then deny Kant's claim that a necessary connection between cause and effect constitutes "the meaning of the concept of cause"? The answer depends on what is meant by "the meaning of the concept of cause," and on what is meant by "a necessary connection." The meaning of the *term* "cause" is, for Hume, simply the idea for which the term stands—in this case, the abstract idea consisting of an exemplar that is associated with a term and a particular revival set. This is why he can remark that "we must not here be content with saying, that the idea of cause and effect *arises* from objects constantly united; but must affirm, that it is *the very same with the idea of these objects*" (*THN* 2.3.1.16; emphasis mine). The purpose of his two definitions of "cause" is precisely to pick out these revival sets. The two definitions do so in ways that are cognitively distinct from one another—since one appeals to the concept of resemblance, while the other appeals to the concepts of determination, idea, impression, and liveliness. Both of these ways are also cognitively distinct from the way in which we capture the revival set in our ordinary use of the term "cause," since that requires wielding no *additional* concepts at all—at least not until we begin to develop and apply the (conceptually formulated) rules for judging of causes and effect.[9] The occurrence of the impression of necessary connection, and its projective mislocation in the objects themselves, plays an important causal role in rendering the resemblance among cause-and-effect pairs more salient, and thus *facilitates* the development of the concept of causation—just as the projective mislocation of the moral sentiments may facilitate the development of concepts of vice and virtue. But the representation of each causal pair as having something *resembling* the impression of necessary connection as an intrinsic part is not essential to the Humean abstract idea of cause and effect itself. To overcome the projective illusion—as Hume implies can be done with care and attention (*THN* 1.3.14.31, 1.4.7.5–6)—is not to change the pairs of objects whose ideas constitute the revival set of the idea of cause and effect, but only to correct the way in which they are represented.

This is not, of course, to deny that causal relations involve a necessary connection in any way. Hume begins his investigation of the causal relation by noting that, in addition to contiguity and priority, "there is a necessary connexion to be taken into consideration; and that relation is of much greater importance, than any of the other two" (*THN* 1.3.2.11); and he later adds that the necessary connection "makes so essential a part" of the causal relation (*THN* 1.3.6.3). However, he regards his own account of the way in which causal inference gives rise to a concept of causation as one that does take this "necessary connexion" sufficiently "into consideration," for it is one that allows judgments of causal relations to be properly considered "necessary." This can be seen clearly from his willingness to treat the satisfaction of his two definitions of "cause" as entirely sufficient to establish the presence of causal necessity, as he does particularly in connection with the necessity of human actions (*THN* 2.3.1–2; *EHU* 8), as well as in his reference to the "absolute impossibility" of miracles (*EHU* 10.27).

We are now in a position to answer the original question of whether Hume "challenged reason . . . to answer him by what right she thinks anything could be so constituted that if that thing be posited, something else also must necessarily be posited." On Hume's account, there are two species of necessity—that is, unthinkability of the opposite—and one of these is causal necessity, grounded in constant conjunction. Accordingly, reason—or rather, a human being when reasoning—is perfectly entitled to think of causal relations as necessary. Since belief in the principle that every event has a cause is itself based on such conjunctions, we are entitled to think of that principle as causally necessary as well. We are not entitled, however, to regard that principle as demonstrable, for we are not entitled to conflate the necessity of causal relations with the ("absolute" or "metaphysical") necessity of relations of ideas, and we are not entitled to assume that the basis of causal necessity is an intrinsic quality lying in individual cause and effect pairs themselves.

HUME'S VIEW OF MATHEMATICAL JUDGMENT

Was Kant right in thinking that Hume in effect took all mathematical judgments to be analytic? In order to answer this question, it is necessary first to apply Hume's theories of concept formation and judgment, as previously developed, to the case of mathematics.

Just as animal minds naturally represent things *as* having nonmathematical qualities and relations (such as being a particular shade of red or being spatially contiguous) but lack the ability to make conceptual judgments ascribing those qualities and relations, so too animal minds can represent things *as* having mathematical qualities and relations (such as having three parts or being congruent in shape) but lack the ability to make conceptual judgments ascribing them. Only human beings make mathematical *judgments*, in a full-blooded sense, for only they have concepts of mathematical qualities and relations. These concepts are, for Hume, abstract ideas for which the relevant aspect of resemblance among members of the revival set is one concerning quantity, shape, or spatial relation. To judge that a particular object has a mathematical quality is to include a lively idea of the object within the revival set of the abstract idea of that quality; to judge that two (three, etc.) objects stand in a mathematical relation is to include a lively idea of that pair (triple, etc.) of objects in the revival set of the abstract idea of that relation. To judge that everything with one mathematical quality also has another, or that every pair of things standing in one mathematical relation also stands in another, is to include a lively exemplar, as associated with the relevant term, and lively versions of the rest of the revival set of the abstract idea of the one quality or relation within the revival set of the abstract idea of the other quality or relation. Thus, the concept of "two" consists, presumably, of a lively idea of some particular pair of things, associated with the term "two" in such a way as to dispose the mind to revive ideas of other pairs as needed; the concept of "two plus two" consists of an idea of one pair of things—an exemplar or other member of the revival set of the concept of "two"—conjoined with an idea of a pair of *other* things (again, either an exemplar or another member of the revival set of the concept of "two"), associated with the term "two plus two" in such a way as to dispose the mind to review ideas of other such pairs of pairs; and the judgment that "two plus two is four" consists of the inclusion of the lively idea of the exemplar of "two plus two" in the revival set of the abstract idea of "four," together with a disposition to include lively ideas of all other members of the revival set of the abstract idea of "two plus two" within the revival set of the abstract idea of "four."[10] Similarly, the judgment that "the shortest distance between two points is a straight line" consists, for Hume, in a lively idea of the exemplar of the abstract idea of "line that is the shortest distant between two points"—itself derived from operations on the revival sets of "point" and "shortest distance"—within the revival set of the abstract idea of "straight line," together with a disposition to include lively ideas of all other members of the revival set of "shortest distance between two lines" within the revival set of "straight line."

True mathematical judgments are, for Hume, knowable intuitively or demonstratively because they are among those truths that depend only on the relations of the ideas. (Other such judgments include "Blue is more like green than it is like scarlet" [*THN* 1.1.7.7n.].) As such, they have a distinctive, noncausal kind of necessity—that is, of unthinkability of the opposite. To say that "two plus two is four" is not only true but necessary is, for Hume, to say not only that every actual pair of pairs is an actual four-membered collection, but also that the contrary of this is unthinkable. This requires, in turn, that even when the mind imagines non-actual pairs of pairs and non-actual four-membered sets, the former are again always among the latter. The necessity of this judgment is *felt* when the attempt to imagine a pair of pairs that is not four-membered consistently fails, despite the mind's best efforts: the mind finds that it can imagine a collection that is not within the revival set of "four" only by *also* making it no longer an example of a pair conjoined with a pair. Similar remarks apply to "the shortest distance between two points is a straight line"—or would, if Hume were convinced that this judgment is precisely true. In the *Treatise* (*THN* 1.2.4, with which Kant was presumably unfamiliar), Hume maintains, in order to avoid what he regards as paradoxes of infinite divisibility, that the axioms of geometry are only *very nearly* true—and sufficiently close to being true as to make little practical difference. That they are at least nearly true, however, is itself necessary and knowable by immediate intuition.

We are now in a position to determine whether Hume would regard mathematical judgments as analytic or synthetic. Kant offers two definitions or characterizations of analytic judgments (e.g., at *Prolegomena*, §2, *AA* 4 266–67). The first is that an analytic judgment is one in which the concept of the predicate is contained and thought in the concept of the subject; the second is that an analytic judgment is one the denial of which is a contradiction.

For Locke, a concept is a single mental particular that is inherently abstract in its representational content. Because such abstract mental particulars may be either simple or complex, many Lockean concepts are literally parts of others: for example, the concept of "extension" is part of the concept of "body," and the concept of "metal" is part of the concept of "gold." Indeed, Locke recognizes a species of knowledge that corresponds precisely to analytic judgments in Kant's concept-containment sense—although it is not what Locke called knowledge of "identity and diversity," as Kant himself supposed (*Prolegomena*, §3, *AA* 4 270), but rather what Locke calls "trifling propositions" (*E* 4.8). Because Humean concepts represent not simply as single abstract mental particulars, however, but rather in virtue of being determinate mental particulars that are associated in a particular way with a term and a revival set, the application of the concept-containment test to them is more complicated. The proper revival set (including exemplar) associated with the predicate need not be contained within the proper revival set (including exemplar) associated with the subject in a true Humean mathematical judgment, but the converse will be true: the proper revival set associated with the subject will always be contained within the proper revival set associated with the predicate. However, *this* latter kind of containment by itself could hardly be sufficient for "analyticity"—for precisely the same inclusion relation between revival sets would occur in *any* true predicative judgment, including such obvious examples of synthetic propositions as "gold is expensive" or "bodies have weight." Rather, what is required for Humean analyticity is a different *kind* of concept containment. Many concepts, for Hume, have revival sets that are effectively picked out by an immediate resemblance, without the mediation of other concepts as criteria. We may call such concepts "semantically simple"—as long as it is kept in mind that the semantic simplicity of a concept or abstract idea is an entirely different question from that of the simplicity or complexity of its exemplar or of the other members of its revival set. (This latter question depends only on the existence of parts within the particular idea in question; and it is in this sense only that Hume himself uses the terms "simple idea" and "complex idea.") Other concepts, however, such as the concept of "bachelor," may be semantically complex because of the way in which the revival set is picked out by using other concepts (such as "unmarried," "adult," "male," and "human") as criteria. A judgment will qualify as analytic if the revival set associated with the subject is contained within the revival set associated with the predicate *because* the subject concept is semantically complex in a way that employs the predicate concept as a constitutive criterion.

Given this understanding of analyticity, standard arithmetical judgments will not be analytic for Hume. In the judgment that "two plus two is four," for example, the concept "two plus two," while depending for its generation on the prior possession of the concept "two," does not depend for its generation on the possession or use of the concept "four"; nor does the generation of the concept "four" depend on the possession or use of the concept of "two" or of "two plus two." Similar remarks apply to the judgment that "the straightest distance between two points is a straight line." Indeed, Hume himself emphasizes that the ways in which the concepts of "straight line" and "shortest line between two points" pick out their revival sets are very different from one another (*THN* 1.2.4.27).

Still, in *An Enquiry Concerning Human Understanding*, Hume remarks that, while to deny a "matter of fact" does not "imply a contradiction," the falsehood of any demonstrable relation of ideas "would imply a contradiction and could never be distinctively conceived by the mind" (*EHU* 4.2). By Kant's second criterion, then, it appears that all demonstrable Humean mathematical judgments, which Hume explicitly identifies as relations of ideas, will be analytic after all. In fact, however, this appearance results simply from a difference in the way in which Kant and Hume conceive of contradictions. Like Leibniz, Kant has a conception of contradiction that is *formal*: all contradictions can be reduced by conceptual decomposition or other form-based transformations to a logical form in which the same thing is explicitly both affirmed and denied. Like Descartes, Spinoza, and Locke, Hume has a broader and nonformal conception of contradiction.[11] For Hume, a contradiction consists of two things that cannot be thought together—as his own elaboration of his point about contradiction by appeal to "distinct conceivability" indicates, and as a survey of his broad range of references to "contradictions" confirms. To say that the denial of "two plus two is four" is a contradiction is, for Hume, to say no more than that, from the nature of the ideas themselves, the mind cannot think something that is both a combination of a pair with another pair and yet is not four-membered. It would likewise be a contradiction for Hume, and for similar reasons, to say that blue is more like scarlet than it is like green—even though no formal contradiction can plausibly be derived from this claim by formal conceptual decomposition or other form-based transformations. Thus, we may conclude, Hume himself already effectively considered many mathematical judgments to be necessary synthetic judgments—without being led thereby to transcendental idealism.[12]

Humean Skepticism

Hume allowed, as we have seen, that reason does in a sense give birth to the concept of causation; that objects or events may be "objectively" related as cause and effect independent of their actual relation to the mind; and that it is correct to ascribe a species of necessity to that relation—even though we often mislocate the impression of necessary connection and consequently conflate causal necessity with the necessity characteristic of relations of ideas. He also allowed, in effect, that mathematical judgments are both necessary and synthetic—without finding a need to explain their necessity through transcendental idealism. Did he neverthe-less, as the result of his failure to discover transcendental idealism, "run his ship ashore . . . on skepticism, there to let it lie and rot?"

The ship metaphor is, of course, Hume's own, presented in the conclud-ing section of Book 1 of the *Treatise* (*THN* 1.4.7.1). In the first half of that section, he writes that his ship is indeed "weather-beaten" and in danger of sinking as a result of his review of the many "infirmities" of human cognitive faculties that he has discovered in the course of his scien-tific investigation of their operations. Among the infirmities he surveys is the susceptibility of the imagination to the "illusion" concerning the impression of necessary connection whereby it supposes that there is some conceivable quality in individual causes and effects themselves—rather than the constant conjunction between them—that constitutes their power or necessity. Yet although his disconcerting discoveries render him, by the end of the section, what he later calls (*EHU* 12.3) a "mitigated" skeptic—that is, one whose general level of assent, along with his confi-dence in his faculties, has been moderated—he has not concluded that his beliefs lack all epistemic merit. On the contrary, he has given positive normative endorsement to a principle of belief I have called "The Title Principle": "Where reason is lively, and mixes itself with some propensity, it ought to be assented to. Where it does not, it never can have any title to operate upon us" (*THN* 1.4.7.11). Having thus determined that we may, with moderation, "assent to our faculties," he is ready to relaunch his ship of inquiry, propelled by curiosity and ambition, into the deep waters of human nature—and he proceeds to do so, carefully and method-ically discovering many truths about the passions and morals in Books 2 and 3 of the *Treatise*.

There are, to be sure, a number of specific points about which Hume is much more skeptical than Kant. For example, while he grants that it is causally necessary both that every event has a cause and that nature is uniform, he doubts—indeed, denies—that these principles of universal causation and uniformity of nature can be established a priori. But in that, Hume seems to be right, not wrong. He also doubts—indeed, de-nies—that space can be known a priori to be perfectly Euclidean. But in that, too, he seems to be right, not wrong. More generally, Hume finds our knowledge of an external world of "continuing and distinct existences" to be problematic. The belief in such existences, while originating in confu-sions and conflations in the imagination, may properly be accepted as the deliverance of our senses, he holds; but he regards the question of whether these existences actually have qualities resembling our impressions of sec-ondary qualities—and, if not, what space-filling qualities they do have—as a vexed and unresolved one that calls into question our ability even to conceive these existences adequately. (Quantum mechanics raises a somewhat similar question about our ability to conceive adequately the properties of subatomic particles today.) Yet on this score—the epistemic merit of beliefs about the qualities of things as they really stand independent of consciousness of them—Hume is still much less skeptical than Kant, who represents himself as extending Locke's denial that bodies have qualities resembling our ideas of secondary qualities to ideas of primary qualities as well.

Finally, if we take into account what Kant allows us to believe on grounds of practical need, then Hume is more skeptical than Kant about God, freedom of spontaneity, and immortality. Concerning these matters, Kant alleges that Hume "overlooked the positive injury which results if reason be deprived of its most important prospects, which can alone supply to the will the highest aim for all its endeavors" (*Prolegomena*, preface, *AA* 4 258n.). But in allowing that Hume's "moral character" was "quite blameless" despite his rejection of these prospects (A746/B774), Kant only sharpens the question of whether faith in them is really a practical need or only a personal want.

CONCLUSION: HUME AND TRANSCENDENTAL IDEALISM

In this volume, Wayne Waxman has presented a compelling account of how Kant could have thought of himself as carrying through a fundamentally Humean investigation, by less empiricist means, to a happier conclusion. Hume, like Kant, investigates the origins of concepts and purported concepts in a way that is intended to clarify their conditions of application. Like Kant, too, Hume critically examines his own cognitive faculties by means of those very faculties and thereby aims to discern their proper bounds while improving both our science and our morals. Kant's "critical" turn to transcendental idealism is certainly one turn that such an investigation can take, a turn that Hume did not foresee. But if what I have argued is correct, then Hume—with an account of objective causes possessing a distinctive species of necessity, an account of mathematical truths as effectively both necessary and synthetic, and a discriminating mitigated skepticism—might not have been obliged to take that turn even if he had seen it; for his own final position was, if sometimes embarrassing to our philosophical pretensions, nevertheless more tenable than Kant supposed.

Notes

1. For conventions adopted in citing Kant and the early-modern authors discussed in this volume, see the list of abbreviations in the front matter.

CHAPTER ONE
KANT'S "I THINK" VERSUS DESCARTES'
"I AM A THING THAT THINKS"

1. Strictly speaking, starting with the "I think" in the Transcendental Deduction text is reversing the chronological order of Kant's references to Descartes in the *Critique of Pure Reason*. For Kant's criticism of the Cartesian move from "I think" to "I am a thing whose whole essence is to think" first occurs in the Paralogisms of Pure Reason, in the A edition of the *Critique of Pure Reason*, whereas explicit reference to the proposition "I think" occurs only in the B edition of the Transcendental Deduction. However, already in the A edition Kant insists on the relationship of all of our representations to the unity of apperception and the "pure representation 'I' " (see in particular A117n.) And it is clear that Kant's criticism of Descartes in the Paralogisms, in the A edition of the *Critique*, is already grounded on Kant's own view of "I" and "I think," which finds a more systematic presentation in the B edition of the Transcendental Deduction.

2. See *DM*, *AT* VI 32 (*CSMK* I 127). *Principles* I.7; Med II, *AT* VII 25; *AT* IX–1 19. References to the *Meditations* include both the Latin text (*AT* VII) and the contemporary French translation, reviewed by Descartes (*AT* IX–1), in addition to the English translation (*CSMK* II).

3. These texts are, respectively, from Med III, *AT* VII 38; *AT* IX–1 30 (*CSMK* II 27). Med IV, *AT* VII 58; *AT* IX–1 46–47 (*CSMK* II 58). See also *Fourth Replies*, *AT* VII 227; *AT* IX–1 176 (*CSMK* II, 160): "And what M. Arnauld adds is not contrary to what I say, namely, that when I think *I come to conclude* that I am" (emphasis mine). On these references, and for an illuminating analysis of Descartes' argument, see Pariente 1988.

4. On this point and for a penetrating analysis of the role of the first person in Descartes' argument, see Pariente 1999.

5. The relation between unity of intuition and unity of apperception is first asserted at B136n. before being fully developed at B160, and B160n.

6. On this point, Kant's distinction, in §19 of the B Deduction, is between the "merely subjective validity" of empirical associations in imagination, and the objective validity of judgments, "even if the judgment itself is empirical, hence contingent" (B141–43). *How*, despite the fact that any empirical judgment is conditioned by the particular standpoint and circumstances of a particular cognitive

subject, we can nevertheless strive to achieve a standpoint valid for all, is of course the object of Kant's investigation both in the Transcendental Analytic of the *Critique of Pure Reason*, and in the *Prolegomena*.

7. Wilson 1978, p. 72.

8. Caveats are called for here. (2) can be endorsed by Kant only if we take "thing" (*res*) to be utterly indeterminate: a mere "something." Whereas for Descartes, although the notion of substance is introduced only in the Third Meditation, already in the Second Meditation "I am a thinking thing" implicitly means, and indeed will turn out explicitly to mean: "I am a thinking *substance*." As for (3), Kant could only *cautiously endorse* some version of it because strictly speaking, as we shall see in a moment, *what kind of thing* I am, and therefore *what is, or what are, my essential* attributes, is not determined, for Kant, by the examination of the proposition "I think." Nevertheless, in discussing the second Paralogism, Kant declares that it is at least possible to suppose that "the same being that as an appearance is extended, is inwardly (in itself) a subject that is not composite, but simple, and thinks." (A360) See also B429: "In the consciousness of myself in mere thinking I am the being itself [*bin ich das Wesen selbst*], about which however nothing is yet given me to think."

9. See chapter 2 in this volume.

10. A346/B404: "At the ground of this [transcendental doctrine of the soul] we can place nothing but the simple and in content for itself wholly empty representation I, of which one cannot even say that it is a concept, but a mere consciousness that accompanies every concept. Through this I, or He, or It (the thing) which thinks, nothing further is represented than a transcendental subject of thoughts = x, which is recognized only through the thoughts that are its predicates, and about which, in abstraction, we can never have even the least concept."

11. Strawson takes the idea of a criterionless consciousness of self-identity to be Kant's groundbreaking discovery in the Paralogisms of Pure Reason. Accordingly, he centers Kant's whole argument in the Paralogisms around this idea: according to Strawson, the core of Kant's argument consists in saying that because consciousness of oneself in the self-ascription of representations is *not* the consciousness of an object obeying criteria of identification and reidentification (which would have to be a *material* object given in space), rationalist psychologists have come up with the notion of another kind of object as the referent of 'I,' the immaterial soul. Strawson praises Kant for having insisted that this criterionless identity of 'I' is made possible by the mere form of the unity of apperception, and is *not* the identity of an immaterial thing. But he criticizes Kant for not having seen that ultimately the consciousness of self present in self-ascription of experiences is inseparable from a consciousness of the identity of oneself as an empirical, embodied subject: a person (see Strawson 1966, pp. 162–69). I do not think Strawson is correct on this last point (namely, in the neglect of the empirical subject he attributes to Kant), but this is not the place to discuss his view. I address this issue in Longuenesse 2005.

12. That the activity expressed in "I think" is an essential attribute of the transcendental subject = x referred to by 'I' is suggested by Kant's striking statement: "In the consciousness of myself in mere thinking, I am **the being itself** [*im Bewußtsein meiner selbst im bloßen Denken bin ich das Wesen selbst*] about which,

however, nothing yet is given to me for thinking." By "Wesen" Kant clearly means something different here than even the pre-categorial *existence* he claims we have access to in thinking "I think." It is "the being itself," namely, its essence, that is present by way of this act. However, he adds, of this essence we know nothing at all. In a similar vein, Kant seems to indicate that although the "transcendental subject = x" referred to by 'I' is unknown to us, we have reason to think that thought is closer to its essence than is extension: see A359–60. I doubt Kant has much justification for such statements (whatever necessity he claims for them from a practical/moral standpoint), but they are the reason why I suggest he would endorse the statement "I am a thing whose essential attribute is to think."

13. My account here differs from Kant's formulation of the Paralogism, in that I talk of "objects," not appearances. This is because I think that in this case, the equivocation on the middle term, which for Kant is characteristic of every Paralogism of rational psychology, is an ambiguation on "outer object," which may mean *either* "object outside the scope of our cognitive capacities" or "outer appearance." See the explanation that immediately follows the statement of the Paralogism at A367–68.

14. See Med III, *AT* VII 40–45; *AT* IX–1 31–34 (*CSMK* II, 27–31). Note that in the case of God, the reasoning *does* give rise to an assertion of existence that is indubitable: indeed, this is the second assertion of existence that escapes doubt, after that of the *Cogito*. This is because, in this case, *no other cause is possible* for the objective reality of the idea of God than God himself. More particularly, the cause of the objective reality of the idea *cannot be found in me*. On the contrary, all other ideas can have their cause in me. The Sixth Meditation, relying on God's veracity, will of course give us ground to believe that *at least in cases where I exercise judgment in the proper way*, the ideas that I take to have their cause outside me mostly *do* have their cause outside—which is all that Kant, too, claims to establish in his Refutation of Idealism, as we shall see shortly.

15. See Med VI, *AT* VII 80ff.; *AT* IX–1 63ff. (*CSMK* II, 55ff.).

16. See B275–76. Kant's Refutation of Idealism alone would warrant a much more substantial analysis and discussion than I can offer within the limits of this chapter. I do hope, however, that the schema I provide captures its general structure.

17. Paul Guyer has argued that Kant was already aware at the time of the publication of the second edition of the *Critique* (1787) that his new refutation of idealism still left to be improved. Guyer provides a careful analysis of Kant's repeated attempts to provide improved versions of his refutation. He argues that Kant succeeded in his attempt by appealing to the *causal* relation between representations and objects distinct from them, as what alone allows us to determine the temporal order of our representations (see Guyer 1987, pp. 297–316). My own view is that even these later versions of the refutation leave us within the scope of what we are *conscious of* or of what we necessarily *experience* as the condition for what we are conscious of, and thus fail to decisively refute the possibility that those objects whose supposition is necessary might be mere intentional objects of our mental states, not objects ontologically distinct from our mental states.

18. See Heidegger [1927] 1962, p. 249.

CHAPTER 2
DESCARTES' "I AM A THING THAT THINKS"
VERSUS KANT'S "I THINK"

1. *A priori* is used in *Burman, AT* V, 153 (*CSMK* III 337). It is opposed to *ab effectu* or *per effectus*, and it means the same as *per ipsam ejus essentiam sive naturam* (by his own essence or nature), *First Replies, AT* VII 120; *AT* IX–1 94 (*CSMK* II 85). (References to the *Meditations* include both the Latin text (*AT* VII) and the contemporary French translation, reviewed by Descartes (*AT* IX–1), in addition to the English translation (*CSMK* II).) Cf. also Descartes to Mersenne, June 16 and July 1641, *AT* III 383 and 395–96 (*CSMK* III 185 and 186).

2. This follows Cottingham's translation; the phrase could also be rendered as "every time [*quoties*] it is by me uttered [*profertur*] or mentally conceived [*mente concipitur*]."

3. Med II, *AT* VII 27 l.13 (*res cogitans, id est*) and 28 l.20 (*res cogitans . . . nempe*); *AT* IX–1 21 and 22 (*CSMK* II 18). Cf. also Med III, *AT* VII 34 l.18 (*ego sum res cogitans, id est*); *AT* IX–1 27 (*CSMK* II 24).

4. Med VI, *AT* VII 78 l.2–20 (*recte concludo meam essentiam in hoc uno consistere quod sim res cogitans*, l.11–12; *certum est me a corpore meo revera esse distinctum*, l.18–19); *AT* IX–1 62 (with two substantial additions, "une chose qui pense <ou une substance dont toute l'essence ou la nature n'est que de penser>"; "moi, <c'est-à-dire mon âme, par laquelle je suis ce que je suis>."

5. Kant, *Critique of Pure Reason*, the Paralogisms of Pure Reason, A343/B401.

6. *Synopsis, AT* VII 13 l.24–25 (*eorum naturae non modo diversae, sed etiam quodammodo contrariae agnoscantur*); *AT* IX–1 10 ("leurs natures ne sont pas seulement reconnues diverses, mais même en quelque façon contraires") (*CSMK* II 10). Cf. Med VI, *AT* VII 85–86; *AT* IX–1 68–69 (*CSMK* II 59).

7. Cf. the definition of the analytic and the synthetic modes of exposition (*rationes demonstrandi*) in the *Second Replies, AT* VII 155 l.23–27; IX–1 121 (*CSMK* II 110 with note 2). It was "this method alone" that Descartes employed in his *Meditations, AT* VII 156 l.21–23; IX–1122 (*CSMK* II 111).

8. In *DM*, part IV, "j'étais une substance" (*AT* VI 33 l.4 (*CSMK* 127)) is rendered in Latin by *me esse rem quamdam sive substantiam, AT* VI 558.

9. Med VI, *AT* VII 78 l.11–12 (*recte concludo meam essentiam in hoc uno consistere quod sim res cogitans*); *AT* IX–1 62 ("je conclus fort bien que mon essence consiste en cela seul, que je suis une chose qui pense, <ou une substance dont toute l'essence ou la nature n'est que de penser>") (*CSMK* II 54). On the addition in the French translation, see note 4. In the seventeenth century, Descartes' translators often used phrases already present in his previously published works to translate works from the Latin to the French, even if nowadays those phrases do not appear to us quite equivalent to the original Latin. But sometimes Descartes took advantage of the opportunity to qualify or modify his own initial formulation when on second thought he judged it more or less mistaken.

10. The full theory of distinctions was completed only in *Principles* I.60–62.

11. Each Meditation is supposed to occupy one day in a continuous series. Cf. Med II, *AT* VII 23 l.23; *AT* IX–1 18 (*hesterna, hier*, yesterday) (*CSMK* II 16). Med IV, *AT* VII 58 l.26; IX–1 46–47 (*hisce diebus, ces jours passés*, these past few days)

(*CSMK* II 41). The role of time in any actual metaphysical progress is explained in *Second Replies*, *AT* VII 130; IX–1 103 (*CSMK* II 94). Readers, particularly the objectors, were surprised and often reluctant to admit the long amount of time explicitly required by the author for understanding and admitting his new philosophy: they objected that a deeper attention, "as of angels," could allow a shorter duration, cf. Sixth Objections, *AT* VII 420–21; *AT* IX–1 224 (*CSMK* II 283–84). Seventh Objections, *AT* VII 494 l.2–7; *CSMK* II 334. On the marathon speed to be maintained throughout the metaphysical progress, cf. Descartes à Huygens, November 12, 1640, *AT* III 241–42: the first five Meditations must be read "*tout d'une haleine*," all in one breath. The situation is different with respect to the Sixth Meditation.

12. The full theory of substance, (principal or essential) attribute, and mode was completed only in *Principles* I.51–65.

13. This traditional Aristotelian or scholastic principle of life is best translated by "âme" in French, or by "soul" in English.

14. *Sum autem res vera, et vere existens; sed qualis res? dixi, cogitans* (ibid., l.15–16).

15. *Manet/maneat positio*, Med II, *AT* VII 27 l.23; *AT* IX–1 21 (*CSMK* II 18 with note 3).

16. It seems to me that Margaret Wilson definitively established this point in her essay entitled "The Epistemological Argument for Mind-Body Distinctness," revisited and reprinted as chapter 6 in Wilson 1999b.

17. "*rem quae per se apta est existere,*" Med III, *AT* VII 44 l.22–23; *AT* IX–1 35 (*CSMK* II 30).

18. Med III, *AT* VII 34 l.18–20; *AT* IX–1 27 (*CSMK* II 24 and note 1). It is not plausible to suppose that the translators are responsible for the addition of love and hate in the French version, even if one takes into account permissive standards of translation in the seventeenth century (cf. notes 9 and 13). This addition seems related to a new concern developed by Descartes the ethicist, a concern for distinguishing between *passions* (of love and hate), a mere subset of feelings (belonging to the mind insofar as it is united with a body, and ultimately caused by the body), and intellectual or inner *emotions* (of love and hate), which are excited directly in the soul by the soul itself, without any causal connection with the body (cf. *Passions* 2.147–48). In any event, insofar as they are conscious, Descartes considered all the affective events in a human life as so many thoughts, directly assigned to a human mind defined as a thinking thing. In contrast, Kant's *Ich denke* is strictly restricted to its function in the faculty of knowledge, the supreme one, and does not interfere with the other two specific faculties or powers of the human soul, the faculty of desire and the feeling of pleasure and pain, whether in their higher (i.e., autonomous) mode or their lower (i.e., heteronomous) mode: cf. Immanuel Kant, *CJ*, introduction, §IX, *AA* 5 195–97.

19. We thus understand why Descartes could substitute doubting for thinking in *The Search for Truth by Means of the Natural Light*, a small uncompleted and undated Dialogue written in French (though its last pages are only known through a posthumous Latin translation). *Te, qui dubitas, esse* (you who are doubting exist) is substituted for "il fallait nécessairement que moi, qui le pensais, fusse quelque chose," *AT* X, 515 (*CSMK* II 409–10). For another instance of the equiva-

lence of thinking and doubting in the *cogito* argument, cf. *DM* IV, *AT* VI 32 1.29 (*CSMK* II 127): "de ce que je pensais à douter de la vérité des autres choses, il suivait très évidemment et très certainement que j'étais," translated in Latin as "*ex hoc ipso quod reliqua falsa esse fingerem, sive quidlibet aliud cogitarem, manifeste sequi me esse*," *AT* VI 558.

20. Cottingham adds this to the Latin neuter pronouns, a grammatical form that avoids many philosophical intricacies.

CHAPTER 3
KANT'S CRITIQUE OF THE LEIBNIZIAN PHILOSOPHY:
CONTRA THE LEIBNIZIANS, BUT *PRO* LEIBNIZ

1. More precisely, one obtains the following results, listed in this order: number of hits in the published precritical writings, the published critical writings, the *Critique of Pure Reason* (B), the Nachlaß and additional notes, the correspondence (1747–1803); overall. Leibniz (212, 84, 20, 86, 13; 395), Descartes (162, 39, 10, 20, 1; 222), Hume (2, 58, 9, 20, 2; 82), Locke (0, 19, 6, 18, 1; 38), Berkeley (0, 8, 2, 2, 0; 10); also of interest: Newton (80, 33, 3, 152, 1; 266), Wolff (43, 71, 6, 48, 7; 169), Plato (5, 55, 13, 60, 4; 124), Spinoza (1, 21, 0, 70, 5; 97). Even if one does not take into account Kant's first publication, the *Thoughts on the True Estimation of Living Forces*, in which alone, due to the subject matter, there are 186 explicit references to Leibniz (and 141 to Descartes), Leibniz still scores highest in the category "published writings."

2. For a prominent reading in the spirit of the popular story sketched earlier, cf. Friedman 1992. With certain qualifications, one can also place Schönfeld's more recent, very thorough study of Kant's precritical philosophy into this category (Schönfeld 2000). Needless to say, neither of these contributions is restricted to the topic of Kant's development in relation to the Leibniz-Wolffian tradition, and both of them provide a much more detailed and richer account of Kant's development and his relation to Leibniz-Wolff than the previous two-sentence summary reflects. But, I think, it is fair to say that on a more coarse-grained level of analysis, the two-sentence summary, and here especially the assertion that by the time of the first *Critique* Kant had radically broken with the Leibnizian philosophy, agrees with the bottom lines of the two interpretations as far as the indicated topic is concerned. By contrast, the bottom line of the reading advertised in this paper does not agree with the two-sentence summary. In general, I should like to emphasize that my reservations about the popular story are not that it is obviously wrong or uninteresting, but rather that, despite being partially right and illuminating on several counts, it has the potential for misleading the reader if it is not supplemented by additional chapters and appendices in several places, in particular regarding Kant's relation to Leibniz, which, it will be argued, should be understood as a continuous and close family tradition rather than as involving a radical break.

3. Maybe it is significant in this context that Kant says of Hume merely that he "interrupted" his dogmatic slumber, while he credits the antinomies with having "first awakened" him from it and "driven [him] to the critique of pure reason itself" (Letter to Garve, September 21, 1798, *AA* 12 257–58).

4. The relation between Leibniz's conception of truth and the principle of sufficient reason is itself quite complicated and deserves a fuller discussion than can be provided here. The general idea is that, from a logical point of view, the reason for the truth of a proposition is its a priori proof, which consists in showing that the predicate is contained in the subject, while from an, as it were, "objective" or "material" point of view, the reason for the truth of a proposition is that there is a real connection between the property expressed by the predicate and the substance falling under the subject concept (cf. *The Nature of Truth*, C 401–3; *Metaphysical Consequences of the Principle of Reason*, C 11; *On Contingency*, Gr 302ff.; *A Letter on Freedom*, B 115; *On Freedom*, F 179). In the case of propositions asserting causal connections between events in the physical world, this parallel between the logical and material perspectives is broken, since, although there seems to be a real connection, it is not the case that the concept of the cause is contained in the concept of the effect (or vice versa). That Kant was aware of this Leibnizian problem as early as 1763 is illustrated by Kant's discussion in *Negative Magnitudes*, AA 2 202.

5. Transcendental idealism can be characterized as the doctrine that empirical objects are transcendentally ideal, i.e., that they are not things in themselves but appearances (of things in themselves), which are given to us through the forms of our sensibility, space and time, upon the affection of our sensibility by things in themselves (cf. note 65). Obviously, the role of Newtonian physics in the development of Kant's natural philosophy is essential, but his natural philosophy only represents Kant's view of the empirical world, the specifics of which, on my reading of Kant, are largely independent of the transcendental idealist doctrine.

6. All translations of Kant are my own.

7. A fully satisfactory defense of these claims obviously requires more than can be delivered in this short essay. Such a more elaborate account, together with a defense of the reading of Kant's philosophical development sketched in the previous paragraph, is presented in two parts in my "Leibniz Freed of Every Flaw: A Kantian Reads Leibnizian Metaphysics" (unpublished manuscript; an extensively revised version of my doctoral dissertation of the same title, in preparation for publication), and "Kant's True Apology for Leibniz" (unpublished manuscript, work in progress).

8. Length considerations must restrict this sketch to a discussion of Kant's objections against Leibnizian teachings in theoretical philosophy. There are also important, if mostly implicit, objections concerning issues in practical philosophy, or the philosophy of religion, most prominently with respect to the Leibnizian conception of human freedom. A discussion of these further objections will have to wait for another occasion.

9. The explicit diagnosis of this fundamental problem with Leibniz-Wolffian philosophy, i.e., that it does not respect the "transcendental" distinction between sensibility and understanding, and between the phenomenal and noumenal realm, appears quite late in the precritical period, namely in Kant's Inaugural Dissertation (*AA* 2 394ff.). But the Leibnizian confusion itself is already involved in most of the other Leibnizian conundrums that Kant grapples with in the precritical period.

10. By "*substantia phenomenon*," Kant means a phenomenal substance or a substance as a phenomenon, i.e., an appearance that falls under the schema of the category of substance, "the real that is permanent in time" (cf. A44/B183).

11. In this assessment I am disagreeing with Rae Langton, who ascribes this very conception of noumenal substances to Kant; cf. Langton 1998, p. 20: "Things in themselves are substances that have intrinsic properties; phenomena are relational properties of substances."

12. A further objection to the preestablished harmony in the precritical period is based on Kant's conception of the nature of force as extrinsic, which implies that the "self-propelled" evolution of isolated substances in conformity with pre-ordained laws, as postulated by the preestablished harmony, is impossible (cf. *Dilucidatio*, AA 1 412).

13. Kant discovered the importance of directional properties in the individuation of phenomenal objects as early as the 1760s (cf. *Negative Magnitudes*, AA 2 171ff.).

14. In his *Monadologia Physica* (1756), Kant expresses this dilemma in vivid terms, cf. *AA* 1 475: "But shall metaphysics be brought together with geometry in this business, since gryphies seem to be more easily combined with horses than transcendental philosophy with geometry? The former persistently denies that space is infinitely divisible, while the latter asserts it with the same certainty as its other theorems."

15. I do not mean to suggest that the antinomies, or, rather, the problem of the infinite divisibility of space and the problem of infinite real wholes, were solely responsible for Kant's breakthrough in 1769. But they were of crucial importance for the introduction of the distinction between the phenomenal and the noumenal world, which is certainly part of the breakthrough. Another "light giving achievement" in the year 1769 might be Kant's recognition of the law- or form-giving function of our cognitive faculties in response to the problem of the applicability of mathematics to the world, as has been argued influentially, for instance, by Kuno Fischer (1860).

16. Cf. B56–57/A39–40: "If they opt for the second party (which several metaphysical teachers of nature belong to), and they regard space and time as relations of appearances (next to, or after each other) that are abstracted from experience, although confusedly represented in this isolation, they are forced to deny the validity, or, at least, the apodictic certainty, of a priori mathematical doctrines with respect real things (e.g., in space), since such certainty is not to be found in the a posteriori."

17. Rae Langton ascribes an explicit argument against the reducibility of relations to Kant that he supposedly provides in the *Nova Dilucidatio* (cf. Langton 1998, p. 119ff.). Although I agree with Langton that Kant rejects the doctrine of reducibility, I cannot find an explicit argument for this rejection in the indicated text; on the contrary, the argument in the relevant passages in the *Nova Dilucidatio* is explicitly introduced as an argument for the claim that in order to establish relations between substances, God needs to do something in addition to determining their intrinsic properties, and not as an argument against reducibility; in order for the explicitly announced intended conclusion to follow, the failure of reducibility must be presupposed (cf. *Nova Dilucidatio*, AA 1 412ff.).

18. Kant attributes the dismal state of Leibniz-Wolffian metaphysics to the fact that the important distinction between synthetic and analytic judgments has not been drawn, and that the critical question "How are synthetic a priori judgments possible?" has not been raised before, which constitute the first two steps toward a critique of pure reason (cf. *Progress*, *AA* 20 265; Letter to Reinhold, *AA* 11 38; *Prolegomena*, *AA* 4 270).

19. Cf. *Discovery*, *AA* 8 247: "[H]e [Leibniz] was poked by many opponents who didn't understand him, but (as a great specialist and deserving laudator of him says at a certain occasion) he was also misused by his alleged followers and interpreters; as it also happened to several ancient philosophers who might have said: God save us from our friends; of our enemies we will beware ourselves."

20. Cf. note 19. The suggestion that Kant is speaking ironically is the option that Henry Allison seems to favor in his study of *On a Discovery*; he reads the closing section of the essay as mainly a "half tongue-in-cheek, half serious" appendix to the main text (cf. Allison 1973b, pp. 46, 101).

21. Surprisingly little is known about which original Leibnizian works Kant actually read, when he read them, and whether he read many of them at all. He did not own a single book by Leibniz—at least, in Warda's inventory of Kant's books, none is listed. But he had access to and evidently made use of the *Acta Eruditorum*, in which many of Leibniz's writings were published, and there was Kanter's well-stocked bookstore in the same house in which Kant used to live for several years. In Kant's precritical writings we find several explicit references to the *Theodicy* and references to Leibnizian doctrines contained in the following Leibnizian writings (which Kant does not explicitly cite): *De Arte Combinatoria, Hypothesis Physica Nova, A Brief Demonstration of a Notable Error of Descartes, Specimen Dynamicum*, an essay on geography, the reply to Bayle's article "Rorarius," and the correspondence with Clarke. It is very likely that Kant read the *New Essays* as well, which were published in Germany in 1765.

22. Representatives of such a "sober" antimetaphysical reading of Kant include, for instance, the Marburg neo-Kantians and their followers, and Peter Strawson and his students (cf. Strawson 1966).

23. It is worth pointing out that in addition to the indicated antimetaphysical tradition in Kant scholarship, there is also a venerable tradition of interpreters who read Kant's philosophy as containing substantive (positive) metaphysical doctrines, or who, at least, stress its continuity, as opposed to its allegedly radical break, with the ontology and metaphysics of its Leibniz-Wolff-Baumgartian predecessors. Such a more metaphysical way of reading Kant seems to be on the rise again, as is indicated by the increasing number of more recent interpretations falling into this category. Early representatives of this tradition include, for instance, Heinz Heimsoeth and Max Wundt (cf. Heimsoeth 1924; Wundt 1924); more recent representatives (disagreements about more particular exegetical questions notwithstanding) are, for instance, Karl Ameriks, Robert Adams, and Rae Langton (cf. Ameriks 1992a, b; Adams 1997; Langton 1998).

24. This is the main thesis of my doctoral dissertation, "Leibniz Freed of Every Flaw: A Kantian Reads Leibnizian Metaphysics," Princeton University, 2004.

25. Such an interpretation is developed in my "Kant's True Apology for Leibniz" (unpublished manuscript).

26. The famous appellation of Kant as *"Alleszermalmer"* ("all-crusher") has its origin in Moses Mendelssohn's *Morgenstunden* (*Morning-Hours*) (1785), in which he refers to Kant as "the all-crushing Kant" (Mendelssohn 1971, v. 3.2, p. 3).

27. In his contribution to the present volume, Daniel Garber casts a critical glance on both of these assumptions.

28. For recent studies in the literature that credit a relatively robust continuity and systematic coherence to Leibniz's thinking, cf., for instance, Adams 1994 or Mercer 2001.

29. On the question of which of Leibniz's writings Kant actually read, cf. note 21.

30. To be as brief as possible, we will restrict our discussion to Kant's and Leibniz's views on space. The case of time is a bit more complicated, but the main lessons are analogous to the ones that can be drawn for space.

31. Cf. McGuire 1976 or Hartz and Cover 1988. Adams accepts the suggested three-level distinction as well, but stresses that the phenomenal level should not be treated as metaphysically isolated from the other two levels, but as "partaking of both," a view with which I concur (cf. Adams 1994, pp. 254ff.). Garber, following Martial Gueroult, draws a threefold distinction between mechanistic physics proper in which all phenomena are explained in terms of the notions of size, shape, and motion, dynamics which treats forces and its bearers, i.e., corporeal substances, and metaphysics which deals with individual substances or monads (cf. Garber 1995; Garber 1985, esp. pp. 203–8).

32. One also might want to add a separate level for God, who is the most real entity in Leibniz's scheme and who exists independently of anything else. For reasons of length, I had to gloss over many details and complications in the following sketch of Leibniz's ontological levels, especially regarding his complex views on corporeal substance.

33. A view of Leibnizian phenomena along these lines has been defended most prominently in recent years by Robert Adams (cf. Adams 1994, chap. 9). I disagree with Adams's identification of aggregates of monads with phenomena in the indicated intentional object sense, which is a central part of Adams's interpretation, but there is not enough room to discuss this disagreement in the present context, so it will be passed over in silence.

Leibniz proposes several criteria for the reality or well-foundedness of the phenomena in addition to their intersubjective perceptibility, which permit a distinction between different degrees of well-foundedness within Leibniz's scheme, e.g., internal coherence, conformity to general necessary truths, or whether the phenomenon in question can be shown to "result from" monads (cf. *On the Method of Distinguishing Real from Imaginary Phenomena*, G VII 319–22; *NE, AL* VI.6 374–75, 392; *Of Universal Synthesis and Analysis*, G VII 296; *Discourse on Metaphysics* (in the following abbreviated as *"DM"*), §14, G IV 439ff.; *Reply to Bayle's Thoughts*, G IV 569; To De Volder, June 30, 1704, G II 268). Fortunately, the details of Leibniz's quite complicated theory of well-foundedness can safely be ignored for our present purposes.

34. To be precise, a corporeal substance of the third kind is composed of an organic body, i.e., a phenomenal entity, and a substantial form, i.e., an element of the substantial level of reality. This means that, strictly speaking, this kind of

corporeal substance does not belong to any one level of Leibniz's ontological scheme, but spans both the phenomenal and the substantial realms. This is the reason for the qualification in the main text that at the third phenomenal level one does not really find corporeal substances, but only their organic bodies.

35. Cf. Notes for a letter to des Bosses, February 5, 1712, G II 438; DM §14, G IV 439; *Theodicy*, §403, G VI 356.

36. It should be emphasized that the phrase "merely phenomenal" is not meant to imply that the phenomena in question are illusory. In my reading of Leibniz, the phenomena of all three phenomenal levels are well-founded, according to some criterion of well-foundedness (cf. note 33), even though not all of them are free from confusion introduced through perception, or from other "ideal" features that are due to the operations of the perceiving mind or soul.

37. Cf. LC 25–26, 89, G VII 363, 415; *Metaphysical Foundations of Mathematics*, GM VII 18; Letter to de Volder, June 6, 1703, G II 253; Letter to de Volder, June 30, 1704, G II 269.

38. Cf. Marginal note to a letter to de Volder, 1704/05, G II 276; Letter to de Volder, October 11, 1705, G II 278–79; Letter to Des Bosses, July 31, 1709, G II 379; Letter to Electress Sophie, *On What Is Independent of Sense and Matter*, G VII 561–62.

39. Cf. LC 67–69, G VII 398–99; *Conversation between Philarète and Ariste*, G VI 583ff.; NE, AL VI.6 153; LC 26, 89, G VII 363, 415. Additionally, the ideality of space—at least in the actual world—can be inferred from the fact that all parts of space are indistinguishable from each other, which means that they do not conform to the principle of the identity of indiscernibles, a nonconformity Leibniz takes to be characteristic of ideal entities (cf. LC 63, G VII 395).

40. I am aware that the claims about extension and (one kind of) *materia prima* implicitly contained in this example are controversial. Unfortunately, there is no room to explain or defend these claims in the present chapter. But whoever is in the position to disagree with these claims should also be in the position to substitute a different example from the Leibnizian philosophy that is acceptable from his or her point of view, which I kindly ask him or her to do.

41. For the claim that space and time involve mental constructions, cf. *Specimen Dynamicum*, part II, GM VI 247 (L 445): "First of all, we must recognize that force is something absolutely real even in created substances but that space, time, and motion have something akin to a mental construction and are not true and real per se but only insofar as they involve the divine attributes of immensity, eternity, and activity or the force of created substances."

42. For the latter sense in which phenomenal space is "anchored" to the material world, cf. LC 70, G VII 400: "It may be said also, without entering into any further particularity, that place is that, which is the same in different moments to different existent things, when their relations of coexistence with certain other existents, which are supposed to continue fixed from one of those moments to the other, agree entirely together. And fixed existents are those, in which there has been no cause of any change of the order of their coexistence with others; or (which is the same thing,) in which there has been no motion. Lastly, space is that which results from places taken together."

43. Cf. Hartz and Cover 1988.

44. Hartz and Cover 1988, p. 502.

45. Robert Adams expresses a similar disagreement with Hartz and Cover regarding their view that there is a "metaphysical apartheid" between the phenomenal and the ideal level (cf. Adams 1994, p. 254). But Adams also seems to think that Leibniz wants to assert that actual bodies, i.e., corporeal substances, are in (ideal) space, an assessment in which I cannot follow Adams.

46. For the distinction between ideal and concrete space on the merely phenomenal level of reality, cf. *LC* 63, *G* VII 395; *Conversation between Philarète and Ariste*, *G* VI 585.

47. Cf. Letter to Des Bosses, May 26, 1712, *G* II 444.

48. Cf. *Anti-barbarus Physicus*, *G* VII 344 (AG 319); Letter to Des Bosses, *G* II 450.

49. Cf. *NE*, *AL* VI.6 81: "Intellectual ideas, from which necessary truths arise, do not come from the senses; and you acknowledge that some ideas arise from the mind's reflection when it turns in on itself." See also Letter to Electress Sophie, *On What Is Independent of Sense and Matter*, *G* VI 505–6.

50. Cf. Letter to Electress Sophie, *G* VII 564: "Both of these foundations [of the order of things, i.e., time and space] are true, although they are ideal. Uniformly ordered continuity, although it is nothing but a supposition and abstraction, provides the basis of eternal truths and of the necessary sciences." Also *NE*, *AL* VI.6 154: "Time and space are of the nature of eternal truths, which equally concern the possible and the actual."

51. Cf. in particular Leibniz's discussion in Book 1 of the New Essays. For the (strikingly similar) Kantian account, cf. especially *Discovery*, *AA* 8 221ff.; Letter to J.W.A. Kosmann, September 1789, *AA* 11 82.

52. Cf. *NE*, *AL* VI.6 50: "From this it appears that necessary truths, such as we find in pure mathematics and particularly in arithmetic and geometry, must have principles whose proof does not depend on instances, nor, consequently, on the testimony of the senses, even though without the senses it would never occur to us to think of them." Abstraction from spatial relations is only part of the original acquisition of the concept of space; the idea of its infinity, for instance, is acquired through reflection on our mind's own reasoning (cf. *NE*, *AL* VI.6 157ff.).

53. For the claim that necessary truths are "grounded" in God, cf. *NE*, *AL* VI.6 149: "Space is no more a substance than time is. . . . It is a relationship: and order, not only among existents, but also among possibles as though they existed. But its truths and reality are grounded in God, like all eternal truth." Also *Monadology*, §43, *G* VI 614; *NE*, *AL* VI.6 227, 447; Letter to Bourguet, 1714, *G* III 572. The appeal to God is, of course, part of the standard rationalist account for the applicability of mathematics to the world. But in addition to this general move, Leibniz can also provide a further, more detailed story, as we will see presently.

54. If God does not describe the spatial orders of all possible worlds in Euclidean terms, does that not mean that Euclidean geometry is merely contingently true, which conflicts with the alleged necessity that Leibniz seems to attribute to it? Yes and no. There is some evidence that Leibniz conceives of the propositions of geometry as hypothetical propositions of the form "Axiom(s) and Definition(s) imply Theorem." Cf. *NE*, *AL* VI.6 447: "As for 'eternal truths,' it must be understood that fundamentally they are all conditional; they say, in effect: given so and

so, such and such is the case. For instance, when I say: Any figure which has three sides will also have three angles, I am saying nothing more than that given that there is a figure with three sides that same figure will have three angles. . . . The scholastics hotly debated de constantia subjecti, as they put it, i.e. how a proposition about a subject can have a real truth if the subject does not exist. The answer is that its truth is a merely conditional one which says that if the subject ever does exist it will be found to be thus and so. But it will be further asked what the ground is for this connection, since there is a reality in it which does not mislead. The reply is that it is grounded in the linking together of ideas." Cf. also NE, AL VI.6 360–61, 450; Principles of Nature and Grace, §5, G VI 600–601. That is, with respect to what we now call "pure" geometry, one could read Leibniz as a proponent of an "if-thenism" view of mathematical truths. And the truth of these hypothetical propositions is, of course, independent of what the actual, or any other possible world is like. If they are true, they are so necessarily. But would Leibniz not also want to say that Euclidean geometry is necessarily true of the actual world? That is not all that clear. If God necessarily created the best of all possible worlds, and if the spatial order of the best of all possible worlds were necessarily Euclidean, and if the actual world were necessarily the best of all possible worlds, then Euclidean geometry would be necessarily true of the actual world. We know from Leibniz's discussions of freedom and contingency that in his view, the first or the third of these conditions fails—more probably the third—although this part of Leibniz's theory is among the most difficult and obscure ones (for a well-balanced, thorough treatment of Leibniz's theory of contingency, cf. Adams 1994, chap. 1). I take it that if Leibniz had been aware of the possibility of non-Euclidean geometries, he would have classified Euclidean geometry as hypothetically necessary, i.e., as necessary given God's (free) choice to create the best possible world. If he regards Euclidean geometry as the only possible geometry, on the other hand, he should also regard it as necessarily true of the actual world, given the assumption that the world must have some geometrical structure, an assumption that seems to be endorsed by Leibniz.

55. Cf. Reply to Bayle's Thoughts, G IV 568 (L, 583): "But space and time taken together constitute the order of possibilities of the one entire universe, so that these orders—space and time, that is—relate not only to what actually is but also to anything that could be put in its place, just as numbers are indifferent to the things which can be enumerated"; LC 42; Principles of Nature and Grace, §10, G VI 603; Theodicy, §8, §119, G VI 107, 169; Letter to Malebranche, June 22/July 2, 1679, G I 331. For God's stepwise procedure in "composing" possible worlds—which steps, of course, occur simultaneously, their order being one of logical but not chronological priority—cf., for instance, Theodicy, §225, G VI 252.

56. For the claim that space and time provide the conditions for the unification of a given collection of bodies in one world, cf. Letter to Des Bosses, October 22, 1706, G II 324: "To remove these [intelligences] from bodies and place, is to remove them from the universal connection and order of the world, which is brought about by relations to time and place." See also Letter to de Volder, 1704/1705, G II 277–78; Letter to de Volder, June 6, 1703, G II 253; Theodicy, §120, §200, G VI 172–73, 236.

57. And, we might add, it will be left to later science to draw attention to the fact that if one wants to defend an idealist view of space and time of this kind, not only the particular arrangement of the phenomena in a universal spatio-temporal order but also the geometric structure of this framework itself needs to be ascribed to God's free decrees or the constitutive function of our minds.

58. How much of a dissimilarity this really amounts to depends on what exactly Leibniz understands concepts to be and what exactly Kant understands intuitions to be, which is a long story that cannot be told in the present context.

59. This cautious formulation is in order, since Leibniz does not deny that space, or our representation of space, possesses these features, but neither plays very much of a role in his theory.

60. Such a more detailed and more nuanced story can be found in chapters 5 and 6 of my doctoral dissertation (Jauernig 2004).

61. Thanks to an anonymous referee for pressing me on the second question, and to Béatrice Longuenesse for pressing me on the first.

62. So, I am not disagreeing with Allison when he claims that "Kant appears to regard these two forms of transcendentalism as mutually exclusive and exhaustive metaphilosophical alternatives" (Allison 2004, p. 20). But I am disagreeing with the view that Kant's explicit characterizations of the distinction between transcendental idealism and transcendental realism about space succeed in providing a partition of all possible positions about the ontological status of space into these two categories.

63. For an informative, more detailed discussion of the proper understanding of transcendental idealism that is not limited to the subject of space, cf. Allison 2004, chapter 2.

64. For our present concerns we can bracket the question of how exactly the distinction between things in themselves and appearances should be understood, and bypass the messy debate between defenders of a "two world" reading and a "two aspect" reading of this Kantian distinction. If our present remarks are defensible, they should apply, *mutatis mutandis*, regardless of which reading is adopted.

65. Cf. A369: "I understand by transcendental idealism of all appearances the doctrine, according to which we regard all of them [the appearances] as mere representations and not as things in themselves, and according to which time and space are just sensible forms of our intuition, but not determinations that are given in themselves or conditions of objects as things in themselves. This idealism is opposed to a transcendental realism, which regards time and space as something that is given in itself (independently of our sensibility). The transcendental realist, thus, imagines outer appearances as things in themselves (if one admits their reality), which exist independently of us and of our sensibility, and which would, thus, also be outside of ourselves, according to pure concepts of the understanding." See also *AA* 18 610: "This is the theory that space and time are nothing but subjective forms of our sensible intuition, and not at all determinations inhering in objects in themselves. . . . This theory can be called the doctrine of the ideality of space and time, since these are regarded as something that doesn't inhere in things in themselves." Also A26/B42–A28/B44; *Prolegomena*, appendix, *AA* 4 374ff.

66. Of course, space understood in this way exists not only in God's mind but also in the minds of monads (and, thus, in the phenomenal world), but God's mind is the ultimate source of its reality (cf. note 53).

67. This essay is written in honor of the memory of Margaret D. Wilson. It was my good fortune to have had the opportunity to take my so-called first-year seminar as a graduate student at Princeton with Margaret. The topic was Locke's *Essay*. My introduction to "analytic style" early-modern philosophy could not have been a better one, and I am grateful for the privilege of having known her, as a wonderful philosopher and as a wonderful person. This seminar turned out to be the last one she ever taught.

I would like to thank two anonymous referees for their objections and suggestions for improvement, the audience at the conference on Kant and the Early Moderns at Princeton University for helpful questions during the discussion period, my "teammate" in the session on Kant and Leibniz, Dan Garber, for his insightful and stimulating paper and his probing comments, my colleague Karl Ameriks for helpful discussions and many comments, especially the ones I could decipher, and here in particular the very clever suggestion to insert a "nothing but" at a crucial place, and, above all, Béatrice Longuenesse for her patience and invaluable help during many discussions of this and other topics in Kant and Leibniz, and for being the nicest chief editor in this best of all possible worlds.

CHAPTER 4
WHAT LEIBNIZ REALLY SAID?

1. In what follows I shall use "*Monadology*" (with a capital letter and in quotation marks) to designate the specific text that usually goes by that name, and "monadology" (with a lowercase letter and without quotation marks) to designate Leibniz's metaphysical account of the world in terms of monads, a theory that appears in many texts. For an account of the diffusion of the "*Monadology*" after Leibniz's death, see Lamarra, Palaia, and Pimpinella 2001.

2. The first edition of the Leibniz-Clarke correspondence was published in London in 1717, under the editorship of Clarke.

3. The *Nouveaux essais* first appeared in Leibniz 1765.

4. For a relatively complete bibliography that indicates when Leibniz's writings were published, see Ravier 1937. The reader should use this with some care, since it is not entirely reliable. See the supplement in Schrecker 1938. It is, of course, quite out-of-date by now, but it is still the best source we have for the publication of Leibniz's writings before 1937.

5. On the genesis of the "*Monadology*," see Pasini 2005.

6. On Brucker and his importance for the history of philosophy, see Braun 1973, pp. 119–37; Bottin, Longo, and Piaia 1979, pp. 527–635; and Schmidt-Biggemann and Stammen 1998.

7. On this see Beck 1969 and Corr 1975.

8. See Wilson 1995, pp. 447–48.

9. See Wilson 1990, pp. 88–89.

10. For a preliminary outline of what such a metaphysics looks like, see, e.g., Garber 1985. I am now working on a much more extended treatment of these issues, where I hope to present a more subtle and nuanced view of Leibniz's thought in his middle years, from roughly 1679 to the mid- or late 1690s and how his earlier thought led him to that view.

11. I would like to thank Paul Lodge for having made available to me his new translation and edition of the de Volder correspondence, soon to be published in the Yale Leibniz series. All of the following translations of the Leibniz–de Volder correspondence used here are his.

12. This letter would have been written between November 14, 1704, and October 11, 1705.

13. This is an unpublished draft of the last letter that Leibniz sent to de Volder, sometime after January 5, 1706. I would like to thank Paul Lodge for providing me with this text and for its translation.

14. This is the view on the relation between monads and bodies that Jauernig attributes to Leibniz in her essay in this volume (see chapter 3). In her dissertation, she argues at greater length for the thesis that this view, which she calls "idealist immaterialism," is Leibniz's considered view. See Jauernig 2004, p. 54. As I understand it, her thesis is that when properly understood, Kant and Leibniz come out rather close on this issue, and in that respect, Kant can be read as a defender of the true Leibnizian philosophy. In the dissertation, though, she treats many other points of contact between the two in defending her general thesis that Kant can be read as a true defender of the Leibnizian philosophy.

15. I would like to thank Don Rutherford and Brandon Look for having made their new edition and translation of the Leibniz–Des Bosses correspondence available to me. It will soon be published in the Yale Leibniz series. All of the translations of the Leibniz—Des Bosses letters that follow are due to them.

16. For a detailed development of the view, see Look 1999.

17. Gerhardt dates this letter as February 5, 1712. Rutherford and Look give convincing evidence for the date of February 15.

CHAPTER 5
KANT'S TRANSCENDENTAL IDEALISM
AND THE LIMITS OF KNOWLEDGE:
KANT'S ALTERNATIVE TO LOCKE'S PHYSIOLOGY

1. Translations from Immanuel Kant, *Critique of Pure Reason*, edited and translated by Paul Guyer and Allen W. Wood (Cambridge: Cambridge University Press, 1998).

2. See also R 4893, AA 18 21. Both of these notes are translated in full in *Notes*, pp. 197, 198.

3. *Met. Mrongovius*, AA 29 763.

4. *Notes*, p. 98.

5. *Notes*, pp. 194–96.

6. *Notes*, p. 206.

7. *Notes*, pp. 261–64.

8. *Met. Vigilantius*, AA 29 258–59.

9. Of course, Locke shared this distinction with other seventeenth-century thinkers such as Galileo, Descartes, and Boyle. See Burtt 1955, chapters 3 and 6.

10. Admittedly, his claim, as it is presented in the fourth and fifth editions of the *Essay*, that "*Bodies* produce *Ideas* in us . . . manifestly *by impulse*, the only way which we can conceive Bodies operate in" (*E* 2.8.11) may sound as if it is supposed to be a conceptual truth of some kind; but Locke has provided no account of any source for such a conceptual truth, and his more extended statement of the point in the earlier editions of the *Essay*—that it is "impossible to conceive, that Body should operate on what it does not touch, (which is all one as to imagine it can operate where it is not) or when it does touch, operate like any other way than by Motion"—sounds very much like an inference from observation of the behavior of perceptible bodies.

11. The literature on Locke's version of the distinction between primary and secondary qualities is far too extensive for me to canvas it here, and therefore for me to defend the present interpretation adequately. Something approximating what I have called a "conceptual" account of the basis for the distinction might be found in Buchdahl 1969, pp. 232–23. The kind of empirical interpretation of the basis of the distinction that I favor is suggested in Mandelbaum 1964, pp. 21–22. In "Did Berkeley Completely Misunderstand the Basis of the Primary-Secondary Quality Distinction in Locke?" (originally 1982), Margaret Wilson discusses the question of whether the foundation of the distinction lies in common-sense observations or scientific theory, but in either case the underlying assumption seems to be that the foundation of the distinction is empirical rather than conceptual; see Wilson 1999a, pp. 215–28.

12. For further arguments of the same kind, see *E* 2.31.12, 4.3.16, and 4.6.11.

13. See *Prolegomena*, §5.

14. I have discussed this argument in detail in Guyer 1987, pp. 354–69.

15. In the *CPrR* (*AA* 5 13), Kant famously asserts that even Hume did not assert that the fundamental propositions of mathematics are empirically known and therefore contingent. That Hume asserted precisely this in the *THN* (1.2.5) is evidence that Kant was not directly acquainted with Hume's magnum opus.

16. See Mendelssohn 1997, pp. 251–306, especially pp. 257–68. Kant had to be familiar with this work, since it triumphed over his own entry in the Berlin Academy's competition on the question of whether the method of metaphysics was the same as that of mathematics and was published along with Kant's own entry, the 1764 *Inquiry Concerning the Distinctness of the Principles of Natural Theology and Morals*. For a detailed comparison of the two essays, see my "Mendelssohn and Kant: One Source of the Critical Philosophy," in Guyer 2000, pp. 17–59.

17. I have argued for this interpretation of at least one central strand of argument in Kant's Transcendental Deduction of the Categories in Guyer 1980 and Guyer 1987, pp. 132–49.

18. An earlier and abbreviated version of this paper appeared under the title "Transzendentaler Idealismus und die Grenzen der Erkenntnis" in Wolfram Hogrebe (ed.), *Grenzen und Grenzüberschreitungen: XIX. Deutscher Kongress für Philosophie* (Berlin: Akademie Verlag, 2004), pp. 89–103.

CHAPTER 6
THE "SENSIBLE OBJECT" AND THE
"UNCERTAIN PHILOSOPHICAL CAUSE"

1. See also *Drafts*, p. 215.

2. E.g., "4° The understanding certainly knows that those Ideas it hath at any time in its self doe at that time actualy & undoubtedly exist there 5° The understanding infallibly knows that those Ideas exist without it. or that those things which affecting the senses always produce those appearances doe exist" (*Drafts*, p. 42).

3. Compare Boyle's explicit refusal to define his notion of quality (Boyle 1991, pp. 28–29; Boyle 1999–2000, vol. 5, p. 314).

4. See also the correspondence with Stillingfleet, *LW* 4 360. One obvious question to ask about Locke's move is how we can be certain that we do not cause the idea in question. Locke, like Descartes before him, assumes that we could not cause such ideas without being aware of doing so.

5. This is the point one is left with if, following Locke's instructions, one substitutes "qualities" for "ideas" in the otherwise perplexing *E* 2.23.1:

> not imagining how these simple *Ideas* can subsist by themselves, we accustom our selves, to suppose some *Substratum*, wherein they do subsist, and from which they do result, which therefore we call *Substance*.

6. See McCann 2001.

7. Contra Bennett 1971 and 1998. I disagree, however, with Ayers's views about (1) why we do need the idea of substance, under actual conditions, and (2) the content of the idea. Ayers 1991, vol. 2, pp. 37, 41. See also Ayers 1975 and 1994.

8. Locke reminds us at *E* 2.2.1 that what is diverse in ideas is unified in things: "[T]he Qualities that affect our Senses, are, in the things themselves, so united and blended, that there is no separation, no distance between them."

9. Implicit here is Locke's assumption that the basic or primary qualities of bodies are categorical properties internally connected to one another, in the way that extension, size, shape, motion/rest, and (arguably) solidity seem to be.

10. For a more extended treatment, see Downing 2001.

11. Except for one case noted later in note 12, all of my references to Draft C are to Ruth Mattern's transcription of selections from Draft C in Mattern 1981.

12. The first (and new) tendency is evident in the primary/secondary quality distinction and real essence discussions, of course. The second is evident to some extent or other in Draft C 1.1.2, Draft C 2.25.51, Draft C 2.7.5, and Draft C 2.7.24, as well as being present in earlier drafts. The first of these references to Draft C is not found in Mattern 1981.

13. See Draft C 2.21.10 and Draft C 2.21.7.

14. Its first clear and explicit appearance is in Locke's abstract of the *Essay* (Locke 1688a).

15. For a more detailed development of this interpretation of Locke's primary/secondary quality distinction, see Downing 1998, pp. 387–96.

16. Compare McCann's assertion (McCann 1994, p. 59) that Locke argues in *E* 2.8 that mechanism reflects our commonsense conception of body. Atherton (1984) and Ayers (1981, p. 229) connect the corpuscularian conception of matter to the nominal essence of matter, as I do.

17. Jacovides (2002, p. 164) objects that Locke's corpuscularian lists of primary qualities are longer than his characterization of the nominal essence of body as "solid extended figured Substance" (*E* 3.10.15) or "something that is solid, and extended, whose parts are separable and movable" (*E* 2.13.11). But surely Locke saw items on the longer lists, such as bulk, motion or rest, and number, as simply following from the core notion of solid extended substance, just as Descartes saw all of the features of bodies as following from extension.

18. As Boyle, who was concerned to show that these Aristotelian notions could be made sense of without appeal to substantial forms, had already established (Boyle 1991, pp. 37–42; Boyle 1999, vol. 5, pp. 322–26).

19. That Locke is limning our idea of matter, and thus giving a nominal essence, is clear in *E* 2.23.15.

20. See also *E* 3.6.21.

21. Locke's initial reading of Newton's *Principia*, it is clear, did not reveal this implication to him. On the contrary, his anonymous review of the *Principia* in Locke 1688b shows that he interprets Newton's attempted neutrality as to the cause of attraction as decided preference for impulse:

> Before beginning this section, the author explains how he understands "attractive force" and "attraction," which should rather be termed "impulse," speaking physically. But the author has kept this popular term in order not to involve himself in philosophical disputes. (Locke 1688b, p. 438)

Despite noting that Newton "proves that the planets are not carried along by corporeal vortices," Locke shows little appreciation, at this point, for the challenge Newton's work ultimately posed to a strictly mechanical worldview. By the time of *Some Thoughts Concerning Education* (published 1693), however, Locke sees Newtonian gravity as having far-reaching implications:

> [I]t is evident, that by mere Matter and Motion, none of the great Phænomena of Nature can be resolved, to instance but in that common one of Gravity. (*TCE*, p. 246)

22. "[H]e is granting to *bodies* what is not even *intelligible*, granting them powers and activities which in my opinion transcend anything that a created mind could do or understand; for he grants attraction to them, even at great distances and without limitation to any sphere of activity, merely so as to uphold a view which is equally inexplicable, namely the possibility of matter thinking in the natural course of events" (*NE*, p. 61).

23. As opposed to his theological righteous indignation.

24. See Wilson 1999a, p. 197.

25. A version of this point is made by Ayers (1981). Here I side with Ayers, to an extent, against Stuart (1998). In Stuart's terminology, I endorse an epistemological reading of many superaddition passages, while noting that when Locke describes God as being responsible for some phenomenon through superaddition, he never rules out that God is so responsible by creating/engineering bodies whose

real essences go beyond our ideas of matter. For a developed version of this last suggestion, applied to Locke's views on thinking matter, see Downing 2007.

26. As he signals clearly enough by writing of "what men can account for from the essence of matter in general."

27. See Guyer 1994, pp. 133–34, and Owen 1991, pp. 105–18.

28. In particular, his examples are not meant to commit him to the claim that the real essences of bodies are exhausted by extension and solidity.

29. See Downing 2007.

30. "*Natural Philosophy*, as a speculative Science, I imagin we have none, and perhaps, I may think I have reason to say, we never shall be able to make a Science of it" (*TCE*, pp. 244–45).

31. I am influenced here by an unpublished paper of Howard Stein's.

CHAPTER 7
KANT'S CRITIQUE OF BERKELEY'S CONCEPT OF OBJECTIVITY

1. One can also see space as "inhering" in things (A39). If space is to be a property of things, it must be something that really inheres in the substances (see B70ff.). In this case, too, the concept of space is self-contradictory, insofar as space is also supposed to be the condition of the existence of all things.

2. This seems to be implied in what Kant writes at A40/B56; cf. also B71.

3. I took over the concept "criteria of truth" from Kant (*AA* 4, 375). I understand a criterion as a necessary and/or sufficient condition. With respect to empirical knowledge—which will be the central issue in what follows—the universal and necessary laws are necessary (not sufficient) conditions.

4. In order to explain Kant's conception of objectivity, one needs to take into account not only the *Critique of Pure Reason* but also the *Metaphysical Foundation of Natural Science* and the *Critique of Judgment*. This does not contradict the claim that Kant thinks of his *Critique of Pure Reason* as the work that formulates an answer to Berkeley, because Kant understands the *Critique of Pure Reason* as providing the basis for what he elaborated in these other writings.

5. This is formulated not only in the *Critique of Pure Reason* (A/B642ff./B670ff.) but also in the *MFNS* (*AA* 4 523–35) and in the *CJ* (*AA* 5 179ff.).

6. In fact, in addition to this idea of a system, Kant also has the notion of a system of concepts and principles which can constitute an empirical science.

7. See, e.g., Kant's statement of the objective validity of the Principles of Pure Understanding at A158/B197.

8. This is a controversial claim which I cannot defend here. See Emundts 2004, chapter 1. Some Kant scholars see the relation to space as something that is made explicitly only in the *Metaphysical Foundation of Natural Science* and in the second edition of the *Critique of Pure Reason*. See Förster 2000, 48–74.

9. That Kant mentions only space (and not time) in contrasting his position from Berkeley's (*AA* 4 374ff.) is grounded in the fact—which I elaborated earlier—that the apriority of space is the condition for the natural laws.

10. In translating "*wirklich*" by "real" (rather than "actual"), I am following Paul Guyer. Note that when I use "real" or "reality" in my text, it is normally to translate the German "*wirklich*" or "*Wirklichkeit*."

11. This similarity between Kant and Berkeley against a skeptical position is highlighted by Turbayne (1955). It has often served as support for the claim that Kant's interpretation of Berkeley as an antirealist is false. Cf. Kemp Smith 1950, pp. 156ff.

12. See, for example, Wolff 2001.

13. For Kant, then, perceptions, understood as the products of a synthetic activity, are never incorrigible data. This is highlighted by Harper 1984.

14. This is made clear in the second edition (B274), but is also true in the first (A377).

15. The dogmatic idealist, says Kant in the fourth Paralogism of the A edition, believes himself able to find a contradiction in the possibility of matter in general (A377).

16. We can here ignore Kant's argument against Descartes to the effect that there must be something real in space if there is to be an empirically determinate consciousness of one's own existence. As Kenneth Winkler shows in his paper (see chapter 8 in this volume), this argument could also be directed against Berkeley's position.

17. This is also true if one assumes that space has its own (Euclidean) structure. It would then be possible in principle to have intuitions without conceptual elements in a certain order. If, however, Kant can show that the rules of the understanding must apply in order to speak of a unified consciousness, the possibility of a merely spatially ordered manifold is for us excluded.

18. This is the reason why Kant claims in the *Prolegomena* (appendix, *AA* 4 375n.): "Genuine idealism always has a visionary purpose and can have no other."

19. Cf. Winkler 1989, pp. 255–63.

20. See also A45/B62. Kant's strategy of using the analogy with secondary qualities when discussing appearances is not necessarily convincing, not least because secondary qualities have not usually been seen as "real" or "objective." I do not want to discuss here whether Kant also wants to introduce the thing in itself through such considerations about secondary and primary qualities (see *Prolegomena*, §13 Rem.2, *AA* 4 289). For a discussion of this question, see Strawson 1966, p. 237.

21. Kant's model here is Leonard Euler, cf. *CJ* §14, *AA* 5 224. I will not discuss here whether Kant has a fully worked out theory about the "real character" of secondary qualities. On this point, see Wilson 1999b.

22. This point is not contradicted by the claim that geometrical and space filling dynamical properties take over in part the function of traditional primary qualities (as claimed by Langton 1998, pp.162–85; cf. also Brittan 1978). Here, too, Kant's empirical distinction between primary and secondary qualities has to be taken into account.

23. For my thesis that according to Kant impenetrability is a property that we know a priori, see Emundts 2004, chapter 1.

24. Intensive magnitudes are also representable in space: cf. A179/B221.

25. Color perceptions, but probably also perceptions of sound, should be distinguished from perceptions of taste and smell, which Kant (correspondingly) calls "more subjective" senses in the *Anthropology* (*AA* 7 157). Accordingly, judgments of taste would be judgments based only on a feeling. Kant provides "sugar

is sweet" as an example of this in the *Prolegomena* (§19, *AA* 4 299). This should also be kept in mind if one wants to locate Kant's position more precisely in the debate over secondary qualities.

26. The use goes back to Kant's Inaugural Dissertation, according to which one can refer to objects as they are in themselves by way of intellectual representations (see, for instance, *Inaugural Dissertation* §26, *AA* 2 413). The questions surrounding the thing in itself are discussed by Kant in particular in the chapter "On the Ground of the Distinction of all Objects in general into Phenomena and Noumena" in the *Critique of Pure Reason* (see A236/B294–A260/B315), where he asks whether we can make use of the categories to cognize something that does not depend on our forms of intuition.

27. I will only discuss the use of the concept of the thing in itself in theoretical philosophy. How we can deal with it from the perspective of practical philosophy is another question. Nevertheless, I want to add that—by the interpretation of the thing in itself which I want to defend—it is (in a way not to be discussed here) possible to refer to things in themselves as existing things from the different—practical—perspective.

28. Allison defends the thesis that one can distinguish between transcendental and empirical affection while maintaining the purely methodological character of this distinction, if one takes the idea of an "affection by the thing in itself" to be a mere abstraction (Allison 1996; cf. also Allison 2004, pp. 35ff.). The problem is that the idea of an affection by the thing in itself remains idle unless one gives it an ontological meaning, where the thing in itself is taken to be the ground of what is given to our senses. Cf., among others, Adickes 1929, pp. 5–26. For another criticism of the double-aspect theory, see van Cleve 1999, chapter 1.

29. If we could not say what we mean here by existing, it would also be unacceptable to conclude that no things in themselves could exist. It would then, however, be senseless to allow the thought of the existence of things in themselves.

30. According to this interpretation, Kant allows the thought of something mind-independent because of the fact that something affects us and he does not take the thing in itself as an abstraction from a given object. This is the reason why I understand this reading as an ontological reading of the thing in itself.

31. As mentioned earlier, the situation is different from the perspective of practical philosophy. In Kant's theoretical philosophy, to speak of the real existence of things means—as spelled out in the first part of this essay—to speak of objects that are given to our outer senses. For this, it is enough to refer to our sensations, our forms of intuition, and the conceptual elements of our knowledge.

32. Or, as Kenneth Winkler puts it in his essay (see chapter 8 in this volume): Berkeley's "failure is not . . . one of insufficient objectivity . . . , but of insufficient humility."

33. Adickes (1929) defends a variant of this thesis, the so-called double affection thesis. In what follows, I make use of another variant, presented by Waxman (2001). For Waxman, on the basis of his distinction between perception and sensation, Kant has the possibility of connecting the concept of existence to sensation, without at the same time being committed to the Berkeleyan consequence that *esse est percipi* because sensation, as the real, can be separated from perception.

34. There are further variants of the thesis that Kant tries to defend the claim that the objects of our experience have to exist mind-independently, which I cannot discuss in detail (cf. Guyer 1987 and 1998).

35. In the explication of this reading, I follow Willaschek 2001.

36. If we claim that this object is not identical with the object of experience, we end up with a Two-Worlds reading of the thing in itself thesis (as in Willaschek 2001). Paton (1936) defends the thesis of a numerical identity.

37. Waxman (2001) uses this to argue against thinking of a particular sensation as corresponding to a particular affection.

38. I am indebted to Sam Quigley for providing a first draft of an English translation. For helpful suggestions and comments, thanks are due to Andrew Chignell, Stefanie Grüne, and, especially, to Rolf-Peter Horstmann. Many thanks are due to Béatrice Longuenesse and Dan Garber for philosophical comments and stylistic help.

CHAPTER 8
BERKELEY AND KANT

1. This quotation from *On a Discovery Whereby Any New Critique of Pure Reason Is to Be Made Superfluous by an Older One* I owe to Langton 1998, p. l, but the translation I use, by Henry Allison, is taken from Immanuel Kant, *Theoretical Philosophy after 1781*, ed. Henry Allison and Peter Heath, trans. Henry Allison, Michael Friedman, Gary Hatfield, and Peter Heath (Cambridge: Cambridge University Press, 2002), AA 8, 250–51.

2. The commentators who come closest to the approach I take in this essay are Allison 1973a (see in particular p. 59) and, more briefly, Ayers 2005. See also Mattey 1983, especially pp. 168–69; Mattey takes up Allison's views on pp. 171–73. Both Allison and Mattey acknowledge their debt to Cassirer 1922–1923, vol. 2, pp. 325–27.

3. Emundts, chapter 7, this volume.

4. Turbayne 1955 and Mattey 1983. Of the works listed, I have consulted only the translation of the *Dialogues* in Eschenbach 1756, a copy of which is in the Wellesley College Library. On the second page of his preface, Eschenbach explains that the basis of his translation was a French translation published in Amsterdam in 1750. The French translation must itself have been based on the first or second English edition (which differs from the first edition only in its title page; see Jessop 1973, p. 14), because Eschenbach's translation does not include long passages added by Berkeley in the third edition of 1734 (among them an important passage distancing him from the "enthusiasm" of Malebranche). Neither Turbayne nor Mattey mentions a German translation of *Alciphron* that appeared in Lemgo in 1737 ([Berkeley] 1737), perhaps because Berkeley's immaterialism makes no appearance in that work. See Stäbler 1935, pp. 44, 96; Jessop 1973, p. 20; and Keynes 1976, p. 51.

5. See Beiser 2002, pp. 99, 619, who cites Warda 1922, p. 46. The volume was Berkeley 1781. Despite its title, only one volume of the 1781 *Werke* appeared, and it contained (aside from a biography) only the *Dialogues* (see Jessop 1973, p.

16). Beiser's chapter on Kant and Berkeley, pp. 88–103, is a broad and useful survey of their relationship.

6. *Met.Herder, AA* 28, 42.

7. See Garve 2004, p. 207.

8. Nor are Guyer and Wood, who also point readers to the Second Antinomy; see their edition of the *Critique*, p. 739, note 34.

9. See Friedman's "Translator's Introduction" to *MFNS* in Kant 2002, pp. 175–76.

10. Thus, the passage moves Norman Kemp Smith to write that "its inapplicability to Berkeley would seem to prove that Kant had no first-hand knowledge of Berkeley's writings" (Kemp Smith 1950, p. 309; see also p. 159).

11. Michael Ayers places Berkeley against the background of this passage in his 2005 essay. He goes on to suggest, as I do, that in light of this background, Kant's interpretation of Berkeley may not be as far off as it is often made to seem. For further discussion of the Battle of Gods and Giants in an early modern setting, see Lennon 1993.

12. A familiar example from outside the British tradition, in the writings of a philosopher more respectful of what the past has to teach us, is the preface to *NE*, where Leibniz aligns Locke with Aristotle and himself with Plato.

13. Much of Hutcheson's history is cribbed, sometimes verbatim, from a similar Latin compendium, Aldrich 1692 (first published in 1691), or from a common source. The close parallels between Hutcheson's sketch and Kant's suggest that they too may have had a common source (or sources), one that reached without much difficulty across national boundaries.

14. Mattey gives a very useful account of the contents of Eschenbach's translation and commentary (Mattey 1983, pp. 164–65), but he says on p. 164 (note 18) that Eschenbach uses *Gedanke* for *idea* "throughout" his translation, which is not the case. More than once he uses *Vorstellung*.

15. For Friedman's remarks on the passage, see his "Translator's Introduction," to *MFNS*, Kant 2002, p. 176.

16. See *PHK* 18, where Berkeley considers whether we can know that there are bodies distinct from our ideas: "either we must know it by sense, or by reason."

17. For a reading, consonant with what I say here, of the opening sections of the introduction to the *Principles*, see Winkler 2004.

18. A great deal of philosophizing only makes the illusion worse, by making it more elaborate. Thus, the "Nature" of which most philosophers speak is a "vain *chimera*" (*PHK* 150).

19. See his notes in his edition of the *Prolegomena*, pp. 44, 45, and 207, as well as his note 42 on p. 479 in Kant 2002.

20. Kemp Smith speaks of "the Cartesian idealism which would convert mere representations into things in themselves" (Kemp Smith 1950, p. 307). McCracken and Tipton (2000, p. 265) offer the same identification. Perhaps it is the dream argument of the First Meditation that leads these commentators to attribute "dreaming idealism" to Descartes. But when Kant discusses the dream argument, for example, in the *Met.Mongrovius* (*AA* 29 927), he takes pains to distinguish bodies from their representations. And in *Met.Herder* (*AA* 28, 42–43), he links the dream argument (quite appropriately) with Berkeley.

21. My understanding of "*dreaming* idealism" is therefore more in accord with Max Apel (1908, p. 144) and Theodor W. Adorno (2001, p. 96). Both link dreaming idealism with Berkeley, though they do so without explanation. In Max Horkheimer and Adorno 1982, the notion of dreaming idealism is adapted (in the form *traümerisch Idealismus*) as a term of cultural criticism, preserving both the link with Berkeley and the contrast with the critical idealism of Kant ("The Culture Industry: Enlightenment as Mass Deception," p. 125).

22. Apart from the lines quoted earlier echoing the *Dialogues*, consider the following paragraph, which reworks several Berkeleyan themes, perhaps under the influence of Hume (who, in the *EHU*, credits Berkeley with some of the arguments):

> The proposition that has long been elaborated in the author's system is in fact the long known proposition that our sensations do not teach us anything of the qualities of things but are merely alterations of ourselves, caused by certain qualities of things unknown to us. Nevertheless (particularly as far as the sense of sight is concerned), these modifications of ourselves appear as objects outside of us. Here, accordingly, is the first and greatest contradiction of sensibility and reason. The former says: there are things and we know their properties, the latter shows clearly that we know nothing of these properties and consequently makes the existence of the things themselves doubtful. (Garve 2000, p. 76)

23. According to Allison, who was the first to bring it to bear on Kant's relation to Berkeley, this fragment was "appended to an earlier and substantially identical draft" of *AA* 4 374–75 (1973, p. 61):

> Berkeley found nothing constant, and so could find nothing which the understanding conceives according to a priori principles. He therefore had to look for another intuition, namely the mystical one of God's ideas, which required a two-fold understanding, one which connected appearances in experience, and another which knew things in themselves. I need only one sensibility and one understanding. (*AA* 23, 58)

24. See the *Oxford English Dictionary*, "eclectic," A *adj*., meaning 1.

25. The reference is worth quoting in full, because although its subject is politics, it notes that Brucker, in line with received opinion, portrays Plato as an unrealistic visionary. "The **Platonic republic** has become proverbial as a supposed striking example of a dream of perfection that can have its place only in the idle thinker's brain; and Brucker finds it ridiculous for the philosopher to assert that a prince will never govern well unless he participates in the ideas" (A316/B372). In this case, Kant is unwilling to follow Brucker. "We would do better to pursue this thought further, and (at those points where the excellent man leaves us without help) to shed light on it through new endeavours, rather than setting it aside as useless under the very wretched and harmful pretext of its impracticability" (A316/B372–73).

26. Brucker cites several authorities for this observation, among them Casaubon 1656. In chapter 1 of his book, Casaubon announces that "no man that hath read him can deny, that *Plato* himself naturally, had much in him of an Enthusiast" (p. 10). In chapter 3 he associates Plato with a distinctively philosophical or "Contemplative" form of enthusiasm (pp. 69–71). Like Brucker, he contrasts Plato's tendency toward enthusiasm with the "sober" rationality of Socrates (pp. 5–7; for "sober" see p. 7). The first edition of Casaubon's book appeared in 1655.

Brucker refers to it under an abbreviated Latin title ("de enthus."), and his page references do not accord with either the 1655 or 1656 edition. He probably made use of a volume of excerpts translated into Latin and published as *Dissertatio de enthusiasmo* in Hamburg in 1696. I have not been able to consult this volume; I owe my brief description to Paul J. Korshin's introduction to the reprint edition of Casaubon 1656, p. viii.

27. There is no such passage in any of the writings now attributed to Xenophon of Athens (the writer Brucker seems to have in mind), nor is the work he names, *Epistolae ad Aeschinem*, among them. Brucker cites "Opp. 1001"—an edition of Xenophon's *Opera*—but I have not been able to trace it.

28. Brucker's source for the turn toward Pythagoras (Brucker 1766–1767, vol. 1, p. 1041) is Cicero, *De finibus*, Book 5, section 29, where Piso says that in his journeys to meet Pythagoreans and others, Plato's aim was "to append to his picture of Socrates an account of the Pythagorean system and to extend his studies into those branches which Socrates repudiated" (Cicero 1914, p. 491).

29. See Dillon's introduction to Alcinous 1995, pp. xli-ii.

30. See Dillon's very informative introduction to Alcinous 1995.

31. See Bracken 1965, pp. 19–20. Leibniz reacted to Berkeley in much the same way: see *AG*, pp. 306–7.

32. Kuehn (2001) shows how strongly Kant was marked by his encounters with fiction, poetry, and philosophy originally written in English, and by conversations with his friend Joseph Green, an English merchant living in Königsberg, where English-language philosophy was intensively studied even in Kant's student days.

33. All quotations from Emundts are from chapter 7 in this volume.

34. See also Gardner 1999, p. 188.

35. For another verdict along the same lines, see Kemp Smith 1950, p. 313.

36. But then, I might be asked, why did Kant not *say* that the proof applies to Berkeley? Why does he take such care to treat Descartes and Berkeley as separate targets? Here is a guess. In Descartes' case, there is a failure to acknowledge immediacy. In Berkeley's case, there is an acknowledgment of immediacy, but a failure to acknowledge that objects are conceived to exist in space. Descartes, by contrast, acknowledges that objects are conceived to exist in space. Only in Kant's view are immediacy and actual existence in space brought together. Kant is not the kind of critic who feels obliged to present a mounting series of arguments against a single view. He prefers interrelated refutations of a range of views, in order to bring out the character and strength of his own position. As a result, particular refutations are often aimed at narrow targets, even if they could be directed more widely.

37. For more on outer sense as a source of objective reality for concepts, see B308, A381–82, B412–13, and B422.

38. In another passage from the second-edition Paralogisms, the concern of the Refutation (the existence of things in space outside me) is brought together in an interesting way with the question of dualism. See B409.

39. See also Gardner 1999, p. 188.

40. In entry 429a (*Bk Works* 1:53), Berkeley adds "or velle i.e. agere."

41. For helpful suggestions I am grateful to Nicolas de Warren, Dina Emundts, Daniel Garber, Paul Guyer, and Wayne Waxman.

CHAPTER 9
KANT'S HUMEAN SOLUTION TO HUME'S PROBLEM

1. I shall use the spelling "reflexion" when this inner sensory apprehension is intended and "reflection" for its usual meaning of a discursive (non-sensory) act of deliberative ratiocination.

2. Kant was well aware of the first of Hume's challenges: "David Hume . . . reasoned as follows. The concept of cause is one that contains the *necessity* of a connection between the existence of distinct things, insofar as they are distinct. Thus, if *A* is posited, I cognize that *B*, something entirely distinct from it, must necessarily also exist. Necessity, however, can only be attributed to a connection insofar as it is cognized a priori, for experience of a combination gives us cognition only that it *is* so, but not that it necessarily is so. Now, it is impossible, Hume asserts, to cognize the combination between one thing and some *other* (or between a determination of one thing and that of some *other*) as necessary a priori if it is not given in perception. Therefore, the concept of a cause is itself fraudulent and deceptive, and, to put it most mildly, an excusable delusion, where a *custom* (a *subjective* necessity) of associating (*beigesellet*) certain things, or their determinations, perceived next to or successively to one another, as regards their existence, so far as *subjective* necessity is insensibly (*unvermerkt*) taken for an *objective* necessity, positing a connection in the objects themselves. The concept of cause is thus acquired surreptitiously and illegitimately, indeed can never be acquired or validated (*beglaubigt*), because it is in itself null, chimerical, requiring a connection that cannot be upheld before any reason, which can never correspond to any object at all" (*CPrR, AA* 5 51).

3. "Hume . . . occupied himself exclusively with the synthetic proposition regarding the connection of an effect with its cause (*principium causalitatis*), and he believed himself to have shown that such an a priori proposition is impossible" (B19–20). "From the incapacity of our reason to make use of this principle beyond all experience, he inferred the nullity of all pretensions of reason in general to go beyond the empirical" (A760/B788).

4. Kant too (*pace* Strawson) was cognizant of this sort of problem: "Proving a synthetic proposition from mere pure concepts of the understanding can never be done, e.g. the proposition that everything that exists contingently has a cause. We can never go further than to prove that, without this relation (*Beziehung*), we could not even so much as *conceive* (*begreifen*) the existence of the contingent, i.e. cognize the existence of such a thing a priori through the understanding. But from this, it does not follow that this same condition is also a condition of the possibility of the things (*Sachen*) themselves" (B289; also A129).

5. Thus "without functions of understanding appearances can certainly be given in intuition. . . . Appearances could very well be so constituted that the understanding did not find them to conform at all to the conditions of its unity, and everything was thence in confusion, for example, nothing might be offered in the sequential series of appearances which might yield a rule of synthesis, and thus nothing might correspond to the concept of cause and effect, so that this concept would be entirely empty, null (*nichtig*), and without meaning. Appearances would

nonetheless offer objects to our intuition, for intuition in no way requires functions of thought" (A89–90/B122–23).

6. "The form of judgments (transformed [*verwandelt*] into a concept of the synthesis of intuitions) produced (*hervorbrachte*) categories which guide all employment of the understanding in experience" (A321/B377–78). The most likely reason Kant stressed logical functions over the other elements in the content of a pure concept of the understanding is that they alone ensure that the Table of Categories is a complete list of fundamental concepts of understanding. No one can doubt that Kant attached the highest importance to being able to prove that his list, by contrast with that of Aristotle, is complete and contains nothing derivative: see, e.g., A80–82/B106–13 and *Prolegomena*, AA 4 324–25.

7. It is worth remarking that even while insisting that the logical functions listed in his Table of Judgments are constitutive of *our* discursive understanding, Kant acknowledged that there is no way of proving this to be true of every discursive understanding: B146 and A230/B283. That is, just as nothing in his system requires that the categories apply to a manifold of space or time, so too nothing necessitates that the synthesis of the manifold of space and time be brought to necessary unity by the logical functions of the table of judgments given at A70/B95 (subject/predicate, affirmation, universality, et al.). The metaphysical deduction proof of the a priori origin of the categories operates at a higher level of generality, requiring only that a sensible manifold of some aesthetic character (spatial, temporal, or whatever) be determined conformably to functions of judgment of some logical character (subject/predicate, et al., or whatever). The categories in Kant's Table are, and need to be, specified only with respect to the forms of judgment constitutive of our mind's capacity to judge (*Vermögen zu unteilen*); they are not, nor (as pure concepts of the *understanding*) should they be, specified with regard to the peculiar spatial and temporal constitution of the sensibility of our minds as well (that would be to move from the categories to their schemata). There would therefore appear to be a precise parallel between the cases of pure intuitions and pure concepts: just as pure intuitions *objectively* (in content) precede all content in sensation (otherwise they would be empirical) but are not possible *subjectively*, as actual representations, until sensations are given (A452/B480n.), so too the categories (and purely intellectual concepts generally, including arithmetic and algebraic) objectively precede all sensible content without exception (a priori no less than a posteriori) but still are not possible subjectively, as actual representations, until the manifold of pure intuition is given for pure synthesis.

8. To this one might object that if Kant had explicated the categories as bound up by content with the a priori sensible manifold and its pure synthesis in imagination, this would render unintelligible any use of the category of cause and effect to conceive a nonsensible (nontemporal, nonspatial) causal efficacy, as is requisite for pure reason to be able to form the idea of freedom (even in the negative sense specified at A553/B581). We clearly need a concept of cause and effect that remains thinkable even after abstraction is made from everything sensible. Though a detailed response to the objection cannot be given here, it suffices to note that Kant offered a second characterization of the categories at B128–29 as rules for fixing the logical place of concepts in judgments so that, for example, by subordi-

nating the concept of body to the category of substance, we preclude it from ever being used as a predicate in cognitive contexts (see also *Prolegomena, AA* 4 324 and *AA* 28–1 472). Taken in isolation, of course, their role in any such proceeding provides no reason for regarding the categories as anything more than logical devices for organizing concepts, subject merely to the whim of the judger. So to secure their status as pure concepts of objects, the B128–29 characterization must be supplemented by the explication of their "transcendental content" (A79/B105) in the metaphysical deduction in terms of the pure manifold of sense, its pure synthesis in the imagination, and the determination of this synthesis conformably to the logical functions of judgment. This, however, is already of itself sufficient to open the way to asking: If the categories as explicated at B128–29 can acquire transcendental content only by being supplemented in the fashion of the metaphysical deduction, might they not acquire other, equally transcendental content by being supplemented in a different, yet no less pure (a priori) manner? The supplementation model implicit in the B128–29 explication of the categories provides all that is requisite to form a concept of nonsensible causality: we simply conceive the supplementation of cause and effect (in its nontranscendental guise at B128–29) by means of something other than the pure manifold of sensibility. Indeed, in the *Critique of Practical Reason*, Kant seems to identify just such an analogue, capable of conferring a positive transcendental, albeit strictly practical, meaning on the categories: "[T]he determinations of practical reason can have place only in . . . conformity to the categories of the understanding, but not in view of their theoretical employment, in order to bring the manifold of (sensible) intuition under one a priori consciousness, but only in order to subordinate the manifold of desires (*Begehrungen*) a priori to the unity of the consciousness of a practical reason commanding in the moral law, or to a pure will" (*AA* 5 65). It should thus be clear how Kant could hold, on the one hand, that the supplemented (but still unschematized) categories of the metaphysical deduction of the first *Critique* are bound up by content with the pure manifold of sense and its pure synthesis in imagination, and still insist, on the other hand, that the relation of practical reason to the capacity of desire suffices to yield a second set of categories adequate to its purely practical purposes.

9. Kant's treatment of space and time is quintessentially psychologistic: by tracing these concepts to an origin in pure intuitions of sensibility and showing that these last are nothing but modes of sensible representation, it follows that space and time can no more be conceived to exist in themselves, or as features of things in themselves, than pain or fear can.

10. "This complete . . . solution of the Humean problem thus rescues the a priori origin of the pure concepts of the understanding as well as the validity of the universal principles of nature as laws of the understanding, yet in such a way as to limit their use to experience, because their possibility depends solely on the relation of the understanding to experience, but with a completely reversed kind of connection that never occurred to Hume: they are not derived from experience but rather experience is derived from them" (*Prolegomena, AA* 4 313).

11. This arises only in empirical thought, under the Analogies of Experience. See also *Prolegomena, AA* 4 321–22.

12. The possibility alluded to here is drawn from Kant's description of a third course between his own epigenetic conception and empiricism at B167–68. As its portrayal here suggests, I think Kant was quite right to assert that any such third course plays right into the Humean skeptic's hands.

13. A more detailed outline of the ideas presented here can be found in Waxman 2005, chapter 3. Their full development will not, however, be available until the second volume of *Kant and the Empiricists*, devoted entirely to Kant, is complete.

CHAPTER 10
SHOULD HUME HAVE BEEN A TRANSCENDENTAL IDEALIST?

1. The accounts of necessity, causal inference, concepts, and causal judgment provided in this and the subsequent subsection are drawn directly from more extensive discussions of these topics in my essay, "Hume's Theory of Judgment: Inference, Judgment, and the Causal Sense" in Ainslie forthcoming. This material appears with permission of Cambridge University Press.

2. In calling the impression of necessary connection a "felt determination of the mind," Hume cannot mean that the mere occurrence of this impression in the mind constitutes immediate knowledge, independent of experience, of the causal relation between an impression or memory and the believed idea that results from the customary transition of thought that he has described. Since *all* discovery of causal relations depends on experience of constant conjunction, according to Hume, the discovery of the causal role of this impression must do so as well. It is nevertheless properly characterized as an impression of the mind's "determination," for one in fact feels this impression whenever the mind makes, or is about to make, a custom- or habit-based inference. Indeed, given its own constant conjunction with the occurrence of such inferences, the impression may well be a state of mind that itself *constitutes* an essential contributing cause to the completion of the inference from the impression or memory to the believed idea; hence, it may even be characterized as "the determination of the mind" itself, and not merely as an impression "of" the presence of such a determination.

3. The term 'relation', Hume claims, may be understood in either of two senses. The first, or "natural," sense is restricted to "that quality, by which two ideas are connected together in the imagination, and the one naturally introduces the other"; this sense includes the three associative relations of resemblance, contiguity, and causation. The second, or "philosophical," sense encompasses more broadly any "particular circumstance, in which, even upon the arbitrary union of two ideas in the fancy, we may think proper to compare them"; this sense includes seven different species of relations, including relations of resemblance, space and time, and causation, but also identity, contrariety, degrees in quality, and proportions in quantity or number (*THN* 1.1.5.1–2).

4. Thus, for example, the abstract idea of the quality *red* is a determinate idea of a particular thing having a particular shade of red but associated with the word 'red' in such a way that the mind is disposed to revive and survey any of a set of other ideas of red things for use as needed. If, for example, one's abstract idea exemplar of red is an idea of a dark red circle, and the claim is made that all red

things are dark red circles, the ideas of red things of other shades or other shapes will immediately come to mind, allowing one to reject the claim proposed. (For further details, see Garrett 1997.)

5. The apparent sizes, shapes, and relative positions of bodies as they are initially sensed must often be corrected, Hume allows, by consideration of the position of the observer (*THN* 3.3.3.2); and the apparent colors, sounds, tastes, and smells of objects must also sometimes be corrected, he notes, for features of the circumstances of observation, including the health of the sense organs. He emphasizes how the immediate deliverances of the moral sense must likewise be "corrected" by taking into account differences of perspective on the individuals judged so as to reduce the "contradictions" in felt response that the same character would otherwise produce among different observers and even within the same observer at different times (*THN* 3.3.3.2). The initial deliverances of the sense of beauty must often be corrected as well, both by a consideration of the physical circumstances of observation (*THN* 3.3.1.15) and by reflectively developed rules of criticism (*THN* 2.2.8.18).

6. These rules include such principles as "the cause and effect must be contiguous in space and time"; "the same cause always produces the same effect, and the same effect never arises but from the same cause"; and "where several different objects produce the same effect, it must be by means of some quality, which we discover to be common amongst them" (*THN* 1.3.15.1–8).

7. Thus, he writes:

'Tis natural for men, in their common and careless way of thinking, to imagine they perceive a connexion betwixt such objects as they have constantly found united together; and because custom has render'd it difficult to separate the ideas, they are apt to fancy such a separation to be in itself impossible and absurd. (*THN* 1.4.3.9)

8. It might be objected that causal pairs resemble each other *solely* in the effect that they produce on the mind. But Hume, at least, cannot allow this objection, for his fifth "rule by which to judge of causes and effects" requires that "where several different objects produce the same effect, it must be by means of some quality, which we discover to be common amongst them. For . . . like effects imply like causes" (*THN* 1.3.15. 7).

Nor need we say that causal relations are *whatever* the causal sense happens to pick out—at least not if this is taken to mean that a difference in what produced association, inference, and the distinctive impression of necessary connection would entail a difference in what the causal relation *is*. Consider an analogy. Suppose that the basis of redness consists in a particular complex (and perhaps highly disjunctive) structural surface reflectance quality. Suppose, too, that, had the human sensory apparatus been different, a different quality of bodies would have produced the impression of red under standard circumstances. Then although it may be true that the quality of redness is what the visual sense of red actually discerns—and that this quality turns out to be a particular complex structural surface reflectance property—it will not follow that redness itself *would* have been a different quality of bodies if the human sensory apparatus had been different. For the referent of 'quality of red' may be fixed rigidly by its relation to the actual present human sensory apparatus—that is, in such a way that redness is whatever quality it is that produces the impression of red through the actual human sensory apparatus under standard circumstances in the actual world now, not whatever *would* produce the impression of red in a different apparatus or under other circumstances. The quality of redness *itself* need not vary with the nature of the mind, even if a change in the nature of the human mind would lead to something other than *redness* playing the role (including producing the qualitatively distinctive "impression of red") that redness plays for us. Similarly, the referent of 'causal relation' may be fixed rigidly by its relation to the actual causal sense—so that the causal relation is, in each possible world, that relation among pairs that produces association, inference, and the impression of necessary connection in normal reflective human beings in the *actual* world, and not whatever relation *would* produce it in that other possible world. So understood, the relation of causation itself need not vary with the nature of the mind, even if a change in the nature of the human mind would lead to a relation other than causation playing something of the role (including the production of association, inference, and an impression of necessary connection) that the relation of causation plays for humans in the actual world.

9. Commentators have generally judged that the two definitions are not even coextensive. However, I have argued (Garrett 1997, chap. 5) that the two definitions of "cause" are each systematically ambiguous between a "subject-relative" reading and an "absolute" reading. On the subject-relative reading, the first definition concerns what has been observed to be constantly conjoined in a given subject's experience, while the second definition concerns the subjects of association and inference in that subject's mind. On the absolute reading, the first definition concerns what has been, is, and will be constantly conjoined through all time, while the second definition concerns the subject of association and inference in the mind of an idealized subject. So understood, the definitions are coextensive on their subject-relative readings and are again coextensive on their absolute readings; whereas the first reading specifies what a subject will include in his or her own revival set for the abstract idea of cause (and hence reflects what he or she takes to be causally related), the second reading specifies what a fully corrected revival set would include (and hence what is in fact causally related).

10. Strictly speaking, this would be Hume's account of the judgment that "two plus two is four" taken as a predication about pairs of pairs; and the reverse inclusion would be required for the predicative judgment "four makes two plus two" taken as a predication about four-membered groups. Both inclusion relations, we may suppose, would be required for the further judgment "two plus two *is* four" understood as a "mathematical identity" or a universal generalization over a biconditional.

11. See Owen 1999, especially chapters 2 and 3, for a good account of nonformalism in early modern logic.

12. Coleman (1979) also notes the broadness of Hume's use of the term "contradiction" and argues—though without developing a Humean theory of concepts or judgments—that Hume should be interpreted as regarding mathematical judgment as synthetic yet necessary a priori. Bayne (2000) claims that geometry is not analytic for Hume in the *Treatise*, but he distinguished the *Treatise* from the *Enquiry* in this regard.

Bibliography

Adams, Robert Merrihew, 1994: *Leibniz: Determinist, Theist, Idealist* (Oxford: Oxford University Press).

———, 1997: "Things in Themselves," in *Philosophy and Phenomenological Research* 57:801–25.

Adickes, Erich, 1929: *Kants Lehre von der doppelten Affektion unseres Ich als Schlüssel zu seiner Erkenntnistheorie* (Tübingen: J. C. Mohr).

Adorno, Theodor K., 2001: *Kant's Critique of Pure Reason*, Tiedemann, R. (ed.), and Livingstone, R. (trans.) (Stanford: Stanford University Press).

Ainslie, Donald C. (ed.), forthcoming: *The Cambridge Companion to Hume's Treatise* (Cambridge: Cambridge University Press).

Alcinous, 1995: *The Handbook of Platonism*, Dillon, J. (ed.) (Oxford: Clarendon Press).

Aldrich, Henry, 1692: *Artis logicae compendium*, new ed. (Oxford: E Theatro Sheldoniano).

Allison, Henry E., 1973a: "Kant's Critique of Berkeley," in *Journal of the History of Philosophy* 11:43–63.

———, 1973b: *The Kant-Eberhard Controversy: An English Translation Together with Supplementary Materials and a Historic-Analytic Introduction to Kant's "On a Discovery"* (Baltimore: Johns Hopkins University Press).

———, 1983: *Kant's Transcendental Idealism: An Interpretation and Defence* (New Haven, CT: Yale University Press).

———, 1996: *Idealism and Freedom: Essays on Kant's Theoretical and Practical Philosophy* (Cambridge: Cambridge University Press).

———, 2004: *Kant's Transcendental Idealism: An Interpretation and Defense*, rev. and enl. ed. (New Haven, CT: Yale University Press).

Ameriks, Karl, 1992a: "Kantian Idealism Today," in *History of Philosophy Quarterly* 9:329–42.

———, 1992b: "The Critique of Metaphysics: Kant and Traditional Ontology," in Guyer, P. (ed.), *The Cambridge Companion to Kant* (Cambridge: Cambridge University Press), pp. 249–79.

Apel, Max, 1908: *Kommentar zu Kants "Prolegomena": Eine Einführung in die critische Philosophie* (Berlin-Schönberg: Buchverlag der "Hilfe").

Arnauld, Antoine, and Pierre Nicole, 1996: *Logic or the Art of Thinking*, Buroker, J. V. (ed. and trans.) (Cambridge: Cambridge University Press).

Atherton, Margaret, 1984: "Knowledge of Substance and Knowledge of Science in Locke's *Essay*," in *History of Philosophy Quarterly* 1:413–27.

Ayers, Michael, 1975: "The Ideas of Power and Substance in Locke's Philosophy," in *Philosophical Quarterly* 25:1–27.

———, 1981: "Mechanism, Superaddition, and the Proof of God's Existence in Locke's *Essay*," in *Philosophical Review* 90:210–51.

Ayers, Michael, 1982: "Berkeley's Immaterialism and Kant's Transcendental Idealism," in Vesey, G. (ed.), *Idealism: Past and Present* (Cambridge: Cambridge University Press), pp. 51–69.

———, 1991: *Locke*, 2 vols. (London: Routledge).

———, 1994: "The Foundations of Knowledge and the Logic of Substance: The Structure of Locke's General Philosophy," in Rogers, G.A.J. (ed.), *Locke's Philosophy: Content and Context* (Oxford: Clarendon Press), pp. 49–73.

———, 2005: "Was Berkeley a Rationalist or an Empiricist?" in Winkler, K. P. (ed.), *The Cambridge Companion to Berkeley* (New York: Cambridge University Press), pp. 34–62.

Bayne, Stephen M., 2000: "Kant's Answer to Hume: How Kant Should Have Tried to Stand Hume's Copy Thesis on Its Head," in *British Journal for the History of Philosophy* 8:207–24.

Beck, Lewis White, 1969: *Early German Philosophy: Kant and his Predecessors* (Cambridge, MA: Harvard University Press).

Beiser, Frederick, 2002: *German Idealism: The Struggle Against Subjectivism, 1781–1801* (Cambridge, MA: Harvard University Press).

Bennett, Jonathan, 1971: *Locke, Berkeley, Hume: Central Themes* (Oxford: Clarendon Press).

———, 1998: "Substratum," in Chappell, V. (ed.), *Locke* (Oxford: Oxford University Press), pp. 129–48.

Bottin, F., Longo, M., and Piaia, G., 1979: *Dall'età cartesiana a Brucker (Storia delle storie generali della filosofia)*, Santinello, G. (ed.), vol. 2 (Brescia: Editrice La Scuola).

Boyle, Robert, 1991: *Selected Philosophical Papers of Robert Boyle*, Stewart, M. A. (ed.) (Indianapolis: Hackett).

———, 1999–2000: *The Works of Robert Boyle*, Hunter, M., and Davis, E. B. (eds.), 14 vols. (London: Pickering and Chatto).

Bracken, Harry M., 1965: *The Early Reception of Berkeley's Immaterialism*, rev. ed. (The Hague: Martinus Nijhoff).

Braun, Lucien, 1973: *Histoire de l'histoire de la philosophie* (Paris: Editions Ophrys).

Brittan, Gordon, 1978: *Kant's Theory of Science* (Princeton, NJ: Princeton University Press).

Brucker, Johann Jakob, 1742–1744: *Historia critica philosophiae a mundi incunabulis ad nostram usque aetatum deducta*, 4 vols. (Leipzig: Breitkopf).

———, 1766–1767: *Historia critica philosophiae a mundi incunabulis ad nostram usque aetatum deducta*, 2nd ed. 6 vols. (Leipzig: Weidemann and Reich).

Buchdahl, Gerd, 1969. *Metaphysics and the Philosophy of Science* (Oxford: Basil Blackwell).

Burtt, E. A., 1955. *The Metaphysical Foundations of Modern Science* (Garden City, NY: Doubleday Anchor).

Casaubon, Meric, 1655: *A Treatise Concerning Enthusiasme* (London: Thomas Johnson).

———, 1656: *A Treatise Concerning Enthusiasme*, 2nd ed. (London: Thomas Johnson; repr. with an introduction by Paul J. Korshin, Gainesville, FL: Scholar's Facsimiles and Reprints, 1970).

Cassirer, Ernst, 1922–1923: *Das Erkenntnisproblem in der Philosophie und Wissenschaft der neueren Zeit*, 3 vols. (Berlin: B. Cassirer).

Cicero, 1914: *De finibus*, Rackham, H. (ed. and trans.) (London: Heinemann).

Coleman, Dorothy, 1979: "Is Mathematics for Hume Synthetic A Priori?" in *Southwestern Journal of Philosophy* 10:113–26.

Cornford, F. M., 1957: *Plato's Theory of Knowledge (The* Theaetetus *and* Sophist *of Plato)* (London: Routledge and Kegan Paul).

Corr, Charles A., 1975: "Christian Wolff and Leibniz," in *Journal of the History of Ideas* 36:241–62.

Downing, Lisa, 1998: "The Status of Mechanism in Locke's *Essay*," in *Philosophical Review* 107:381–414.

———, 2001: "The Uses of Mechanism: Corpuscularianism in Drafts A and B of Locke's *Essay*," in Newman, W., Murdoch, J., and Lüthy, C. (eds.), *Late Medieval and Early Modern Corpuscularian Matter Theory* (Leiden: E. J. Brill), pp. 515–34.

———, 2007: "Locke's Ontology," in Newman, L. (ed.), *The Cambridge Companion to Locke's* Essay Concerning Human Understanding (Cambridge: Cambridge University Press), pp. 352–80.

Emerson, Ralph Waldo, 1982: "The Transcendentalist," in *Selected Writings*, Ziff, L. (ed.) (Harmondsworth: Penguin), pp. 239–58.

Emundts, Dina, 2004: *Kants Übergangskonzeption im Opus postumum. Zur Rolle des Nachlaßwerkes für die Grundlegung der empirischen Physik* (Berlin: Walter de Gruyter).

Enfield, William, 1791: *The History of Philosophy, from the Earliest Times to the Beginning of the Present Century; Drawn up from Brucker's Historia critica philosophiae*, 2 vols. (London: J. Johnson).

Eschenbach, Johann Christian, 1756: *Samlung der vornehmsten Schriftsteller die die Würklichkeit ihres Eignenkörpers und der ganzen Körperwelt Läugnen* (Rostock: A. F. Rose).

Fischer, Kuno, 1860: *Immanuel Kant und seine Lehre. Entwicklungsgeschichte und System der kritischen Philosophie* (Heidelberg: C. Winter).

Förster, Eckart, 2000: *Kant's Final Synthesis: An Essay on the Opus Postumum* (Cambridge, MA: Harvard University Press).

Friedman, Michael, 1992: *Kant and the Exact Sciences* (Cambridge, MA: Harvard University Press).

Garber, Daniel, 1985: "Leibniz and the Foundations of Physics: the Middle Years," in Okruhlik, K., and Brown, J. R. (eds.), *The Natural Philosophy of Leibniz* (Dordrecht: Reidel), pp. 27–130.

———, 1995: "Leibniz: Physics and Philosophy," in Jolley, N. (ed.), *The Cambridge Companion to Leibniz* (New York: Cambridge University Press), pp. 270–352.

Gardner, Sebastian, 1999: *Kant and the* Critique of Pure Reason (London: Routledge).

Garrett, Don, 1997: *Cognition and Commitment in Hume's Philosophy* (Oxford: Oxford University Press).

Garve, Christian, 2000: "The Garve Review," in Sassen, B. (ed.), *Kant's Early Critics: The Empiricist Critique of the Theoretical Philosophy* (Cambridge: Cambridge University Press), pp. 59–77.

———, 2004: "The Göttingen Review," in Hatfield, G. (ed.), *Prolegomena to Any Future Metaphysics*, rev. ed. (Cambridge: Cambridge University Press), pp. 201–7.

Guyer, Paul, 1980: "Kant on Apperception and A Priori Synthesis," in *American Philosophical Quarterly* 17:205–12.

———, 1987: *Kant and the Claims of Knowledge* (Cambridge: Cambridge University Press).

———, 1994: "Locke's Philosophy of Language," in Chappell, V. (ed.), *Cambridge Companion to Locke* (Cambridge: Cambridge University Press), pp. 115–45.

———, 1998: "The Postulates of Empirical Thinking in General and the Refutation of Idealism," in Mohr, G., and Willaschek, M. (eds.), *Klassiker Auslegen. Kritik der reinen Vernunft* (Berlin: Akademie Verlag), pp. 297–324.

———, 2000: *Kant on Freedom, Law, and Happiness* (Cambridge: Cambridge University Press).

Harper, William, 1984: "Kant on Space, Empirical Realism and the Foundations of Geometry," in *Topoi* 3:143–61.

Hartz, Glenn A., and Cover, J. A., 1988: "Space and Time in the Leibnizian Metaphysic," in *Noûs* 22:493–519.

Heidegger, Martin, [1927] 1962: *Being and Time*, Macquarrie, J., and Robinson, E. (trans.) (San Francisco: HarperSanFrancisco).

Heimsoeth, Heinz, 1924: "Metaphysische Motive in der Ausbildung des kritischen Idealismus," in *Kant-Studien* 29:121–59.

Horkheimer, Max, and Adorno, Theodor, 1982: *The Dialectic of Enlightenment*, Cumming, J. (trans.) (New York: Continuum).

Hutcheson, Francis, 1756: *Logicae compendium* (Glasgow: R. and A. Foulis).

Jacovides, Michael, 2002: "The Epistemology under Locke's Corpuscularianism," in *Archiv fur Geschichte der Philosophie* 84:161–89.

Jauernig, Anja, 2004: "Leibniz Freed of Every Flaw: A Kantian Reads Leibnizian Metaphysics." Ph.D. dissertation, Princeton University.

Jessop, T. E., 1973: *A Bibliography of George Berkeley*, 2nd ed. (The Hague: Martinus Nijhoff).

Kemp Smith, Norman, 1950: *A Commentary on Kant's "Critique of Pure Reason,"* 2nd ed., rev. and enl. (New York: Humanities Press).

Keynes, Geoffrey, 1976: *A Bibliography of George Berkeley, Bishop of Cloyne* (Oxford: Oxford University Press).

Kuehn, Manfred, 2001: *Kant: A Biography* (Cambridge: Cambridge University Press).

Lamarra, Antonio, Palaia, Roberto, and Pimpinella, Pietro, 2001: *Le prime traduzioni della Monadologie di Leibniz (1720–1721)* (Florence: Leo Olschki).

Langton, Rae, 1998: *Kantian Humility: Our Ignorance of Things in Themselves* (Oxford: Clarendon Press).

Leibniz, G. W., 1765: *Oeuvres philosophiques latines et françaises de feu Mr. de Leibnitz . . .* , Raspe, R. (ed.) (Amsterdam: chez Jean Schreuder).

Leibniz, G. W., and Clarke, Samuel, 1717: *A Collection of Papers, Which Passed between the Late Learned Mr. Leibnitz, and Dr. Clarke* . . . , Clarke, S. (ed.) (London: James Knapton).

Lennon, Thomas M., 1993: *The Battle of the Gods and Giants: The Legacies of Descartes and Gassendi, 1655–1715* (Princeton, NJ: Princeton University Press).

Longuenesse, Béatrice, 2005: "Self-Consciousness and Consciousness of One's Own Body: Variations on a Kantian Theme," forthcoming [*sic*] in *Philosophical Topics* 33(2).

Look, Brandon, 1999: *Leibniz and the "vinculum substantiale"* (*Studia Leibnitiana Sonderheft* 30) (Stuttgart: F. Steiner).

Mandelbaum, Maurice, 1964: *Philosophy, Science, and Sense Perception: Historical and Critical Studies* (Baltimore: Johns Hopkins University Press).

Mattern, Ruth, 1981: "Locke on Power and Causation: Excerpts from the 1685 Draft of the *Essay*," in *Philosophy Research Archives* 7:836–939.

Mattey, G. J., 1983: "Kant's Conception of Berkeley's Idealism," *Kant-Studien* 74:161–75.

McCann, Edwin, 1994: "Locke's Philosophy of Body," in Chappell, V. (ed.), *The Cambridge Companion to Locke* (Cambridge: Cambridge University Press), pp. 56–88.

———, 2001: "Locke's Theory of Substance under Attack!" in *Philosophical Studies* 106:87–105.

McCracken, Charles, and Tipton, Ian (eds.), 2000: *Berkeley's* Principles *and* Dialogues: *Background Source Materials* (Cambridge: Cambridge University Press).

McGuire, J. E., 1976: "'Labyrinthus Continui': Leibniz on Substance, Activity, and Matter," in Machamer, P. K., and Turnbull, R. G. (eds.), *Motion and Time, Space and Matter: Interrelations in the History and Philosophy of Science* (Columbus: Ohio State University Press), pp. 291–326.

Mendelssohn, Moses, 1971: *Gesammelte Schriften, Jubiläumsausgabe*, Bamberger, F., et al. (eds.), continued by Altmann, A., et al. (eds.), 24 vols. (Stuttgart-Bad Cannstatt: F. Frommann).

———, 1997: *Philosophical Writings*, Dahlstrom D. O. (ed.) (Cambridge: Cambridge University Press).

Mercer, Christia, 2001: *Leibniz's Metaphysics: Its Origins and Development* (Cambridge: Cambridge University Press).

Owen, David, 1991: "Locke on Real Essence," in *History of Philosophy Quarterly* 8:105–18.

———, 1999: *Hume's Reason* (Oxford: Oxford University Press).

Pariente, Jean-Claude, 1988: "Problèmes logiques du Cogito," in Grimaldi, N., and Marion, J.-L. (eds.), *Le Discours et sa méthode* (Paris: Presses Universitaires de France), pp. 229–69.

———, 1999: "La première personne et sa fonction dans le Cogito," in *Descartes et la fonction du sujet*, Ong-Van-Cung, K. S. (ed.) (Paris: Presses Universitaires de France), pp. 11–48; repr. in Pariente, *Le langage à l'oeuvre*, pp. 89–113.

———, 2002: *Le langage à l'oeuvre* (Paris: Presses Universitaires de France).

Pasini, Enrico, 2005: "La Monadologie: histoire de naissance," in Pasini, E. (ed.), *La Monadologie de Leibniz: Genèse et contexte* (Paris: Mimesis), pp. 85–122.

Paton, H. J., 1936: *Kant's Metaphysic of Experience*, 2 vols. (New York: Macmillan).

Ravier, Emile, 1937: *Bibliographie des oeuvres de Leibniz* (Paris: F. Alcan).

Schmidt-Biggemann, Wilhelm, and Stammen, Theo (eds.), 1998: *Jacob Brucker (1696–1770): Philosoph und Historiker der europäischen Aufklärung* (Berlin: Akademie Verlag).

Schönfeld, Martin, 2000: *The Philosophy of the Young Kant: The Pre-Critical Project* (Oxford: Oxford University Press).

Schrecker, Paul, 1938: "Une bibliographie de Leibniz," in *Revue philosophique de la France et de l'étranger* no. 126, *Année* 63:324–46.

Stäbler, Eugen, 1935: *George Berkeley's Auffassung and Wirkung in der Deutschen Philosophie bis Hegel* (Zeulenroda: B. Sporn).

Stanley, Thomas, 1655–1660: *The History of Philosophy*, 3 vols. (London: Humphrey Moses and Thomas Dring).

Stanley, Thomas, 1662: *The History of Chaldaick Philosophy* (London: Thomas Dring).

———, 1687a: *The History of Chaldaick Philosophy*, 2nd ed. (London: Thomas Bassett).

———, 1687b: *History of Philosophy: Containing the Lives, Opinions, Actions, and Discourses of the Philosophers of Every Sect*, 2nd ed. (London: Thomas Bassett).

Strawson, Peter F., 1966: *The Bounds of Sense: An Essay on Kant's "Critique of Pure Reason"* (London: Methuen).

Stuart, Matthew, 1998: "Locke on Superaddition and Mechanism," in *British Journal for the History of Philosophy* 6:351–79.

Turbayne, Colin M., 1955: "Kant's Refutation of Dogmatic Idealism," in *Philosophical Quarterly* 5:225–44.

Van Cleve, James, 1999: *Problems from Kant* (Oxford: Oxford University Press).

Warda, Arthur, 1922: *Immanuel Kants Bücher* (Berlin: Breslauer).

Waxman, Wayne, 2001: "Kant's Refutation of Berkeleyan idealism," in Schumacher, R. (ed.), *Idealismus als Theorie der Repräsentation* (Paderborn: Mentis), pp. 77–99.

———, 2005: *Kant and the Empiricists*. Vol. 1, *Understanding Understanding* (Oxford: Oxford University Press).

Willaschek, Marcus, 2001: "Affektion und Kontingenz in Kants transzendentalem Idealismus," in Schumacher, R. (ed.), *Idealismus als Theorie der Repräsentation* (Paderborn: Mentis), pp. 211–31.

Wilson, Catherine, 1990: "Confused Concepts and Darkened knowledge: Some Features of Kant's Leibniz-Critique," in MacDonald Ross, G., and McWalter, T. (eds.), *Kant and His Influence* (Bristol: Thoemmes), pp. 73–103.

———, 1995: "The Reception of Leibniz in the Eighteenth Century," in Jolley, N. (ed.), *The Cambridge Companion to Leibniz* (Cambridge: Cambridge University Press), pp. 442–74.

Wilson, Margaret Dauler, 1978: *Descartes* (London: Routledge and Kegan Paul).

————, 1999a: *Ideas and Mechanism. Essay on Early Modern Philosophy* (Princeton, NJ: Princeton University Press).

————, 1999b: "The 'Phenomenalisms' of Berkeley and Kant," in Wilson, *Ideas and Mechanism*, pp. 294–305.

Winkler, Kenneth, 1989: *Berkeley: An Interpretation* (Oxford: Clarendon Press).

————, 2004: "Berkeley, Pyrrhonism, and the *Theaetetus*," in *Pyrrhonian Skepticism*, Sinnott-Armstrong, W. (ed.) (New York: Oxford University Press), pp. 40–67.

Wolff, Christian, 1720: *Vernünftige Gedanken von Gott, der Welt und der Seele des Menschen* (Halle: Rengerische Buchhandlung).

Wolff, Michael, 2001: "Geometrie und Erfahrung. Kant und das Problem der objektiven Geltung der Euklidischen Geometrie," in Gerhardt, V., Horstmann, R.-P., and Schumacher, R. (eds.), *Kant und die Berliner Aufklärung. Akten des IX. Internationalen Kant-Kongresses* (Berlin: Walter de Gruyter), vol. 1, pp. 209–32.

Wundt, Max, 1924: *Kant als Metaphysiker; ein Beitrag zur Geschichte der deutschen Philosophie im 18ten Jahrhundert* (Stuttgart: F. Enke).

Contributors

Jean-Marie Beyssade is Professor of Philosophy (emeritus) at the Université de Paris-Sorbonne (Paris IV). His recent books include *Descartes au fil de l'ordre* (Presses Universitaires de France, 2001) and *Etudes sur Descartes, Histoire d'un Esprit* (Seuil, 2001).

Lisa Downing is Professor of Philosophy at the Ohio State University. Her articles (on Locke, Berkeley, and Malebranche, among others) focus on mechanist conceptions of body and their justification, debates surrounding gravity/attraction, and changing conceptions of scientific explanation in the early modern period. She is working on a book on empiricism and Newtonianism, among other projects.

Dina Emundts is Wissenschaftliche Mitarbeiterin at the Humboldt Universität in Berlin. She is the author of *Kants Übergangskonzeption im* Opus postumum (W. de Gruyter, 2004), coauthor of *G.W.F. Hegel. Eine Einführung* (Reclam, 2002), and editor of *Immanuel Kant und die Berliner Aufklärung* (L. Reichert, 2000). She has also published several articles on topics in classical German philosophy. She is currently working on a book on Hegel.

Daniel Garber is Chairman and Professor of Philosophy at Princeton University. He is the author of *Descartes' Metaphysical Physics* (University of Chicago Press, 1992) and *Descartes Embodied* (Cambridge University Press, 2001), as well as numerous articles in the history of early-modern philosophy. He is currently finishing a monograph on Leibniz's views on body, substance, and the physical world.

Don Garrett is Professor of Philosophy at New York University. He is the author of *Cognition and Commitment in Hume's Philosophy* (Oxford University Press, 1996) and the editor of *The Cambridge Companion to Spinoza* (Cambridge University Press, 1995). He has served as coeditor of *Hume Studies* and North American editor of the *Archiv für Geschichte der Philosophie*.

Paul Guyer is the Florence R.C. Murray Professor in the Humanities at the University of Pennsylvania, where he teaches the history of modern philosophy, especially Kant, and the history of modern aesthetics. He has written nine books on Kant, most recently *Kant's* Groundwork for the Metaphysics of Morals*: A Reader's Guide* (Continuum, 2007) and *Knowledge, Reason, and Taste: Kant's Response to Hume* (Princeton University Press, 2008). He is the cotranslator of Kant's *Critique of Pure Reason* (Cambridge University Press, 1998), *Critique of the Power of Judgment* (Cambridge University Press, 2000), and *Notes and Fragments* (Cambridge University Press, 2005), and editor of six anthologies on Kant. He is currently writing a history of modern aesthetics.

Anja Jauernig is Assistant Professor of Philosophy at the University of Notre Dame. She works on Kant, early-modern philosophy (especially Leibniz), philosophy of science, and post-Kantian German philosophy.

Béatrice Longuenesse is Professor of Philosophy at New York University. Her books include *Kant and the Capacity to Judge* (Princeton University Press, 1998), *Kant on the Human Standpoint* (Cambridge University Press, 2005) and *Hegel's Critique of Metaphysics* (Cambridge University Press, 2007). Her current work focuses on issues concerning self-consciousness and personal identity, drawing on post-Kantian philosophy in both the "continental" and the analytic traditions of philosophy.

Wayne Waxman is the author of *Kant and the Empiricists*, of which one volume has appeared, *Understanding Understanding* (Oxford University Press, 2005). He is currently at work on the second volume, *Time out of Mind*.

Kenneth P. Winkler is Professor of Philosophy at Yale University. His books include *Berkeley: An Interpretation* (Oxford University Press, 1989) and an abridgment of Locke's *Essay concerning Human Understanding* (Hackett, 1996). From 2000 to 2005 he was editor, with Elizabeth Radcliffe, of the journal *Hume Studies*. A collection of his papers, *Matters of Reason: Essays in Early Modern British Philosophy*, is forthcoming from Oxford University Press. He is now at work on a study of personal identity in eighteenth-century British philosophy.

Index